Journalism of Ideas

Journalism of Ideas is a comprehensive field guide for brainstorming, discovering, reporting, digitizing, and pitching news, opinion, and feature stories within journalism 2.0. With on-the-job advice from professional journalists, activities to sharpen your multimedia reporting skills, and hundreds of story ideas ripe for adaptation, Daniel Reimold helps you develop the journalistic know-how that will set you apart at your campus media outlet and beyond.

The exercises, observations, anecdotes, and tips in this book cover every stage of the story planning and development process, including how news judgment, multimedia engagement, records and archival searches, and various observational techniques can take your reporting to the next level. In addition to these tricks of the trade, *Journalism of Ideas* features an extensive set of newsworthy, timely, and unorthodox story ideas to jumpstart your creativity. Reimold also provides tips about how to successfully launch a career in journalism, including the ins and outs of pitching stories, the process of getting published, blogging and social media, internships, and the post-graduation job search. The conversation continues on the author's popular blog, College Media Matters.

Daniel Reimold is an assistant professor of journalism and a student newspaper adviser who has taught reporting, editing, and new media courses at universities in the U.S. and Southeast Asia. He maintains College Media Matters (www.collegemediamatters.com), a student journalism industry blog affiliated with the Associated Collegiate Press, the largest and oldest U.S. student media organization. He is also the "Campus Beat" columnist for USA TODAY College and a contributor to Poynter, PBS MediaShift, and *The Huffington Post*. He is the author of *Sex and the University: Celebrity, Controversy, and a Student Journalism Revolution*.

Journalism of Ideas

Brainstorming, Developing, and Selling Stories in the Digital Age

Daniel Reimold

 Routledge
Taylor & Francis Group

NEW YORK AND LONDON

First published 2013
by Routledge
711 Third Avenue, New York, NY 10017

Simultaneously published in the UK
by Routledge
2 Park Square, Milton Park, Abingdon, Oxon OX14 4RN

Routledge is an imprint of the Taylor & Francis Group, an informa business

Library of Congress Cataloging in Publication Data
Reimold, Daniel, 1981–
    Journalism of ideas: brainstorming, developing, and selling stories in the
    digital age/Daniel Reimold.
    pages cm
    Includes bibliographical references and index.
    1. Online journalism—United States.   2. College student newspapers
    and periodicals—United States.   3. Web publishing—United States.
    4. Citizen journalism.   I. Title.
    PN4784.O62R45 2013
    302.23′0973—dc23
    2012039558

ISBN: 978-0-415-63466-3 (hbk)
ISBN: 978-0-415-63467-0 (pbk)
ISBN: 978-0-203-09432-7 (ebk)

Typeset in Aldine 401 BT and Helvetica Neue
by Florence Production Ltd, Stoodleigh, Devon, UK

For Jacqueline Koch and Rosemary Boccella,
my favorite teachers, who challenged, energized,
and inspired me

Table of Contents

Acknowledgments

My first thank you extends to Yee Hung Lim. He is a master artist whose vision and illustrative talent led to images that leap off the page. He is a true gentleman, one of the kindest and hardest-working individuals I am blessed to know. Yee Hung, I do not possess your visual skill. I only have a way with words. The eight words I share with you here: Thank you. I am forever in your debt.

I am equally grateful to Routledge editor Erica Wetter for her belief in this project, the freedom she granted me to pursue it with gusto, and an overseeing editorial style that was appreciably upbeat and über-professional.

Separately, to my dearest friend Serene: You are my primary unofficial editor and daily inspiration. My sincere, eternal thanks.

My thanks as well to the many, many contributors who gave moments, hours, and days of their lives in various ways for this project, notably Sonny Albarado, Lori Brooks, Meredith Cochie, Caley Cook, Kelly Furnas, Sara Ganim, Brian Haas, Holly-Katharine Johnson, Frank LoMonte, Megha Mansharamani, Michelle Monroe, Bryan Murley, Audrey Scagnelli, Brooke Scherer, Mike Trobiano, Brian Thompson, and Anna Young.

Thank you Logan Aimone at ACP and Patrick Foster at USA TODAY for supporting my writing. Thank you Judy Hayden and John Capouya for your friendship and counsel. And to my parents, thank you, for everything.

CHAPTER 1

The Idea Stage

Illustration by Yee Hung Lim

"I saw stories everywhere. At dinner parties, I would leave with two or three story ideas. Every phone conversation, every movie or play, every walk down the street or trip on the subway brimmed with possibilities. I wrote down every idea that occurred to me, on scraps of paper that I stuffed into my jacket pockets. When I arrived at the office, I would empty my overflowing pockets and sort through the scraps."

Arthur Gelb, former *New York Times* managing editor, reflecting on his days as deputy metro editor

In space, astronauts occasionally hover around a kitchen table.

There is no practical need for a table in a spacecraft. In fact, in a zero gravity environment, a table doesn't make any sense at all. But NASA engineers found astronauts missed having the equivalent of a kitchen or dining room table in their space habitation modules ("the box where the crew lives").

Their longing wasn't *really* for the table. It was for the comfort and familiarity the table brought—part of a larger yearning for at least some semblance of home while in orbit. "We're humans," said science writer Mary Roach. "Human beings want to sit around a table and gossip and talk about stuff and eat and drink."

So a table was permanently added into the shuttle design scheme—simply to keep the astronauts happy.

This is one of the hundreds of "takeaway facts" shared over the past two-and-a-half years on *99% Invisible* (99percentinvisible.org). Hosted and produced by Roman Mars, the self-described "tiny radio show" has gained a massive, impassioned following. It tells stories and shares a smorgasbord of "discoveries that make you stop and re-examine the objects you see and touch every day"—from toothbrushes, stamps, and steering wheels to escalators, airports, and the Teddy bear.

While branded upfront as a program on architecture and design, Mars declares his true central focus is "the 99 percent invisible activity that shapes our world." Basically, he explores concepts and things that don't scream newsworthy, but still greatly influence or interact with many aspects of our daily lives.

For example, in an episode last May, Mars looked into queue theory, the study of how we wait in lines. Think it has nothing to do with you?

Consider how often you sit in traffic, wait for an elevator, choose a check-out aisle at the grocery store, head to a fast food drive-thru, get placed on a course wait-list or stand in line at the bank, the ballpark, the airport, the movie theater, or even the happiest place on Earth.

Among other facts, Mars discovered nearly 20 employees at Disney work solely to ensure visitors to its theme parks remain entertained and satisfied while waiting in line for shows and rides. As an expert at MIT nicknamed Dr. Queue tells him, "They have mastered the idea that people can be happy waiting 40 minutes in line for a four-minute ride."

Each episode of *99% Invisible* is a four-to-15-minute ride that airs on a radio station in San Francisco and as a podcast. It typically contains one big idea, an interesting "takeaway fact," two or three anecdotes, and "a person exhibiting geeky enthusiasm." (See Dr. Queue.) After the reporting for each episode is complete, Mars spends roughly two days mixing and editing—often at night after putting his kids to bed.

This formula has rocketed the show to an almost-unparalleled stratosphere of success. It has earned awards, enormous praise from radio industry veterans, a super-high iTunes podcast ranking, and a rabid fan-base known as The Invisiblers. Last summer, a fundraising campaign on the website Kickstarter brought in more than $170,000—the most money pledged for a journalism project in Kickstarter's history.

99% Invisible is the epitome of new journalism. It is a terrestrial–online hybrid. It is independently produced, from home. It is crowdfunded, and at times crowdsourced. And it presents episodes and extras that can be listened to, read, viewed, downloaded, shared, and commented upon.

Yet, beyond all the innovation, the most visible element of its success is simple—and old school. As one writer explains, "[I]t tells the types of stories that you can't wait to share with someone else."

"Stories are super satisfying," said Mars. "I think that narratives are what you naturally do in your brain . . . Tapping into that is important . . . There's a little bit of voodoo in the magic of it. Everyone wants to be a storyteller . . . It makes you feel like you're doing something important. Because stories are so important."

■ Over the past decade, digital tools and platforms have rocketed journalism to a universe of innovation, interactivity, and immediacy once unimaginable. Yet, without stellar content, journalism 2.0 is not worth the effort to read, watch, listen, contribute to, or connect with. Everything journalism was, is, and will be rests on our ability to tell a story. **And every story starts with an idea.**

WOW STORIES

In February 2012, a working hot tub mysteriously appeared on the roof of the University of Michigan computer science engineering building. Then, roughly 48 hours later, just as mysteriously, it vanished.

"People were kind of flabbergasted," a university spokesman said at the time. "It was obviously unexpected. It was pretty creative and now it's gone. It left a buzz in its wake."

Staffers at *The Michigan Daily*, the school's student newspaper, were the first to grab the scoop about this buzz. They were clued in after seeing photos of the machine posted anonymously to a blog. They also heard murmurings of a Reddit discussion thread that revealed its location.

The paper's subsequent story earned local and national attention, including an Associated Press report and a mention in the "Weird News" section of *The Huffington Post*.

Now, check out the infamous Michigan hot tub in the photo on the previous page. Really soak in the image. Enjoy looking at it, because you will hardly ever be in it.

The *Michigan Daily* story is the anomaly. In Occupy Wall Street terms, this is the one percent. When you are on deadline or in your story ideas meeting each week, hot tubs hardly ever fall from the sky and provide you with a memorable, newsworthy story.

Instead, we are often stuck, staring at the world (wide web) without a plausible or publishable idea and no real clue how to even begin searching. Nervousness leads to guilt, then fear, and finally outright desperation.

One example: a public request submitted by a student named Haylee. A while back, the budding journalist was facing a deadline crunch and a story shortage. In an entry posted on the community sharing site Yahoo! Answers—under the headline "Any Journalism Story Ideas?"—Haylee wrote, "My journalism teacher said that we need to have like 'WOW' stories for the next newspaper. I reaalllllllllllllly need an idea. Does anyone have any?"

This textbook is aimed at answering that question with a huge YES, thousands of times over. It is also aimed at teaching, inspiring, and prompting students, advisers, professors, and professionals to come up with endless WOW stories on their own. Why? Because many jobs within journalism depend upon harnessing and unleashing this WOW factor.

IN OTHER WORDS

Illustration by Yee Hung Lim

"Reporters should learn from the get-go that uncovering story ideas is their job. Any editor worth his or her salt will make it clear that reporters who have no story ideas will not be reporters for long."

Doug Cabral, editor, *The Martha's Vineyard Times*, Mass.

"Ideas are your currency, so always be pitching them, researching them, and refining them."

Robert Terry, managing editor, *Washington Business Journal*, D.C.

PUBLISHED GOLD

Journalism of Ideas is a comprehensive field guide for brainstorming, discovering, reporting, digitizing, and pitching news, opinion, and feature stories within journalism 2.0. It presents advice from more than a hundred professional journalists, student journalists, journalism professors, and student media advisers and advocates. It boasts hundreds of story ideas ripe for adaptation. And it connects the advice and ideas with a slew of interactive exercises, assignment prompts, ethics and cliché alerts, and blueprints for building innovative multimedia stories.

The exercises, observations, anecdotes, and tips touch on every stage of the story planning and development process, including how news judgment, multimedia engagement, records searches, and various observational techniques can help spin a brainstorming session into published gold. Separate advice focuses on the storytelling methods involved in data journalism, photojournalism, crime reporting, and commentary writing.

A concluding segment shares the secrets to establishing a presence and launching a career in journalism—the ins-and-outs of pitching stories, getting published, and navigating the internship and job search. Related tips touch on the art of freelancing 2.0, starting an independent blog or site, constructing a quality online portfolio, and building a social media following.

JOURNALISM OF IDEAS, ONLINE

The textbook is ultimately the foundation for a storytelling conversation that continues on my blog, College Media Matters. College Media Matters is the country's leading student journalism blog. It is affiliated with the Associated Collegiate Press (ACP), the largest and oldest U.S. student journalism organization.

Visit the blog for many more journalism ideas, college media breaking news, extended Q&As with top student and professional journalists, career prep advice, and the chance to be featured or submit ideas of your own.

- Check out my blog: collegemediamatters.com
- Follow me on Twitter: @collegemedia
- Subscribe to my Facebook page: facebook.com/collegemediamatters

A THUMPING PULSE

The blog is one part of my larger college media reporting, researching, and presenting work, a professional journey that has brought me across the U.S., Southeast Asia, and to the Kurdistan region of Iraq. As the *Student Press Law Center Report* notes, "Reimold's work allows him to track the pulse of America's college papers and identify student press trends."

In recent years, the pulse has been thumping. Student journalists have been reporting upon oodles of highly relevant and crazy cool stories. Among the highlights: features on student Adderall addicts, grade inflation, campus gun rights, rising dropout rates, "point, click, and cheat" trends, student debt, fake IDs, legacy enrollees, and the rise in phenomena such as dubstep dance parties, paintball clubs, Quidditch teams, and online anonymous flirting.

Yet, even after a single semester practicing the craft, most student journalists realize the ideas for stories like those and all others do not simply scream at you until they grab your attention. They do not reveal themselves during clandestine meetings in dark parking garages. And they rarely, if ever, just pile up in your email inbox, begging to be discovered.

Instead, they play out low-key, within quietly emerging trends, monotonous meetings, numbers buried in budget documents, and idle chatter. They require good reporters to recognize them, dig to uncover them, figure out a fresh way to tell them, and flesh them out.

With this book, I am assisting and pushing you to do all those things and more. By the time you are done reading, my ultimate hope: If someone brings up a person, place, thing, event, trend, viewpoint, document, law, word, or even a single letter, you will bring up an idea—a good one, a newsworthy one, one worth reporting.

This is journalism at its purest. This is the journalism of ideas.

A STANDOUT STORY IDEA

Every quality story or WOWzer of an idea possesses all or most of the following buzzwords.

- Innovative
- Impacting
- Accurate
- Timely
- Interesting
- Fresh
- Objective
- Informative
- Concrete

IN OTHER WORDS

Illustration by Yee Hung Lim

"Every story, big or small, daily or enterprise, should **answer the 'so what?' question**. Otherwise, why are we doing it? If you keep that question in mind while brainstorming story ideas, it will help you focus. Ask it while reporting, and the questions you should be asking become clearer. And always ask yourself before writing and you'll better communicate the impact of the story to your readers."
Daniel Thigpen, former staff writer, *The Record*, Calif.

"From an old journalism professor: You have to **hit readers in the heart and the checkbook**. From my dad, an editor: Great stories are the ones that make people laugh and cry."
Jenna Johnson, higher education reporter, *The Washington Post*

"Pretty much every story out there has been told. It has been done and redone. You must bring **a fresh perspective** to each story you report. The difference is how you see the story and how you share it."
Aric Crabb, multimedia reporter, Bay Area News Group, Calif.

"While it's impossible to start reporting a story without some preconceived idea of where it is going, it's imperative that you're willing to let your preconceptions go as you investigate more. The point is not to fit the story into your idea of what it should be, but to **let the story be what it is**. That sounds simple enough, but it's often hard for journalists to accept their preconceptions were wrong."
Glen Starkey, journalist and lecturer, California Polytechnic State University

"Don't write for your portfolio, your editor or yourself. **Write for the readers**."
Michael Lello, legal news editor, LexisNexis

"Journalists get caught up with the big assignment—the World Series, the earthquake in Haiti, anything in Africa. What we fail to see and cover well is our own backyard, and that produces some of the best stories of all. Look at your town. **Make the big time where you are**."
Aric Crabb

"Many years ago, an editor at *The New York Times* told a foreign correspondent to report on the events as if he were writing letters home to a friend. Strive for that level of effectiveness and **familiarity with your readers**. They'll appreciate it."

Ethan Magoc, journalist and graduate student, University of Florida

"We need to tell better stories. **Don't write articles. Tell stories**. Write your story like you're talking to a friend and telling them about something you are both interested in. Garrison Keillor calls the reader 'the friend I haven't met yet.' "

John Smalley, editor, *Wisconsin State Journal*

"Any real worthy story needs to **have both the sizzle and the steak**. It needs to be flashy and have the required tension, but also have some serious facts and reporting to back it all up."

Matt Kettmann, senior editor, *The Santa Barbara Independent*, Calif.

"*Under Siege 2: Dark Territory* was a lousy movie, but one of its characters provided the sagest advice for journalists I've heard: 'Assumption is the mother of all f***-ups.' In other words, **don't ever, ever assume—ever**."

Christian Hill, staff writer, *The News Tribune*, Wash.

"We live in an on-demand, personalized world. Between Facebook, DVRs, and iPhones, we can always pick and choose just what we want, when we want it. Good journalists keep this in mind when developing story ideas. If the reader cannot tell from the first beat **how the story matters to them**, they are not going to stick around for very long."

Brandon Szuminsky, columnist and copy editor, *The Uniontown Herald-Standard*, Pa.

"In today's world, people expect to see more than just text. They want slideshows, videos, podcasts, graphics, timelines, related tweets, and more. It's key to always be thinking of multiple ways to tell a story **beyond the written word**."

Callie Schweitzer, director of marketing and projects, Vox Media

CHAPTER 2

A Journalism Life

Illustration by Yee Hung Lim

The croutons were blackened crisps.

During finals week in fall 2011, George Washington University student Audrey Scagnelli and friends accidentally burnt the croutons they were toasting in a campus apartment oven. She describes the scene that followed as truly "one of those *this-only-happens-in-the-movies* kind of moments."

Flames roared from the oven, triggering a fire alarm that led to a full building evacuation. A pair of fire trucks and what Scagnelli described as "an army of firemen" arrived and secured the scene. Students huddled outside in 40-degree weather. The apartment was left covered in soot, down to the doorknobs and bedspreads. And the blackened breaded bits remained, drizzled in now-smoldering olive oil.

Embarrassed, the political communication major and her pals brought the firefighters some raspberry napoleons. They also turned the experience into a magazine spread.

Scagnelli is the co-founder and editor-in-chief of *College & Cook* (collegeandcook.com), an online student magazine that premiered in spring 2012 in part to prove college students should not be "stereotyped by Easy Mac and cold pizza."

Early issues included stories on a campus sustainable food project, food allergies, a self-taught student cook, restaurant tipping, windowsill gardening, and the origins of foodie phrases such as *couch potato* and *that's the way the cookie crumbles*.

But Scagnelli's favorite feature remains the one about burnt croutons, a story that also touches on the rise in campus dorm fires like the one she experienced.

"When I'm asked what story kind of sums up *College & Cook*, I think most people are surprised to hear it's the fire story," she said. "I love that it's a spread for a few reasons. We are college students. I don't claim to be this chef. I'm a college kid. Everyone involved in this magazine, we're all college students. It just kind of shows who we are."

Scagnelli's summation is on-point: The search for stories begins with you.

■ Your own experiences—successes, failures, trips, classes, check-ups, jobs, hobbies, downtime, dates, commutes, and burnt croutons—often serve as the foundation for ideas worthy of being fleshed out. Friends, family, colleagues, relationship partners, and fellow subway riders can all act as initial, informal sources for stories you may later professionally report. Journalism is not just a job or a craft. It is a way of life. Ideas are its lifeblood.

IN OTHER WORDS

"Don't lose your childish curiosity. Question everything and then question that. I'd say more than 50 percent of my story ideas come from things I see or wonder about on my free time. You're never off the clock when it comes to collecting story ideas."

Aimee Heckel, youth, fashion and features writer, *Daily Camera*, Colo.

Illustration by Yee Hung Lim

"The best advice any editor ever gave me: 'Go have a beer with your friends.' As he told me, 'Go have a beer and just listen to what people are talking about. Eavesdrop. And see what you come up with.' That advice stuck with me. It was the first time I'd thought about journalism being something you could do all the time, not just in the newsroom from 9 a.m. to 5 p.m. You could find stories in the bar with your friends. You could find them at Target while buying T-shirts. You could think of them while you were brushing your teeth. **The best journalists live a journalism life**."

Adam Wisneski, multimedia producer,
Tulsa World, Okla.

"The cool thing about journalism is that it gives you an excuse to ask questions about things that interest you. Whether it's an issue at school, my kids' health or a family trip, I always try to leverage my curiosity into a story. When I was eight months pregnant and broke my ankle on the ice, I remember thinking on the way to the emergency room: This will make a great story. Later that year, I wrote a health story for *The Washington Post* about the impact of pregnancy on your balance and bones."

Caralee Adams, freelance journalist
based in Bethesda, Md.

"Quality stories are everywhere. It's just a matter of being curious. A reporter at *The Philadelphia Inquirer*, Gil Gaul, once donated his blood and walked away wondering what would happen to it. The answer netted him a Pulitzer Prize."

Pete Boal, news editor, *The Philadelphia Inquirer*

THE ALWAYS LIST

- **Always** consider yourself on the clock.
- **Always** have a notebook, pen, and camera phone nearby.
- **Always** see potential stories in your personal journeys.
- **Always** be up for politely eavesdropping on strangers and friends.
- And **always** engage in campus life and quality conversation instead of lazing alone in your dorm.

THE NEVER LIST

- **Never** lose your sense of wonder.
- **Never** talk more than you listen.
- **Never** discount your initial instinct about a story idea's potential.
- And **never** ever forget to write a cool idea down.

CURIOSITY IS KING

Exude curiosity.

Whether looking at a Facebook photograph, a financial disclosure statement, a billboard or someone's tattoo, tears, or scars, the key is being curious, intensely curious—and then possessing the guts, wherewithal, and passion to follow up on that curiosity and get your story.

"Among all things, curiosity is still king," says *Wisconsin State Journal* editor John Smalley. "Why did that happen? How come? When did that change? What's going on over there? What does it take to do that? How many? How much? You get the idea. Curiosity is the fuel that keeps our engine cranking. We need curious people who look at the world around them and ask questions, not because we're paying them to, but because it's just what they do. Be curious."

Journalist Andy Kirkaldy puts it more simply. "Curiosity killed the cat," he said. "**Lack of curiosity killed the reporter**."

Prominent writer Malcolm Gladwell knows about the internal battle between boredom and curiosity. He remembers once trying to convince himself that writing about shampoo and hair dye would be interesting. As he wrote in his book *What the Dog Saw*:

"The trick to finding ideas is to convince yourself that everyone and everything has a story to tell. I say trick but what I really mean is challenge, because it's a very hard thing to do. Our instinct as humans, after all, is to assume that most things are not interesting. We flip through the channels on the television and reject 10 before we settle on one. We go to a bookstore and look at 20 novels before we pick the one we want. We filter and rank and judge. We *have* to. There's just so much out there. But if you want to be a writer, you have to fight that instinct every day. Shampoo doesn't seem interesting? Well, dammit, it must be, and if it isn't, I have to believe that it will ultimately lead me to something that is."

■ In the spirit of Gladwell's shampoo journey, here is your first assignment.

ASSIGNMENT ALERT!

The Wallet Exercise

 "A college instructor at the University of Pittsburgh asked each student to bring his or her wallet to a newspaper reporting class. We did, and he promised, before we had opened them, that each of us would find 10 story ideas in our wallets. And we did—about how we spent our money, our credit-card use, club memberships, what the ticket stubs and photos we carried said about us, and how various age groups differed from others. I'd been dubious at the start. I was a budding sportswriter and carried no sports-related items in my wallet, so I couldn't imagine such an exercise would be of interest to me. It ended up not just interesting, but enlightening. I'd grudgingly offered my curiosity, and was rewarded many times over. Don't limit curiosity to those few things in which you believe you'll make your career, or those relatively few things that hold your interest today. There's a whole world of interesting subjects out there. Be curious, about everything. Start with your hip pocket or purse."

Matt Martin, managing editor/sports, *Erie Times-News*, Pa.

Your Assignment

Follow Martin's lead. Look inside your wallet, purse, or backpack and brainstorm five to seven story ideas from the items you find—and don't find—inside. Do the same with the wallet, purse, or backpack of a trusted friend.

THREE NOTES

Graphic by Michele Boyet

"Two words: BE THERE. I used to have a yellow sticky note saying that on my desk. I know it sounds stupid, but it's all too easy to pick up the phone. If you're there in person, you can observe gestures, the surroundings, etc. You'll meet an extra source or two, often someone off the beaten path. **And who knows, something extraordinary could happen**. Once, while doing the second story on a bicyclist killed in a hit-and-run, I went to the crash site, intending to do knock-and-talks in the neighborhood. Instead, I ran into the victim's sister. It made for a very powerful story."

Kyle Odegard, sports writer,
East Valley Tribune, Ariz.

WALLET EXERCISE IN ACTION

While rifling through her purse as part of the exercise, a journalism student at a Midwest school pulled out assembly instructions for a mini-shelf she had recently purchased from Ikea and built in her dorm. She quickly scribbled five buzzwords: Ikea, self-assembled, clutter, storage, and, just for fun, shelvin' it.

1 IKEA HACKS

After some industrious Googling, she comes across "Ikea Hacks." It is a phenomenon students greatly enjoy, involving the creative repurposing of Ikea furniture.

2 CAMPUS CYBERSECURITY

The second part of the phrase "Ikea Hacks" reminds her of a recent hacking incident at her best friend's college, resulting in the public exposure of students' personal information. She wonders about the cybersecurity procedures at her own school.

3 INTERNET ADDICTION

She chats about her first two ideas with classmates. Someone mentions HackCollege, a cult site aimed at helping students help themselves. She visits the site, quickly stumbling onto a post topic that spurs a story idea: students who become so fanatical about the Internet that logging off leads to "withdrawal symptoms similar to drug addicts or smokers going cold turkey."

4 STREET HARASSMENT

She also clicks on a playful post indirectly connected to one of her buzzwords, shelvin' it, focused on the art of trash talking. It triggers an idea for a serious story about a form of verbal sexual abuse known as street harassment that is increasing on college campuses.

5 TEXT SPEAK

After receiving a garbled Gchat message from a friend, her thoughts about trash talk turn to text speak. An idea surfaces about students' evermore mangled writing and speaking in the digital era. She finds academic studies confirming the influence of texts and tweets on undergrads' declining language skills.

6 CULT of LESS

Next, she reviews news reports, which reveal a HackCollege-IKEA connection: Its founder is a principal member of a movement popular among students called Cult of Less. According to Wikipedia, it embraces removing nearly all furniture and worldly possessions from your home, except for a few digital tools, in part to clear physical clutter from your life. She finds several students who have adopted aspects of its philosophy.

7 DO-IT-YOURSELF FASHION

Soon after, on a walk around her dorm, she spots friends involved in a different movement: do-it-yourself fashion. It is an offshoot of an economic-driven style trend, recession chic.

8 ONLINE BREAK-UPS

In a final brainstorming session, she glances once more at the buzzwords she had jotted down, while thinking about her own life. The "shelvin' it" phrase again strikes a chord. Her mind races to her recent romantic break-up, and the fact that it had occurred on Facebook. A directed online search confirms she is far from the only undergrad to suffer this digital adieu.

SO IN THE END . . .

She brainstormed and uncovered a bunch of ideas that could be transformed into full stories featuring students and staff at her school: Ikea Hacks. Campus cybersecurity. Internet addiction. Street harassment. Text speak. The Cult of Less. Do-it-yourself fashion. And online break-ups. It all started with a set of instructions in her purse. Among the sources to which she turned: Google, the news media, academic research, Wikipedia, the Internet at-large, classmates, friends, personal observation, and her own life. Story ideas are everywhere. You just have to know where and how to look. **LET'S GET STARTED.**

Graphic by Mike Trobiano and Brooke Scherer

"Jack Nelson, the late, great *Los Angeles Times* reporter and D.C. bureau chief, hated it that *The Washington Post* and *New York Times* were dominating the Watergate story in 1973–'74. So he put a note on every reporter's desk with GOYAKOD. The acronym meant: 'Get off your a**, knock on doors.' The truth of that stunt: People want to talk. No matter what the story is, somebody is willing to talk about it, if you can find them. Woodward and Bernstein held the field on Watergate because they went door to door, looking for people in the Nixon election campaign who would talk about the slush fund. And they finally found a few. I've always reminded myself of that when facing a story that doesn't seem to have an entry point. Just start calling people who might have been at the scene or in the know. **If you are persistent enough, you will find them.**"

Peter Roper, news reporter,
Pueblo Chieftain, Colo.

"It was a slow day, not much going on. I heard over the scanner that there was a bank robbery, so I headed out. I figured at the very least it would be good for source building. I showed up and talked to the detectives. They were all laughing. The robber had given the teller a note demanding money that he actually signed, 'P.S., Kevin.' Even the teller laughed him out of the bank, without giving up any money. I had myself a great little story, just by showing up. But it got even better. As I chatted up police, I heard one officer yell, 'He's in the bushes, sleeping, passed out!' The guy hadn't made it 50 feet from the bank when he passed out in some bushes. **I showed up. I had a great story.**"

Brian Haas, crime reporter,
The Tennessean

IDEAS, ONLINE

College Problems

"Your roommate never leaves the room . . . So much homework that you don't know where to start . . . The only thing lower than your GPA is your bank account balance . . . Study abroad where you're legal to drink. Come back home and you're still not 21 . . . Professor says the test is easy. Lies."

The endless and often hilarious difficulties associated with being a student now have an online home: College Problems (collegeproblems.org). Its tagline: "Everyone's got them. Tell me yours." The popular Tumblr site started and maintained by Boston University student Madeline Huerta collects brief student-submitted complaints and confessions about the complications of collegiate life.

From a journalism perspective, the problems are wonderful prompts for potential stories—providing clues about what is angering and frustrating undergrads everywhere.

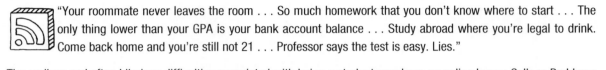

collegeproblems #952
roommate is a slob. embarrassed to have friends over.

collegeproblems|tumblr

collegeproblems #941
learning more from google than from your textbooks.

collegeproblems|tumblr

collegeproblems #769
commuter campus. not enough parking for residents.

collegeproblems|tumblr

collegeproblems #624
spend $200 on a fake ID. it says you're 30.

collegeproblems|tumblr

THE STUFF OF LIFE

A to-do list, the top item stating simply, "Dump Adam."

A handmade warning sign announcing, "Within 100 meters from here, I noticed a coyote which . . . has lost its fear for humans." A birth control pill case, a week's worth of pills remaining. A black-and-white photo of a boy in jean shorts and a sweatshirt with an airplane on it, crying while plopped in some hay. A slightly crumpled piece of paper, containing the same sentence over and over, written by a punished student:

I will control myself.
I will control myself.
I will control myself.
I will control myself.
I will control myself.

These items and many, many more are part of the popular media phenomenon *FOUND Magazine* (foundmagazine.com), which also includes a blog, books, and online videos. *FOUND* is a long-term crowdsourcing project of sorts focused on scooping up and sharing the staggering amount of eclectic items left in public without explanation that provide "a glimpse into someone else's life."

The *FOUND* collection has been dubbed "the ultimate reality programming," "little vignettes into the human soul," "a formidable stash of the blurry, the mysterious, the touching, and the unexplainable," and "a quirky lens into the flotsam and jetsam of humanity."

The phenomenon's popularity and staying power is also quirky proof of the power embedded within dirt-level reporting. It is the craft of looking under every crack and crevice and noticing the little things others have forgotten, cast aside, left behind or taken for granted.

Many great stories are in the details—those that are sought out, found, verified, made meaningful, and brought to life. Mixed in with the main facts, figures, quotes, characters, and scenes, details can powerfully connect with readers, satiate their curiosities, offer them an additional sliver of understanding, and whet their appetites to read more. As Stewart Warren, a former reporter for *The Herald-News* in Illinois, shares, "The stuff of everyday life can be very, very interesting to many people."

ASSIGNMENT ALERT!

A Dirt-Level Report

 Follow in *FOUND*'s footsteps. Embark on your own dirt-level report, viewing that which has been tossed or spurned, someone else's trash, as a journalist's possible treasure. You have one week to scour your campus, surrounding community, and hometown for items discarded, abandoned, or forgotten in public that might provide "a glimpse into someone else's life." Take photos of the items you come across or collect them, depending on their size, weight, legality, and feasibility for transport.

After the hunt, analyze your "finds" in a fun, short show-and-tell video, blog post, or photo slideshow. Scrutinize what your finds might tell you about the individual, group, or event responsible for their creation and current trashed state. Also, brainstorm story ideas inspired by your trash-treasures. For example, a student of mine who once stumbled upon an amateur magic kit came up with a pair of story ideas: a profile of local street magicians and a feature on campus fraternity members who use magic to pick up dates.

ETHICS ALERT!

Similar to *FOUND Magazine* contributors, don't break any laws to obtain your items, including stealing and trespassing on private property. Avoid actual trash rummaging and picking up items of possible harm. And turn over any items of great financial or personal value (such as a smartphone or house keys) to local authorities or their original owners.

IN OTHER WORDS

"As a journalist, you have an excuse to talk to anyone you want. Use it. If you keep your ears open and **heed that tingle**, there are amazing stories all around you."

Carl Ciaramella, former staffer, *U-T San Diego*, Calif.

Illustration by Yee Hung Lim

ASSIGNMENT ALERT!

The Reporter and the Record Egg

 "My former editor Tom Heslin once told me a great story I think about often. He was a young reporter at a small paper in Maine. A man, a farmer, called the city desk with a story idea. He said his chicken had hatched what he believed was a record egg. He thought it was a story.

"The editor dispatched Tom, who was also taking his own pictures. Tom reluctantly went, thinking that this had to be a career low—writing about an egg. He got out there, looked at the egg and listened to the farmer go on and on with pride. To Tom, it looked like, well, just a big egg, so he took his picture and went back to the newsroom, loudly laughing and complaining to his colleagues.

"A few weeks later, he got a job at another daily. At his going-away party, someone gave him a copy of a picture of the egg in a frame as a joke gift. Tom went on to bigger things. But several years later, he was going through some old boxes and found that picture and he started crying.

"For the first time, he looked at the hands that were holding the egg. They were the farmer's hands—old, incredibly worn, covered with calluses and dirt in every crevice.

"He thought, here was this crusty man who worked so hard with his farm and who was so proud that one day he picked up the phone to call his local paper about an egg. And all Tom had seen was this stupid egg, not the man who was holding it. *He* was the story. So don't get blinded by the egg."

Jennifer Levitz, staff writer, *The Wall Street Journal*

Your Assignment

 Play the egg game with a friend or willing accomplice. Look them over, within reason. Pick out less noticeable characteristics about their appearance or what they have with them. Among the possibilities: clothing, jewelry and other fashion accessories, scars, tattoos, wrinkles, tan lines, make-up smears, hair frizz, items in their pocket, wallet, schoolbag, and purse, books in their hand, bookmarked sites on their laptop, pictures in their wallet or on their tablet, songs and podcasts on their MP3 player, and apps on their mobile phone. Most important, once identified, connect these items and attributes to the human story. Consider how they relate to—and what they say about—the person who wears, carries or uses them.

CHAPTER 3
People Stories

Illustration by Yee Hung Lim

Kristina Hacker was determined to become an expert on blackouts.

For her first college newspaper reporting assignment, she was tasked with writing a story on a series of statewide electrical outages. "I spoke with numerous officials at the university and at the state level," said Hacker, now top editor at California's *Turlock Journal*. "I read every news story written on the subject and was briefed by the local electrical company. I spent at least 20 hours researching and writing the 40-inch story. I proudly turned it in and waited for the praise to begin."

But instead of praise, the lights went out. "The editor tore the story to pieces," she confirmed. "She said I turned in an essay on blackouts, not a news story. She proceeded to ask: What are the students doing to prepare for the blackouts? How do they feel about blackouts? Are they afraid? Upset with the lack of energy management? I had forgotten the most important thing: community reaction. The heart of any news story is the people affected. I have never again forgotten the people."

Neither should you.

> ■ People are paramount to quality reporting. They are essential news sources. They are the audience we are striving to serve. And they are the heart of almost every quality story. As *Independent Record* city editor Pete Nowakowski puts it, "If you want to be a journalist, a true journalist, then remember that stories are people."

PEOPLE OFTEN PROFILED

The Influencers: people who are successful, rich, powerful, and the focus of continued speculation and intrigue.

Examples

- Best-selling novelist
- College president
- Millionaire Internet entrepreneur
- Snooki
- Star athlete

The Unorthodox: people slightly or fully outside their coverage area's mainstream due to their lifestyle, mental and physical capabilities, or interests. A few examples: the Amish, amnesiacs, Arctic explorers, hoarders, and a second-grader with a genius IQ.

Example

There are a very small number of atheist and agnostic students at Baylor University, the largest Christian Baptist school in the world. As *The Baylor Lariat* explained in a fall 2011 report, "It can be hard fitting in at a university where many of the people you meet believe you're going to burn in hell." While the student atheists and agnostics say their undergraduate experiences are not majorly impacted by their beliefs, they do often hide them while on campus "because of the possibility of tension with members of the faculty or student body."

The Man on the Street: people whose everyday lives equate to newsworthiness, even though they are hardly ever in the public eye. They are picked to tell the larger story of the age bracket, economic class, profession, religion, or ethnic group to which they belong. Or they find themselves in the spotlight due to extraordinary events, including their heroism in a dramatic moment.

Examples

- Graduating senior facing enormous loan debt comparable to many students
- Illegal immigrant working odd jobs under the table like many in his situation
- Longtime bus driver who saved passengers' lives after a crash
- Married couple who met on dating website, without knowing they lived a block apart

The Perseverant: people who complete a monumental journey, carry out a thankless task, or endure a notable long-term hardship, at times out of the spotlight and without full knowledge of their own newsworthiness. Two examples: a secretary who has served 10 university presidents and a military veteran who road-races with prosthetic legs.

Example

During the spring 2011 softball season, Florida A&M University's Tenisha Dixon lost her spot on the team due to an unplanned pregnancy. The birth of her son months later caused a facial paralysis so severe Dixon had blurred vision, trouble eating, and "no longer recognized herself in the mirror."

As *The Famuan* reported, "To some people, these events were the beginning to a life clouded by shattered dreams and struggle. There was Dixon, a 21-year-old single mother with a numbing disorder and a demanding class schedule. And softball—the sport that paid for her education—was ripped away."

But Dixon soldiered on, using her newborn as motivation. She stayed in school, recovered from the worst of the paralysis to the point of "living nearly symptom-free"—and regained her place on the softball team.

THE ALWAYS LIST

- **Always** present people as actual human beings. Tell a story. Be engaging and creative.
- **Always** provide warts-and-all glimpses of the people whose stories you are telling. You are not creating their Facebook profile. Get beyond the superficial or most idealized versions of what they want to share with the world. Heroes are for film scripts. News profiles deserve real people, flaws and all. Readers are savvy enough to know no one is perfect.

- **Always** interview and shadow people in spots where they are most comfortable and spend a lot of time. Also, whenever possible, encourage them to engage in an activity that will reveal more about who they are. During your time together, take notes of not just what they say, but what they do.
- **Always** talk to people who are close to the person you are profiling—friends, family, colleagues, exes, teachers—to get a more complete picture of who they are and who they used to be. Most people are not the most knowledgeable or objective source about themselves. Talking to others who know them provides a more well-rounded view, possibly bringing up characteristics, anecdotes, and past events your profile subjects are unwilling to share or not self-aware enough to see.

THE NEVER LIST

- **Never** present a one-dimensional character. Every person you profile is as complicated as you are. You are most likely focusing on someone for a specific reason, but provide readers with a deeper sense of who they are, away from their most famous achievement or newsworthy characteristic. Above all else, do not stereotype people by their jobs or level in school. A profile is about a human being, not a "cop," "soldier," "mayor," "teacher," "thief," or "incoming freshman."
- **Never** accept people's stories at face value. False modesty, inflated egos, faulty memories, and charged emotions occasionally make the people you are profiling unreliable sources about themselves. Check out facts. Request verification. Probe deeper. Search for holes. And get the other side of every story, especially if it paints something or someone else in a negative light.
- **Never** strive to present people's comprehensive histories, unless you truly have the time, drive, and resources. Profiles are not biographies. A large majority of people's stories are snapshots, offering a close-up of who someone is at a certain moment and fragments of who and what shaped them along the way.
- **Never** overlook the incredible responsibility you hold in sharing someone's story. As Wendy Reuer, a reporter at *The Forum of Fargo-Moorhead*, shares, "A journalist needs to remember that to you, it may just be another story, another source, another day. But to the source who has accomplished something or lived through an interesting enough experience, meeting you and seeing their name in print will most likely be a once-in-a-lifetime experience. While you may move on to the next day and the next story, **they will hold that story with them forever**."

IN OTHER WORDS

Illustration by Yee Hung Lim

"Strike up conversations with complete strangers, waiters, people who work the drive-thru, ticket takers, and security guards. There are a few billion people on the planet and we all have stories to tell."

Brandon Szuminsky, columnist and copy editor,
The Uniontown Herald-Standard, Pa.

"If you talk to anyone long enough, you'll have a story."

Jackie Borchardt, education reporter,
Casper Star-Tribune, Wyo.

"Everyone has a great story hidden somewhere inside. It's your job to find it. Back in the days when staffs were huge and newspapers actually covered travel expenses for a non-sports or non-election story, a reporter for one of the big papers had a human interest series going. **He'd go to a new city, open a phonebook, put his finger down at random, and write about whatever he found**. Much to his colleagues' surprise, he always found something amazing. Until one day, when he landed on the doorstep of what must have been the most boring couple on the planet. He interviewed them for hours, looking for a thread, even the whisper of a story. He used every trick, asked every question, and nada. He finally decided his colleagues had been right. His previous stories hadn't been a matter of skill, but merely luck, and his extraordinary lucky run was over. He said a sad goodbye to the couple. He closed his notebook, paused, and asked, 'Is there anything you'd like to tell me that we haven't talked about already?' The wife turned to the husband and said, '**Honey, did you tell him about the graveyard in the garden?** The one where our murdered son is buried?' Everyone has a graveyard in the garden."

Jackie Burrell, food editor, Bay Area News Group, Calif.

The Graveyard in the Garden

As outlined by Burrell, play a version of the phonebook game. Select students and staffers at random during a stroll around campus or by browsing through your school's online directory or Facebook network. Interview them, ask, ask, ask, and uncover something newsworthy about them not many people know—a hobby, obsession, physical quirk, lifelong dream, or memorable moment that qualifies as their graveyard in the garden. As Burrell puts it, "If you don't have a story, you haven't asked the right questions."

Playing a version of the game on campus last fall, my introductory journalism class quickly came across a student cliff diver, dolphin trainer, certified quilting instructor, MMA fighter, autopsy specialist, champion dirt bike rider, and competitive wiffleball player. They interviewed students whose lives are defined by their addictions to caffeine, Subway sandwiches, Batman, films by the Coen brothers, the singer Jack Johnson, zebras, pigs, and the Miami Heat.

They spoke to students afflicted with intense bouts of sympathy pain, seasonal affective disorder, inappropriate laughter syndrome, legal blindness, kidney stones, scars from a Rottweiler attack, and such severe obsessive–compulsive disorder that the young woman can only eat food in increments of two and must spit in the sink every time she washes her hands.

A separate student discussed once building a stripper pole in his family's living room—gathering the scrap wood and steel tube himself—at his parents' urging. (Hmm.) Another student told the tale of rescuing her neighbor's dog from a house fire, racing into the flames. And yet another proudly showed off his ability to blow fire from his mouth after gargling lighter fluid. My advice: Do not try the last skill yourself.

STEREOTYPED SOURCES

In the photo, the two students are leaning toward each other.

Their eyes are locked amorously. Their lips are puckered in anticipation. And their hands are blocking their mouths.

The odd last detail is a playful symbol of the couple's vow to save their first kiss until after marriage.

The image ran alongside a spring 2012 report in *Ball Bearings Magazine* at Ball State University. The story focused on the small segment of college students who pledge to refrain from kissing until their wedding day, even as hook-ups and one-night stands take place in bars and dorm rooms all around them.

During her reporting, Lindsey Gelwicks, at the time a Ball State junior, found that for students waiting to smooch "a kiss isn't just a kiss." There are religious considerations, family expectations, peer pressures, emotional intimacy issues, and the media-created fairy tale of what the experience is supposed to be.

She also found another layer of complexity: the students waiting to kiss or be kissed are not who many people expect them to be. "My boyfriend had read several drafts of the story as I was writing it, so he had an image of these students in his head," she said. "When he saw the magazine with the pictures for the first time, he turned to me and said, 'Wow, these people are actually really attractive.' He wasn't the only one to say this to me. Because sex is so prominent in our culture, I think we have this stereotype in our heads about those who don't partake in physical activity. Sometimes we automatically assume that something is wrong with them or that they are just unattractive and 'can't get any.' This isn't the case. They are just like everybody else. They have just chosen a different path than most."

Ugly Virgin. Ditzy Blonde. Socially Awkward Asian. Rude Frenchman. Homophobic Christian. Dumb Jock. Science Nerd. Crotchety Old Person. Haughty Ivy Leaguer. Slutty Sorority Girl. Fat Slob. Shady Politician. Carefree Hippie. Muslim Terrorist. Anorexic Model. Troubled Loner.

Every age group, body type, geographic region, ethnicity, religious denomination, hobby, sport, academic major, profession, and political party contains eye-roll-worthy, popularized, and hard-to-shake stereotypes. Most have become so deeply entrenched in our culture they are simply accepted as true.

Many of us fall within various groupings ourselves, forced to either put up with or constantly fend off the spate of stereotypes that come with them. These stereotypes often add up to some semblance of a version of us—at least the "us" people superficially see and make immediate judgments about. As an author explains, "Show a people as one thing, only one thing, over and over again, and that is what they become."

Along with educating the public, exposing wrongs, and telling truth to power, journalists must strive to find and present more in-depth human stories, to show people as many, many things. Let's start with the toughest groups to scrub fresh: the stereotyped.

ASSIGNMENT ALERT!

A Trip to the Corner

 Interview numerous people about the stereotypes they feel cornered into. Discuss the relative truths of these stereotypes, their most inaccurate and offensive aspects, how they have helped or hurt them, and what is being done or should be done to change them.

Check out recent related news reports and media depictions to help determine how and how much pop culture props up the stereotypes or attempts to cut through them. Talk to experts and review research determining the stereotypes' factuality and their effects on a mass scale or over time.

Talk to a sampling of students on campus and the public at large to grasp the everyday perceptions about the stereotypes. Also, think about your own initial perceptions of the people you chose to interview and whether the stereotypes you held about them have been strengthened or changed through your reporting.

IDEAS, ONLINE

The Gavin Project

 Gavin is a Yale University student who likes dogs, The Beatles, and Barack Obama. He plays poker for money. He appears to have cheated on at least one of his exes. He may illegally stream television shows and illegally download music online. He once Googled the phrase "proof for alcohol to be flammable" for reasons one can only imagine. And he has the founder of Reddit, a former Mexican president, and former New York governor Eliot Spitzer on his smartphone contacts list.

In spring 2011, a small group of Yale undergrads uncovered these facts about Gavin and much, much more, while enrolled in a computer science course focused on privacy in the digital age. For a final project, the students dived into the mobile phone, Gmail account, and Facebook account of a peer—with his full permission. They publicly dubbed the student "Gavin" to protect his identity.

They read his emails. They examined his Facebook messages, wall posts, and photos. And they scrolled through his smartphone texts, apps, contacts list, call logs, and mobile web browsing and search history. As they shared on a website called The Gavin Project (thegavinproject.com), the students' efforts revealed an incredible amount about Gavin—including information most would consider intimate and embarrassing.

According to the students, "Our goal in compiling this project was to determine the answer to two questions: 'what source of personal information is the most revealing?' and 'which source of personal information would you least like to reveal to the world?' "

Along with the phone, email, and social media details, the students searched for information about Gavin through Google, Yahoo!, and Bing, in part to note the contrast between our public and private Internet selves.

"[A] simple Google search won't reveal the extent of Gavin's romantic encounters, his music tastes, grades, and questionably legal activity," the students reported. "Each of Gavin's technological media that most of society would regard as private—his cell phone, Facebook account, and Gmail account—exposed different aspects of Gavin's private life . . . Perhaps the more philosophical question should be where *is* the real Gavin?"

Your Assignment

Conduct your own personal data collection experiment on a willing participant. Respectfully request temporary access to some or all of the following: their main email account, Facebook account, other social media accounts, blog, mobile phone, tablet, laptop, iPod, and digital camera. Then, dive in.

Find out as much as you can about the individual through their digital presence and devices. Along with basics such as age, appearance, year in school, and hometown, see if you can obtain details about their academic performance, dating life, family history, illegal or morally questionable behavior, sleep and communication patterns, close friends, entertainment fixes, creative endeavors, and religious and political affiliations.

Determine the account or device that revealed the most and least about your Gavin. Consider how many private details were uncovered about *other* people somehow connected to Gavin. Also, nail down what you did *not* uncover about your Gavin.

Then, conduct an extensive Google search—comparing the public results that pop up with your own private findings. Finally, share your findings and get a reaction from your Gavin, including whether their perspectives on privacy or digital identity have shifted.

ETHICS ALERT!

 Similar to the Yale Gavin team, set ground rules with your participant in advance, including what data or details are off limits for your search and public reveal. And err on the side of caution when presenting information that may disclose the person's identity, get them in trouble, or disclose the identity of someone they know or once interacted with.

THE LITTLE GUYS

The people most often profiled are the biggies, those who operate at the extremes.

They are the most successful, powerful, wild, strange, courageous, selfless, soulless, destitute, or just plain lucky individuals walking the Earth. Profile them. Enjoy. But don't overlook the unsung, oft-forgotten little guys.

In a spring 2012 commencement speech at Barnard College, President Barack Obama shared, "People ask me sometimes, 'Who inspires you, Mr. President?' Those quiet heroes all across this country . . . no fanfare, no articles written about them, they just persevere. They just do their jobs. They meet their responsibilities. They don't quit. I'm only here because of them. They may not have set out to change the world, but in small, important ways, they did."

On the journalistic front, *Harvard Independent* president emerita Susan Zhu shares advice echoing Obama's sentiments: "Look for the little guys, the underdogs. The big names will always have an outlet and a voice. It's our responsibility to make sure that they don't drown out everyone else."

ASSIGNMENT ALERT!

Quiet Campus Heroes

 In an adaptation of Obama's turn-of-phrase, find and profile some quiet campus heroes—people putting in a full day or making a difference in some small way, but receiving little, if any, recognition from their peers or the press. To start, consider focusing on individuals in one of these groups.

- Adult students
- Athletic trainers
- Cafeteria workers
- Cleaning crew
- Commuter students
- Groundskeepers
- Remedial students
- Security officers on graveyard shift
- Waste management employees
- Webmasters

IDEAS, ONLINE

Crowdsourcing

 The police officer asked for 500 rupees. Last August, a resident of India said a constable came alone to his home and calmly requested compensation in that amount if he wanted his passport application approved. As the resident shared, "I was shocked the way he is [*sic*] demanding bribe without fear."

The resident's complaint is one of more than 20,000 shared by individuals across India on I Paid a Bribe (ipaidabribe.com). The website is described as "the only forum for citizens to air their grievances when they grease palms." Specifically, it enables the public to document all instances in which they are forced to bribe officials to obtain clearances, licenses, and assistance for everything from purchasing property, operating a business, and winning a court case to getting good grades, having a baby, and keeping their electricity turned on.

In the site's first two years, people have shared stories of bribes totaling the equivalent of roughly $8.4 million. Their enraged accounts of how the payoffs were demanded by officials occupying positions of trust have raised awareness about the country's massive graft problem and the public's desire to do something about it.

As its founders contend, the secret to I Paid a Bribe's success has been "harnessing the collective energy of citizens."

This collective energy is at the heart of crowdsourcing, the ultimate people-first digital journalism method. As Robert Niles explains in *Online Journalism Review*, "Crowdsourcing, in journalism, is the use of a large group of readers to report a news story. It differs from traditional reporting in that the information collected is gathered not manually, by a reporter or team of reporters, but through some automated agent, such as a website."

Some crowdsourcing projects share the public's responses or bootstrap reporting about a single issue or event. A few examples: personal stories of post-college debt, eyewitness video of a major disaster, hashtagged tweets during Homecoming weekend, or even regular updates on local gas prices (gasbuddy.com). Other projects proactively solicit so-called citizen journalists to help with a more massive investigation, such as digging through government documents for clues of corruption. Still others are more general and freestanding, built to capture the public's take on news of the day or the quirks of a particular locale.

For example, Overheard in New York (overheardinnewyork.com) features regular updates of dramatic, funny, inane, and vulgar conversations spoken by people in The Big Apple. The conversations are submitted by hundreds of "spies and eavesdroppers" roaming the streets. Three very quick examples:

- Gentleman on B7 bus: "She's vegetarian?! I thought she was an alcoholic?"
- Twentysomething intellectual at a private party in Brooklyn: "Facts are such a distraction from the essence of what's really happening."
- Woman at an eatery on Manhattan's West Side: "I am dating two different guys with kids and no one will take me to see *Harry Potter*. Now *that's* f***ed up."

One writer smarmily praises the site as "an immense grassroots sociological experiment, a deeply profound (and yes, often moronic) verbal profile of the 21st-century urban-American street."

ASSIGNMENT ALERT!

Overheard on Campus

Much like city streets, college campuses feature a bevy of bizarre, hysterical, and insightful conversations every day—in classes, cafeterias, dorms, elevators, and house parties and on athletic fields, construction sites, sidewalks, and late-night shuttles. The constant chatter—the small talk, philosophizing, and flirting provides a unique glimpse into the experiences, fears, beliefs, and thoughts of the countless people who compose the heart of higher education.

Bottom line: The campus is talking.

Your Assignment

 Listen in. And report on what you hear. In the spirit of Overheard in New York, temporarily tune into the speeches, shouts, and conversation snippets spoken in your presence on campus. Capture the especially outrageous, heartfelt, hilarious, and memorable quotes. Also, take note of the speakers' general descriptions and the setting in which the words are spoken. And submit your quotes collection to the public via a blog or appropriate social media platform.

CHAPTER 4

Fresh Perspectives

Illustration by Yee Hung Lim

Nigerians do not know how to use a stove.

They cannot speak English. They listen to "tribal music." And they are in need of saving from themselves—their poverty, "senseless wars," and scourges such as AIDS.

In a public talk in 2009, Nigerian novelist Chimamanda Ngozi Adichie recounted that, years before, her American college roommate actually believed these and many other falsities about her and her African homeland.

"She had felt sorry for me even before she saw me," said Adichie. "Her default position toward me as an African was a kind of patronizing, well-meaning pity."

Why? From Adichie's perspective, it is because the only narrative her roommate and many other Westerners have ever been fed about Africa is one of "catastrophe" and a lifestyle incredibly different and somehow beneath those practiced in the First World.

The reality, of course, is much more complicated—dependent on the stories being told and the voices doing the telling. Yet, there is often only one dominant perspective that weaves its way into the cultural sphere to the discounting or elimination of all others, including at times the truth.

Adichie calls it "the danger of a single story."

College media face their own set of similar dangers: the SOS SASS. The acronym I've coined is short for the Same Old Stories, Semester After Semester Syndrome. There are simply some stories reported upon by student journalists again and again, sometimes with a fresh spin, but always with the same core issue or topic intact.

SOS SASS is not always a negative. The college audience—at least the main student one—is always changing, ensuring new eyes for "old" stories. And some issues deserve repeated reporting and editorializing, like the incarcerated main character Andy in *Shawshank Redemption* writing his weekly letter for years in order to finally secure funding for the prison library.

But in reality, the same old stories tend to be published semester after semester simply because students are not aware or do not care that they have already been covered. The result: an archived stories set that starts to look awfully familiar. During an interview with a former editor-in-chief of a top-notch campus newspaper, I pulled up the website of the paper he once ran. His first reaction upon seeing the lead story on the homepage: "Well, the headline's different, but we basically wrote the same thing five years ago."

Here are seven Same Old Stories, with their most common news angles listed beneath them:

1. **Student Drinking**
   (Dangerous Behavior)

2. **Study Abroad**
   (Life-Changing Experience)

3. **Campus Parking**
   (Tough to Grab a Spot)

4. **Student Fees**
   (Being Raised, Some Concerns)

5. **New Staff Hire**
   (Smiley, Eager to Pitch In)

6. **Visiting Speaker**
   (Crowd Gathered)

7. **Freshmen Orientation**
   (Bonding, Starting Year Off Right)

Even on the tightest of deadlines or the seemingly most boring story, don't suffer from SOS SASS, or what is also commonly called cliché of vision. You do not have to write the narrative you think you are supposed to write. If you begin reporting already knowing how a story will turn out, stop being a journalist. You might as well be inputting numbers at an accountancy firm.

■ Break free. Search for the unexpected. Keep your eyes open. Maintain your sense of wonder. Even on what appear to be the most obvious stories, through your reporting, your perspectives can and will change.

IN OTHER WORDS

"The best advice I have for a beginning student journalist is this: If you're at the Louvre, don't look at the Mona Lisa. It's always important to find a fresh angle on a story, but as a starting journalist it's paramount you prove that you can find unique stories, too. Sure, the Mona Lisa has an interesting story, but it's been covered, read, and absorbed. Turn around. Are there new paintings? Are any missing? Who is looking at the Mona Lisa? Who isn't?"

Emily Handy, former managing editor,
The Oracle, University of South Florida

"In college, I once heard a *Wall Street Journal* editor say that there are two types of stories: a 'no sh*t' story (you know, flu season is coming, blah blah) and an 'oh sh*t!' story (something amazing and beyond the mundane). He said he always pushes his reporters to do the 'oh sh*t!' story. He's right. Now there will be plenty of lame stories in your career, and when you're at a smaller newspaper sometimes you get more than your fair share of lame stories. But there are usually more innovative angles to take, people to talk to, and ways to make it more interesting for the reader and for you to write."

Kate Kompas, news editor,
St. Cloud Times, Minn.

Illustration by Yee Hung Lim

THREE PERSPECTIVES TO SEEK OUT

Brainstorming a story idea does not just involve choosing a person, place, thing, issue or activity to focus upon.

It also includes selecting and sharing a perspective. A huge factor separating no sh*t stories from oh sh*t stories is the reporter's ability to tell them in a new, newsworthy way. Give readers a view of someone or something they otherwise would never see, have never seen before, or have never stopped to take a close look at.

Here are three perspectives to seek out as you get started.

The Turnaround: a literal and metaphorical twist, focusing on people, places, and things not often featured or on the fringes of major events and phenomena.

Example

The number of students leaving school prior to graduation has risen so dramatically in recent years that the U.S. now boasts the highest college dropout rate in the industrialized world.

Yet, dropouts rarely receive press attention, and the few related stories that are published often frame them in a failing light.

As a onetime dropout wrote last year in *The Mooring Mast* just prior to his own commencement from Pacific Lutheran University, "[W]hile the graduates are treated as people, the rest of us are treated as statistics. Every year, analysts write about why some of us failed to complete all four years of our degree. Nobody writes about all the work we did to make it through one year, or two, or three."

The Obstructed View: a purposeful attempt to report from a vantage point that is limited or offbeat, dropping journalism's standard "eye of God" pretense.

Example

In spring 2011, New York University sophomore Taylor Myers lived in the school's main library for five days.

His brief stay in the facility, named Bobst, was a test-run to see if he could stomach a long-term living situation. Due to financial aid problems, he had been considering staying there permanently the following fall. He called it a "sacrifice that must be made" for the sake of his education.

Myers's suitemate Andrew Duffy created a short documentary film about the experiment, titled "Bedless in Bobst." According to *The Washington Square News*, NYU's student newspaper, Duffy and a small crew "recorded seven hours of audio and took hundreds of photographs, and even stayed overnight with Myers in Bobst's lower levels." To enhance the authenticity of their report, they wanted to see what it was truly like to live in the library.

The Story Behind the Story: a glimpse behind the scenes of a newsworthy figure, event, location, or trend aimed at showing them in a new light and providing added context.

Example

It's a fascinating—and horrifying—thought to some students: Professors used to be young. In their current roles, of course, they teach. They publish. They advise. They hold office hours at weird times. And they fail to grasp the concept of a Twitter hashtag. But before they were professors, they were students.

What were they like then? Did they party? Did they study abroad? Did they switch majors more than clothes? In general, did they enjoy the "stereotypical college experience" or something far from it?

In spring 2011, *The Columbia Daily Spectator* sought to answer those questions and more. The campus newspaper offered six Columbia University professors the chance to "reflect on their days as students."

The main revelation: Most professors are not born with tenure and a silver spoon. For example, renowned Columbia sociologist Herbert Gans recalled attending the University of Chicago mainly because it was within walking distance of home—he didn't have the money for room and board at a school any farther away.

THE ALWAYS LIST

- **Always** keep an open mind about how or through whom you can tell a story.
- **Always** be sure the perspective fits the story and what your editors want. If you are assigned to cover the State of the Union, reporting upon it from the vantage point of protestors near the White House may not be permissible every time out.
- **Always** witness or participate in a perspective firsthand, when possible. For example, if you are reporting on America's growing soccer fever, attend English Premier League match viewing parties at local bars. If you are reporting on a campus security ramp-up, go on patrol with the officers.
- **Always** attempt to surmount the limits of your own perspectives. Recognize how your age, education, past travels, political stances, religion, and more shapes what you know and don't know—and how you view the world.

THE NEVER LIST

- **Never** accept the first perspective you come up with. In almost all cases, there is a better one waiting to be brainstormed or captured.
- **Never** be afraid to physically embrace the fresh perspective hunt. Cock your head sideways. Lie down and look up. Move to the back of the room and squint your eyes. Climb a ladder, safely, to the top and look around. Or shut your eyes and simply listen—just get down from the ladder first.
- **Never** run from who or what is most unpopular or hated. Their perspectives carry credence, may help ease the fervor surrounding them, or at least open the door for a glimpse at their humanity.
- **Never** forget all perspectives are relative. One country's terrorist is another country's freedom fighter. During a political debate, a book-smart professor may come across as more intelligent than a local mechanic with a high school degree. But just wait until the professor's car breaks down. In the end, it's all a matter of perspective.

ASSIGNMENT ALERT!

The Groundhog Day Story

Inspired by the classic Bill Murray film *Groundhog Day*, take part in a faux sci-fi adventure. The gist: You wake up, charged with covering an event. The next morning, you wake up once more like normal, but discover it is the same day—and you are charged with covering the same event again. And again, and again, and again.

You are stuck reporting upon the same news story, over and over. And the kicker: You must figure out a way to tell it from a different perspective each time.

To jumpstart the adventure, attend an event on campus or in the community. Subsequently, brainstorm how you would report on it over many, many days. Or imagine yourself as a reporter writ large, at the scene of a major event like the Super Bowl or a supremely historic moment like the moon landing or the fall of the Berlin Wall.

Regardless of which actual or imagined news happening you chose, the ultimate question you want to answer is the same: How many different ways—and from how many different perspectives—can you tell stories about it?

For each *Groundhog Day* story, create a perspectives list. Start updating it with ideas right away. After all, your very long day is just beginning.

In the long term, use the exercise as inspiration. Consider creating a perspectives list for each story you are assigned or pitch, in part to help you brainstorm possible sources to track down, storytelling methods to employ, and related issues and angles to report upon.

THE OPPOSITE ATTRACTION

Joe Fox once went out of his way to attempt to hate cats.

According to the Ohio University student, the "adorable little demons have to be stopped."

In a column last spring for *The Post*, OU's student newspaper, Fox cited six main reasons cats unnerve, anger, and annoy him. "I hate their cute little paws, their perky ears, and the way they gracefully leap between pieces of furniture as if the floor was lava," he wrote. "I hate that they always land on their feet . . . and I hate the way they lie on their backs and look up into my soul as if by not petting their bellies immediately I am sending them into an inescapable spiral of depression. And most of all, I hate it when they rub up against my legs and emit coy meows. It's unbearably adorable."

To be clear, Fox actually loves cats.

He has two pet cats right now, and a third deceased cat he still misses dearly. Their names: Proton (his parents both studied chemistry in college), Electron, and Jasper. He also owns three books about cats and feels he would do well in "a feline trivia contest."

But in the spirit of quality journalism, he wanted to briefly take an opposing stance and see things—and in this case felines—from another perspective.

It's a tack he sometimes took with his *Post* column. For example, as he recalled, "I was fed up [a while back] with people who ride really loud motorcycles. So I wrote a column that was from the perspective of someone who rides a really loud motorcycle—just trying to get inside the head of someone who is obnoxious enough to drown out everything going on around them and figure out why they might do that."

The public, and the press, are most often focused on who and what is most popular, pervasive, expected, and ordinary. What get drowned out are the so-called opposites—the perspectives, people, behaviors, and beliefs that stand apart due to their rarity, strangeness, or high disapproval ratings.

ASSIGNMENT ALERT!

The Game of Opposites

Follow Fox's MO. Figure out what we all seemingly hold dear, take for granted as accurate, and simply accept as the way things are done. And then take the opposite tack.

Play the game of opposites in three steps. First, make a short list of people, places, items, trends, and ways of life that fit into the popular, pervasive, expected, and ordinary categories.

Next, determine who and what fits into the opposite category. Then brainstorm as many story ideas as possible related to those opposites.

Here are two quick examples to get you started.

Everyone Googles

What about individuals who lack Internet access or search engine know-how or those who dislike Google specifically or what it stands for generally?

An initial brainstorming session resulted in stories on those who prefer old-school research methods, the current state of university libraries and encyclopedias, the invisible web and what does *not* pop up on Google, the growing number of competing search engines, and online reputation managers paid to either prop up someone's Google history or make it go away.

Everyone enjoys a night out

What about those unable, unwilling, or not allowed to enjoy it and the many hurdles and enticements standing in people's way?

An initial brainstorming session resulted in stories on homebodies and individuals with social phobias, people who work at night and must socialize during the day, parolees and others legally restricted from leaving their residences beyond regular work hours, the increasing sophistication of home entertainment options, and the latest trends in digital hang-outs such as chat rooms, wikis, MMORPGs, and online speed dating forums.

THE INANIMATE PERSPECTIVE

A 26-inch inflatable boat. Crème brûlée cooking lessons. Chinchillas. And an earwax-removal training exercise.

The strange diversity of items, activities, and even animals that individuals are looking to peddle or purchase has not abated in the online age.

As a feature in *Inside* magazine at Indiana University begins, "Newspaper classified ad sales might be floundering, but that hasn't stopped people from buying and selling their junk. The adage 'one person's trash is another person's treasure' couldn't be truer in the world of cyber classified ads. Every lost ring, found wallet, and free couch has a hidden history."

In the piece, the staff writer uncovers the histories behind some of the more intriguing ads posted on an IU-only classified ads site. The individual snippets are alternately fascinating and hilarious. Most seem deserving of their own full reports.

All told, the tales are a published reminder. As you search for the proper prisms through which to tell stories, remember inanimate objects have (shelf) lives and perspectives all their own—even the most insignificant stuff.

ASSIGNMENT ALERT!

The Story Ideas Sack

Attack the sack. Specifically, brainstorm a pile of ideas related to items unloaded from a special story sack. To start, ask a friend, classmate, or colleague to fill a Santa-like sack with an array of quirky contents. The sack should contain things found around the house, purchased cheaply from a thrift shop, and borrowed from the vehicle, schoolbag, basement, and closet of a close acquaintance. The key: Stay in the dark about what's put inside.

Subsequently, alone or in a small team, pull out each item individually and launch into a series of speedy, intense brainstorming sessions. Conceive of ordinary and offbeat ideas related to each object until your brain hurts, tongue tires, or writing hand goes limp.

Build your ideas off each item's name, intended and unofficial uses, shape, size, age, cultural significance, and simply the first thing that comes to mind when it is flashed before your eyes.

When the sack, and your head, is emptied, identify the most promising ideas. Run them by a journalism professor, veteran journalist, or senior student newspaper staffer to determine if any are especially newsworthy and fresh.

Here are some items placed into a sack attacked last year by a small group of student journalists, along with a small sampling of ideas they conceived.

- Lava lamp
- "Keep Calm and Carry On" poster
- Used evolutionary biology textbook
- Flirty note from someone's ex
- Nintendo Wii guitar
- Halloween mask
- Illegal hot plate
- LEGO building set
- Knee brace
- Shot glass

Among the ideas brainstormed: an investigation into the campus construction contract bidding process (building off the LEGO set), a feature on the local glass art movement (the shot glass), a profile of students with early onset arthritis (knee brace), and a report on an area liposuction facility seemingly always busy, night and day (the lava lamp).

If an actual sack and physical stuff are non-starters, go virtual. Select items featured on Pinterest, Amazon, or eBay, throwing up screenshots or active pages on a laptop, tablet, or projector screen.

PHANTOM STORY SYNDROME

Sometimes, we feel a buzz when one does not exist.

There is a phenomenon in the digital age centered on an odd occurrence shared by many people: a sudden feeling that our mobile phones are vibrating in our pockets, bags, or purses, followed by a quick check revealing there had been no call, text, or alert.

It is known as phantom vibration syndrome. There is no scientific explanation. It seems the high-tech world and our human instincts simply go haywire every once in a while, producing an empty sensation.

There is a news media equivalent: the phantom story syndrome. Simply put, sometimes there is no story. It is an essential perspective to master. Know when a story is boring, insignificant, based on a PR stunt, painfully obvious, redundant, outside your scope, or not as relevant as the five other stories on your to-do list.

As Shaun Smith, a staff writer for New Jersey's *Current Newspapers*, notes, "Sometimes a story idea is a bad one. Reporters may spend hours, days, even weeks working on an assignment that might not turn out. Sometimes the story is that there is no story."

In many newsrooms, there are fewer reporters trying to cover more stories with more multimedia amid a constant deadline and real-time feedback. Faced with this reality, the ability to recognize a buzzworthy story from an empty sensation is an incredibly important skill. One journalist and techie calls it "innovation-by-omission."

Now to be clear, the phantom story syndrome is not an excuse to beg off a tough project or any other story whose awesomeness is not apparent the first moment it crosses your path. Many initially "bad stories" can be saved through an innovative approach, extra effort, or an especially spirited brainstorming session.

But we can no longer fall prey to what is known as "the journalism of filling space and time." Every story needs to matter.

ASSIGNMENT ALERT!

Same Old Stories

Scan campus, local, and national news outlets for stories that, well, don't matter. Or at least ferret out a few that suffer from the clichéd affliction mentioned at the chapter's start: the Same Old Stories, Semester After Semester Syndrome (SOS SASS). Then, reshape them. Brainstorm fresh angles for their main topic areas. Make them once again newsworthy, innovative, timely, and relevant to readers.

To get your brain synapses firing in the right direction, start by providing these especially heinous stories (certified victims of the SOS SASS) with fresh perspectives.

- **Campus Construction**
  (Some Headaches, Excitement for What's to Come)
- **Student Political Apathy**
  (Cynical About Candidates, Unsure How to Register)
- **Course Selection Trouble**
  (Some Students Locked Out, Issues with Online System)
- **Students Download Stuff Illegally**
  (They Just Don't Want to Pay, School is Monitoring)
- **Greek Life More Than Hazing, Drinking**
  (Charity Events, Lifelong Friendships Formed)

AN EXCHANGE OF IDEAS

A Matter of Opinion

 The exchange is a recurring feature in the book and on my blog, spotlighting advice and exercises from top journalism students, professionals, educators, and advocates.

This exchange comes from Brian Thompson. Thompson is a columnist and former editor at The St. Augustine Record. *He is the adviser of* The Gargoyle *student newspaper at Florida's Flagler College, where he also serves as news and information director, alumni magazine editor, and a visiting instructor.*

His exchange focuses on column and commentary writing, or in the context of this chapter, the opinionated perspective.

I have written more than 700 opinion columns in my career. Every single week I owe an editor a newspaper column. I have done radio commentaries. I have won Florida Press Club awards for commentary three years in a row. I even teach a college opinion writing class.

Yet, every week it is a struggle to come up with a new idea.

Why is opinion so hard?

Maybe it is because you are not writing about what other people think. You are writing about what *you* think. And putting your opinions out for public consumption—or ridicule— can be downright scary.

In addition, what you write has to be compelling and persuasive. It has to be unique and interesting. It has to be something your readers will relate to, read all the way to the end, and then want more.

That's a tall order, but it's not impossible.

Writing opinion doesn't have to be so nerve-racking, pressure-filled, and terrifying. Over the years, I've learned some key tips and tricks that will help you write opinion that truly matters.

"People-ize" Issues

Often, opinion writers concentrate all their attention on studies, legislative actions, statistics, or other tidbits from the news. They forget it isn't the issues we care about—it's the people affected by them. That's why it is so important to bring a human element into everything you write. Good opinion needs to be issue-based, but people-focused.

Find New and Fresh Angles

Most problems have already been written about in the same boring way. Through your own personal experiences with an issue—or how you've seen it impact someone else—take an old issue in a direction people haven't thought about before.

Write About Issues You're Interested In

Sounds obvious, right? But too often writers forget this. It doesn't mean something has to affect you personally, but good opinion usually comes from topics that cause our blood to boil or make us want to shout from the rooftops. After all, if *you* are not excited about an issue, how can you expect your readers to be?

Ask Yourself One Key Question

One of the biggest mistakes writers make is forgetting to ask themselves the simple, but critical, question: What's my point? Or put another way: What is it you are trying to say? In addition, ask yourself, what should readers take away or better understand about it? And what do you want people to do about it?

Take a Stand

Opinion is about, well, having an opinion! This means taking sides and jumping into the fray—even if it makes some people angry. Don't beat around the bush or ask a lot of questions like, "Shouldn't we care about the Australian shallowback hooknose penguin?" or "What do you think about it?" Instead, explain to readers what *you* think about it. Take a stand on the issues.

Don't Just Rant

Readers are looking for more than just complaints and frustrated rants about parking problems. They can do that themselves. What they want are insights, solutions to problems, and a push to take action.

Do Your Research

Just like a news story, you have to back up your opinion with good research and reporting. It isn't enough to take a stand on an issue. Know your stuff and share with readers the trusted sources and information that led you to your position.

Inject Your Voice into Everything You Write

Nothing is worse than stiff, scholarly, boring-as-oatmeal opinion writing. Readers want personality. They want to hear the voice of the writer in every piece. The goal isn't to sound like everyone else. It is to sound like you. Be conversational. Be colorful and lively. Be creative, even funny. Just don't be boring.

Have Confidence in Your Writing

Believe you have something important to say. As Pulitzer Prize-winning columnist Connie Schultz once told a group of young journalists, "Speak your mind even if your voice shakes."

Read it Aloud—Even if You Hate the Sound of Your Voice

We hear problems with our pieces when we read them aloud. It is a great editing tool that will help you figure out what needs to be cut or smoothed out.

Be Persuasive

Pulitzer Prize-winning editorialist Michael Gartner once said editorials and columns are not stories, but arguments. In an argument, you try to convince someone to see things your way. That is the goal of all opinion. Your other goal: Convince someone to stand up and take some action.

Break Out of the Box

Not all opinion has to be poured from the same mold. Every once in a while, get out of the box and experiment with new styles of writing. Give humor and satire a shot. Personal essays can also be a great way to tackle an issue that has affected you. You will find others have been through similar situations, and will relate on a personal level.

Have Fun and Write with Passion

Otherwise, don't write. Get a hobby. Learn how to weave baskets. If you don't love it, there are much easier ways to spend your time.

To view an archived set of Brian Thompson's columns, visit *The St. Augustine Record* website at staugustine.com/entertainment/brian-thompson.

ASSIGNMENT ALERT!

One Word Focus

Need help focusing the topic or angle of your opinion? Try boiling it down to a sentence, or even a single word.

On my first trip to Cuba as a journalist, I struggled with a column. I wanted to write about Cubans usingrafts to try to make it to U.S. shores, but I didn't know how to start it and I grew frustrated. Then, as I was standing on Havana's waterfront overlooking the Florida Straits, I realized it all came down to this: distance.

When I had been in Key West, Fla., Cuba always seemed so close—only 90 miles away. In the U.S., 90 miles is nothing. But standing on the shores of this Communist nation, hearing the stories of those who had braved the waters on rickety oil drums lashed together as rafts, 90 miles seemed like forever.

"Distance" was a matter of perspective, not to mention life and death. That one word helped me find focus and a place to start writing.

Your Assignment

 Boil down an opinion of your own to a single word. Brainstorm a few to start, testing out their merits with yourself and others, before selecting a winner. Then list the angles and arguments that spin out from the word. Also, jot down an opening sentence or nut graf built around the thrust of what the word means to the opinion you want to present. Or set an online countdown timer and simply free-write for 10 to 15 minutes, using the word as the starter prompt.

IDEAS, ONLINE

One Word

The premise is simple: For 60 seconds, you should do nothing but write your heart out. For inspiration, you are given a single word.

Icicle. Autumn. Alarmist. Profound. Those are just a few of the many writing prompts at the heart of oneword (oneword.com).

The interactive forum is built around one new word each day. The words are triggers, pushing you to briefly brainstorm and write, write, write, without over-thinking, losing focus, or falling prey to other tasks.

The game is perfect for days in which your creativity has fled or your brain needs a chainsaw rev-up. It allows you to flesh out ideas in a raw, spontaneous format, built atop a word that is typically general enough to be looked at from many different perspectives. The key is pouring out your thoughts in an uninterrupted burst, with no worries about misspellings and grammar snafus.

The site's motto: "Don't think. Just write."

CHAPTER 5

Words, Letters, and Lots of Ideas

Illustration by Yee Hung Lim

Music. Sunshine. Vivacious. Exquisite. Jedi. Anthropomorphic. Zany. Spiffy. Weightless. Mentor. Mensch. And Kanye!

These nouns, adjectives, and verbs (some sporting exclamation points) are among the roughly 1,500 selected since 2008 by incoming freshmen at California's University of the Pacific to describe themselves. They are featured in the One Word Project (pacificoneword.org), a student-run initiative aimed at capturing the essence of first-year students through their own definitions.

A related website features a scrollable photo slideshow of each student, posing next to their superimposed chosen word. A pop-up then provides a first-person explanation about the word's meaning and significance to the student.

The explanations are helpful, especially when the words defy convention—or are not even traditional words at all. For example, junior Fatima Carpenter selected F@+!M@, a typographical adaptation of her first name. "It is spelled differently because it describes my personality," she writes. "I am spontaneous! I chose my name as my one word because there is a sentimental meaning behind it for me. When I was born I had heart-lungs-bypass and there was a small chance for me surviving. So one day my mom went to church and prayed for my survival. She promised to name me after Our Lady of Fatima. After that I gradually started to recover and now I am a living proof of an answered prayer."

In a larger sense, the One Word Project is interactive proof of one of journalism 2.0's core content bases: features focused on words, lots and lots of words, old and new, common and rare, everyday and quirky, all competing for attention.

According to the Global Language Monitor, there are more than 1 million words in use in the English language. A new one is coined roughly every 90 minutes. As the American Dialect Society confirms, "language change is normal, ongoing, and entertaining."

It can also be newsworthy.

■ The path to new trends, issues, and types of individuals can often be tracked through the words, acronyms, and phrases created or popularized to describe them. As writer and cultural critic Touré shares, "The words we coalesce around as a society say so much about who we are. The language is a mirror that reflects our collective soul."

SOME WORD STORIES

Buzzwords: old, new, and obscure words suddenly gaining traction, stirring controversy or shifting in meaning. Some examples of fairly recent vintage: FOMO, true conservative, Occupy movement, Kony, Katniss, and pinning.

Example

Feathering is a popular fashion trend that has some crying fowl. For a few years now, a healthy slice of female students have been adding "shiny, long, speckled," and colorful feather extensions to their bangs or the bottom layers of their hair.

The process is inexpensive, only takes a few minutes, and is less permanent than a full dye or cut. It is also apparently quite inhumane for the animals involved.

As a PETA representative told *The Daily Titan* at California State University, Fullerton, "[R]oosters are typically confined for 30 weeks—the majority of their short lives—in tiny, stacked cages inside deafeningly loud barns before they are killed and skinned."

Wordplay: larger issues and trends impacting modern language and communication. Related stories often focus on everyday language shifts (such as the rise in multilingualism), ways of communicating (such as graffiti), and digital language phenomena (such as textspeak and wikis).

Example

A "compliments culture" is quietly spreading on many campuses. Specifically, students at a rising number of schools are earning kudos and attention simply for doling out compliments—in person and online.

For example, during a recent semester at UCLA, a student trio became known as "The Compliment Guys." They spent an afternoon each week standing at a high-traffic campus walkway, firing off spirited bursts of sincere flattery to students while wearing colorful costumes.

The students were not part of a fraternity or other formal campus group. They were not raising money or awareness for a larger cause. They just enjoyed giving compliments—and hoped others would enjoy receiving them. As one of the Compliment Guys said, "It's an involuntary bonding experience. UCLA is very fragmented. People are isolated in their social groups, and there isn't much mingling. When we give compliments, it's one of the few times people are receiving something just for being a student."

Wordsmiths: individuals and groups whose work, culture, or life is centered in some way on language. A few examples: speechwriters, the deaf, foreign language translators, hip-hop artists, and debate teams.

Example

In fall 2011, a New Jersey high school student enrolled in a local college course earned international attention after his professor asked him to no longer speak in class. The student has "a profound stutter that makes talking difficult, and talking quickly impossible."

The professor felt his attempts to ask and answer questions were disruptive to his classmates. As *The New York Times* reported, "His classroom experience underlines a perennial complaint among stutterers, that society does not recognize the condition as a disability, and touches on an age-old pedagogical—and social—theme: the balance between the needs of an individual and the good of a group."

THE ALWAYS LIST

- **Always** think of creative ways to use words as 'ins' to stories.
- **Always** consider what a new word, phrase, hashtag, and acronym says about society and how it connects to a larger group, trend, or issue.

- **Always** keep an eye out for words and language patterns that are fading or have disappeared entirely, along with those growing in popularity.
- **Always** recognize the power of words expressed in non-text and non-story forms, including the spoken word, sign language, photography, fashion, art, and computer code.

THE NEVER LIST

- **Never** fail to recognize the bigger picture changes in expression that may be occurring far beyond the introduction of a single word.
- **Never** overlook the potential cultural impact of even the silliest words and phrases.
- **Never** stop reading and looking up words you do not know.
- **Never** forget to focus some stories on the words students create, including in their status updates, first-person essays, and academic research. At times, they can tell you a ton about their creators and the larger college culture.

ASSIGNMENT ALERT!

Brainstorm Something

 Every word can and should trigger inspiration. Words can be the foundations for brainstorming sessions. They can be associated with newsworthy events, issues, trends, and individuals. They can be built upon and with the right reframing or fresh perspectives configured into publishable stories.

In the spirit of the popular mobile app Draw Something, let's play Brainstorm Something. The exercise involves formulating as many quality story ideas as possible linked to the words you select.

The key to success: See beyond a word's direct, literal meaning or the first thing you associate with it in your head. Instead, seek out all its possible usages and its connections, however remote, to other people, places, trends, and principles.

For example, the word Manhattan can be brainstormed in the context of many things, including a borough (of course in New York), a full-blown city (most prominently in Kansas), a classic film, a bridge, a bagel company, a cocktail, a college, and a once-secret government project of nuclear proportions.

Now, play Brainstorm Something yourself.

BRAINSTORM
SOMETHING

Select a word from one of the sets below and immediately start brainstorming. Conceive of at least a dozen related ideas as quickly as you can. Rank them in order of their newsworthiness and how creatively they connect to your chosen word. Subsequently, share them with a friend, classmate or colleague. From the ideas you pitch, can they guess the word you picked?

EASY: Baby
MEDIUM: Records
HARD: Download

EASY: YouTube
MEDIUM: Rollercoaster
HARD: Zombie

EASY: Nurse
MEDIUM: Marathon
HARD: Scissors

EASY: Lion King
MEDIUM: Star Wars
HARD: Fight Club

EASY: Debt
MEDIUM: Homeless
HARD: Dubstep

EASY: Gambling
MEDIUM: Tattoo
HARD: Bandwidth

EASY: FarmVille
MEDIUM: Guitar Hero
HARD: Fruit Ninja

EASY: Valley of the Dolls
MEDIUM: The Da Vinci Code
HARD: Singin' in the Rain

EASY: Racism
MEDIUM: Capitalism
HARD: Plagiarism

Next, create your own version of the game. Come up with words specific to your campus or coverage area. Bonus points for especially offbeat, timely or newsworthy selections. And extra kudos for motivating yourself or your peers to choose the "Hard" options each time out.

Graphic by Mike Trobiano and Brooke Scherer

POST-MORTEM

 Post-Mortem is a recurring feature in the book and on my blog, telling the story *behind* **a story, series, or website—in the words of the reporter or editor responsible for creating it.**

WKU, A to Z

A is for Ambassador. B is for Band Member. C is for Chess. D is for Dubstep. E is for Event Planner. F is for Forensics. G is for Guns.

Those are the first seven headlines in a yearlong 26-part series put together in 2011–2012 by *The College Heights Herald* at Western Kentucky University.

"WKU, A to Z" featured students and a few faculty whose side-jobs, club activities, life passions, sexual identities, genetic anomalies, and professional goals could all be categorized under different letters of the alphabet.

Former *Herald* features editor Emily Patton, the series leader, said part of the paper's aim was to highlight people with slightly unique abilities or sensibilities whose names and faces would not otherwise be considered newsworthy.

"We wanted to take snapshots of individuals' lives, regular Janes and Joes," she said. "A lot of times people don't get in the paper unless they're doing something incredibly unique or bad or really good. So I think this series simply recognizes all the people who are special just for being themselves."

For every letter, there is a story. R is for Racquetball. S is for Saxophonist. T is for Twins. U is for Umpire. V is for Violinist. X is for Xylophone . . .

In this Q&A, Patton discusses the series' start, standout stories, and reporting methods. She also offers advice for student journalists interested in similarly exploring their campuses—from A to Z.

How did the series come about?
It was actually really simple at first. It came down to basic mathematics. We have 26 Friday issues a year. We were looking for a way to have a series that would run on those 26 Fridays where we could be proactive and we wouldn't have to worry about whether we had a story to run based on outside events . . . There are 26 letters in the alphabet so it was just kind of "OK, 26, what can we do with that?"

We wanted to look at students who people see all the time on campus and have questions about and make up stories about in their head, like, "Oh, he's doing that for this reason." For example, I was stopped at a red light on campus one day at a crosswalk and this guy who walked by my car was juggling. He was just doing it like it was normal, like he does it all the time. I had no idea who he was. But then days later I overheard people talking about "the guy who juggles." I thought, "Wow, that could be the same guy I saw." Then, more people came up to tell me about him. I sent a couple of reporters on my staff out to find this guy. It wasn't hard. In an hour, they found "the guy who juggles" and we [published] a story about him.

It's those kinds of stories that I know people will pick up and read. It's those kinds of stories that keep journalism around. We want to read about other individuals and stuff that impacts us or walks right by us every day.

How did the brainstorming for each letter and story work?
Some of the letters got done early. Some of them we knew in advance. And a lot of times we'd change letters mid-semester. Something came up or something caught our eye . . . When we were trying to come up with stories for "Q," we started by brainstorming words beginning with that letter. Queen was one of them, but we immediately shook the idea off because we thought about Homecoming Queen or Beauty Queen. We felt like those had been done before. They always got coverage when Homecoming comes around or Miss Kentucky was a Western student. So we shot it down.

For the longest time, we had planned to do Quarterback. There was a back-up quarterback. He had been injured. That was our go-to story. Then this local drag queen theater popped up. We heard people were going to it. So all of a sudden Q was for drag queen.

At first we thought it was still way too far-fetched. It was crazy. We can't do that. But then we found people who do this on campus and that it was a fairly common thing among a certain group of students . . . It was such a last-minute thing. It was in the middle of the day and we needed to shoot a drag queen in full costume and make-up. It was a struggle, but it ended up being a great story and photo.

Ultimately, any idea that my staff brought to me, I wanted it. I can't preach that enough: Any idea you think won't go anywhere, that's a starting point. And we can take it somewhere.

What's your advice for those who want to carry out a similar A-to-Z series?
Definitely plan ahead, but be willing to be flexible. In addition, be creative. Be very creative. The more creative you are, the more people gravitate to it.

Also, look for what's right in front of you. That's what other people see every day and that's what people want to read about. Since it's right in front of them and they might not know the whole story behind what they're seeing, it's your job to tell them.

IDEAS, ONLINE

Wordy Web Checks

There are many ways to monitor newsworthy word use online. Here is a sampling of regular web checks to carry out to spot trendy verbiage, language shifts, and emerging lingo significant enough for related features or even their own investigative reports.

- **Keep tabs on the most popular words, acronyms, and phrases** of the moment through spots such as Twitter, Google News, and the Merriam-Webster Online "Trend Watch" (merriam-webster.com/trend-watch).
- **Stay abreast of the newest crowdsourced slang** through websites such as Urban Dictionary (urbandictionary.com) and Word Spy (wordspy.com).
- **Learn the latest words in the web and mobile worlds**, starting with a stop at NetLingo (netlingo.com).
- **Check out Words of the Day**, including those featured on sites such as Dictionary.com, *The New York Times* Learning Network (nyti.ms/7j2xPB), and the Oxford English Dictionary (oed.com).
- **Keep track of Words of the Year**, most prominently those highlighted by the American Dialect Society (americandialect.org/woty). Over the past decade, the American Dialect Society's words of the year include those touching on major technological, political, social, and militaristic trends and events—from bailout, subprime, app, and metrosexual to tweet, WMDs, 9–11, and occupy.
- **Hunt for words that need to go**, in part through the "Banished Words List" put out annually by Lake Superior State University (lssu.edu/banished). Recent inductees: baby bump, man cave, the new normal, bff, ginormous, viral, and epic.

READ EVERYTHING

A man in Chile sports 83 tattoos, all depicting Julia Roberts.

Fox hunting has been illegal in England since 2004. King Juan Carlos of Spain earned criticism last year for hunting elephants in Botswana while his people suffered through a recession back home. He ended up suffering too, returning to Madrid earlier than planned to have surgery after falling and fracturing his hip.

Lebron James is the most popular athlete on Twitter. Foodies in New York's West Village have their choice of 173 different hamburgers. A small group of journalists hold the job title surfer photographer. Only 7 percent of the 34,000 students who applied to join Stanford University's class of 2016 were admitted. And, when they started dating, South Carolina governor Nikki Haley asked her husband to begin going by his middle name, Michael, instead of his actual first name, William— simply because he seemed more like a Michael to her. He agreed to the switch.

New York Times Magazine staffers know all this and much more due to a quirky assignment they sometimes blog about: Editors and reporters gamely attempt to read every word—every last word—of a variety of magazine issues. The cover-to-cover read-throughs have included editions of *Psychology Today*, *House Beautiful*, *The New Yorker*, *Real Simple*, *Sports Illustrated*, *Surfer Magazine*, *Vice*, *Vogue*, *The Economist*, and *Bloomberg Businessweek*.

The knowledge bits they glean are scattered and often delivered tongue-in-cheek. But the assignment's apparent point is serious and easy-to-spot: Even silly, dense, effete, and niche publications provide a bunch of intellectual and entertaining goodies that might trigger ideas worthy of a cover story—or at least a midday blog post.

The larger storytelling lesson it embodies: You can get a lot out of reading, really reading, anything and everything, down to the last word and letter. Others' words are incredibly powerful platforms from which to grab ideas, learn new writing styles, and come up with fresh reporting methods or ways of looking at the world.

IN OTHER WORDS

Illustration by Yee Hung Lim

"Absorb as much information as possible: The best journalists read everybody else's work, so they know what's been covered and where the holes are."

Lydia DePillis, staff writer,
Washington City Paper, D.C.

"READ! Read the newspaper. Read magazines. Read alternative publications. Read blogs. You need to understand the varying writing styles and who is the audience of each."

Tracy Collins, reporter,
Fox 30 Action News, Jacksonville, Fla.

"Read publications that don't reinforce your opinions. Get outside your comfort zone of views."

Hank Stern, former managing news editor,
The Willamette Week, Ore.

"In the moments when you're creatively stuck, which seems guaranteed to happen to journalists at every level, look for innovation. Save the stories—whether they are articles or interactive media or videos—that inspire you as a reader or viewer, and take note of what it is about that story that captivated you. Being aware of what makes a story powerful is incredibly helpful when you're trying to achieve the same effect."

Alisha Green, former capitol correspondent,
Michigan Information and Research Service

"Devour inspiration to build a foundation in your craft. You must seek out the best, consume it, and digest it. When you run across something that tickles you, figure out why. Take it apart, put it back together, tinker with it. Take it all in. Be inspired."

Brian Kennedy, online editor,
Napa Valley Register, Calif.

ASSIGNMENT ALERT!

Cover to Cover

 In the spirit of the *New York Times Magazine* assignment, grab and read the current issue of a popular or obscure magazine title. *Really* read it, cover to cover, including the masthead, advertisements, and letters to the editor. Pick out every interesting and newsworthy factoid. Then, use those facts as triggers to brainstorm quality story ideas.

For example, in a recent introductory journalism class of mine, students delving into a range of magazines found facts about the recent rise in mannies (male nannies), digital personal trainers, and men purchasing accessories such as bracelets, scarves, and shoulder bags (an apparent sign of economic recovery).

They learned about the invention of an inflatable abdominal tourniquet known as the "soldier saver" because of its potential to help injured military personnel in the field. They discovered broccoli consumption in the U.S. has risen dramatically in the past 30 years. They came across a statistic confirming 20,000 children are rushed to the emergency room each year due to sledding-related injuries. They read up on the most popular student laundry habits not involving the washer and dryer (including the "sniff test"). And they giggled at the official job title of a gentleman in Canada: Bear–Human Conflict Avoidance Educator.

A bevy of story ideas quickly followed.

AN EXCHANGE OF IDEAS

From One Word to 1,500 Words

 The exchange is a recurring feature in the book and on my blog, spotlighting advice and exercises from top journalism students, professionals, educators, and advocates.

Anna Young is a writer, designer, and photographer currently freelancing while attending graduate school in Colorado. While at James Madison University, she won scholarships and awards for writing and photography from organizations such as the Society of Professional Journalists and the American Copy Editors Society.

Her exchange focuses on the brainstorming, reporting, and writing steps needed to transform a single word into a polished story.

In summer 2010, during an internship with UPIU [since renamed UPI Next], the student arm of the international news service UPI, top staff approached me with a single-word story prompt: autism. "OK," I thought, "What *about* autism?"

Three weeks later, I published a news feature focused on young adults with autism.

How did I go from a one-word assignment to a 1,500-word article? Here are the steps I followed:

1 Audience

I had to narrow down the topic of autism to appeal to the primary readership of UPIU, which includes college students and twentysomethings. I asked, "What do young adults want to know about autism and why should they care?"

2 Research

I started researching autism and how it affects young adults. I asked, "What are the most pressing issues young adults with autism are facing?"

3 Topic

Through my research, I discovered one of the most pressing issues young adults with autism face is their struggle to transition into adulthood. I asked, "Is this an interesting topic for UPIU?"

4 Sources

After determining it was a good story for UPIU, I made a list of about 20 possible sources. On my list, I had government officials, school administrators, nonprofit employees, autism experts, and families of autistic young adults. I asked, "Even if I don't use all of these sources, does this list include all possible angles of my story?"

5 Facts

I tracked down facts and statistics from federal government reports and agencies, as well as nonprofit organizations and other advocacy groups. I asked, "Where is the best information I can find to include in my story to give it depth and credibility?"

6 Reporting

I spent a solid week on the phone and out of the office speaking with sources, compiling information, and composing an outline. The outline was crucial in helping me organize all of my information into a coherent storyline. Then, I reviewed the outline with UPIU mentor Krista Kapralos and set a deadline for my article. I asked, "What information is missing from my reporting?"

7 Shoe-leather

I didn't sit at my desk and send emails to gather all of my information, a lazy method of reporting often called "armchair journalism." Instead, I spoke directly to my sources, found a newsworthy event that brought life to my story, and attended it in person. This direct, traditional style of reporting is known as "shoe-leather journalism." With my notepad and pen, a digital voice recorder, and a camera, I attended a graduation ceremony for two autistic students who had completed a program helping them learn skills needed to get competitive jobs. I asked, "Is this the event that is going to make my general story on autism newsworthy?"

8 Follow-up

I followed up after the graduation ceremony in two ways. First, I interviewed a family I met at the ceremony by going to their home and getting additional information, photos, and audio. In addition, I interviewed many of my sources a second time, getting more information on everything relevant to the program and event. I asked, "Do I have all the information I need?"

9 Write

After transcribing 10 pages of interviews with more than 20 sources and organizing page after page of research, I spent about three days narrowing down my information—writing, editing, and rewriting my article. I asked, "Will others be informed and entertained by my story?"

10 Fact-check

Krista and I thoroughly edited and fact-checked my story several times. I sent a source list to Krista that included the names and titles of my human sources and the research and text sources for all cited facts. I asked, "Am I being as credible and clear with my reporting and writing as I can be?"

11 Finish

I took the edits and suggestions from Krista seriously and, after several draft versions, I finally finished the three-week project of researching, reporting, and writing about autism. I asked, "What stories can I work on next?"

To learn more about Anna Young, visit her portfolio page at missannayoung.com.

IDEAS, ONLINE

Six-Word Memoirs

Everyone has a story to tell. According to *SMITH Magazine*, some of the sweetest, most heartrending, and hilarious personal narratives can be told in six words, no more, no less. Six words: It's the story of a life.

For years, *SMITH* editors (smithmag.net/sixwords) have been collecting thousands of memoirs from celebrities and everyday people. All of them sum up their life's journeying in six words.

Some examples: "Cursed with cancer, blessed with friends"; "I like big butts, can't lie"; "No wife. No kids. No problems"; "Happily married, until the paternity test"; "Cinderella story, only edgier, more subplots"; "Discarded, adopted, couldn't trust, hurt, rage"; "All my stuff is in storage"; "After nine months, found true love"; "Catholic school backfired. Sin is in!"; and, from Stephen Colbert, "Well, I thought it was funny."

In journalism, the best reporting is clear. It is concise. It evokes emotion. It provokes thought. It extends knowledge. And it packs a punch in the fewest words possible. Enter the six-word memoir.

Your Assignment

 Collect six-word memoirs from your family members, friends, fellow students, and complete strangers. Help them explore their passions, experiences, inspirations, life stages, past hurts, and future dreams—summing themselves up in exactly six words, no more, no less. And to buttress this mini-profiling, the last memoir in your set should be your own.

CHAPTER 6
Timely Ideas

Illustration by Yee Hung Lim

Cardboard boats don't always float.

At 10 a.m. on a Homecoming weekend in a small Michigan college town, scores of students in boats made of cardboard and duct tape paddled down a local pond—and occasionally sank.

At 2 p.m., not far from the water, a kind-eyed, bearded mechanic at a small muffler shop worked on repairing his own car—hours after hitting a deer on the highway.

At 5 p.m., just a short drive from the shop, harried employees at a packed restaurant expertly aligned cheese, dough, and sauce, at times topped with pepperoni—cranking out an endless supply of pizzas to hungry customers.

At 9 p.m., near the restaurant, "hyperactive teenagers" scooted around a roller skating rink beneath flashing lights and pop music—a 12-year-old girl giggling at one point while admitting "I have met many of my boyfriends here."

At 11 p.m., just up the road from the rink, members of a local church cooked and handed out hundreds of "Jesus Dogs" to students craving a snack—at the same time serving up music and a bit of "God's love."

The dogs, pies, paddling, skates, and mechanic were among the many people, places, events, cuisine, and routines featured in a special report by *Central Michigan Life* at Central Michigan University.

In October 2009, the student newspaper spread staffers across Mount Pleasant, Mich. They spent 24 hours documenting the sights, sounds, smells, tastes, and personal touches in place during Homecoming weekend.

As the paper stated in its introduction, "New York is not the only city that never sleeps. Even a city of 26,675 people ticks every hour of the day."

The *CM Life* project is built atop an immutable journalism truth: Sometimes an idea is all in the timing. Along with people, places, perspectives, traditions, fads, and the items in your pocket or purse, the passage of time is bursting with story potential.

Related ideas often focus on extra-special moments, reflections of time gone by, real-time accounts of significant or entertaining events, and glimpses at points in time that most people are not awake or typically interested to see.

■ The wonderful reality of most coverage areas is that they are alive 24–7, in pockets, with different groups coming, going, and abuzz on their own personal circadian rhythms. Quality stories depend on how, and when, you tune in.

TIMES WORTH FEATURING

The Big Time: moments or days of monumental significance in which the daily routine is shattered or put on hold.

Examples

- Commencement
- Death of someone significant
- Election Day
- Natural disaster
- Wedding day

The Random Time: quiet, offbeat or in-between moments not often featured in stories.

Examples

- Commuting time
- Employee break times
- Life around town at dawn
- Online browsing time
- Time it takes to fall asleep

The Old Time: the recent or distant past, made newsworthy through a recurring calendar date, breaking news event, or ongoing new trend.

Examples

- Collapse of bridge built 90 years ago
- Museum exhibit opening
- New Abraham Lincoln films
- Thrifting
- Veterans Day

The Changing Time: the evolution of someone or something over time—from aging and a semester abroad to technological advancements and global warming.

Example

"The Mindset List" (beloit.edu/mindset) is an iconic annual reflection of what incoming undergraduate students most likely know and don't know about the world. Produced by a pair of staffers at Wisconsin's Beloit College, it shows the extent to which the world and its younger generation have changed.

For example, the list featured in 1998 mentioned buzzwords such as Reagan, the first Gulf War, AIDS, VCRs, and the compact disc. By comparison, the list released in 2012 begins, "This year's entering college class of 2016 was born into cyberspace and they have therefore measured their output in the fundamental particles of life: bits, bytes, and bauds . . . They have never needed an actual airline 'ticket,' a set of bound encyclopedias, or *Romper Room*."

THE ALWAYS LIST

- **Always** bring time back to people. A few examples: a birthday cake, terminal illness, late-night shift, graduation ceremony, first kiss, and a fresh batch of soldiers marching in step.
- **Always** know when the time is right for features such as previews, reviews, follow-ups, spin-offs, and real-time reports.
- **Always** look back to report in the present. The past is a powerful point of comparison because of the effects people are living with. As Daniel Patrick Sheehan, a reporter for *The Morning Call* in Allentown, Pa., advises, "Learn history. Not just American or world history, but the intimate history of the place you cover. Some things can only be learned through time and experience, but studying the history of a place can speed that process along. History provides context, and context gives depth, and a sense of authority, to storytelling."

THE NEVER LIST

- **Never** forget about the long-term impact of an event. Recognize the ending of a story—an accident, shooting, winning shot, and wedding—is often the beginning of another story. Use it as a jumping point to tell the story *after* the story.
- **Never** fear slowing time down. At moments of historic significance, sheer excitement, unmatched intensity, and immense intrigue, readers want to know every detail, every thought, every action and reaction, to the second.
- **Never** forget time is a tricky concept to pin down. There are differing opinions on everything from proper cooking, sleep, and recovery times to the dates of historic events and the proper age to begin voting, drinking, driving, and enlisting. Don't declare something past its prime, timed just right, ahead or behind the times or out of time without verifiable proof or immense confidence in your prognostications.

THE POWER OF OLD

Civil War has begun!

In April 2011, *The Daily Tar Heel* featured those four words at the start of a fascinating series commemorating the 150-year anniversary of the historic North–South conflict.

Using information gathered from the University of North Carolina at Chapel Hill campus library, the student newspaper published numerous stories on various parts of the Civil War and its immense impact on the university.

The most innovative part of the series: The stories carried datelines from the 1800s, reporting on events as if they had just happened and "presented as they might have appeared in a student newspaper."

For example, an opening story based in April 1861 focuses on the Battle of Fort Sumter, the official start to the war. Separate reports detail the dramatic drop in enrollment at UNC due to military enlistment. And a May 1865 article details the impending marriage of the university president's daughter to a Union general—an act some locals viewed as a betrayal to their beloved Confederacy.

The series overall is time-tested proof of the power of old—the olden days, days gone by, yesteryear, and time immemorial. The past is a mosh pit of endless newsworthy potential. It is filled with stories that with the right reframing or extension can have major relevance in the present.

As Confucius once advised, "Study the past if you would divine the future." Or as Shakespeare noted, "What is past is prologue." Or as Walt Whitman once asked, "For what is the present after all but a growth out of the past?" Or as a commenter beneath one of the *Daily Tar Heel* Civil War stories exclaims, least eloquently of all, "This is [a] great, wonderful article! [R]eflecting on our past once in a while should (hopefully) be beneficial!"

These reflections can educate others about the way things used to be. They can provide context for why things are the way they are now. And they can serve as the foundation for a continuing story, one that is not yet complete.

The bottom line: If news is worth initially reporting, it is most likely also worth following up on. Certain news events deserve extended looks that are not possible in a single piece or they scream for a status update a few semesters—or even 150 years—after they first occur.

Status Update Examples

- You report on a hip social network started by students. Reach out for a progress report when they celebrate signing up their 100,000th member.
- A student is killed in an accidental campus shooting. Revisit the family and report on how gun laws have changed on what would have been his birthday.
- Students start a campus Quidditch team. Pen a follow-up piece on the anniversary of the release of *Harry Potter and the Philosopher's Stone*.
- In 1992, Hurricane Andrew upended major chunks of Miami, Fla., including the University of Miami. Last August, on the storm's 20th anniversary, *The Miami Hurricane* reflected on the campus damage Andrew caused and the emergency management procedures and residence hall retrofitting now in place.

ASSIGNMENT ALERT!

Time for a Follow-Up

 "Don't forget 'update stories.' If it has been a slow week, I look back on articles I have written within the past few weeks or months. I check to see if police have any leads on a crime I reported on, for example, or if circumstances surrounding the subject of a past feature story have changed and could be newsworthy."

Canda Harbaugh, reporter, *The Western News*, Mont.

"Follow-ups can make a much more interesting story than a flashy beginning."

Michelle Monroe, copy editor and page designer, *The Santa Clarita Valley Signal*, Calif.

Your Assignment

 Follow this Monroe doctrine. Drop the flash and look to the past. Cull the archives of your campus or local press and uncover a set of stories in need of updates. For each article, put together a reporting plan of attack on how to go about your follow-up reports—the angles to tackle, the sources to track down, and the most newsworthy and timely questions to answer.

SPECIAL DAYS

Some days stand out.

Anniversaries, holidays, and the days when significant school, community, and national events occur are excellent idea fountains. Some reporters and editors literally maintain a datebook or smartphone calendar app to ensure they remember these special days.

To start, here is a quick-hit list of the holidays and campus events most often and extensively covered by college media.

- Homecoming
- 9/11
- Finals
- Commencement
- Orientation
- Parents and Family Weekend
- Spring Break
- Valentine's Day

- Annual Parade
- Martin Luther King, Jr. Day
- Halloween
- Athletic Recruit Signing Day
- April Fools' Day
- Prospective Students' Weekend
- Anniversary of Tragic Crime, Event
- Early and Regular Admissions Selection Days

Due to school breaks, cultural ignorance, and other journalism priorities, a number of religious, ethnic, and political holidays and campus events are often left out of college media's coverage mix. Depending on your publishing schedule and competing stories, they might be worth at least a smidgen of coverage.

Here is a list of the days student journalists most commonly minimize or miss.

- New Year's Day
- Easter
- Diwali
- World Water Day
- Fourth of July
- Passover
- Cinco de Mayo
- Christmas
- School President's Birthday
- Frat and Sorority Bid Day
- Dead Week
- Earth Day
- Mother's Day
- Thanksgiving
- World AIDS Day
- Black Friday
- Tax Deadline Day
- Founder's Day
- Ramadan
- Veterans Day
- Kwanzaa
- Hanukkah

ASSIGNMENT ALERT!

A Special Edition

Some moments require months of advance planning and extended coverage. One example: In fall 2011, on the 10th anniversary of the September 11 attacks, many student newspapers published special editions or sections.

The papers used the milestone as motivation for a look at how the country and their campuses had changed. They also provided glimpses into the lives of current students, who make up what is being called the 9/11 Generation.

The State News, Michigan State University

The East Carolinian, East Carolina University

Your Assignment

Scan the campus, community, and general holiday calendars for an event or day worthy of enormous coverage. Once selected, plan a full-bore news package. Brainstorm a bevy of straightforward and offbeat stories, multimedia options, and real-time reporting focuses.

For inspiration, turn to *The Orange County Register*. On opening day of the 2012 Major League Baseball season, the *Register* formed a high-profile "news mob" to cover the game between the Los Angeles Angels and Kansas City Royals.

Indiana Daily Student, Indiana University

The Daily Iowan, University of Iowa

Building on heavy advance coverage, more than 100 *Register* staffers "descend[ed] on Angels Stadium," providing a nonstop torrent of stories that made the standard definition of comprehensive seem obsolete. "I like flash mobs, I like cash mobs, and what I've been telling people is this is an overwhelming choreographed allocation of news resources," said the paper's Angels editor Keith Sharon. "I want everybody who sees our website, our print product, our iPad product, our mobile device product to think: '**They thought of everything. I mean everything**.'"

STRANGE DAYS

Certain annual cultural events and unofficial holidays defy normality. Yet, however far out they appear at first glance, there are story ideas leaping from these bizarre calendar items—campus trend pieces, student profiles, man-on-the street features, and social media movements.

CHECK OUT THIS CALENDAR FOR A GLIMPSE AT OUR SOCIETY'S WACKIER CULT CELEBRATIONS.

JAN
9 Play God Day
15 Hat Day
23 Handwriting Day

25 Opposite Day
31 Backward Day

FEB
2 Groundhog Day
5 Weatherman's Day
11 White T-Shirt Day

20 Love Your Pet Day
21 International Mother Language Day

MAR
2 Old Stuff Day
6 Frozen Food Day
14 Pi Day

21 Fragrance Day
22 Goof Off Day

APR
4 Tell a Lie Day
9 Name Yourself Day
19 High Five Day

20 Look Alike Day
26 Hug an Australian Day

MAY
3 Lumpy Rug Day
8 No Socks Day
10 Clean Up Your Room Day

22 Buy a Musical Instrument Day
27 Sun Screen Day

JUN
4 Hug a Cat Day
17 Watergate Day
18 International Panic Day

29 Camera Day
30 Meteor Day

JUL
3 Disobedience Day
7 Global Forgiveness Day
8 Video Games Day

13 Embrace Your Geekness Day
14 Nude Day

AUG
12 Middle Child's Day
15 Relaxation Day
16 Tell a Joke Day

18 Bad Poetry Day
26 International Day Against Nuclear Tests

SEP
5 Be Late for Something Day
16 Play-Doh Day
19 Talk Like a Pirate Day

27 Ancestor Appreciation Day
28 Ask a Stupid Question Day

OCT
12 Moment of Frustration Scream Day
17 Thrift Shop Day
18 No Beard Day

24 Bologna Day
31 Increase Your Psychic Powers Day

NOV
1 Men Make Dinner Day
10 Forget-Me-Not Day
13 World Kindness Day

17 Take a Hike Day
24 Celebrate Your Unique Talent Day

DEC
1 Phony Smile Day
14 International Shareware Day
21 Humbug Day

22 Roots Day
26 Whiner's Day

Graphic by Mike Trobiano and Brooke Scherer

ASSIGNMENT ALERT!

Harness the Strangeness

Building off this quirky calendar rundown, brainstorm a slew of Strange Days stories. Spin out ideas from the days' names, intended purposes, confirmed or likely participants, larger causes, and cultural connections.

For example, Lumpy Rug Day and Clean Up Your Room Day could be the groundings for a look at dorm decoration trends. Roots Day should inspire a piece on your school's legacy enrollees. Sun Screen Day is screaming for a story on tanorexics. Look Alike Day should spur a profile on student twins.

Meanwhile, Name Yourself Day is ripe for a spin-off feature on student nicknames. Pi Day can be the impetus behind a profile of a standout math major. Frozen Food Day is an excellent foundation for a report on residence hall eating habits. Bologna Day could lead to an investigation into the care of meat sold in the cafeteria.

Separately, start a social media push for everyone to submit a photo they snapped on Camera Day. Or have them share "crazy ex" stories on Forget-Me-Not Day. Man-on-the-street interviews with students can use prompts such as Play God Day, Ask a Stupid Question Day, and Moment of Frustration Scream Day. And fashion trend pieces can surge from these wacky dates—Hat Day, Thrift Shop Day, No Socks Day, and, ahem, Nude Day.

THE LONG NEWS

The O.J. Simpson trial. The Aurora movie massacre. Hurricane Katrina. The Abu Ghraib prison scandal. The bird flu, swine flu, mad cow, and SARS outbreaks. The Anthony Weiner Twitter sex scandal. The athletic dominance of Usain Bolt, Michael Jordan, Michael Phelps, and Tiger Woods. The stunning popularity of *Harry Potter*, *Twilight*, *Fifty Shades of Grey*, and *The Hunger Games*.

In recent years, these stories and many like them have provoked tons of news coverage, commentaries, online and industry gossip, and social media chatter. But do any of them *really* matter? And will they even be remembered or cited as significant a few decades, generations, and millennia from now?

Advertising guru and big thinker Kirk Citron would argue no. In a February 2010 TED talk, Citron laid out the basics of The Long News (longnews.org), a movement devoted to promoting stories that matter far more and will matter far longer than the many items that drown them out on a daily basis.

"What we're looking for is news stories that might still matter 50 or 100 or 10,000 years from now," said Citron. "You look at the news through that filter, a lot falls by the wayside."

From The Long News perspective, even seemingly major stories like the fighting in Afghanistan, the economic recession, or Michael Jackson's death will be filtered out over time—all but forgotten or reduced to historical footnotes. Yet, in the present, these stories and many others like them are the ones that garner all the airtime, trending alerts, and column inches.

By comparison, the stories about people, things, and ideas with the true capacity to impact us greatly, globally, and for many generations to come do not get any attention—or at least not the attention they deserve.

For example, scientists are developing micro-robots with the potential to travel through our brains and bloodstreams to target and cure disease. Agricultural researchers are working on creating genetically modified crops that will feed our exploding population. And researchers have separately discovered everything from water on the moon to the Higgs boson (the so-called God particle), which may immensely alter how we understand everything from the outer reaches of the solar system to the very core of the universe's mass.

Still think Usain Bolt's sprinting or Anthony Weiner's tweeting is big news?

The bottom line: News is mainly focused on the now. This leaves many significant events, incidents, individuals, inventions, and trends off the front page or unrecognized by the masses for the major role they may play in our near and distant future. In Citron's words, "In the long run, some news stories are more important than others."

ASSIGNMENT ALERT!

The Next Millennium News Game

You are living in the distant future, roughly a thousand years from now, in a galaxy far, far away. You have traveled back to present-day America—to play editor.

You are on a quest to rearrange our news of the day. You want the top headlines, the most in-depth investigations, and the fiercest debate to reflect The Long News, the news that will matter most to you in the next millennium.

Illustration by Yee Hung Lim

To get started, read and scroll through a variety of campus, local, and national news outlets. Look past the celebrity gossip. Shrug at the sports page. Roll your eyes at the arts and entertainment updates. Search only for items with the greatest potential for long-term national and global impact.

Next, create a mock newspaper, blog, pinboard, or Twitter feed highlighting the individuals, events, trends, and innovations you feel will in some way be newsworthy—or at least lead to something newsworthy—in the next millennium.

Explain your selections, outlining their implications for society in the near and faraway future. Compare them with the stories currently dominating the news landscape. And figure out how to report on your chosen items in the present so they can better compete for attention in your coverage area or among your core audience.

If you need a leg-up, my advice: Focus on science, technology, health, environmental, political, and military news. Those fields often boast breakthroughs and dabble with decisions that can most dramatically and long-lastingly change our world and lives.

IDEAS, ONLINE

Real-Time Reporting

Certain ongoing incidents, big-time events, and moments in which each millisecond counts deserve real-time coverage—from a shuttle launch, social movement like Occupy Wall Street, and natural disaster to a major speech, court case, and sporting event.

Full stories, video news reports, and multimedia packages come later. In real time, rely upon bursts of brief, accurate, easy-to-read, and easy-to-access updates.

In that spirit, here are brief bursts of advice about the art of real-time reporting.

Dan Reimold @collegemedia
Plan ahead. If possible, research the event so you have a sense of what you will be covering and how best to cover it. Once it begins though, be prepared for the unexpected and roll with the chaos.

Dan Reimold @collegemedia
Never hold anything back for fear of losing a full story scoop. But be careful about reporting upon speculation without confirmation.

Dan Reimold @collegemedia
Post updates in complete sentences. Ensure almost every update can be understood on its own, even when appearing in a larger stream.

Dan Reimold @collegemedia

Focus on the scene, action, people, and quotes, along with unscripted small moments that may not work their way into stories the next day.

Dan Reimold @collegemedia

Be upfront with people about your real-time coverage plans and that what they say or do may become public, immediately. At the same time, respect what is private or might hurt innocent people if shared. Err on the side of humanity.

Dan Reimold @collegemedia

Always be updating. The point of real-time reporting is to engage people in the moment. Too many missed moments will motivate people to read something or someone else.

Dan Reimold @collegemedia

Utilize multimedia when needed or for a change of pace, including photos and raw audio or video.

Dan Reimold @collegemedia

Join the larger conversation about what you are covering. Interact with other reporters and readers via retweets, shares, and hashtags. Use Storify (storify.com) to find and feature related social media chatter. Always give full credit to others who post a scoop or original insight.

Dan Reimold @collegemedia

Maintain a consistent tone. Determine beforehand how much commentary or sarcasm you might include—dependent in part on your news outlet's identity, readers' expectations, and your own strengths or brand.

Dan Reimold @collegemedia

Never shy from covering an event in real-time even if you're not attending in person or not close to the action. Cover what you see on TV or through web streaming. Or provide an offbeat perspective, such as a real-time concert review from the stadium's last row or updating from the end of the line outside an Apple store prior to a new product release.

Dan Reimold @collegemedia

Finally, select the right real-time reporting tool. As news media guru David Simpson (@adviserdavid) implores, "Embrace Twitter during live events! It's a medium built for immediacy and the quick, concise writing that journalists do better than anyone." CoveritLive (coveritlive.com) and Scribblelive (scribblelive.com) are two other respected live-blogging platforms, although both are mainly pay services.

Your Assignment

Cover *The Little Mermaid*. Or *Goodfellas*. Or *The Avengers*. Select a new or classic film for a real-time reporting exercise of cinematic proportions. Pretend the events depicted on screen are happening in present day, in real time. And provide running updates on a mock Twitter account. Focus on major plot points, featured and secondary characters, settings, memorable and "newsworthy" quotes, smaller details that stand out, and possibly production elements such as special effects.

Employ as much humor as you need to make the exercise enjoyable, but focus seriously on the task at hand: telling the story of what's happening on screen in brief bursts of real-time coverage.

Ask for feedback from friends after the credits roll. Among those who have seen the film, how well do they feel you captured the big moments and most telling details? Among those previously unfamiliar with the movie, how well did you make them feel part of the show and in the loop about what was happening? Also, ask yourself: What were the toughest parts of the experience?

CHAPTER 7

Trendy Ideas

Illustration by Yee Hung Lim

Think Twice.

Daily Pennsylvanian staffers Hayley Brooks and Ali Kokot share this simple, effective reporting philosophy. Last spring, the good friends encountered an array of trends their student peers at the University of Pennsylvania did not give a second glance. By contrast, in a shared column, Brooks and Kokot looked close—and asked questions.

Among them: Why are so many students wearing pajamas around campus and to class? Why do some college partygoers strive to become so drunk they black out? Why do Spring Breakers care so much about showing off their trip photos on social media? In between classes, why can't students talk about anything but academics and pre-professional plans? Why have young adults "become excessively needy and dependent upon socializing" and not missing out, to the point of sleeping next to their mobile phones and pitying a peer who chooses to eat alone?

"We're just trying to really think twice about social norms and question them, as opposed to simply subscribing to them," said Brooks, an English and cinema studies student from Fort Lauderdale, Fla. "We step back for a second and ask, 'Why is this happening? What is that about?' It's all about us trying to push the envelope about why social norms are the norm, and does it have to be that way, and why and why not."

The first norm they tackled in their *Daily Pennsylvanian* column is also the most pervasive within the college clubbing and party scene: grinding. As Brooks and Kokot write, "[B]ooty-shakin' has overshadowed all other forms of dance on college campuses. We're saturated by images in popular culture, music videos, and advertising campaigns. Grinding is so ingrained in our culture that we don't stop to question it."

Brooks and Kokot did stop, however. They asked in their piece, headlined "Get Low? Hell No," "Why has doggy-style dancing become so public, so ubiquitous, and so nonchalant?"

The questioning is in keeping with their reporting philosophy, and their column's name: "Think Twice."

The two-word phrase is one of the keys to spotting and sharing quality trend stories. It fits snugly into my so-called big five:

Head out. Tune in. Step back. Think twice. Wonder why.

What should you be wondering about? It may be a fad, a custom, a tradition, a quirk, a behavior, a belief, a philosophy, a passion, a passing fancy, a prevailing mood, an outright diversion, an activist stance, a style, a sport, a toy, a tech gadget, an old-school group, a newfangled network, a monomania, a comeback, the next big thing, an astonishing growth, a steep decline, a subtle shift, a full-blown disappearance, the first or last of its kind, or an idea whose time has finally come. (Try saying all that out loud without taking a breath.)

■ Trends encompass more than a single person, place, or pre-scheduled event. They almost always occur in between the lines. They touch on the social, sexual, philosophical, political, and digital experiences that saturate our lives or no longer preoccupy us. They are so subtle, pervasive, or seemingly obvious no one typically bothers to even give them a second thought—except for good reporters.

COMMON TREND STORIES

The Popular: things suddenly happening much more frequently, exploding in acclaim or entering their heyday.

Examples

- Cable cord cutting
- Extreme couponing
- Fair trade clothing movement
- Planking
- Scarification

The Vanishing: things happening much less frequently, becoming much less popular, or going entirely extinct. A few examples: landline phone use, marrying young, and heading to the library to do research.

Example

Bottled water is bad. That is the thrust of the many campaigns collegians have recently been waging in an attempt to stop the product from being sold on their campuses. Inspired by a larger movement triggered by Food & Water Watch, students have been aiming to enlighten their peers about the apparent wastefulness and pointlessness of buying something they can already get for free.

The student activists' gist: Bottled water is not healthier than tap water, and at times is simply tap water repackaged. The plastic bottles are environmental boondoggles. And the entire bottled water industry is a cash cow at consumers' expense.

As The Salt, National Public Radio's food blog, reports, "Bottled water is trickling away from college campuses nationwide, thanks to the efforts of student activists and the nonprofit groups that support them."

The Alternative: activities, issues, and groups of people relatively unknown or occupying niches within society.

Examples

- Riding Segways
- Riot grrrl movement
- Scientologists
- Vinyl record collectors
- Virginity pledges

The Routine: traditions, common behaviors, and evergreen issues—typically those that have stood the test of time, continue to be debated, or have changed dramatically in the digital age. A few examples: studying abroad, Social Security, letter writing, and tattoos.

Example

At colleges and universities worldwide, a significant number of students continue to engage in the Seven Deadly Sins of academic dishonesty.

As one student notes, these include "cheating (on tests), plagiarism, fabrication, obtaining an unfair advantage, aiding and abetting, falsification of records and official documents, and unauthorized access to computerized records."

Like everything else, these dishonest acts are also increasingly going digital, built atop cheating websites, social networks, and texting schemes.

Separately, cheating is becoming more complicated to define, in part through an increase in international student enrollment. "International students are more likely to cheat than their American counterparts," *The GW Hatchet* at George Washington University shares. This behavior at times stems from cultural misunderstandings—apparently what is considered cheating in some societies is deemed A-OK in others.

THE ALWAYS LIST

- **Always** recognize real trends from isolated incidents. A single event, individual, or circumstance does not equal a fad or craze. The journalism adage: One means nothing. Two is a coincidence. Three *could* be on the way to a trend. But nowadays that adage is regarded mainly as tongue-in-cheek. The truth is that there is no set number—more, more diverse, and more trusted is best. Bottom line: Be sure something is happening—truly happening—to a degree you feel comfortable having your name in the byline of a story containing the word *trend*.
- **Always** secure verified data to back up what you are seeing or what people are saying is happening. Relying on anecdotal evidence, social media chatter, and an observation session or two is rarely, if ever, enough. Hard numbers—from a focused research study, the Census, or publicly available reports—are always the best way to make your case about a trend's existence, time and point of origin, and current strength.
- **Always** establish an unofficial focus group. Seek out a mix of everyday people ensconced in your coverage area who can give you the skinny on what's shaking, shifting, being gossiped about, or being shunned. Check in with them regularly.

- **Always** be searching. Don't expect trends to grandly, proactively announce themselves. Often, they form slowly, sans buzz. It takes some serious legwork to uncover them and recognize their newsworthiness.
- **Always** look back. Trend reporting is often about catching onto the present "in thing" or predicting what will come next. In order to do both, you need to know what came before. Study the trends that have previously played out within your coverage area. There is nothing worse than running a story about the next "in thing" only to discover it already earned that label a few years before.

THE NEVER LIST

- **Never** buy into the hype of a supposed new fad. Just because everyone seems to be doing or talking about something does not mean it is actually as impacting or widespread as it seems. Challenge common wisdom and popular conceptions.
- **Never** forget the other side. Every noticeable trend has a myriad of potential sources and story focuses. Consider taking the hard road and reporting from a less-traveled perspective, such as profiling people hurt by a trend everyone loves or someone who hates what everyone else is really into.
- **Never** invent a trend, but don't dismiss your gut instinct about something you feel is emerging.
- **Never** report on a trend without seeing it with your own eyes. Ensure that what people are saying is happening matches what is actually happening.
- **Never** forget to connect a trend with a larger portion of society or a way of life. Along with providing evidence it is occurring, you must also explain why it matters and what it means.

SPRING CLEANING

The toughest trends to spot are the ones that have been around forever. They fall into the extremely ordinary, taken-for-granted, goes-without-saying category.

Ferreting out these seemingly built-in behavior patterns, routines, philosophies, and perma-crazes requires active searching, news judgment, and human instincts. The key: knowing when it's time to call something out, give it a fresh once-over, or adopt a new stance toward it.

In recent years, *The Washington Post* has adopted an especially interesting stance toward these taken-for-granted trends. The *Post* publishes an annual "Spring Cleaning" feature that asks a select group of thinkers to nominate "an idea, a tradition, a habit, a technology . . . that we'd all be better off tossing out" from society at large.

Since its start in 2009, writers have proposed everything from engagement rings, tipping in restaurants, and premium gas to chick flicks, small talk, and the vice-presidency be given the boot.

The selections are at times humorous and the arguments full of holes, but the larger point of the series has real value: While many longstanding trends are so omnipresent they are almost invisible, that should not make them invincible or free from scrutiny.

ASSIGNMENT ALERT!

Reexamine, Reinvent, or Scrap

 In the spirit of the *Post*'s real-world recommendations, create a campus spring cleaning guide of sorts. Put together a list of academic, social, residential, and fashion trends and traditions taken for granted that you feel should be reexamined, reinvented, or simply scrapped.

Follow in the footsteps of student columnists worldwide who regularly argue that certain parts of the college experience should be tossed or overhauled, including unpaid internships, deadbeat professors, bad grammar, nice guys finishing last in the dating game, and essay writing.

As a student at England's University of Leeds wrote about the latter, "Why on earth are we still writing essays? Once we graduate, will we ever find ourselves in the situation where our supervisor/manager/mom asks us a difficult question and gives us three months to prepare an answer, write it down, with a word limit, one-inch margins and font size 12? I don't think so. And once the paper is written, the euphoria of having it done makes us think that the whole world will read it, but it's not, it is read by an audience of one (our lecturer, who knows far more than we attempt to know already), and it's then lost in the cyberspace of Turnitin . . . I think that the style of essay writing is nonsense; it achieves nothing but confusion, and the over-use of the synonyms function."

Remember, the anger and annoyance you personally feel toward your selections are secondary. The primary point: They are on your mind. Are they on the minds of your readers as well?

TRENDSPOTTING FEVER

The sad truth: In the press, many things declared trends are not truly trends.

Instead, they are reportorial inventions. As longtime media critic Jack Shafer once explained, "The bogus trend story thrives thanks to the journalists who never let the facts get in the way when they think they've discovered some new social tendency."

Shafer began tracking bogus trend stories in 2003. He has come across a ton of dubious published reports, including stories on "people giving up bathing, women riding bikes, the connection between crime and Yankees caps, the emergence of flat-chested pride . . . Christian fight clubs, home barbering, DIY burial . . . [and] dudes with cats."

The problem with many trend stories is that reporters base their assumptions on scant evidence, vague references about something's mass popularity, and a few examples that barely qualify as proof of anything.

As Shafer advises tongue-in-cheek, "How to write a bogus trend story: Start with something you wish were on the rise. State that rise as a fact. Allow that there are no facts, surveys or test results to support such a fact. Use and reuse the word *seems*. Collect anecdotes and sprinkle liberally . . . Finish with an upbeat quotation [that underscores the apparent existence of the trend]."

Daniel Radosh, an Emmy-winning writer for *The Daily Show with Jon Stewart*, ranted famously about faux trends in the late 1990s. As he wrote in *GQ*, "It wasn't so long ago that big news meant Great Men and Major Events. IKE INVADES NORMANDY. DEWEY DEFEATS TRUMAN. Big news was concrete. It was dramatic. It involved action and information . . . There was simply no room or imagination for exposition along the lines of, *Lately there is a vague sense that more and more people seem to be doing or thinking or buying something or other that might possibly reflect the mood or psyche or spirit of the nation as a whole.* That wasn't news; it was small talk . . . American media have become obsessed with deconstructing the nation's social and personal habits, revealing their hidden patterns and reading them, entrails-like, to divine our fortunes. Call it trendspotting fever. While you're at it, call this the Trendspotting Generation."

To be clear, journalists who attempt to discover and define trends deserve immense respect. Trend reporting requires courage. Unlike the historic events Radosh describes, trends are not concrete, easily observable entities. But readers still want and need to know about them. Someone has to head out, tune in, step back, think twice, and wonder why. But it is imperative to avoid catching trendspotting fever. Never place a trend before the truth.

ASSIGNMENT ALERT!

Cure the Fever

Help cure trendspotting fever. Collect trend pieces recently aired or published on local and national news outlets across a variety of media. If possible, specifically seek stories discussing apparent student trends. For each story, carry out your own independent gut-checks and fact-checks, in part by utilizing your peers and professors as sources. Determine each piece's level of trustworthiness and factual accuracy.

Ultimately, decide which stories hold up and which fall into Shafer's bogus trends category. If helpful, employ a trend-story rating system introduced in summer 2012 by *The Atlantic Wire*: "Probably True, Plausible, and You're Kidding."

IDEAS, ONLINE

The Spirit of the Times

Increasingly, trends are emerging first, spreading faster, and stretching farther online. To the digital-savvy reporter, trends now reveal themselves most often through the wisdom, inanity, and insanity of the digital masses— what they are reading, watching, sharing, hyperlinking, "liking," pinning, hashtagging, status updating, and searching for.

Most websites and social networks sport sections devoted to what's popular or lists hinting at what's trending. For example, YouTube sports a "Trending Videos" page. Pinterest features a "Popular" pinboard. Twitter and Google+ sport real-time lists of trending people, places, events, movements, words, phrases, acronyms, and hashtags. Facebook features an annual "Memology" review of "the most popular topics and cultural trends" popping up within the status updates of its 800 million users worldwide.

Meanwhile, the Yahoo! Buzz Index (buzzlog.yahoo.com/overall) reveals "what the world is searching for" with a daily list of top terms. Microsoft's Bing has a shorter, similar teaser list on its homepage. And Google has a more compelling Hot Searches page (google.com/trends/hottrends) and an interactive Trends portal, both falling under a larger Zeitgeist index (google.com/zeitgeist).

" 'Zeitgeist' means 'the spirit of the times,' " the search engine giant explains, "and Google reveals this spirit through the aggregation of millions of search queries we receive every day. We have several tools that give insight into global, regional, past, and present search trends. These tools are available for you to play with, explore, and learn from. Use them for everything from business research to trivia answers." And story ideas, lots of story ideas.

SITE ALERT!

Here is a quick breakdown of three other online trend spotters, definers, and organizers, touching on breaking news, pop culture, fashion, media, technology, and business.

Trendsmap (trendsmap.com), "a real-time mapping of Twitter trends across the world." It features the terms and hashtags most frequently discussed and retweeted in specific countries, states, cities, and parts of the world, including potentially your coverage area.

trendwatching.com (trendwatching.com), "an independent and opinionated trend firm, scanning the globe for the most promising consumer trends, insights, and related hands-on business ideas. For the latest and greatest, we rely on our network of hundreds of spotters in more than 120 countries worldwide."

Trend Hunter (trendhunter.com), "the world's largest, most popular collection of cutting-edge ideas, crowdsourced by [more than 100,000] trend hunters. As MTV puts it, 'At Trend Hunter, find out what's cool before it's cool.' "

Criminal Ideas

"Wait, wait, wait, he burned down his *own* house—because he didn't get any Christmas gifts?"

I still remember my editor's words vividly. It was a chilly late December morning. I was a reporting intern covering the police beat for a suburban daily newspaper outside Philadelphia. I had just grabbed some police reports from the newsroom fax machine. As I read through the first few, my head slowly cocked to the side and my lips pursed—forming the word that finally escaped them: "Whaaaatttt?" Some follow-up calls confirmed the seemingly unthinkable. Soon after, I told my editor.

The story: A young man, angry at receiving no gifts from his parents on Christmas morning, set fire to his family's home. It burnt down. Police arrested him. He told officers he was going to kill their families. At an evening arraignment in court, he threatened to burn the Bible used to swear in witnesses. He asked, at one point, "So what if I burned my house down? It's my house."

He was placed in county prison, on charges of arson and criminal mischief. His parents temporarily moved in with relatives. And I had a front-page story—and a lifelong motivation to be extra generous to my loved ones around the holidays.

Crimes, fires, accidents, and the legal and law enforcement apparatuses that attempt to stop, control, defend, and prosecute them are by far the most fascinating elements of the news. *Las Cruces Sun-News* online editor Jason Gibbs advises, "Mine the court and crime beats—these are your best breeding grounds for the odd, weird, and just plain astonishing material that will be read."

As *Oklahoman* staff writer Michael Kimball shares, "Some of the most-viewed stories I've ever written include crime briefs about a drunken woman who crawled through her car's window and into a McDonald's drive-thru window because she was upset about being asked to pay for her order and an intoxicated woman who gave a police officer a candy wrapper and a credit card when he asked for her license and proof of insurance."

This type of silliness is coupled with stakes that are often as high as they come—life and death, the control and loss of wealth and personal property, and the comfort and security we all take for granted until it is suddenly gone. According to Glenn Smith, veteran crime reporter for *The Post and Courier* in Charleston, S.C., "No beat provides as much human drama and opportunities for narrative storytelling as the crime beat."

This storytelling involves a unique set of skills and know-how. As Smith states, it is "a lot more complicated than listening to a scanner and running out to car wrecks and shootings."

AN EXCHANGE OF IDEAS

Paper, People, Victims, Context

 The exchange is a recurring feature in the book and on my blog, spotlighting advice and exercises from top journalism students, professionals, educators, and advocates.

Brian Haas is a crime reporter at The Tennessean *in Nashville, Tenn. Over the last ten years, he has covered crime at the* South Florida Sun Sentinel, The Bradenton Herald, *and the* Star Democrat *in Easton, Md. He has reported on more than 200 homicides and high-profile cases like the 2007 death of Anna Nicole Smith and the 2004 abduction and murder of 11-year-old Carlie Brucia in Sarasota, Fla.*

His exchange focuses on the essential characteristics of crime and courts reporting.

There are four keys to covering crime and courts: paper, people, victims, and context.

First, Paper

Learn about every document you have access to in the criminal justice system. Arrest affidavits are great. And find out where your court stores the search warrants, which in many states are public records once they've been served. There are some fascinating cases I've written about using search warrants. But search warrants are just the tip of the iceberg—there are also internal affairs reports, audits, depositions, memos, databases, and more. Learn what your sources keep on paper and regularly mine that paper.

Second, People

You need to get to know as many key people on your beat as possible. Crime-wise, it's the street-level cops and their immediate supervisors who have the best handle on what's really going on. Often, lieutenants and above are far more in the political machines of a given agency. Homicide detectives are great. Street-level drug guys and vice squads are not only a blast to hang out with, but they also provide a lot of the criminal intelligence that the homicide guys end up using to bust murderers.

Also, make nice with your local records clerks. If you are doing your job well, they are going to be seeing a lot of you. And it never hurts to have someone who isn't afraid to slip you something for free or, even better, something you aren't supposed to see.

Also, cozy up to your local medical examiner. They are an amazing source on a range of issues like homicides, suicides, and drug deaths (a good indicator of local drug trends). And don't forget private investigators. They often work for civil attorneys investigating civil rights abuses, police corruption, and wrongdoing, and can be amazing sources. In the courts, get to know the District Attorney's investigators, the people who go out and do prosecutors' grunt work—often, they are retired homicide or violent crimes cops.

On any beat, know that most government agencies today are run like corporations. They tend to filter all media requests and interviews through PR-type "media relations" folks. There are some damn good ones out there. The best ones step out of the way and get you to the right person to speak with. The bad ones are barriers we must jump so we can get to the right source. Either way, on stories of importance, do not settle for a spokesperson. You will likely be wasting a lot of time and won't get the quality information you really need. They tend to be fine for the routine stuff, though.

Third, Victims

Talk to as many victims as you can. It is easy to write about crime in the academic sense—citing statistics and generalities—but the real stories are told from the victims' perspectives. While our interest may end with an arrest or conviction, many live with the effects of these crimes on a daily basis. Some may be victimized once by a criminal and then again by police, prosecutors, or an intimidating and unwieldy criminal justice system. In short, if you have no empathy and interest in victims, you have no business writing about crime or criminal justice.

Finally, Context

It is easy to publish a bunch of "if it bleeds it leads" stories. You show up on the scene, interview the victims, interview cops, write 12 inches of news copy, and you're done. But those types of stories do very little to inform the community about how safe they are or how well the criminal justice system is functioning.

Crime reporting without context can easily lead readers and viewers to assume crime is out of control. You ask a typical citizen and they probably think crime is the worst it's ever been. That simply isn't the case. Crime rates from the 1980s and 1990s are astounding compared to the minuscule crime we see today, but rarely is that reported.

You must provide context by tracking trends. Learn Excel and take a basic statistics or computer-assisted reporting course. Learn about the FBI's Uniform Crime Reporting (UCR) program and its National Incident-Based Reporting System (NIBRS). Find ways to take stories beyond the individual crimes to tell larger narratives about your community. Let people know whether something is an isolated incident or part of a larger issue that the public needs to know about.

To learn more from Brian Haas, follow him on Twitter @brianhaas. To utilize the UCR and NIBRS, start by visiting fbi.gov/about-us/cjis/ucr.

EVERYDAY CRIMES

Last summer, an American University student "touched off a small firestorm in the music industry."

During an internship with National Public Radio, Emily White leapt into the ongoing economic, existential, and generational debate over online music consumption. In a post for NPR's music blog,

All Songs Considered, White, general manager of AU's student radio station WVAU, confessed that even while loving music she has hardly spent a cent to acquire her massive song and album collection.

"I am an avid music listener, concertgoer, and college radio DJ," she wrote. "My world is music-centric. I've only bought 15 CDs in my lifetime. Yet, my entire iTunes library exceeds 11,000 songs. I've never supported physical music as a consumer. As monumental a role as musicians and albums have played in my life, I've never invested money in them aside from concert tickets and T-shirts."

White explained that digital natives recognize "the gravity of what file-sharing means to the musicians," but they are simply too enamored with the ease through which they can acquire free music, instantly. "I honestly don't think my peers and I will ever pay for albums," she contended. "I do think we will pay for convenience . . . All I require is the ability to listen to what I want, when I want, and how I want it. Is that too much to ask?"

Within days of its posting, White's write-up garnered more than 900 comments, lots of blogosphere chatter, and outside media coverage including a *New York Times* recap. The most impassioned respondents branded her a crook or musical Judas—professing to be a true music aficionado but refusing to support the artists who create it. As one commenter noted, "I am shocked by this blog post. Emily, you are stealing. Stealing is dishonest. And it is a crime."

Yet, White has not been arrested, charged, or punished for her actions. Many people feel she is not doing anything wrong at all. Some even applauded her for openly discussing what is happening en masse. And others are simply blasé, arguing whether we like it or not, free music file-sharing and downloading is an unstoppable force—making anger or some type of symbolic crackdown not worth the fuss.

Why not? Because the admittedly illegal activity falls into the category of what I call "everyday crimes."

As opposed to the most heinous of criminal offenses—homicide, hate crimes, human trafficking, rape, sexual assault, and aggravated assault—there is an enormous amount of wrongdoing rarely noticed, stopped, punished, or covered by the press. According to one student newspaper, many of these crimes are "everyday activities not commonly viewed as unlawful." They are quiet protests against the system, tiny breaches seen worth the risk or thoughtless misdeeds spurred by ambition, desperation, or a desire for convenience.

For example, a spring 2012 report in *The Mooring Mast* revealed that at Washington's Pacific Lutheran University an eye-opening number of students are stealing food and drinks from campus markets. They are also swiping friends' ID cards at the cafeteria instead of using their own. And they are convincing friends who work in dining services to pretend to ring them up for purchases without making them pay.

Among the reasons students cite for such behavior: rising food prices, a lack of spare cash, the ease with which they can get away with it, and their meal plan restrictions. As one student who confirmed she occasionally stole from the PLU markets asked, "Isn't making me pay $10 for food that I'm not going to eat $10-worth-of stealing too?"

ASSIGNMENT ALERT!

Everyday Crime Report

Investigate an everyday crime on your campus or within your community. Explore how, how often, where, and when it tends to happen. Focus on some individuals who engage in it most often, or most creatively, and pinpoint their rationales for carrying it out. Determine its financial or social impact. Track trends or changes related to it over time. Gauge the responses of campus security, school administrators, the police, the press, and the public. Search for online communities or activist groups that particularly embrace it or rail against it. And look up all related laws, possibly consulting an expert or professor to translate what they specifically allow and restrict.

To get started, select an everyday crime from the following list. One thing to remember: Even amid their ordinariness, many carry serious, sometimes long-lasting repercussions.

- Copyright infringement
- Disorderly conduct and indecent exposure
- Drunk driving
- Email and social network hacking
- Fake ID creation, purchase, and use
- Fire code violations and fireworks possession
- Gambling
- Getting paid "under the table"
- Hazing
- Illegal prescription drug use and sales
- Illegal streaming, downloading, and file-sharing
- Jaywalking
- Littering
- Marijuana sales and use
- Noise ordinance violations
- Parking violations
- Pet violations, such as leash and licensing laws

- Profanity violations, such as cursing in public
- Public intoxication and urination
- Room squatting
- Shoplifting and petty theft
- Skateboarding and bicycling violations
- Smoking in non-designated areas
- Speeding
- Texting while driving
- Trespassing
- Underage drinking
- Vandalism
- Weapons possession
- Wireless piggybacking (stealing Wi-Fi)

IDEAS, ONLINE

Interactive Campus Crime

In recent years, University of Illinois at Urbana-Champaign journalism students enrolled in classes led by Eric Meyer have created and maintained a comprehensive website devoted to criminal activity at UIUC.

CampusCrime.net presents interactive maps, statistics, video, audio, and short text breakdowns of reported crimes, the campus crime alert system, student crime victims, and the occasionally combustible involvement of alcohol use and racial tension.

The students have embraced non-linear storytelling for the site's presentation. As the "About" page explains, "Rather than create text-based narratives that force readers to follow only one pathway through the material, they presented without comment audio highlights of hundreds of interviews they conducted and created interactive features that allow readers to query the data their research uncovered in whatever manner the readers desired."

For example, all reported campus crimes over the past decade can be analyzed by factors such as the days of the week and times they occurred and the victim's age, gender, affiliation to UIUC, and whether they had been drinking. Separate interactive quizzes ask students about the definitions of various crimes and invite them to respond to faux campus crime situations, comparing their answers with those provided by a campus security officer.

POST-MORTEM

 Post-Mortem is a recurring feature in the book and on my blog, telling the story *behind* **a story, series, or website—in the words of the reporter or editor responsible for creating it.**

Move the Story Forward

Sara Ganim is, quite simply, a phenomenal journalist. As a crime reporter for *The Patriot-News* in Harrisburg, Pa., Ganim broke the story on what became the Penn State sex scandal and has continued digging into it with unmatched vigor and ingenuity.

Her investigative tenacity has been praised as "every bit comparable to the guts and drive of *The Washington Post* in breaking the Watergate scandal."

As she explains on her personal website (saraganim.com), "Jerry Sandusky was convicted [last] June of sexually abusing boys he met through his children's charity. The arrest of the former Penn State assistant football coach, 68, caused a rippling fallout that engulfed the university, Pennsylvania politics, and started a national conversation about child sex abuse and college athletics. It led to the firing of iconic coach Joe Paterno, the university president, and the dismantling of his children's charity, The Second Mile."

But Ganim was tracking the story long before Sandusky's arrest and the scandal's global spread. Her early inquiries and initial scoop were actually met with fierce criticism from members of the PSU community unable to believe the worst about a local hero. Competing news outlets and the national press also shied away, most not reporting anything at all about the abuse allegations.

As her editor told *Glamour* magazine, "It felt like we were living in *The Twilight Zone*."

Ganim persevered and pushed the story forward, in part through what she calls traditional journalism—"knocking on doors, talking to people face-to-face, running into a lot of brick walls, and coming up with creative ideas to get around them."

She also benefited from the belief her editors placed in her, and the freedom they bestowed upon her to keep investigating even through numerous dead-end days. As she shares, "It's not about the masthead. It's about the work you do."

Ultimately, her work exposing the Penn State sex scandal earned her a 2012 Pulitzer Prize, the profession's highest honor. Twenty-four years old at the time, she became the third-youngest journalist to receive the award.

In a Q&A last summer, Ganim, now a CNN correspondent, outlined her investigative reporting philosophy and techniques, how they applied to her Pulitzer Prize-winning series, and what student journalists can learn from them when embarking upon large-scale projects of their own.

How do you approach and conceptualize such a massive, long-term investigative report?
People have asked me many, many, many times if I saw this playing out the way that it did. No. The answer is we didn't. We were following the facts. It was just another crime story, to be honest with you. It became this [huge story]. And because we were in the community and because we did not project our reporting on some idea of what it should be, we were able to stay ahead and to follow it step by step.

I kind of see this as a two-part story. It was this investigation that no one else was working on, that no other journalist in the state wanted. We were the only ones on it. We were getting criticized because of who [Sandusky] was and because it was just unimaginable . . . I mean, I had people coming up to me saying, "You should investigate this—to prove he's *innocent*." It was that far to the extreme.

So it was this very traditional journalism—knocking on doors, talking to people face-to-face, running into a lot of brick walls, and coming up with creative ideas to get around them. There was no Twitter. There was no blogging. There was no online anything. We weren't even writing stories for the paper. It was lots of lawyers, lots of "let's hold it one more day," lots of "let's make one more call," lots of old-school journalism.

And then there was this turning point. When he was charged, it became what journalism is more like we know it to be today.

What are the keys to maintaining focus and confidence when you're running into brick walls?
I think you need to find a sounding board in your newsroom, someone who you can bounce ideas off of. It's good for two reasons. One, when I talk out loud, it helps me process stuff. But you're also talking to someone who doesn't know the story or new details as intimately as you do, who is going to show you a little bit more. Sometimes you're in the weeds and you need the big picture.

How proactive are you about your investigative work? Do you come into the newsroom each morning knowing what you'll be working on, where things are heading?
We've always had this philosophy in our newsroom: **Move the story forward**. There are a lot of obvious details in every story, which a lot of people can get. You can walk into the courthouse or look at public records and get the obvious. But the real question: What can

we tell you that you can't get otherwise? We've always had that philosophy in our newsroom. I think that was a big part of our success.

[For the sex scandal investigation] it was constantly "OK, in the last 24 hours *a lot* happened. You can read about it on Twitter. You can read about it on our website, because we're constantly updating it. But in tomorrow's paper, we are not just going to rehash that." That is what a lot of people were doing, just kind of putting it altogether. Our philosophy: What can we tell you that you didn't hear in the last 24 hours?

How do you meet today's demand for real-time coverage while reporting on such a complicated and explosive situation?
There was definitely no holding back. Once we have it, and we're confident we have it, we put it out there. Not before we're confident though. One example: the night Joe Paterno died—or didn't die. And everyone killed him. We didn't. And for 18 hours I was getting yelled at—we were the only ones in the world that didn't have it. We just didn't have it, so I wasn't going to write it. It turned out, instead, we were the first ones to have that he was still alive.

What do you do off the clock or around the edges of an investigation that helps you when the real reporting ramps up?
I think it's just about calling sources when you don't have a question. It's cultivating relationships and talking to people. There's a difference between people who sit on Twitter, reading other people's stuff, and writing stories and people who go out there and are the ones doing the real work and sending out the tweets.

What is your advice for student or beginning journalists interested in undertaking a longer-term investigative report?
A lot of it is frustrating and every single one doesn't turn out to be huge. I had a boss, not this one, but the one before, who said to me "You should put in some 'right to knows,' just for the heck of it. Look at some stuff. Take some time to do investigations that we know will go nowhere." So I did them on Saturdays and Sundays and at midnight on Fridays. And a lot of them went nowhere. But the practice helped a lot, and when I stumbled onto the right story at the right time, **I did know what to do because I had done it before— on stories that went nowhere**.

CRIMINAL ELEMENTS

"Good morning, my name is Lars Peterson, and I used to be a dumbass."

In spring 2011, the reformed ex-convict greeted Virginia Tech criminology students with those words.

More than a decade ago, authorities put Peterson in prison stripes for his part in a botched robbery and abduction. Prior to his arrest, he had been a drug dabbler and disaffected college student.

Once incarcerated, his priorities shifted. As a profile in *The Collegiate Times* at Virginia Tech shared, Peterson took part in college classes and vocational training, options most prisoners decline. He earned slightly early release for good behavior. In the shadow of the school's horrific mass shooting, he applied and earned acceptance at Virginia Tech—after numerous checks, required counseling, and a semester of community college classes.

He graduated in May 2011, filled with promise, yet knowingly burdened by his past. "I'm on my way to bigger and better things," he told the *CT* at the time. But as he also confirmed, "My record is completely clean except for one hour, but I will forever be known as Lars Peterson the ex-felon."

Peterson is one of many, many people who live forever in the shadow of a single crime or a past streak of criminal behavior. They include the victims, victims' families and friends, the police and private investigators, the prosecution and defense teams, emergency responders and medical personnel, prison officials, eyewitnesses and innocent bystanders, the criminals' friends and families, and, of course, the criminals themselves.

These individuals and a number of others are often overlooked or forgotten soon after crimes have occurred—or after a verdict is reached, a funeral is held, sentencing is handed down, and a prison sentence begins.

Recognize that the moment of greatest press and public fascination—the crime itself—is almost always both the end and beginning of separate stories that deserve just as much attention and care in their telling.

Look especially closely into the longer-term fallout from crimes. Determine how they continue to influence individuals who were directly and indirectly involved. Dig deeper. In some cases, the impact is noticeable and easy to define. In other cases though, the scars are less visible and may even be unseen or unfelt by the people who have them.

ASSIGNMENT ALERT!

Nearby, Offenders

 In spring 2011, *The Daily Emerald* at the University of Oregon reported that more than 30 registered sex offenders lived relatively close to the school. Additionally, law enforcement had reached out to 16 sex offenders in the past two months on campus. Seven were arrested on other outstanding criminal activity. Four resisted arrest.

UO is not an anomaly. Convicted sex offenders live and work near many college and university campuses. It is a fact confirmed by the FBI Sex Offender Registry (fbi.gov/scams-safety/registry). The registry exists because law enforcement has deemed individuals who commit certain sexual crimes dangerous enough to warrant public knowledge of their general whereabouts.

While there should be no rush to judgment and no begrudging of rehabilitation, a report indicating the number of sex offenders near your campus or within your coverage area may help others stay safe and open a valuable discussion about the fairness and effectiveness of having their homes in a public database.

Your Assignment

 Utilize the FBI Sex Offender Registry to determine the number and types of registered sex offenders living and working locally. Examine the monitoring efforts of law enforcement and campus security. Find out if and how the individuals' sex offender status affects employment and college admissions prospects. Profile individuals identified in the registry as sex offenders, along with those who work to catch, prosecute, defend, and help rehabilitate them. Separately, if possible, focus on sharing the story of a sex crimes victim.

ETHICS ALERT!

 The names of people on the offenders' list should not be included in any reports without their permission or a true journalistic rationale. Also, recognize the range of activity that constitutes sex crimes. Along with the most monstrous behaviors, they may also involve someone sending sexual text messages or an older college student dating a high school senior.

POST-MORTEM

 Post-Mortem is a recurring feature in the book and on my blog, telling the story *behind* **a story, series, or website—in the words of the reporter or editor responsible for creating it.**

The Tweetalong

During the 2011–2012 academic year, Stephanie Schendel, the cops and courts reporter for *The Daily Evergreen* at Washington State University, participated in occasional "tweetalongs." During these weekend ridealongs with officers from the Pullman Police Department, she tweeted live observations, providing the paper's Twitter followers with a candid, witty glimpse of after-hours community goings-on.

Schendel had a four-fold goal for the innovative reporting effort: to build a relationship with local law enforcement, to begin learning the police beat, to heighten the paper's social media buzz, and to provide readers with a nighttime narrative of life in and around WSU.

More than anything else, the real-time reporting experiment revealed one immutable truth: After dark, some people in Pullman, Wash., are a bit bonkers. For example, during a tweetalong last year, Schendel reported, "Girl just went by on a bike. No pants . . . Someone got into a fight with a vacuum cleaner. The vacuum lost . . . Group of girls screaming, don't worry—it was just a puppy . . . Girl passed out in the women's transit car."

In this Q&A, Schendel discusses the characteristics of a quality tweetalong, including the ethics and audience engagement issues involved.

How do you determine what is appropriate to tweet?
The first time I did it was probably the toughest. I had no idea what was going to happen. I honestly didn't really know what goes on in terms of crime and what police respond to. I remember being incredibly overwhelmed because you would go to a funny interaction— for example, my first night there was a guy in a gnome costume rapping to the police officers. Then . . . we got called to an overdose, not someone I knew but essentially someone who was my age, who was a classmate of mine.

It was really shocking for me as a student, as a person, as a civilian, to see that. So I immediately made the decision that victims and people who are arrested for MIPs [a charge of being a minor in possession of alcohol] or other minor crimes, their names are not important in these stories, even though some of it is public record. In terms of publication, we made the decision that it's completely irrelevant. The stories I tried to create from these tweetalongs were about the issues and general things that happened to students. It was not about the individual.

In what ways do readers interact with you during the tweetalongs?
What I realized is that a lot of alumni follow our Twitter account. A lot of them are like, "Oh, I miss Pullman. I miss WSU." And a lot of them would retweet some of my quirkier tweets and the funnier things that happened. But then as it went on people started tweeting in incidents, like, "I just saw a police officer arresting someone for an MIP."

There were a couple of times, actually, when I've gotten tweets about incidents before someone even called the police. There was one incident where someone was shooting a gun in an alley, shooting it up in the air. I started getting tweets about it and I thought, "Well that's weird. I haven't heard anything." So I tweeted out, "I don't know anything. I haven't heard anything." Two minutes later, the call came over the dispatch.

How did the sarcastic tone of the tweetalongs come about?
I went with the same two police officers each time. I think a lot of my tweets matched their personalities. They are very sarcastic and have good senses of humor. I think you would have to in their line of work. My personality, I felt, really meshed with theirs. No one wants to be overwhelmed with tweets about overdoses and student falls and tragic things.

Even though that's a really important part of [the officers'] job, there are some positive things that happen and positive interactions. I really wanted to mirror that difference, that change where they can go from laughing to five minutes later be called to a scene where sometimes my reaction was like, "I want to cry. This is horrible what's happening to people." I just really wanted to capture that.

At the start, what reporting ground rules did the officers lay out for you?
A lot of it was up to my best judgment. I think after the first tweetalong they really trusted my judgment. There was only one instance in which they asked me not to tweet something out and that was when [an officer] needed to get a search warrant for something. It was in between the point when he smelled marijuana and was going to the police station to get a search warrant. That was the only time they asked me not to tweet anything out. I mean, I was once kind of on scene for a stabbing and was kept in the loop on a lot of information that otherwise would not have been told to me if I was a reporter calling the next day to ask for information. They never asked me to keep certain things to myself.

How did the extended time you spent with the officers help your crime reporting overall?
Before I started covering this beat, I didn't know any police officers. The police in our town, students don't really look favorably at them. They are kind of seen as party busters . . . So people's perceptions of them weren't that good. As a student, I sort of had that perspective too. Once I met them and spent more than an hour with them, my perspective on everything was completely different. There are a lot of things civilians will never understand about what police officers do.

CHAPTER 9

Location, Location, Location

Illustration by Yee Hung Lim

Jordan Bentz once journeyed to hell.

It is also known as Warm Springs Indian Reservation. Warm Springs is a cold place. Rez life, as the natives call it, on the Oregon tribal land reeks of rampant crime, poverty, alcohol and drug addiction, and a shockingly high youth mortality rate that has branded it "the deadliest place for children" statewide.

In spring 2011, Bentz explored this American Indian sovereign state. For an award-winning report in *Flux Magazine* at the University of Oregon, Bentz sketched a bleak scene, "an expanse of one-story houses and worn brick buildings where more than 40 percent of the population is below the poverty level . . . Domestic abuse, fatal driving incidents, and random acts of violence often overshadow the reservation's rich cultural heritage."

As he stated more simply, "For some, Warm Springs is hell."

Bentz's focus on this hell, and its inhabitants, adheres to a deeper maxim at home within journalism (and real estate): Often, it's all about location, location, location.

More specifically, the settings for many newsworthy moments, cultures, individuals, and issues are not just the stages upon which stories play out. They are also stories themselves.

> ■ From the hyperlocal to the international, on the main streets and side streets, news and feature stories often center on their surroundings. It boils down to simple news judgment. Occasionally, the energy, activity, mood, movement, chatter, and look of a place twist and shout together as a story's most newsworthy angle—a principal character all its own.

Certain location–location–location stories strive to educate readers about unfamiliar, controversial, and oft-forgotten places. Others attempt to pinpoint changes in places over time. And still others bring to life a place's inherent complexity.

To this end, the Warm Springs story encompasses much more than simple hellishness. It also involves a new generation of local Native Americans somehow able to look past the "recurring tragedy"—and see home. As a recent UO graduate who returned to the reservation shared, "It is the only place I feel like I belong, the only place where I really feel whole."

Within journalism, great place stories also accomplish this wholeness—telling the tales of people, trends, events, and perspectives through the prism of the one thing they all have in common: the settings where they occur.

SOME FEATURED PLACES

The Place to Be: the halls of power, latest hangouts, and other especially lively spots where the masses gather or significant events are staged.

Examples
- Airport customs
- Broadway
- Bustling marketplace
- Harvard University
- Student center

The Forgotten Place: a location cast aside, overlooked, off the beaten path or simply not often viewed as newsworthy. A few examples: the poor part of town, a remedial class, and a theater's backstage.

Example

"My most memorable story came after a fellow reporter told me he had fallen asleep, drunk, on a BART [Bay Area Rapid Transit] train from San Francisco one night. He had missed his stop in Oakland and awakened at the end of the line in the deep suburbs. On two subsequent nights, I rode the final trains of the night and interviewed the similarly stranded. I talked to station agents who knew of the phenomenon and opportunistic cab drivers who waited around for the sleepers. I even gave one young man a ride home. It turned into a front-page story: 'BART, from A to ZZZZZ.' It always reminds me of how fun the job can be if we follow our instincts into the field, and it reminds me to pursue stories even if they don't come out of typical places like City Hall or the courts."

Demian Bulwa, reporter, *San Francisco Chronicle*

The Meaningful Place: a spot that holds special significance for a large or small group of people.

Examples
- Church
- Dead child's bedroom
- Grand Canyon
- Memorial site
- Protected wetlands

The Changing Place: a general area or specific site being redefined, for better or worse—from campus construction projects and natural disaster recovery to political redistricting and urban poverty growth.

Example

In fall 2009, *The Review* at the University of Delaware published a special report on "the Chrysler property," a once-bustling, recently belly-up automobile assembly plant in Newark, Del., eyed by UD administrators as "a gateway to the university's main campus." As the introduction explains, "It sits on South College Avenue, a sprawling, 270-acre reminder of both dreams ended and dreams about to take off."

The Virtual Place: a location lacking a verifiable, physical structure, but whose existence is quite real within us, believed to be all around us, or waiting for us.

Examples
- Afterlife
- Dreams
- Emotional states such as depression
- Hallucinations
- Internet and virtual reality

THE ALWAYS LIST

- **Always** see a place for yourself. No amount of background research or interviews can equate to the power of seeing the spot you are reporting upon with your own eyes.
- **Always** connect a place's successes, plights, or shifts to the external forces that have some part in shaping them. Nowadays, not even the most remote islands or North Korea are cut off from the world.
- **Always** obtain a complete picture of a place. Even for a snapshot profile, you need to know how it developed, what is missing, what is nearby, and what is happening underground (figuratively or maybe literally).
- **Always** strive to peek behind the curtains, providing a glimpse inside the most prominent, protected places that the public rarely, if ever, has access to see.
- **Always** look for the places adjacent to those sporting the most buzz or apparent newsworthiness. As *New York Times* media reporter Brian Stelter once shared, "Go where the silence is."

THE NEVER LIST

- **Never** brush off places that seem dead or boring at first glance. Even in the absence of activity or grandiosity, there is life—and news. Keep digging.
- **Never** stereotype a place. A place means different things to different people. What some cast off as a slum, others embrace as home, sweet home.
- **Never** overlook the physical tales a place can tell, including through its wildlife, plant life, natural light, and manmade build-up and blight.
- **Never** forget those without a place to call home or temporarily or permanently away from their native lands—exiles, immigrants, the homeless, even commuter students.
- **Never** get caught up solely in a place's big picture. The lifeblood and most powerful stories of many spots are in the details.

Illustration by Yee Hung Lim

IN OTHER WORDS

"Pay attention to the details. It may sound simple enough, but in reality it takes a keen eye, ear, and sometimes nose to get the most from a story . . . Close your eyes for a moment at the scene. What do you hear? What do you smell? Open your eyes and write down the action you see."

Paul D'Ambrosio, director of news and investigations,
The Asbury Park Press, N.J.

"When I was with The Associated Press and working on the AP's foreign desk in New York, I was tapped to go to Cuba for what was to be a historic visit by an American religious leader. I knew little about Cuba and less about religion, so I turned to the AP's deputy foreign editor for advice. He told me, 'Just write what you see.' It worked, and it has worked over and over since then . . . The essence of a lot of reporting is showing people through your reporting what it is like to be there."

Tina Susman, national correspondent, *Los Angeles Times*

ASSIGNMENT ALERT!

The Dartboard of Observation

Take a fresh, detailed look at a common place. Soak it in. Really study it. And show readers what it is like to be there.

To start, affix a map of your campus or community to a dartboard and safely toss a dart at it. Travel to the place it pierces—whether it is the campus cafeteria, the chemistry lab, the local library or the Little League baseball fields. Observe the location in minute detail, search for stories, and take note of everything you see.

To spot ideas and set the scene, employ your six—yes, six—senses: sight, hearing, smell, taste, touch, and sheer wonder. According to Susman, "The power of observation is crucial. I notice every color, every item of clothing someone is wearing, the street signs, the jewelry on a dead body, and the types of trees growing on the side of the road. I note the smells and the sounds, and the kinds of dogs, cats, or other animals roaming nearby. If they bark, howl, meow, or moo, I notice it."

Along with these detailed bark-howl-meow-and-moo observations, think story building. Embrace the native-land-through-foreign-eyes concept. **Pretend your darted spot is a foreign country**. Uncover stories that might interest readers "back home." Interview and report upon the people who are employed, living, visiting, or simply hanging out there. Document the place's power structure, work and social routines, major imports and exports (even if they are just spreadsheets and pizza), defined borders, rebels and castaways, tourist spots (say, a smoking lounge), weather patterns (a faulty air conditioner, perhaps), and official and unofficial rules.

For example, a past student who carried out a dartboard observation of a campus chemistry building brainstormed ideas on the laboratories' cleanup procedures and hazardous materials storage; the fun students and staff have with chemical abbreviations, hazard symbols, and other lab lingo; the odd environment that at times required freezing temperatures or air duct shutdowns; and the basic experiments serving as rites of passage for introductory students (such as T-shirt Chromatography and a High Performance Liquid Chromatography analysis of soda).

OVER & BACK

In fall 2010, *The Daily Bruin* took its readers 8,000 miles and a world away.

A pair of staffers at the student newspaper reported on a place that has indirectly led to raucous cheers on campus—even though most at the University California, Los Angeles, probably cannot spell it, pronounce it, or even know it exists: Yaoundé, Cameroon.

The capital city of 2.5 million has produced two players on UCLA's men's basketball team. As the paper reported, "Fans go crazy when a talented student-athlete from an unknown place takes a college campus by storm. But what happens to international student-athletes before they reach a Division I university remains largely invisible to even the most die-hard college sports fans across the nation."

For "Over & Back" (overandback.dailybruin.com), a special report funded by the Bridget O'Brien Scholarship Foundation (rememberingbridget.com), student journalists Matt Stevens and Maya Sugarman made Yaoundé visible—through stories, audio, video, and photos focused on its native basketball culture.

In a full month of on-the-ground reporting, the pair uncovered a dispiriting number of obstructions standing between talented young Cameroonian hoopsters and a chance at basketball stardom and a better life. These include "rigid American visa policies," corrupt middlemen, poverty, broken homes, and even a heart condition "endemic to Africa."

The power of their award-winning report is its firsthand perspective. They bridged readers' awareness and knowledge gap about Yaoundé by seeing the city with their own eyes.

Quality reporting about an invisible or unfamiliar place often requires this type of direct, prolonged exposure. To be an intermediary for your readers, to understand a culture's hierarchy, customs, rhythms, and rules, you must experience it for yourself—even when you wipeout.

Cut to Cailly Morris, in fall 2011:

"Standing waist deep in the frothy water, I stare at the four-foot wave tumbling toward me. I pause, close my eyes, and recite my mantra one more time—push, jump, stand up . . . Simple enough. An icy wave forms behind me, barreling toward my back. I take a deep breath and push off with my board, feeling the whoosh of the water graze my side. **Push. Jump. Wipeout**."

Morris's watery collapse was part of her storytelling adventure in the "Malibu of the Midwest." For an online magazine report, the University of Wisconsin-Madison student explored the surfing culture in Sheboygan, Wis., "one of the state's best-hidden secrets . . . a world where the sun-bleached, laid-back California surfer meets rugged beer-bellied cheese lover."

Morris interviewed a local surf guru along the Lake Michigan coastline. She observed surfers in action. She picked up the lingo of what should and should not be spoken—including the accepted term *bitchin'* ("cool, awesome"). And she donned a wetsuit, grabbed a board, and paddled into the water herself.

Her surfing results: wipeout. Her story: bitchin'.

Seek out a place you have never been, one that is literally or metaphorically foreign to you or most readers in your coverage area. It does not have to be 8,000 miles away. Spend time at a local cultural center, religious site, international school, international restaurant or grocery store, dance school, foreign embassy, or cigar factory. See it with your own eyes. Experience it, however you can. And interact with the people, listening to their stories and perspectives.

ASSIGNMENT ALERT!

The International Exchange

 In spring 2011, just before graduating from the University of Pennsylvania, Wiktoria Parysek called out American students for not knowing or asking much about international students like her.

As the German resident shared, "[T]here's a lot that American students aren't aware of when it comes to us students from a little further afield, even though they are almost certainly sitting next to us in class. Without sounding too dramatic, I truly believe there's a fundamental gap in our intercultural communication here . . . Yes, international students can drive. Yes, we can work. Yes, it's extremely complicated—why don't you ask me about it sometime?"

Your Assignment

Accept Parysek's challenge. Ask international students about their experiences. Dive into their back-stories, including what brought them to the states and your school specifically. Uncover the advantages they enjoy and challenges they face day-to-day due to their outsider status. And inquire about their thoughts on the school, its students, U.S. higher education, and America overall.

QUESTIONABLE PLACES

There are spots in nearly every coverage area spoken about in hush-hush tones.

They often accrue complaints about their squalid states or words of warning about traveling there alone or after dark. The fright, uneasiness, or decrepitude that accompanies them, however, does not diminish their potential newsworthiness.

Here are three examples of these types of newsworthy places featured in stories by student and professional journalists.

The Bridge

Once out of jail, roughly 70 of Florida's registered sex offenders stay beneath a bridge in Miami. Due to laws limiting them from living in spots frequented by children, the bridge is located in one of the few areas of the city they are allowed to settle. In a report for the *Tampa Bay Times*, staff writer Lane DeGregory paints a bleak picture: "Home now is a spit of sand beneath a highway overpass. It's the punishment after the punishment . . . There is nowhere to escape heat or bugs or storms. No electricity, except for a communal generator plugged into a tangle of extension cords . . . On the underside of the bridge, someone has spray-painted reminders: 'They don't want us to make it.' 'We R not monsters.' And, simply, 'Why?'"

The Testing Facility

In early 2012, protestors at Harvard University condemned the school's affiliated animal testing facilities. At the time, nine animals had died within them over the previous two years, including some through alleged negligence involving mistaken medicine doses and one brief escape. Most distressing to the protestors and activists: The failure of staff at one facility to notice a primate's abnormal behavior and death, to the extent that its carcass was left in a cage being cleaned in a mechanical washer that doused it with extremely hot water. According to the executive director of the activist group Stop Animal Exploitation Now, "If the university complex has had this many negligent deaths in this amount of time, there is clearly something very, very wrong. The public needs to be skeptical of what's going on here."

The Fishing Village

In an extremely remote village in Cambodia, residents are overrun by "poor sanitation, polluted water, and raw sewage." Literally, as Susana Cobo described last spring in *Tusk Magazine* at California State University, Fullerton, the fishing slum of Pak Long is awash in mud, mosquitoes, feces, pigs, corrugated tin roofs, and an abundance of trash such as "a ceramic pot, a rubber slipper, [an] IV bag, and decomposing dog teeth." As one local fisherman says, "It's a self-struggle. No one is going to come and help us."

Take readers places like these and others they may be afraid to go or have stopped going or have never gone. Take them places where the going is tough. And take them places aligned with a sexual, ethnic, political, religious, environmental, or economic viewpoint or way of life that may scare, dismay, or disgust them.

Often, telling the story of a place humanizes it and connects it to other people and places. It gets readers beyond their most misguided stereotypes. It calls out the fear mongering. It shows that while we do not have to like every spot we read and learn about, there is still something to gain from it. It serves as a reminder that an avoidance or hush-hush mentality does not mean it is going away—and that a greater understanding may lead to progress, change, and some manner of grudging respect.

As former *Daily Bruin* senior staff photographer Maya Sugarman recognized upon her arrival home from Yaoundé: Even 8,000 miles and a world away, there is more that connects than divides us.

As she wrote, "Many Cameroonian coaches and players laugh at the same jokes we do; we even make the same jokes. We are frustrated by the same problems in basketball; we also have our disagreements and our arguments. We give each other relationship advice. What makes us different from each other? As far as I can tell, nothing."

IN OTHER WORDS

Illustration by Yee Hung Lim

"After the 2005 earthquake in Pakistan, I was in Kashmir near the political line of control between India and Pakistan when a resident asked me a sincere question: 'Mr. John, what do Americans think of the situation in Kashmir?'

"I paused, realizing that I couldn't lie to him. **'Most Americans, unfortunately,' I began, 'think Kashmir is a sweater**. They couldn't find it on a map.' I went on to explain that 'international' news in most papers in our country is relegated to a half page inside the paper above the auto repair ads. That's all the play the rest of the world gets from the perspective of Americans, unless it involves our banks, troops, or other U.S. involvement.

"But I told my questioner that Americans aren't so different from residents of Kashmir: They love their children and want the best for them. That means safe streets, good schools, and a chance to go to college and have a chance at a better life than their parents had.

"That's my inherent philosophy about covering international news: **People are mostly the same**. While they don't share the same language, customs, and religions, there is more that joins them than sets them apart. And while I look for stories to report to the folks back home about how the big wide world outside their backyards is different from what they know, I also try to focus on common themes.

"In Kashmir, I wrote about business owners trying to restart their lives following the disaster. I wrote of a small town where the school had collapsed atop scores of small children. As they waited for the heavy machinery to arrive to remove the structure, many parents could only sit and stroke the dead hand of a son or daughter that jutted from the rubble that was too heavy for them to move aside. That poignant moment of loss can be felt by any reader, in any nation."

John Glionna, national correspondent, *Los Angeles Times*

IDEAS, ONLINE

Worlds Without People

In South Dakota, a rusted metal swing-set sporting a pair of white plastic seats stands alone amid yellowed grass in an unused playground. In the Georgian city of Tbilisi, an aged stone statue of Vladimir Lenin's face sits in front of an empty factory—his eyebrows, nose, ears, and chin scuffed and a large acorn-shaped hole in his right cheek. In Spain, a small cat pauses along a worn, shoddily paved road, the empty expanse of an economically flummoxed town in the background.

These images are among those included in "A World Without People," an online *Atlantic* feature focused on "nuclear-exclusion zones, blighted urban neighborhoods, towns where residents left to escape violence, unsold developments built during the real estate boom, ghost towns, and more."

Aimed at providing a glimpse of "what the world might look like if humans were to vanish from the planet," the photo collection is a full-color rendering of solitude and alienation. As one commenter responded beneath the feature, "I can feel the loneliness in these pictures."

In every coverage area, there are abandoned, out-of-the-way, and forgotten buildings, intersections, and entire communities where people rarely live, work, visit, or generally want to be. These lonely places—these small worlds without any or many people—deserve greater attention. There are stories embedded in their silence and emptiness.

Your Assignment

Tell the stories of places known for not having people in them for years or months at a time or during long stretches of each day or night. Visit them during their down-and-empty periods. Capture their isolation with words, photos, video, and even audio.

Here are a few places to get you started, campus spots known for being devoid of people or activity at certain times of the day or semester.

- Anatomy lab and campus morgue
- Animal research lab
- Back stacks of library
- Band practice room
- Cafeteria kitchen
- Campus radio station
- Campus security lost and found
- Data center or server room
- Health center waiting room or exam areas
- Popular late-night diner, in the early afternoon

MAPPING

In spring 2011, a tornado leveled parts of Tuscaloosa, Ala., with an historic torrent of wind and rain.

Following the storm, *The Crimson White* at the University of Alabama, located in the city, published and posted a prodigious amount of stories, videos, photo sets, and invaluable tweets.

Among the paper's most viral efforts was a Google map providing a geographic breakdown of everything tornado-related, including the path it took, the lives it claimed, the communities it affected, the buildings it leveled, and the volunteer opportunities available to help locals lessen its impact. Brandee Easter, the CW staffer who created the map, even received recognition from a United Nations representative for her work.

It is a powerful example of the power of online maps. When used correctly, they crystallize the geographical specs of a location, on a micro and macro level. They visualize quirks or trends that otherwise might not emerge or be as noticeable. They show the scope of a journey, the repetition of a corrupt act, or the connection between people, places, events, and mountains of information. And they serve as portals for additional newsworthy exploration, especially when embedded with related text, photos, audio, video, and other multimedia elements.

Here is a quick rundown of the more popular types of online maps created and published by the student and professional press.

Location Listings

- Campus crime
- Handicapped parking spaces
- Local landmarks
- Study abroad programs

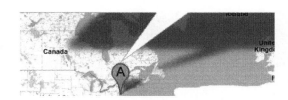

Paths Taken

- Sports team travel throughout season
- Projected or actual storm path
- Criminal car-chase route
- Protest march

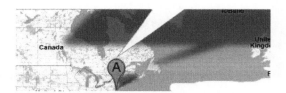

Data Distribution

- Population density and shifts over time
- Campaign contribution totals by constituency
- Temperature change in various spots over time
- Unemployment or inflation levels nationwide

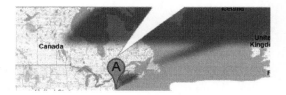

Social Mapping

- Interconnections between school donors, top administrators, and board of directors
- Geographic display of real-time social media response to crisis or major event

SITE ALERT!

 Here is a sampling of popular online mapping creation, editing, and embedding sites and programs.

Geofeedia (geofeedia.com), "quickly find and curate social media from locations where breaking news is happening"

Google Maps (maps.google.com), "a web mapping service application and technology provided by Google"

OpenHeatMap (openheatmap.com), "turn your spreadsheet into a map"

quikmaps.com (quikmaps.com), "maps for the masses"

ZeeMaps (zeemaps.com), "create, make, and publish interactive, customized maps"

CHAPTER 10

The Local Angle

Illustration by Yee Hung Lim

"Cover what you do best. Link to the rest."

In February 2007, digital media guru Jeff Jarvis famously advised news outlets to do this to succeed within journalism 2.0. It is still relevant, on the student and professional levels. Follow this mantra in your brainstorming sessions and coverage of all "mega-big" stories.

Never shy from reporting on the outside world—even the events, issues, and trends that appear to exist beyond your reportorial skills, knowledge base, or coverage area. But when you do attack the mega-big stories, always strive to find your niche, the angle, the slice of information, or the follow-up no one else can offer as well as you.

Most important to recognize: Students absolutely have something to offer. As Vox Media marketing and projects director Callie Schweitzer confirms, "Age should never be something that holds you back. Instead, it should push you forward. In our ever-evolving society that moves at the speed of light, young people are uniquely qualified to comment on and analyze a changing world—from a youth perspective."

For example, in spring 2011, even at the top Ivy League schools, student newspaper readers were not expecting an exclusive, behind-the-scenes, blow-by-blow account of how U.S. military forces discovered and killed Osama bin Laden. Those expectations instead fell on *The New York Times*, *The New Yorker*, *Time*, CNN, *The Washington Post*, and a few other prestigious national news outlets. But that does not mean students did not or should not have reported upon it.

Take *NextGen Journal* (nextgenjournal.com). At the height of its popularity *NextGen*, a student-run news and commentary site, featured student contributors from colleges and universities across the U.S. and Canada. Amid the conversations—and celebrations—that erupted in the wake of bin Laden's death, *NextGen* published more stories from more student angles than any other news outlet in the world.

The site featured dispatches on student reactions at roughly two dozen schools—from West Point cadets running around in "crazy patriotic costumes and underwear" to Stanford University students who "roasted s'mores, drank beer (mostly the American variety), and chanted 'U-S-A U-S-A!'"

NextGen contributors soon after debated the merits of the country's celebratory mood, including a Michigan State University student who decried the "Osama circus" atmosphere and a Tulane University student who separately described the national party as "perhaps the only time that I've felt proud to call myself a young college student."

NextGen also reflected on the meaning of the terror kingpin's death for current students who were in grade school when the September 11 attacks occurred. It gauged the impact of the military strike on the 2012 presidential election. And it ran a reminder op-ed that "terrorism does not die with Osama bin Laden."

Similar stories were run throughout the professional press—but hardly any from the student angle.

As *NextGen Journal* founder and top editor Connor Toohill, a student at the University of Notre Dame, said, "Our best pieces, our most popular pieces—whether it's Egypt or the State of the Union or health care reform or the Super Bowl—really look at, what is the impact here for students? What is the significance for our generation? We've seen there is really a demand for that."

Your task: Meet that demand.

■ To start, recognize rule one: Every story contains ideas for a dozen more. It links to an old-school five-syllable word memorized, repeated, and practiced by many journalists: localization.

TO FIT YOUR READERSHIP

Localization is the process of adapting an existing story to fit your readership, reporting style, coverage area, or deadline.

It is *not* stealing. Do not steal others' stories. There is a four-syllable word for that: plagiarism. And that often leads to a three-syllable phrase: You're fired.

Instead, localization typically involves mining others' work for one of four things.

A Narrower Focus, one that will specifically interest your target audience. It often requires making a big story smaller, fitting it to your location or main readership demographic.

Example

Last spring, local newspapers throughout Virginia reported on the new budget approved by the state's General Assembly. At the College of William and Mary, *The Flat Hat* student newspaper published a story specifically focusing on how the budget would affect the school.

A Closer Look at one portion or person within a larger story, typically someone or something given scant attention or a supporting role.

Example

In a local news report about a ban on panhandling on or near your campus, you spot the name of a recent alumnus from your school, now homeless. You track him down at a local shelter and share the story of how he's fallen on such hard times.

A Fresh Concentration on an angle, individual, or issue other stories are leaving out.

Example

In Tampa, Fla., local press outlets annually cover the Gasparilla Pirate Festival, a mass celebration that takes over a chunk of the city one weekend each year. For a complementary report in spring 2011, University of Tampa student journalist Amanda Sieradzki focused on what happens to the party beads used in the festival after the parade and public and private soirées are over—including those used as "cheap home décor."

An Independent Story organically inspired by—and sporting only a loose affiliation with—the original.

Example

A viral video is making the rounds showing a college student saying a gleeful yes to a surprise marriage proposal during a class. The video motivates you to explore the lives of married and divorced students on campus and to interview a professor who studies the country's changing relationship trends.

THE ALWAYS LIST

- **Always** consider what every story you read means for your own audience, beat, or coverage area. Determine how you may be able to localize it. Think beyond direct connections.
- **Always** cite or link to the original source that inspired your localized story. Online, this is known as a hat tip.
- **Always** check facts independently. Do not simply assume that because another news outlet reported something it must be true.
- **Always** use others' stories as inspiration or as a foundation for additional interpretation, not replication. I cannot stress enough: Do your own reporting. Adapt. Don't steal.

THE NEVER LIST

- **Never** assume your story will or should look similar to the one that inspired it. Your sources may have different opinions. You may bring up issues the reporter for the original story did not even think to search for. You may stumble across different information. Bottom line: Keep an open mind about the direction in which your localized story might go.
- **Never** lose faith in the power of the student angle. You cannot yet boast 20 years of experience, but your undergraduate status may provide you with a perspective, established contacts, access, or insider knowledge that veteran reporters lack due to their older age or off-campus location.
- **Never** base your reporting too much on others' work. There is power in adaptation. But fresh creation is also powerful.
- **Never** rely solely on national outlets or the professional press for localization. The student press can help as well.

ASSIGNMENT ALERT!

Localize *This*

Let's practice some localization. Select a story or two from the following list, which features events, issues, and trends that received especially enormous bursts of national news coverage last year and earlier this year. For each selection, brainstorm 10 localized story angles for your campus readership or students nationwide.

- Aurora movie massacre
- Health care debate and Supreme Court decision
- Superstorm Sandy
- Kony 2012 movement
- Pope Benedict's resignation
- Manti Te'o online love hoax
- The Oscars
- Pinterest
- Presidential election
- Summer Olympics
- Super bowl

Next, conduct an online news search of a current trending topic or big event. Again, brainstorm localized angles. Focus on stories you do not see highlighted within the current coverage or that students would be especially interested in.

POST-MORTEM

Post-Mortem is a recurring feature in the book and on my blog, telling the story *behind* a story, series, or website—in the words of the reporter or editor responsible for creating it.

The Tucson Shooting

On a Saturday morning in January 2011, top editors at the *Arizona Daily Wildcat* were preparing for a staff meeting. Reports started streaming in about a shooting at a Safeway grocery store not far from the University of Arizona campus.

The meeting never happened. Instead, the reporting began, and temporarily continued nonstop. After the shooting—which killed six and injured 13, including U.S. congresswoman

Gabrielle Giffords—*Daily Wildcat* staffers presented a myriad of stories, commentaries, photos, and tweets about the incident, its aftermath, and its impact on UA and Tucson, Ariz.

In this Q&A, Michelle Monroe, the paper's editor-in-chief at the time, discusses the benefits and difficulties of being at a campus newspaper while reporting upon such a monumental event. Monroe is now a copy editor and page designer for *The Santa Clarita Valley Signal* in California.

For a student news outlet, what are the challenges of reporting upon such an impacting, real-time story?
The biggest challenge was verifying the facts . . . With a story as big as the Tucson massacre, we were especially on edge about errors. Being a student newspaper is not a defense when you misspell a victim's name or get the facts wrong. If anything, you're working with the fear that if you mess up, you're putting a bad face on all student newspapers. There's nothing more infuriating than people sneering at you because you work for a college paper and not a "real" paper, and we didn't want to give anyone the satisfaction of proving their assumptions right.

So when reports first started airing that Rep. Gabrielle Giffords died, it caused a standstill in the *Daily Wildcat*. Someone monitoring Twitter saw the first post and shouted out the news. We didn't immediately retweet or update our story. We stopped working and had a discussion about it. There was no attribution except to other newspapers—our reporter at the hospital couldn't confirm—but on the other hand the race to be the most updated lingered over our heads.

Conflicted, we finally agreed to a solution our news editor, Luke Money, came up with. We would update the story online, reporting that other newspapers were reporting that she had died, but that we could in no way verify that information.

Minutes later when our reporter on the scene called saying they were prepping her for surgery we updated the story saying despite other reports that she had died, our reporter confirmed Giffords was going into surgery.

The challenge in part was that **bigger news organizations get treated better than student organizations**. There is a real possibility that the hospital would tell CNN before they would even think about returning our calls. We had a reporter at the hospital for obvious reasons, but also because we feared getting ignored or pushed to the side for media callbacks and we wanted to try and get the information as quickly.

One other issue was that the shooting happened during Winter Break. With a full staff we have . . . around 50 or 60 on the editorial side. When the January 8, 2011 shooting occurred we were lucky to have 12 people in Tucson able to come to the newsroom . . . School wasn't set to begin until January 12, so while some of our staff was able to drive from their respective cities to campus early, others had flights that couldn't be changed.

A professional news outlet might have a few people out on vacation, but **we had around 80 percent of our people out of town**. We only had one reporter with a car who we could send out so she drove back and forth across town. She would leave the hospital to go to a police press conference and have to rush back to the hospital dictating information on the phone to the editors. That was definitely a challenge only a student newspaper would have to deal with.

By comparison, what are the advantages of being a student news outlet while covering a story like this?

The advantage of being a student news outlet is that it's easy to find people who have been personally affected by this tragic event. Gabrielle Giffords is a huge part of Tucson's identity and she has a significant impact on the university. Many of the students on campus interned with her, including members of our student government.

It was helpful to be a student outlet because we have contact information for almost every member of the Associated Students of the University of Arizona Senate and executive branch, and they have strong ties to the local and state government.

Daniel Hernandez Jr. [the individual who helped save Giffords' life] is a very well-known student. Many people at the newspaper had personal connections with him and were able to provide his contact information to an unbiased reporter immediately.

The university is also a center of the town, so we are in close proximity to the hospital where the victims were taken. Also, as students, we were able to know the correct people at the university to call immediately when the memorial was announced. We have a very distinct culture and community on campus and as a student news outlet it was helpful to have such a multitude of sources and angles in such a concentrated area.

Did you cover the story mainly from a student or UA perspective or go toe-to-toe with the professional outlets and report from all angles?

As stated in our purpose, the *Daily Wildcat* is dedicated to reporting on campus and world affairs with a specific university focus. Generally, if there is no campus connection, we don't print it in our paper. We chose to cover the story from the student and UA perspective. We have a unique audience that we cater to, so we try to tailor our ideas to fit that niche. I don't have a specific count, but I believe we had more than 20 articles written on the subject [the first week after the shooting] from a variety of angles with a campus focus.

An editor-in-chief before me once told me that in *The New York Times* newsroom there are six clocks, each displaying a different time zone. But the *Las Vegas Sun* newsroom has six clocks, all set to Las Vegas time, because staffers there know **their strength is in being masters of their own community**. I like to apply that message to the *Daily Wildcat*.

PEER-TO-PEER STORY SHARING

One student angle deserves another.

Localization frequently occurs among student news media. An insightful report by a college newspaper far away featuring a pertinent student issue can easily be localized to your own school or spun-off with a fresh twist.

For example, since fall 2011, *The Daily Collegian* and *Onward State*, a pair of student news outlets at Penn State University, have been comprehensively covering the high-profile child sex abuse scandal, its related football fallout, and its lingering impact on Happy Valley and the PSU brand.

The outlets' hard-nosed, on-point, wide-ranging editorial slates should serve as inspirations to journalists everywhere. In addition, through their extensive reporting, they are providing glimpses at a variety of individuals, activities, and issues deserving closer inspection on many campuses.

Here is a sampling of the many Penn State scandal stories that have the potential to be localized.

Retired Staff

One eye-catching detail reported during the scandal's initial hysteria: convicted abuser and former assistant football coach Jerry Sandusky had "remained a presence around Penn State." He had even been spotted in a PSU weight room only a week before charges against him were filed. He had not officially worked at the university since 1999. Related questions for a report at your school: What access are retired officials and professors granted on campus? How often do they take part in meetings, trips, and other school business? Are any still on the active payroll? And, more generally, how does staff retirement work at your school?

Criminal History

Prior to his arrest, Sandusky had allegedly engaged in despicable activity for years without prosecution and criminal punishment. But what about those who have been caught and convicted of wrongdoing in the past and are now applying to attend or work at your school? Specifically, what is involved in the vetting process for new faculty and staff hires? And what are the guidelines for determining the admittance of student applicants with a criminal history?

Presidential Roles

Along with being ousted as Penn State's president, Graham Spanier resigned or was booted from other organizations on which he held leadership positions—most prominently U.S. Steel and college football's Bowl Championship Series. What outside boards and committees do the president and other high-ranking administrators at your school serve on? Who approves the affiliations? And how are conflicts of interest handled? More generally, in what ways do faculty and staff earn outside money during the academic year or semester breaks?

Campus Crime Reporting

According to *The Chronicle of Higher Education*, "In the wake of the scandal over child sex-abuse allegations at Pennsylvania State University, colleges across the country are reviewing their policies regarding what their employees are required to do when they witness or receive information about suspected abuse of children." What are your school's regulations for reporting crimes or other suspicious activity, whether it involves children or not? What are the rules for RAs and other student leaders specifically? And how have people actually responded to criminal behavior they spotted in the past?

Brand Management

As the scandal unraveled, a number of high-profile companies that advertised with or sponsored Penn State disassociated themselves from the Nittany Lion brand. What companies are aligned with your school, and in what ways? What demands do the companies make in exchange for advertising or sponsorships? How much money does your school receive from such arrangements? And, most importantly, how is that money spent once it is received?

ASSIGNMENT ALERT!

Student Press Visits

Visit some or all of the following websites for 30 of the top student newspapers within the U.S., Canada, England, and Singapore. Scroll through the papers' current and recent content. Similar to the Penn State examples, find potential stories that can be localized or otherwise adapted. Along with news reports, remember to look at commentary pieces—worrying not about the slants or specific points made but the issues and themes they address.

- *Arizona Daily Wildcat*, University of Arizona (wildcat.arizona.edu)
- *The Columbia Daily Spectator*, Columbia University (columbiaspectator.com)
- *The Crimson White*, University of Alabama (cw.ua.edu)
- *The Daily Californian*, University of California, Berkeley (dailycal.org)
- *The Daily Collegian*, Penn State University (collegian.psu.edu)
- *The Daily Emerald*, University of Oregon (dailyemerald.com)
- *The Daily Illini*, University of Illinois at Urbana-Champaign (dailyillini.com)
- *The Daily Northwestern*, Northwestern University (dailynorthwestern.com)
- *The Daily Pennsylvanian*, University of Pennsylvania (thedp.com)
- *The Daily Princetonian*, Princeton University (dailyprincetonian.com)
- *The Daily Reveille*, Louisiana State University (lsureveille.com)
- *The Daily Tar Heel*, University of North Carolina (dailytarheel.com)
- *The Daily Texan*, University of Texas at Austin (dailytexanonline.com)
- *The Diamondback*, University of Maryland (diamondbackonline.com)
- *The Harvard Crimson*, Harvard University (thecrimson.com)
- *The Independent Florida Alligator*, University of Florida (alligator.org)
- *Indiana Daily Student*, Indiana University (idsnews.com)
- *Iowa State Daily*, Iowa State University (iowastatedaily.com)
- *The Lantern*, Ohio State University (thelantern.com)
- *Leeds Student*, University of Leeds (leedsstudent.org)
- *The McGill Daily*, McGill University (mcgilldaily.com)
- *The Minnesota Daily*, University of Minnesota (mndaily.com)
- *The Nanyang Chronicle*, Nanyang Technological University (ntu.edu.sg/chronicle)

- *The Oklahoma Daily*, University of Oklahoma (oudaily.com)
- *The Pitt News*, University of Pittsburgh (pittnews.com)
- *The Red and Black*, University of Georgia (redandblack.com)
- *The State News*, Michigan State University (statenews.com)
- *The University Daily Kansan*, University of Kansas (kansan.com)
- *Varsity*, University of Cambridge (varsity.co.uk)
- *Yale Daily News*, Yale University (yaledailynews.com)

IDEAS, ONLINE

Daily College Checks

Along with student newspapers, there are a number of other high-profile regional, national, and international news outlets focused on higher education that are the perfect starting points for localized stories.

Here is a sampling of related news and commentary websites, almost all of them appearing in a bookmark folder on my main web browser named "Daily College Checks."

The Chronicle of Higher Education (chronicle.com), "the No. 1 source of news, information, and jobs for college and university faculty members and administrators"

Her Campus (hercampus.com), "a collegiette's guide to life"

Huffington Post College (huffingtonpost.com/college), "college news and more"

Inside Higher Ed (insidehighered.com), "the online source for news, opinion, and jobs for all of higher education"

IvyGate (ivygateblog.com), "a news, gossip, and commentary blog that covers the Ivy League"

The Nation "Extra Credit" (thenation.com/blogs/extra-credit), "campus-oriented news, first-person reports from student activists and journalists about their campus

The New York Times "Colleges and Universities" (nyti.ms/MvnNmP), "news about colleges and universities"

USA TODAY College (usatodayeducate.com/staging), "blog, news, and information for today's connected college students powered by *USA TODAY*"

The Wall Street Journal "Higher Education" (on.wsj.com/Ny6hfv), "information, news, and pictures"

The Washington Post "Campus Overload" (wapo.st/TCQDC8), "a syllabus for navigating the high-powered campus social scene"

CHAPTER 11
Building a Beat

Illustration by Yee Hung Lim

Establish a beat.

It is one of the best idea-generating and career-making moves a young journalist can make. A beat is a general or specific coverage area tackled by the same reporter, story after story after story.

Working the same beat for an established outlet or an independent website you create enables you to become a mini-expert about a small slice of our world. It gives your reporting a sense of identity and purpose. And it builds a knowledge and contacts base that will breed confidence and better journalism.

■ Over time, your stories will have more depth and be more accurate. You will gain more access and grab more scoops. Soon enough, you will be happily drowning in a sea of newsworthy ideas. In many ways, a quality news beat is a self-sustaining story ideas machine.

MOST COMMON BEATS

Among journalists, some things simply get more coverage.

Certain parts of our lives and the world as we know it boast such massive significance and provoke such endless fascination they require constant reporting. At times, dedicated beats are established to ensure someone is always exploring them.

Here is a list of the most common general news beats, on and off campus.

- Academics
- Admissions
- Alumni and development
- Arts, entertainment, culture and media
- Business and employment
- Construction and planning
- Crime and courts
- Environment
- Faculty and staff
- Family and parenting
- Fashion
- Food
- Greek life
- Health and wellness
- Housing
- International
- Love and sex
- Military and security
- Politics
- Religion and multicultural
- Science
- Sports
- Student life
- Tech
- Transportation

BREAKING DOWN A BEAT

There are some keys to mastering a beat.

Covering an essential, popular beat requires building and sustaining relationships with specific sources, following the right real-world and online chatter, attending and seeking access to key public and behind-the-scenes events, and remaining focused on a single set of guiding questions.

To help with all those things, before you begin reporting, break down your chosen beat. For example, here is a brief admissions beat breakdown.

Admissions

- **The Gist**: This beat explores the university recruiting, admissions, and enrollment process and the impact of that process on students and schools.

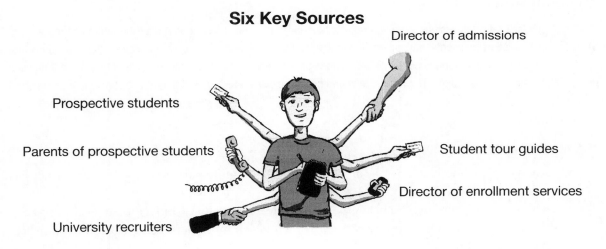

Six Key Sources

Director of admissions

Prospective students

Parents of prospective students

Student tour guides

Director of enrollment services

University recruiters

- **Also, Don't Forget**: prospective students whose applications are rejected, admitted students who have chosen to enroll elsewhere, transfer students, high school guidance counselors who mentor students on college selection, staffers at standardized testing prep centers, and the team that creates the admissions brochures and other materials.

- **Five Guiding Questions**: Who is applying to my school, and why? Who is *not* applying? How is my school promoted to prospective students, and who is behind that promotion? What does my school envision as its perfect student body, and how do they go about selecting students to fulfill that vision? And in what ways do the weak economy and digital media explosion impact the admissions game?

- **Five Key Events**: admissions open houses, campus tours, admitted students weekend, off-campus recruiting trips, and individual student admissions interviews.

- **Five Online Areas to Monitor**: admissions portion of school website, social media and online forums in which applicants (and their families) interact, sites sporting the latest school rankings, news outlets focused on academia such as *The Chronicle of Higher Education* and *The New York Times* blog The Choice (thechoice.blogs.nytimes.com) which is aimed at "demystifying college admissions and aid."

ASSIGNMENT ALERT!

The Beat Blueprint

Similar to the Admissions sample, create a blueprint for a specific beat you might be interested in tackling. List the sources, events, and online content that will be most helpful, along with the big-picture questions that should guide you during your reporting. In addition, monitor current coverage of the beat by local and national news outlets and the blogosphere. Note the stories and perspectives you feel are left out, underrepresented, or reported inaccurately.

THE ALWAYS LIST

- **Always** learn the history of your beat, including reading past stories your own outlet has published.
- **Always** check out how the beat is currently covered on a local and national level. Also keep abreast of related international coverage to lend even more depth and breadth to your beat expertise.
- **Always** learn the lingo employed by individuals on your beat, along with the routines they follow and traditions they hold sacred. The goal: Ensure your sources and readers trust you as someone knowledgeable about what you are covering.
- **Always** maintain a presence at key events and hangouts related to your beat. You will pick up a slew of ideas you could never find online. In addition, you will become the first person sources think of and decide to contact when they have a big scoop.

THE NEVER LIST

- **Never** forget to reach out to prominent people on your beat when writing a story that will impact them or make them angry at not being included.

- **Never** become so insulated within your beat you lose sight of what's newsworthy to regular readers. In the end, you are reporting for them, not the newsmakers and sources you interact with every day.
- **Never** overlook what needs to be explained in simpler terms in order to be understood by people outside your beat.
- **Never** ignore the people and parts of your beat no one else is covering or that have been unfairly stereotyped by news media in the past.

THE MICRO-BEAT

Along with beats, there are micro-beats.

Coined by Andy Rossback, the editor-in-chief of *The Daily Emerald* at the University of Oregon, the term describes a coverage area more specific or timely than the common catch-all beats. Yet, similar to a regular beat, a micro-beat is still complex and newsworthy enough to require a staffer, section, blog, or website all its own. For example, technology is a beat. Potential micro-beats include everything from viral videos, MMORPGs, and Google to cloud computing, cybersecurity, and your school's information technology department.

A micro-beat also encompasses an event, project, trend, or issue that pops up and exerts heavy influence for a finite period of time. For example, politics is a beat. Potential micro-beats include everything from specific election cycles, Supreme Court decisions, and the Occupy movement to the Tea Party, an Anthony Weiner-style scandal, and the formation, passage, and enactment of a single bill.

Lastly, a micro-beat is at times tied to a project, group, person, or phenomenon especially impacting or unique to an individual campus or coverage area. For example, sports is a beat. Potential micro-beats include each of your city's major professional and college teams, the nearby horse racing park, a local waterway often holding regattas, your university's sports research center, campus intramural sports, and a major stadium construction project.

ASSIGNMENT ALERT!

Pick a Beat, Any Beat

 Take a second look at the list of common beats. Pick one. Brainstorm 10 to 15 related micro-beats specific to your campus, coverage area, or college students in general. Bonus points for ferreting out a few that are especially timely or often overlooked.

Post-Mortem is a recurring feature in the book and on my blog, telling the story *behind* **a story, series, or website—in the words of the reporter or editor responsible for creating it.**

The Homicide Beat

Homicide Watch D.C. (homicidewatch.org) is an independent online reporting project that aims to do nothing less than cover every murder in Washington, D.C. "from crime to conviction." Its tagline: "Mark every death. Remember every victim. Follow every case."

Launched in fall 2010 and run by journalist Laura Amico, HWDC utilizes "primary source documents, social networking, and original reporting to build one of the nation's most comprehensive public resources on violent crime."

As *Nieman Journalism Lab* confirms, "It's been lauded for its devotion to blanket coverage and for its ability to build communities of interest around the kind of crime stories that might get a few inches of coverage—if that—in the local daily."

The site is proof that with vision, drive, web savvy, and reporting chops, you can carve out an original, innovative, and interactive micro-beat that makes a true, sustainable difference in your coverage area.

In this Q&A, Amico discusses the difference Homicide Watch D.C. has made since its inception and the benefits and challenges of operating independently and online.

What is HWDC doing that sets it apart from other outlets and sites?
We are merging very traditional crime reporting with new tools in a way that creates one of the most comprehensive views of homicide available. We use primary source documents—and publish them online—whenever we can. That means funeral programs, arrest warrants, press releases, and more. We have used DocumentCloud (documentcloud. org) to build an integrated and searchable library of these documents.

We are database driven. This means every homicide has certain required information and helps us see where the holes in our reporting are. It also creates a reporting tool to use for investigative stories.

We capture community reaction to homicides and homicide news in real time by pulling comments posted on Twitter, Facebook, and more into a narrative (using Storify) and posting it online. Those posts elicit further comments and reaction, ranging from memorial messages to news tips. We map each case with a searchable database that allows users to interact with the information geographically or topically. A user can search by neighborhood or type of homicide. We provide a photo gallery of victims' photos. Users can flip through and see who the victims are. It has been one of our most popular features.

We commit to following every case through investigation, prosecution, and sentencing. Most news outlets will follow a handful of cases in this way every year. Our theory is that in a homicide case, if a defendant's name is published, it is responsible to follow up regularly on where the case stands. Who knows? That person could be acquitted and it's only fair to clear their record publicly, and mark that the case remains unsolved. Individually, these reporting methods are not unique to Homicide Watch D.C. **What has set us apart is the integration of all of them**.

What are the advantages of working independently and online?

Working for myself, I've had complete control over how I want the project to look and feel. As the project has developed, I've been able to make decisions quickly, without having to go to a committee or find a consensus. I know what all the moving pieces are and how each decision that I'm making fits into the wider picture of what I want to accomplish.

I am also able to approach a very sensitive subject without some of the confines of legacy media. I have not inherited anyone else's community or history. That also means I am responsible for creating Homicide Watch's community and history. Because nothing I do has precedent, everything I do sets precedent, and I have to do that mindfully and carefully.

What has been a particularly memorable moment for you?

Soon after I got underway with Homicide Watch, I was talking to a victim's brother who had used the site to announce a vigil and funeral. The brother happened to also have been a witness to the homicide and I was interviewing him in preparation for a preliminary hearing. I was asking a lot of sensitive questions about the crime, and you never know how a person will react. This man was more than helpful, answering each question.

At the end of the interview, he thanked me for listening to his story. I thought he had been helping me with my reporting, but he really needed someone to listen to the tragic story of what his family had been through. Again and again since then, I've realized families so often want to tell the stories of what has happened and for their pain to be recognized. So often, they are grateful to have the chance to talk about it.

What has surprised you?

I had no idea how much business and public relations work the project would be when I started it. I wish I had more experience with grant writing, that I knew how to write a business proposal and negotiate contracts, and that I had a better idea of how to promote the site. Having a good idea gets you a long way, but it takes a business plan and PR work to get you home.

What is your advice to those looking to launch a similarly independent, niche, news-oriented site?

There's a phrase that's useful in web development: "always in beta." That's how Homicide Watch has grown. We are constantly fine-tuning the technical, editorial, and business operations. I tell people interested in online journalism projects to trust that things will fall into place, but do what you can to make sure the pieces fall in the right places.

If I had it to do over again, I would bring a finance person on board as soon as it became clear there was a future for the site and business. **There are three legs to the stool: editorial, technical, and financial**. It's hard because these three pieces grow at different rates and are related to each other, but one should never be so far behind the others that it threatens to topple the stool. Having a plan—even if you change it—for all three is important.

BABYSITTING A PIECE OF GLASS

Select a beat. Break it down. Get up to speed on how it should be covered. And then head straight to the source.

Sources are journalists' most sacred treasures, especially when working a beat. According to Sara Ganim, who broke the Penn State sex scandal while covering the crime beat for Harrisburg's *Patriot-News*, "Polishing sources is like babysitting a piece of glass. It takes a lot of care. I spend a lot of time just listening to people and chatting about things. But once you've got their respect, it all pays off. Instead of chasing stories, stories chase you."

Surprisingly, this babysitting is often left out of journalism class lessons. As journalist Glenn Wallace shares about his professional start, "I was caught by surprise by the importance of learning a beat and fostering sources. No one ever taught me any tips or guidelines for how to build trust with official sources, or how the simple act of getting on a first-name basis with an executive's secretary would one day become a deadline-saving move. I live and die by my beat connections, whether it's getting that 'heads up' call about certain issues, or having that personal cell number for that crucial source that I can call waaaay past business hours."

Source discovery and development is an in-between-the-lines art. It requires people skills, unimpeachable professionalism, genuine compassion, and an ability to look someone in the eye and tell them the full truth—even when it might hurt them. These are all tougher to master than you think.

Here is the scoop from top journalists on cultivating and polishing sources.

Think About Your Best Friend

"Think about asking a complete stranger or your best friend to trust you. Which one do you think would trust you more? It is your best friend, because you have built that relationship of trust. Building a relationship with a stranger will allow you to have more intimate moments and better access."

Jason Halley, staff photographer,
Chico Enterprise-Record, Calif.

Show Off Your Work

"I've dropped off packages of my stories at homes before, just to show that if they want to talk to me, I'll give them a fair shake. If they see your work, they're connecting with you, which helps make an 'in.'"

Andy Boyle, news applications developer,
The Chicago Tribune

Weigh Sources Over Scoops

"Don't practice what I call hit-and-run journalism, which is getting what you want from a source any way that you can, without regard for whether you'll need that person's help again. If you burn your sources and they do not trust you, then you are out of business. Never sacrifice someone who could be a long-term source just to get a one-day scoop."

Lea Kahn, staff writer,
The Lawrence Ledger, N.J.

Err on the Side of a Full Explanation

"Be upfront with your sources about your story and your intentions, especially with people who aren't media-savvy."

Kathleen Richards, co-editor,
East Bay Express, Calif.

Go Out of Your Way

"If you can't get somebody on the phone or by email, and the story could hurt their reputation, go to their office or their house. Leave your card. Bug their secretary. Try really hard to find them. It's only fair."

Carol Carnevale, managing editor,
Palm Beach Daily News, Fla.

Look in the Mirror

"If you keep having the same problem with your sources—they don't want to talk, they're not returning phone calls, the information they give is garbled, etc.—the likelihood is that it's not the sources who are all afflicted with the same problem. Maybe it's the other common denominator: you."

Natalie Kennedy, editor,
The Wellsboro Gazette, Pa.

ASSIGNMENT ALERT!

Find Common Ground

"You have to cultivate sources, which means distinguishing yourself from the other reporters who cover the same beat that you do. One way to do that is to find common ground with that source. My father was a member of the local Masonic Lodge and I would look to see if my source was wearing a tie clip or a ring with the Masonic emblem, and use it as an icebreaker."

Lea Kahn

Your Assignment

Seek out a set of complete strangers in a safe, social setting. Sit and chat for a bit. See how long it takes to find common ground, such as a shared interest, activity, background, fashion sense, pop culture obsession, or daily routine. Notice how the commonalities are uncovered. Did they emerge from things you visually noticed about the other person or vice versa? Did they crop up from you talking more or listening more? And were they stumbled upon via specific questions or general conversation?

Start with the Secretary

"If you really want to know and understand what is happening, ask the secretary. They're the ones completing all the paperwork and they know how to put it in plain language."

Natalie Kennedy

Then Try the Clerks

"Take the time to get to know clerks—court clerks, local government clerks, anybody whose job involves serving as an intermediary between you and information you need. Selfishly, those connections could give you access to documents you might not get otherwise. These people also often know a lot about what's really going on and might be more willing to talk about it than the officials you're meeting with or interviewing. They also tend to be interesting people."

Zaz Hollander, freelance writer,
The Alaska Star

Also Shoot for Primary Sources

"When you are writing about a subject, first attempt to reach the subject. If the story is about gangs, talk to gang members. If a story is about a criminal who was arrested, visit the person in jail. If the story is about teen drinking, talk to teen drinkers. Too often, we as journalists fall back on secondhand sources like documents and attorneys."

Demian Bulwa, reporter,
San Francisco Chronicle

Dress a Few Steps Lower

"If I was interviewing the mayor, I would wear a tie. If I was in a courtroom, I'd wear a nice dress shirt and tuck it in, usually into jeans and nicer shoes. But I always tried to dress a few steps lower than the people I'd be dealing with. If you dress nicer than them, they sometimes won't open up as much. You look too much like authority. If you look like a guy they'd run into at a bar and do a couple shots of Jameson with, they might open up more."

Andy Boyle

Become Comfortable with Everyone

"Young reporters need to be comfortable interacting with a wide variety of sources—from highly-educated politicians and business types to working-class folks who live paycheck to paycheck. A reporter needs to learn how to quickly develop a rapport with these folks. Sometimes, it can mean changing your speech patterns just a bit, or taking a patient, deliberate approach to asking questions."

Matt Garfield, former chief political reporter,
The Herald, S.C.

Treat Everyone with the Same Respect

"We see a lot of people at the best times of their lives and the worst. We meet people who are super rich and those that are dirt poor. We meet people who are saints and those who have done the most heinous things. And mostly we deal with everybody in between. No matter who they are, or what their station in life is, I treat them with the same respect. I'm there to tell their story. And I listen to them. In order to know their story, you have to listen to them tell it."

Christopher Chung, staff photographer,
The Press Democrat, Calif.

ASSIGNMENT ALERT!

Colorful, Happy Memories

"Back in my cub reporter days, I was assigned to follow the life of an everyday senior citizen for one year. Each month, a photographer and I met 'Buzz' at his home, the senior center, and other local haunts for regular catch-ups. At the end of the year, I was having a hard time condensing Buzz's story into an interesting, concise narrative, so my editor told me to go back and ask Buzz what he felt were the highlights of his year. Turns out it wasn't the 'topical' themes I'd planned to focus on—the senior health care safety net, family relationships, and the financial troubles faced by most local seniors. Buzz could only remember the week he went to Padres spring training, the time he found a $50 bill on the sidewalk, and the week his granddaughter was visiting from Arizona. These were colorful, happy memories that resonated for him. Using these memories as my framework, I built the story around them, and it later won a regional journalism award. My lesson: When in doubt, go back to the source and use their words—not your own—to paint the picture."

Pam Kragen, arts and features editor, *North County Times*, Calif.

Your Assignment

Interview someone solely about memories. Seek out their personal reflections on the highlights and lowlights of their previous day, week, semester, year, or even entire childhood. Possibly focus your chat around a general emotional prompt, such as asking for their happiest, saddest, scariest, or most romantic memories. Spot the themes that emerge in what they share and leave out. If feeling especially ambitious, shape an entire feature around their recollections. For example, tell the story of a senior student's college career through a glimpse back at the experiences that stand out most in their memory.

Keep an Ethical Distance

"Your sources are not your friends. It's OK to like them, but remember they are business connections."

Carol Carnevale

Shuck the Awe

"Please, please, please don't be in awe of the people you are covering. Never ask them for their autograph or jersey, a photo with them, or other things like that. You can and will lose your job due to a lack of professionalism."

Christina Dunmyer, sports writer,
The Daily American, Pa.

Follow Up

"I find that following up with the people I interview is always helpful and pays off in the long run. I send a simple 'Thank You' email after every interview and usually send a web link to the piece I interviewed them for. People like to feel appreciated and, in turn, appreciate the writer right back. I continue to build connections with those who I've met and am amazed at the writing opportunities that come my way as a result."

Dani Burlison, staff writer,
The Pacific Sun, Calif.

CHAPTER 12

Records Reporting

The million-dollar story began with a one-sentence tip.

Early last year, while working as an enterprise reporter for *The Daily Kent Stater* at Ohio's Kent State University, Doug Brown investigated the past legal troubles of Jason Cope.

At the time, Cope, a Kent State alumnus, was preparing to donate $1 million to the university athletics program. In return, school officials were planning to name the campus basketball court after him. Brown initially leapt into the story after the *Kent Stater*'s web editor received an email from a stranger with a single tip: "Google Jason Cope v SEC."

What Brown discovered: Twelve years ago, as branch manager of a financial firm, Cope was part of a Ponzi scheme that defrauded investors out of close to $9 million. He was found guilty of breaking federal securities laws that "involved fraud and deceit" and ordered with his co-defendants "to pay a total of more than $19 million in penalties."

Brown's investigation into this criminal activity prompted Cope to suddenly renege on the $1 million gift. His subsequent story led to questions about Kent State's decision to accept a donation and align itself publicly with someone best known for bilking others of their investments.

As a *Kent Stater* editorial contended, "We're wondering why Kent State would knowingly accept money from someone with a disconcerting financial background. At first glance, it makes us question the athletic department's ethical standards. Sure, the university can accept the money, but should it? It doesn't quite seem right."

In piecing together what ultimately became a nationally lauded two-part report, Brown relied most heavily on public records, including analyzing school officials' email messages, recordings of meetings, and documents available through the SEC and FINRA.

"I didn't use any speculation," he said. "Literally every statement in my article was according to some document or according to this litigation . . . I really love getting public records. Because the more you have, the less you can be pushed around."

■ The use of public and private records to build stories and confirm facts is a time-honored journalism practice. Messages, documents, data, and recordings are chock full of newsworthy information, damning evidence, and endless million-dollar story ideas. You just have to know where and how to request, uncover, and interpret them.

Let's learn more from a journalism and law expert, known to many as "the hardest-working man in the free speech business."

AN EXCHANGE OF IDEAS

A Reporter's Main Course

 The exchange is a recurring feature in the book and on my blog, spotlighting advice and exercises from top journalism students, professionals, educators, and advocates.

This exchange comes from Frank LoMonte, Esq. LoMonte is the executive director of the Student Press Law Center, the country's leading legal assistance agency for scholastic and college journalists. Along with experience as a commercial litigation attorney and federal judge clerk, he was previously an award-winning investigative reporter and political columnist in state capitol bureaus in Florida and Georgia, and in Washington, D.C.

His exchange focuses on the rules, resources, hurdles, and storytelling potential of records reporting.

When a government agency creates or keeps *anything* that documents information—a memo, a recording of a meeting, an email, or a database—that is a "record." At every level of government, from the Pentagon to the county school board, records are presumed to belong to the public unless the agency can prove some exemption applies.

Public records are the main course on an investigative reporter's dinner plate.

For example, they are what enabled reporters for *The Daily Campus* at Southern Methodist University to document last spring that, out of a hundred campus rapes reported over a 25-year span, only *one* resulted in a successful criminal prosecution.

The information from government records can often produce or lead to these types of jaw-dropping results. And, unlike personal interviews, records don't change their stories.

The Basics

Every state and the District of Columbia has a public disclosure law. It may be called the "Sunshine Law," the Open Records Act, or the Freedom of Information Law, but no matter. They all work the same way. (We'll use the blanket term FOI law—for freedom of information—just to keep things simple.)

Under these laws, a citizen—and it can be any citizen, not just a journalist—may make a request for particular records or for records containing certain information. The agency must then respond by either granting access to the records or by pointing to a specific exemption in the law allowing the records to be withheld.

The decision to withhold can sometimes be appealed to a state agency, such as a freedom of information commission, but often must be challenged in court. The federal government has a comparable law—the Freedom of Information Act—that works the same way.

For the purposes of college journalism, requests almost always will be made under the *state* law, since public colleges and their state-level oversight bodies (such as a board of regents) are covered by state law. Police and sheriff's departments also fall under state law.

Common Types of Record Stories

You have most likely already benefited from a public records law without even realizing it. When you publish the football coach's salary or your college's student loan default rate, you probably first saw those numbers because your college was legally required to disclose them.

There are a few go-to public records every student journalist should be aware of. Let's start with the easy ones.

Salary Information

How the government spends money is a classic public record—and that includes salaries, consulting contracts, expense reimbursements, and more.

At a public college, some salary stories are worth redoing every year. Start with these questions: How much did faculty and staff make last year at your school? What kind of raises did top administrators—and coaches—receive compared with ordinary employees? And what kind of perks—housing, car, travel, and country club memberships—come with being your school's president or chancellor?

Health Inspections

In 2010, ESPN turned stomachs coast-to-coast with an investigative series focused on health department inspections of sports stadiums nationwide.

Its reporters found a parade of horrors, including roaches and mice in the kitchens, food service workers who did not wash their hands, and food stored at unsafe temperatures.

All public eating establishments, on and off campus, must be regularly inspected for health and safety conditions. A county health department usually carries out the inspections, but a state agriculture or health department sometimes oversees the process instead. So become familiar with how your state works.

It is also worth asking who inspects campus housing, including Greek houses, for sanitary and fire safety conditions. Colleges at times handle these inspections internally with very little independent accountability.

Purchasing and Contracting Information

If you were starting your own college, think for a second about all the stuff you would need to buy. Buildings, of course. And paving, lots of paving. Library books. Gym equipment. Park benches. Computers. Don't forget the frozen pizza.

All that stuff and more is typically bought from outside vendors and, chances are, some of it is not purchased properly. Through dishonesty or just plain laziness, school and government officials sometimes do not make the best deal for taxpayers or students.

When a public college purchases anything—a product (canned tomatoes) or a service (legal advice)—the purchase leaves a trail of public records. A similar trail exists for any deals the college signs with food service companies, bookstore operators, and other vendors that commonly set up "privatized" shops on campus.

Public records—such as contracts, bid documents, and audits—enable you to keep watch over how effectively and honestly the college is spending money.

When a big new purchase is made, or a new corporate partnership is announced, **be on the lookout initially for three main things**:

Competitive Failures

Failing to obtain competitive bids before making a purchase, or awarding a contract to a company that is not the lowest-cost bidder.

Breakups

Breaking up contracts with the same vendor into bite-sized pieces that fall beneath the threshold for mandatory bidding—for instance, signing two contracts for $49,999 instead of one for $100,000.

Double Dips

Contracting with "double dippers" or recently retired college executives brought back as "consultants" to do the same work they were doing on the government payroll—while also collecting a pension at the same time.

Form 990

Remember that private colleges and universities—even ones that take millions in federal aid—are not considered government agencies, so state and federal Freedom of Information (FOI) laws don't cover them. But *every* nonprofit corporation, including a private college, must file a yearly Form 990 tax return with the IRS.

Form 990 offers a pretty revealing financial snapshot. Among the many questions it answers: How much did the college pay its top executives? Did its investments make, or lose, money last year? And does the college have "insider" contracts with its own trustees?

By law, the college *must* turn it over on request.

SITE ALERT!

 You can also check out your school's Form 990 online by starting a free GuideStar account at guidestar.org.

Pocket FOI Laws

Besides the general Freedom of Information Law, the lawbooks are full of "pocket" disclosure laws that require agencies to compile and share specific types of information. What is especially great about these "pocket" FOI laws is that they also cover any private institution that accepts federal aid.

Here are three of the most useful ones:

Clery Act

After 19-year-old Jeanne Ann Clery was strangled to death in 1986 in her Lehigh University dorm room, her outraged family took action. They persuaded Congress to enact a federal disclosure law that bears her name.

The Clery Act applies to any school that accepts federal aid, public or private. It is a lifeline for police reporters for two chief reasons. First, it requires an annual statistical report each October showing the last three years' worth of serious crimes—violent crimes, property crimes, drug crimes—reported to campus security personnel. Second, it requires a rolling log, updated at least every 48 hours, showing the what/where/when of all crimes reported to campus law enforcement.

Student journalists are the public's best defense against campus crime under-reporting. So if the numbers look too good to be true—or if crime logs are not kept up to date and made immediately available upon request during nine-to-five business hours—the U.S. Department of Education should be notified.

The DOE can, and does, penalize colleges that fail to fully disclose crimes—as it did in 2009 at Tarleton State University after student journalists discovered at least three rapes and one robbery were left off the Texas school's annual report.

SITE ALERT!

 To quickly look up the past three years of Clery Act crime reports, check out the DOE's Campus Safety and Security Data Analysis Cutting Tool at ope.ed.gov/security.

Equity in Athletics Disclosure Act

Due to concerns women's sports programs were getting shortchanged, Congress passed the Equity in Athletics Disclosure Act (EADA). The EADA requires colleges to file yearly reports with the U.S. Department of Education showing what they spend on each sport, what they earn, and how many students are participating.

The "equity" story is an obvious and easy one—EADA reports almost always show that women's team coaches make substantially less than their male counterparts—but don't stop there. EADA figures can also help debunk the myth of college athletics as a cash cow.

Except for a handful of national football and basketball merchandising powerhouses such as the University of Texas and the University of Florida, most colleges and universities lose money on athletics. Some schools even lose millions annually—money that must be covered by state taxpayers or through student tuition and fees.

SITE ALERT!

 To access colleges' reports on athletic spending and revenue, participation in sports by gender, and coaches' salaries, utilize the DOE's Equity in Athletics Data Analysis Cutting Tool at ope.ed.gov/athletics.

Credit Card Accountability, Responsibility and Disclosure Act (CARD Act)

Who's in your wallet? It might be your alumni association. Stemming from concerns that colleges were profiteering from pushing high-interest credit cards on vulnerable student consumers, Congress voted in 2009 to require credit card issuers to submit annual disclosure reports to the Federal Reserve that includes copies of any "affinity" agreements with colleges. This includes private colleges and the private affiliates of public colleges, including foundations, alumni associations, and Greek houses.

Using contracts obtained under the CARD Act, *The Huffington Post* exposed the unseemly fact that some colleges actually received a "bounty" from credit card issuers if their students maintained extra-high credit card balances.

SITE ALERT!

 To view the annual report of "affinity" marketing agreements between colleges (and their affiliates) and credit card issuers, visit the Federal Reserve Board's College Credit Card Agreements at federalreserve.gov/collegecreditcardagreements.

Side Doors and Back Windows

Many records requests are met with a flat-out "no." Or they are met with a response that is the practical equivalent of a "no," including that the request will cost tens of thousands of dollars or take half a year to fulfill. When adversity strikes, remember the first "no" is just the start of the conversation and not the end. Take it as an invitation to negotiate.

Pushing Back

Understand the Charges

Know what the law does and does not allow the agency to charge for. In many states, costs are capped at a minimal per-page copying fee. Even in states where labor costs can be assessed, you should pay only the hourly rate for a clerical person, not a $100-an-hour vice president.

Don't Worry about a Justification

Remember, you do not need to have a "justification" for wanting public records. Being a nosy citizen is reason enough. And the agency may not deny or unnecessarily delay your request simply because it dislikes how you plan to use the records.

Don't Accept Blanket Excuses

Blanket excuses for noncompliance ("that's personnel!" is a perennial one) are rarely legally correct—even some personnel records are normally disclosable. It is always the agency's burden to point to a specific exemption in the law that justifies concealment.

Don't Fall for the Policy Excuse

"That's not our policy" is also a popular, and wrong, answer to a records request. Agencies do not get to make "policies" that are inconsistent with the law. If the law says a police department must release all incident reports, then the department cannot enforce a policy of secrecy.

Know the Difference between Can't and Won't

With very rare exceptions, public records laws are a floor and not a ceiling. For example, a memo to the mayor from the city attorney about strategy in a lawsuit probably is exempt from the FOI law because it contains confidential attorney–client communications. But if the mayor hands it to you, she is not "breaking the FOI law." Government officials can almost always give you more than they absolutely have to. This means that when they say, "I can't give you that," your first response should be, "No, you *won't* give me that."

Accepting Half a Loaf

Consider Redacted Records

If confidentiality is an obstacle, consider whether your purposes can be achieved with "redacted" records that remove only the most sensitive information. Sometimes, statistics—for example, a report detailing how many students were disciplined for hazing—are almost as useful as individual case files.

Roll with It

If the request has multiple parts, ask for a "rolling production" of documents so you can obtain the first wave of easily accessible records before the last one is prepared.

Get around Copy Fees

When quoted a jackpot fee for making copies, try first asking to inspect the originals and flag only the most important pages for duplication. Also, under most state laws, if the agency keeps the information in electronic form, you are entitled to an electronic copy—which should greatly reduce copying charges. In respect to the latter option, just be sure to ask for the records in a format your own computer can actually read!

Running around the Runaround

Seek Out Other Record Holders

Always consider who else might have a copy of the records you want. For example, reporters in Pennsylvania got past a porous state FOIA law that exempted Penn State University by requesting documents from the state Department of Education's higher-education division instead. Officials at the DOE were copied in on numerous Penn State emails in the weeks following disclosure of the child sex abuse scandal implicating former coach Jerry Sandusky—emails that would not have been available directly from Penn State.

Know which state and federal agencies—including committees in your state legislature—regulate the university system. They are often less motivated to conceal embarrassing information. Be especially aware of who audits the university—both "financial audits" of how the college manages money and "performance audits" of how effectively its programs work—and ensure you are getting all their audit reports.

Come to the Courthouse

The courthouse can be a goldmine of public information. Make it a habit to stop by the civil division of the clerk's office at your state and federal courthouses. Run a check in the case names—using the public-access computer terminals available in most offices—for the college's name and the names of key administrators, including the chair of the trustees or other governing board.

If you see a newly filed case, "Smith v. Homestate University," ask the clerk to pull the case file and dig in. Start with the Complaint—that's how all lawsuits begin—and determine who is claiming what. Of course, remember they *are* just claims, not proven facts.

The file should also have the names and contact information for every lawyer who is involved. Call them before you write a related story—lots of case files are confusing and lack context that may be essential to know before publishing or posting.

Write About What's <u>Not</u> There

When all else fails, write about the absence of information or the inability or refusal to produce it. If you ask for a list of employees who have been issued government cellphones and you are told no list exists, that's a story: "Central State College does not know how many employees have state-paid cellphones or who they are." Chances are, as soon as you start reporting that story, the list will "miraculously" appear.

SITE ALERT!

 For additional assistance navigating FOIA roadblocks with U.S. government agencies, turn to the Office of Government Information Services at ogis.archives.gov.

The FERPA Fallacy

When seeking records about the public's business, don't take "FERPA" for an answer. The Family Educational Rights and Privacy Act (FERPA), a federal confidentiality law, prohibits the release of "education records" such as transcripts and test scores. But FERPA is *not* a blanket excuse for schools to simply withhold anything they find embarrassing on the grounds of "student privacy."

Courts have almost unanimously rejected colleges' attempts to expand FERPA secrecy beyond the core academic and disciplinary records maintained in a college's central records office. In recent years, courts have emphatically said lawsuit settlements, professors' emails, reports of employee misconduct, and student parking tickets are all public records and not confidential FERPA records—even if student names are mentioned.

In a related sense, do not *ever* let a college say that police reports—or student names in police reports—are off limits because of FERPA. In fact, Congress has said exactly the opposite: Law enforcement records are specifically excluded from FERPA. So "student privacy" is never a good excuse for withholding them.

One Last Tip

Public records are the meat inside the sandwich. But they are not sandwiches themselves. To make a complete journalistic meal, you need to sandwich those records around research and interviews—both beforehand (to find out what information the government agency has and how it might be useful) and afterward (to make sure you fully understand the context of what the records appear to be telling you).

For more advice from Frank LoMonte and resources related to records reporting and journalism legal issues at large, visit the Student Press Law Center website at splc.org.

IDEAS, ONLINE

The April 16th Documents

In December 2008, roughly 20 months after the tragic mass killing at Virginia Tech University, *The Collegiate Times* posted online roughly 750 pages of what the student newspaper called the "April 16th Documents." *The Roanoke Times* labeled the material, more simply, the "shooting papers."

Stored on a permanent special section of the *Collegiate Times* website, the massive information release—reminiscent of newspapers' handling of the Pentagon Papers and "The Starr Report"—is known within digital journalism as a document dump.

A doc dump is a posting of often-copious amounts of primary source information, typically gathered through internal leaks or public records requests.

While at times accompanied by an introductory news summary or snippets to add context, the dumps mostly display the records without a filter. They let the public, watchdogs, and other media analyze them in their original state.

At Virginia Tech, the *Collegiate Times*' posting came one day after the documents were made available to families of the victims by the university through a "password-protected electronic archive."

The emails, memos, and other records cover many thoughts, reactions, and plans of action at the university before and after the campus shooting on April 16, 2007. For example, there is correspondence mentioning earlier faculty concerns about the student shooter and docs "detail[ing] techniques and approaches to dealing with the image of a mass shooting on campus" by University Relations.

ASSIGNMENT ALERT!

Performer Contracts

Condoms. Blue Solo cups (not red, blue). Homemade cookies. Pop-Tarts®. Socks. And soup. Those items were among performer Mac Miller's formal requests included in a contract for a spring 2012 concert at Pennsylvania's Allegheny College. As a report in *The Allegheny Campus* explained, the requests were part of Miller's contractual rider, "a list of items he asked the school to give him while he's in town . . . [A]rtists have always submitted riders before a concert, which often contain items that the school refuses to provide."

Your Assignment

 Carry out a similar contractual exploration of entertainment programming on your campus or organized by your school. Examine who and what is involved in the selection and staging of outside performer visits. Detail the money allocated and spent on the performances each academic year. Compare the amounts with those of nearby schools or schools sporting similar enrollments. Determine where the money comes from and how much input students have in the funding and performer selection decisions. Also, explore how performer contracts are negotiated. Confirm the oddest and most common items and services listed in the riders of performers, including those rejected by the school.

CHAPTER 13
Data Journalism

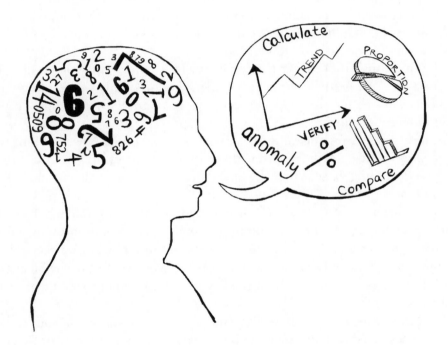

What does it cost to replace *Romeo and Juliet*?

What happens to a lost *Harry Potter*? How about a late *Lord of the Rings*? Or a beat-up *War and Peace*?

An explosive report last year by Britain's Press Association dealt with those questions and more while focused on a normally quiet spot: the library.

Buttressed by Freedom of Information (FOI) requests, the national news agency reported on a seemingly runaway library fining system within UK higher education and revealed a shocking number of students unwilling or unable to return loaned books. Specifically, over the course of six recent academic years, British colleges and universities raked in roughly $78 million in charges for late or lost books.

"With fines as little as 10p [about 15 cents] a day per book, it seems that students are returning thousands of books late each year," *The Guardian* confirmed. "But many are never returned—more than 300,000 books nationally are unaccounted for." Each of those unaccounted titles and late penalties costs the students—holding up their library access, course registration clearance, and at times even their graduation.

According to the Press Association, the University of Leeds led the high fine society. Over six years, students and staff at the large public research university roughly three hours north of London paid the equivalent of $2.78 million in library fines. Please read the previous sentence again. *$2.78 million*. In library fines. At one school. In six years.

What do the fines fund at Leeds? It is unclear. An FOI request and follow-up interviews by reporters for the *Leeds Student*, the campus newspaper, produced only vague allocations—leading to questions about oversight, transparency, and basic financial fairness toward student patrons already burdened with numerous school fees.

As the headline of one *Leeds Student* story sums things up, "Book, Fine, and Sinker."

The eye-opening figures, and the reporting that ferreted them out, are hardback proof that even a world of words—including those penned by Shakespeare, Rowling, Tolkien, and Tolstoy—often boils down to numbers.

It is the same with almost every area of our lives—from our checking account, Twitter followers, and apartment square footage to our wake-up time, blood pressure, and unread emails.

Two numbers, in particular, scrape and claw for utmost power and control within our increasingly digital existence: zeros and ones. These are the components of the binary code that—stripping away all the geek talk—basically runs every tech device and program that matters in and out of our solar system.

"Your career history, 300,000 confidential documents, who knows who in your circle of friends can all be (and are) described with just two numbers: zeros, and ones," journalist and educator Paul Bradshaw writes. "Photos, video, and audio are all described with the same two numbers: zeros and ones. Murders, disease, political votes, corruption, and lies: zeros and ones."

Bradshaw shares this numerical truth in the introduction of *The Data Journalism Handbook* (datajournalismhandbook.org), a free online guide posted last year "for anyone interested in the emerging field of data journalism."

> ■ Data and journalism have always coexisted, but in the digital sphere they can be more easily and often combined to produce startlingly powerful reports—comprehensive, interactive, visual, unquestionably accurate, and, above all, newsworthy.

Let's learn more about story ideas, zeros, and ones from a pair of leading journalism educators and advocates.

AN EXCHANGE OF IDEAS

Numbers *are* the Story

 The exchange is a recurring feature in the book and on my blog, spotlighting advice and exercises from top journalism students, professionals, educators, and advocates.

This exchange comes from Bryan Murley. Murley is an associate professor of new and emerging media in the journalism department at Eastern Illinois University, where he also advises The Daily Eastern News. *He is the primary blogger for the Center for Innovation in College Media and the former webmaster for the College Media Association.*

His exchange focuses on defining and practicing data journalism, including helpful tools and sample story focuses to get you started.

The saying goes that journalists don't do numbers. That's why they become journalists. Journalists like to tell stories to inform the public. But increasingly, numbers *are* the story, and serve as rich sources of information that—when handled correctly—will inform in ways words alone cannot.

That is why something called data journalism has become such a crucial part of the journalist's toolkit.

What is Data Journalism?

I break down data journalism into three parts: gathering, analyzing, and presenting numerical information in a way that allows readers to grasp the bigger picture of a phenomenon. Let's look at each of these parts in a little more depth.

Gathering

Modern society runs on numbers. Managers generate reports on sales. The federal government collects data from the Census. Marketers and polling companies collect survey results to test products and politicians. State governments collect statistics on poverty. Local police departments collect information on every arrest. Universities collect and assemble information on every student.

All of this information helps generate a "big picture" of what is going on around us. The wonderful thing for journalists is that much of this information is available to the public (with a few notable exceptions like medical records and personal identity information) and much of it is already in a format that can be manipulated by software (like spreadsheets, databases, and PDFs).

When the data is not available in readily accessible formats, journalists can use a variety of tools to input the data into a format that can be manipulated.

Example

Beginning in 2009, the investigative journalism group California Watch spent 19 months examining and exposing troublesome gaps in school earthquake safety. The award-winning series (californiawatch.org/earthquakes), built atop data gathered through Freedom of Information requests, included "a searchable database of an estimated 10,000 public schools showing their potential seismic safety hazards." It led to changes in California's system of school inspections and funding for repairs.

Analyzing

Almost all the data a journalist will handle contains far more information than you will need to answer the specific questions you are asking. Refining this mountain of information, sifting through it to find the key bits you are after, is the second part of data journalism. This may be as simple as reordering a spreadsheet according to ZIP codes or as complex as extracting a subset of records from a database.

Presenting

Unstructured data—reams of records filled with information—doesn't tell a story. Even if you have analyzed the data and arranged it in a manner coherent to you, it likely won't make sense to most people.

You need a way to share the information so readers can grasp its main news thrust and lasting implications. It's all about the presentation. There are a number of ways to present unstructured statistics or a rash of records, but one thing is clear: Simply writing about the information in paragraphs filled with verbiage doesn't cut it.

Example

Last spring, *The New York Times* analyzed data from a variety of sources for a series about skyrocketing college student loan debt, which currently totals more than $1 trillion nationwide. As part of the series, the paper created an interactive graphic about U.S. student debt levels. It features information in chart and map form.

SITE ALERT!

 Check out the interactive graphic included in the *New York Times* report at nyti.ms/JOPvGn. Among other clickable options, it breaks down debt by schools' enrollment size, graduation rate, athletic conference, and the percentage of graduates currently living with debt.

How to Do Data Journalism

Start Small

If your media outlet hasn't ever done data journalism, or hasn't done any in a long time, it can seem very daunting to get started. There are mountains of information out there and a plethora of ways to present it.

The best suggestion is to start small. Pick a topic you can research fairly easily, where the data is readily available, and make a simple spreadsheet, map, or timeline. Every small project will boost your confidence and build up to larger projects.

For example, *The Collegiate Times* at Virginia Tech started with a database of faculty salaries, which are accessible at almost all public universities. The database was such a success, the staff expanded it to cover more than 40 universities nationwide.

Following in the *CT*'s footsteps, find the salary information for faculty, administrators, and staff at your school. Place it online, and then start finding interesting stories in the data.

SITE ALERT!

 Check out the *Collegiate Times* public school salary database at collegiatetimes.com/databases/salaries. The paper's database section also includes a breakdown of campus crime and grade distributions in all Virginia Tech classes.

Always Think About Data When Researching a Story

This sounds simple, but it is amazing how many reporters do not think about this. For example, if you are doing a story about the rise in tuition, it is relatively easy to come up with the percent it has increased over last year. But what about the total increase over five, 10, and 20 years? How do those increases compare with inflation? And how do they compare with the amount of state funding increases or decreases over the same time period?

Example

The Daily Toreador at Texas Tech University thought about data when researching a story about, of all things, a parking garage near campus. After acquiring and analyzing data in emails, lease and deed of trust agreements, and tax records, the *Toreador* discovered the school's leasing of roughly 1,000 spaces in the garage is a major money-loser and existed as a "sweetheart deal" between the university and alumni members of a Texas Tech fraternity. For its efforts, Investigative Reporters and Editors (IRE) bestowed the paper its top student journalism award in 2011.

Choose the Right Visual for Presentation

Just as a screwdriver isn't a good tool to drive a nail into a piece of wood, and a putter isn't a good club for hitting a golf ball off the tee, different types of data visuals are not as useful for certain analyses. For example, a pie chart is not a good visual to represent the locations of most campus crimes—a map is a much better choice for that data.

Make Sure the Data is Credible

Just as you would check the source for all information in a written story, you should check the source of your data in a data-driven story. Individuals and groups interested in hiding or exaggerating the truth can manipulate data in many ways.

An example of this is the campus crime report every college and university must file with the federal government. There are numerous methods campus safety and school officials employ to "massage" the numbers to downplay problems with campus crime. Gather the crime data for your campus and compare the year-to-year reporting. Also, compare it with city police reports. Search for interesting stories in the numbers or comparisons that do not add up.

Make Sure the Data Says What You Think it Says

Along with outsiders "massaging" the data, it is also very easy for journalists to inadvertently mislead with statistics and charts. To this end, work overtime to ensure your graphics are accurate. Make an effort to understand how different graphical representations of data tell a story and the limitations of certain types of visual elements.

If you are uncertain about a visual, check with an expert—maybe in your school's math department. Don't take anything for granted. Even maps can be deceptive.

During U.S. presidential elections, for instance, the public often sees graphic maps—called choropleths—of each state in either red or blue to denote which candidate the majority of voters in that state supported.

But taken in on a national level, those maps do not tell the real story of voter preferences. As University of Michigan professor Mark Newman explains, the iconic red-state–blue-state map favored by the press "fails to allow for the fact that the population of the red states [the 'Republican states'] is on average significantly lower than that of the blue ones [the 'Democratic states']. The blue may be small in area, but they represent a large number of voters, which is what matters in an election."

Make Your Web Data Interactive

If you are going to present information online, make sure there are ways for viewers to "drill down" into the information for greater insight. Take advantage of the capabilities the web gives you to expand the information and make the reader's exploration of it more compelling and interactive.

Data Journalism Tools

There are a number of excellent programs and platforms to help get you started with data journalism. Here are a few:

Google Docs (docs.google.com): a free tool that includes a spreadsheet function. You can create forms to input information into the spreadsheet and make graphs and charts from the resulting data.

freeDive (multimedia.journalism.berkeley.edu/tools/freedive): a tool to create searchable databases using information stored in a Google Doc spreadsheet.

Many Eyes (ibm.co/bUxl0J): a set of tools allowing users to create a variety of visualizations from data uploaded to the site. Once a visualization is created, it can be embedded on a website and updated continuously.

Tableau Public (tableausoftware.com/public): a Windows-only downloadable software that helps create data visualizations and puts them on the web.

Zoho (zoho.com): a large suite of online applications, free for limited use. Of particular interest is Zoho Creator, which creates a database that can be displayed on websites.

DocumentCloud (documentcloud.org): a platform allowing you to upload documents to its servers and then utilize its software to run the docs through OpenCalais (opencalais.com) to extract meaningful information about people, places, and dates. The best thing about DocumentCloud is that it works on PDFs. It is free, and run by the IRE.

For more digital journalism advice from Bryan Murley, visit the Center for Innovation in College Media website at collegemediainnovation.org.

IDEAS, ONLINE

Data Visualization

 Canada has the most fruit drinkers of any country in the world. The United States has the most serial killers. Saudi Arabia has the most oil. Argentina has the most horsemeat. Luxembourg has the most tractors. And Ireland has the highest quality of life.

These are a few of the nearly 200 facts featured on "International Number Ones." The data map on the website Information is Beautiful (informationisbeautiful.net) lists what nearly every nation worldwide boasts more of than everyone else. The map's tagline doubles as the rationale for its creation: "Because every country is the best at something."

Data is at its best when it is visualized. It connects with readers more powerfully than words. It displays the connections between seemingly disparate statistics and information scraps. And it tells multiple stories, those projected by the news outlets and those discovered by readers mining the data.

This particular visualization is strong for a number of reasons. It is pleasing to the eye, easily scannable, quickly understandable, and built atop accurate and verifiable sources (including the CIA World Factbook). It is focused on something of at least some news value and of interest to readers. And it offers the potential for further exploration, including through a Google spreadsheet listing.

SITE ALERT!

Along with Information is Beautiful, Bryan Murley suggests checking out a few other websites offering data visualization news, resources, and examples:

Flowing Data (flowingdata.com), "explores how designers, statisticians, and computer scientists are using data to understand ourselves better"

Guardian Datablog (guardian.co.uk/news/datablog), a blog on data journalism and data visualization maintained by UK's *The Guardian*, which Murley dubs "one of the media outlets at the forefront of innovative data journalism"

Online Journalism Blog (onlinejournalismblog.com), "publishes comment and analysis on developments in online journalism and online news," including data journalism and computer-assisted reporting

AN EXCHANGE OF IDEAS

The Relational Element

The exchange is a recurring feature in the book and on my blog, spotlighting advice and exercises from top journalism students, professionals, educators, and advocates.

This exchange comes from Kelly Furnas. Furnas is an assistant professor of journalism and associate director of publications at Kansas State University. He also serves as executive director of the Journalism Education Association, a national scholastic journalism advocacy and education organization.

His exchange focuses on the reporting capabilities and storytelling potential of online databases.

A good reporter will use plenty of figures and statistics to provide the documentation and context for a well-rounded story. Data goes a long way toward backing up, or refuting, your sources' claims. Numbers can identify trends your audience should be concerned about or quantify inequities in your community.

But statistics also can create problems for journalists. First, they can be used selectively, only telling a part of the story that coincides with your source's narrative. Second, even if used objectively, too many numbers can become overwhelming in a basic news story.

Online databases offer your audience the ability to not only check the facts and context of a story you are presenting, but also to create and develop their own narratives—seeing connections that may have never been the intent of your original news peg.

Most of the websites you visit on a daily basis are run off a database, which is simply a set of records containing the same fields. Your Facebook page, for example, is a record of you, with fields for your name, your birthdate, your employer, and so on.

What makes a database powerful is its ability to recognize relationships, so when you click on the name of your employer, you can see a list of other Facebook users who work there as well.

It's the relational element that becomes really interesting for journalists. Here is an example.

Grading Breakdown

The scenario: You submit a Freedom of Information request to your school, asking for the number of As, Bs, Cs, Ds, and Fs given in each section of every course offered by your school, as well as the related semesters and the names of the teachers for the sections.

You get back a spreadsheet that has hundreds of lines of data looking like this:

Course	Section	Semester	Instructor	A	B	C	D	F
Reporting 1	A	Fall	Jones	2	7	6	3	0
Reporting 1	B	Fall	Smith	8	4	2	1	1
Reporting 1	A	Spring	Jones	4	5	8	3	1
Reporting 1	B	Spring	Smith	6	3	2	1	1
Reporting 2	A	Fall	Nelson	3	4	2	1	3
Reporting 2	B	Fall	Smith	5	1	1	1	0
Reporting 2	A	Spring	Jones	3	4	2	1	3
Reporting 2	B	Spring	Nelson	4	2	1	6	1

As a reporter, what is the story here?

To figure that out, the first thing you need to do is to make the data you receive match the data you want. This is called "data cleansing."

Sometimes this means standardizing the data so values match across records. (For example, if one semester of the course was referred to as "Reporting II" instead of "Reporting 2," you would want to correct that so it's easier to compare one record to the next.)

Another common type of data cleansing is adding fields that use existing data to calculate new data. This would be very useful in the current example to calculate the average GPA of each section of each class.

In the spreadsheet, we would simply create a new column that would take the sum of As multiplied by 4, Bs multiplied by 3, Cs multiplied by 2, and Ds multiplied by 1, and then divide that sum by the total number of students in the class. In doing so, we get the following average GPAs:

Course	Section	Semester	Instructor	Avg. GPA
Reporting 1	A	Fall	Jones	2.44
Reporting 1	B	Fall	Smith	3.06
Reporting 1	A	Spring	Jones	2.38
Reporting 1	B	Spring	Smith	2.92
Reporting 2	A	Fall	Nelson	2.23
Reporting 2	B	Fall	Smith	3.25
Reporting 2	A	Spring	Jones	2.23
Reporting 2	B	Spring	Nelson	2.14

Most reporters who look at the data would quickly spot the eyebrow-raising trend: Smith's grades are significantly higher than those given by other teachers—even those teaching the same course.

Armed with this data, you could write up a pretty good story, fleshing out the numbers with interviews with Smith, Jones, and Nelson about their teaching philosophies and chats with students in each of their classes.

And yet that's not the whole story. Look closer at the numbers and you will spot other trends. Perhaps the high GPAs should not be attributed to Smith's grading philosophy, but instead to the number of students enrolled in the class. (Smith has significantly fewer students in each class than the other teachers.)

Or perhaps there is a story in the fact that grades in the fall are on average slightly higher than grades in the spring.

At some point, you will notice, the data becomes too overwhelming to include in a traditional news or feature story. This example looked at only one department, three teachers, two courses, and two semesters.

Think of the hundreds of interesting comparisons you could make if you expanded this data over multiple years, with every course at your school, including hundreds of teachers and dozens of departments. What if you started including other schools, too?

The best solution is to turn over all the data to your audience. There are several online resources to help develop searchable databases once you have the data in hand. Or if you or someone at your school is versed in MySQL (mysql.com) and PHP (php.net), you can probably develop the database yourself. But as a journalist, you will want to decide two important things prior to any development: how you want your users to be able to search for data and how you want the resulting data displayed.

Which of the fields in the grades example—course, section, semester, instructor, GPA—do you think your users would be searching in? And what information would they want to see once that search is done?

To learn more about Kelly Furnas and the Journalism Education Association, visit the JEA website at jea.org.

ASSIGNMENT ALERT!

Start with the Census

If you are searching for a trusted, free, and easily accessible set of numbers to kick off your data searching, start with the Census (census.gov).

The decennial Census is arguably the most comprehensive and compelling data set for U.S. journalists working today. Doug Haddix, the director of Ohio State University's Kiplinger Program in Public Affairs Reporting, heralds it as nothing less than "a treasure chest of story ideas for every community in America."

Statistics from the 2010 Census, released in chunks throughout 2011 and into last year, reveal local, state, and national glimpses at how we are living, working, loving, and learning, along with who we are through the prisms of gender, race, age, income, sexual persuasion, and much more.

Mine the data for stats that leap out or to summon ideas for stories related to your state, county, hometown, Congressional District, college community, demographic, or coverage area. Comb through past Censuses as well to check on changes over time.

Review local and national news coverage of the Census over the past two years to determine how others utilized the data and to spot what numbers and trends have been overlooked or underreported.

Separately, consider how you would visualize various parts of the data set. And brainstorm the types of expert sources and everyday people you would need to locate to shed light on the significance of various parts of the data or to bring out the human side of the hard numbers.

SITE ALERT!

Here are a pair of tools enabling quicker and more proficient searching of 2010 Census data, the first set up by the government and the second by Investigative Reporters and Editors (IRE).

American FactFinder (factfinder2.census.gov), "your source for population, housing, economic, and geographic information"

Census.ire.org (census.ire.org), "designed to provide journalists with a simpler way to access 2010 Census data so they can spend less time importing and managing the data and more time exploring and reporting the data"

CHAPTER 14

Photojournalism Ideas

Illustration by Yee Hung Lim

"Katrina hit everybody."

Matt Stamey uttered these words about the historic 2005 hurricane, still the costliest and one of the deadliest in U.S. history. At the time, as the chief photographer at a newspaper in Houma, La., about an hour from New Orleans, he calculated the enormity of Katrina's impact by the endless stream of Big Easy evacuees arriving in Houma—in some cases without the ones they loved.

"It was quickly clear to me after the storm that the wind and floodwaters didn't separate blacks or whites or rich or poor," said Stamey, now a photographer and videographer for Florida's *Gainesville Sun*. "After the waters started to rise, many people fled New Orleans by any means possible. Many families were split apart without any way of contacting each other. It crushed me to see mothers not knowing where their children were. I wanted to help."

Stamey quickly set up a makeshift studio—white backdrop, white lighting—and began snapping portrait shots of New Orleaners displaced to Houma shelters. "Within minutes, I had a huge line of people waiting to be photographed," he recalled.

He posted the photos on multiple websites, placing people's names and the contact information for their shelters in the captions, in hopes it might reunite them with relatives, neighbors, colleagues, or friends.

He called the project "Faces of Katrina."

One of the faces he photographed was Alicia Seeden, then 17, temporarily staying in a recreation center with the rest of her family after they had lost their home and all their belongings.

Stamey's simple portrait of Alicia captures her standing straight, arms at her side, a close-mouthed smile expressing an infectious sliver of happiness at a moment for many of pure despair.

Once posted online, the image reached and genuinely touched churchgoers in Kalamazoo, Mich. The congregation raised money to build the Seeden family a home and moved them to Michigan. A few months later, according to Stamey, Alicia graduated from a Kalamazoo high school.

"Journalism and photography is powerful," he said. "It can influence. It can create change. And it can help others."

■ Power. Influence. Help. Change. Stamey's "Faces" project is proof of photojournalism's unrelenting impact—even amid tragedy, chaos, and a changing media landscape.

"Pictures will never die," said Katie Paysinger, a photographer based in Oregon. "Whether in print, online, on your tablet, on your phone, on whatever comes next, there will always be someone who wants to see something other than what is in front of his or her face. That's where photojournalists come in."

In this chapter, a range of photographers and photojournalists share advice, observations, and anecdotes about the endless search for meaningful images and strong conceptual ideas to go with them.

Their words are supplemented by my own, offering occasional assignment prompts and glimpses at a few digital movements and tools. These are aimed, as always, at helping you brainstorm and discover the most innovative, visual ideas possible.

WHERE THE ELEPHANTS ARE

A Camera is Only the Start

"Everyone has a camera. It's your EYE that is what you are paid for as a journalist. You see different. You must train yourself to SEE."

David L. Ryan, photographer, *The Boston Globe*

"I hate high-impact, technically beautiful photos that don't say anything. Get out there with your camera and say something, scream it from the rooftops: Come take a look! Photojournalism is a full-contact sport. Grow a thick, bulletproof skin and take risks."

Alex Hicks, freelance photographer based in Wichita, Kan.

"Stop thinking so much about photography. Instead, concentrate on storytelling. Little moments make powerful and informative news photos—not apertures, shutter speeds, or cool camera equipment."

Brian Blanco, professional photojournalist based in Tampa, Fla.

"Whatever it is a photographer shoots, it has to mean something to someone."

Afton Almaraz, photo editor, Getty Images

"One of my first photo editors told me, '**To shoot elephants, you have to be where the elephants are.**' You have to be at the right place at the right time. Always strive to put yourself in the best possible position to get the most storytelling image."

Christopher Chung, staff photographer, *The Press Democrat*, Calif.

"Don't just snap a photo. Capture the emotions you see in front of you. Great photographers don't just document the moments. They tell a story."

Kimberly Yama Tamaoka, special sections editor, *The Garden Island*, Hawaii

"You can have a great looking image, but without its second layer, it doesn't go beyond the 'ooh' and 'ahh.' The stories behind the images are the photos that drive viewers to act and to call for action."

Jason Halley, staff photographer, *Chico Enterprise-Record*, Calif.

Minimum of Equipment

"Use a minimum of equipment in the beginning so you are really learning the craft of photography itself, and thinking more about what you are trying to communicate than how to work a new camera or lens."

Tammy Lechner, author and photojournalist
based in Laguna Beach, Calif.

"A camera is a box. It's not a life. I think of the old Roman words, 'They worshiped the creation rather than the Creator who is blessed forevermore.' I do not want to do that."

Mikayla Mackaness, writer and photographer
based in Charleston, S.C.

The Pull of the Gadget

"With the advancement of digital cameras, photojournalists now have that dream-come-true opportunity of immediately checking a camera's display to see the pictures they've taken. That fantastic option, though, sometimes turns into a shortcoming. In 2002, during Michael Jordan's stint with the Washington Wizards, I was sent to cover his first game back in Toronto. Photographers were seated behind the basket line, taking pictures of the game. At one point, there was a decent dunk by a Toronto Raptors player, followed by a timeout. All my colleagues immediately started 'chimping'—checking the pictures they had taken, selecting some, deleting others. At that moment, by contrast, I kept looking through my lens. Suddenly, Jordan, in frustration, stabbed his index finger in the chest of a younger teammate. I pressed the shutter. I was the only guy in the building who captured that moment. The picture was subsequently widely used across the U.S. *The Washington Post* featured it on its front page. Had I succumbed to the pull of the gadget and chimped along with all other photographers, I would have missed it."

Zoran Bozicevic, associate photo editor,
National Post and *Financial Post*, Canada

"Be aware of everything, and learn that every little thing can be important. When you arrive at a spot news scene, become aware of the situation so the moments can present themselves. When you shoot a feature on someone, be obsessed with knowing about that person before you go. This is how insignificant mug shots can turn into full-blown photo essays."

John Flavell, journalism instructor, Morehead State University

"Remember to check in with yourself emotionally as you are pursuing a story. Is it making you feel something? If so, you are probably on the right track. Follow that gut instinct."

Sonya Hebert, official photographer,
The White House

"People have told me 'photograph with emotion.' I didn't know exactly what that meant until I realized the statement had more to do with my own emotional availability than any technical piece of advice. A photograph is only as good as my ability to connect emotionally with the people I am photographing. If I'm emotionally open and available to people, they are more likely to be the same in return. If I'm closed off, and hiding part of myself, the photograph will show that distance as well."

Dania Patricia Maxwell, staff photographer,
Naples Daily News, Fla.

The Thrust

"Know why you are being assigned to take a photo in the first place. What is the thrust of the story? Why is the person or event important? In order to have any hope of capturing an image that conveys the entire message of the article it accompanies, the photographer must fully understand why he is there to begin with. Calling some of the assignment notices photographers receive from editors 'brief' is generous. It is up to you as the photographer to talk to the writer, the subject, and any other relevant individuals who might be able to better enhance your understanding of the story."

Viktors Dindzans, former senior photo editor,
The GW Hatchet, George Washington University

"Develop a sense of the natural flow of events. Every scene or situation is like a film—it has a rising point, a climax, and a falling point. Whether you are covering a local school pageant, a violent protest, or a political campaign, everything follows these rules. Become tuned into them."

Shane Dunlap, staff photographer,
The Evening Sun, Pa.

ASSIGNMENT ALERT!

Capture the Change

"Find a person who's going through some sort of change and follow him or her for a while, with a camera of course. Photograph the process of the person going through that change."

Dania Patricia Maxwell

Your Assignment

Accept Maxwell's challenge. Select, shoot, and feature an individual, athletic team, town, class, family, fraternity, or other group undergoing a physical, emotional, intellectual, or economic change. A few examples: a young couple falling in love or breaking things off, a fresh college graduate adapting to the real world, and an introductory dance class going from awkward to in-step. The possibilities are surprisingly endless.

LOOK LOOK LOOK

Seeing through the Shrapnel

"Look for moments between moments, gestures, and metaphors rather than nouns. Keep looking through your viewfinder after you capture an image. **Push beyond your first idea and leave room for serendipity.**"

Emilio Bañuelos, documentary photographer and photography instructor based in California and Mexico

"LOOK LOOK LOOK. It's the part of the job that is fun. What other job is there where you get to watch people and life and then get to snap the moment . . . and get published?"

David L. Ryan

Five Minutes Ago

"As a photojournalist, there is one refrain I have heard more than any other in my 25-year career: 'You should have been here five minutes ago.' The number of times you will hear that remark from an event organizer or news scene bystander can be disheartening. And perfect punctuality makes no difference. It doesn't matter when you arrive at a scheduled event or get to a breaking news story. According to someone nearby, the good stuff already happened. Of course, most experienced photographers still find plenty that's photo-worthy, but it still stings, just a little, to be told so consistently you've missed the real action. The solution? I haven't found it yet, but maybe setting your watch five minutes fast may help."

Glenn Callahan, photographer, *The Stowe Reporter*, Vt.

"Sometimes I'll go to an assignment and be trying to make pictures and there is nothing there— **a visual wasteland**. I'm constantly looking for pictures, really concentrating. I may only be there for an hour, but I'm exhausted. Being on and trying to 'see' takes a lot out of you. It's really draining, but you've got to be looking ALL THE TIME."

J.L. Sousa, photo editor, *Napa Valley Register*, Calif.

"Have all your senses heightened to survey the scene around you. Be looking for clues, listening for sounds, smelling and feeling what's around you. When I first approach an event, I reach an almost higher state of consciousness, where many of my senses are so heightened that I'm not actually paying attention to what I'm doing. Many times, people will stop me and tell me I look lost or confused, or I will wander around and stare quite a bit, to the point that it worries people. But it's OK. I'm just closing off some of my mental faculties and focusing on my natural abilities to sense my surroundings and process visual information."

Josh Birnbaum, photojournalist and
adjunct faculty member, Ohio University

"At a breaking news event, it can be madness. My job is to see through all the shrapnel and pull out one compelling image that tells the story. That's my goal: Capture all the madness in one rectangle."

J.L. Sousa

ASSIGNMENT ALERT!

The Eye Test

"As an intern, my photo editor once told me, 'Any time two people make eye contact, take a photo.' Photojournalism is about telling the human story and there is an innate human reaction to eye contact between two people. You will find that you have more usable photos from a take when you practice this simple rule."

Max Becherer, freelance photojournalist
represented by Polaris Images

Your Assignment

Follow Becherer's lead. While on a stroll across campus or your hometown, capture photos of people making eye contact. Attempt to grab the images from angles that tell a story or resonate as powerfully as possible with viewers. Follow proper photojournalism procedures and get names and basic identifying information for everyone featured. If possible, take it to the next step—think themes, say flirty looks, heated stares, or awkward strangers-on-the-street glances.

Stick and Move

"It's like being a boxer—stick and move. That's how you really work an assignment. Work an angle, get the shot you're after, then move onto another angle. I can't stand when I edit another photographer's take and there are 50 shots of the exact same thing. Grab one shot, then move onto the next. Give your editor some options."

Christopher Chung

"Move around and don't let readers know how tall you are. In other words, change perspective. Work as many angles as possible."

Cindi Christie, chief photographer,
Contra Costa Times, Calif.

"Once you have the shot, get three more. When working, as soon as I have the shot I was going for, I am often tempted to stop. Really working the subject and pushing myself to get at least three other unique angles, I almost always get a better shot than I thought I could."

Allison Lazard, photographer and visual designer

Pay Attention to the Frame

"Use one of my own personal acronyms, F.A.S.T.—Frame, Area, Subject, Take the Shot! Composition is a major component to every photograph, and I'm always mindful of what touches the frame of my image and what is contained within it before I hit the shutter. An amateur just shoots, but a photographer will take a couple extra seconds to pay attention to the frame and decide what to include and what not to include."

Zachary Ordonez, photographer and
photography instructor based in Fla.

"Pre-visualize. Imagine in your head what an image will look like, considering composition, quality, and direction of light. My best images have come from consciously putting myself in the right situations to make the images I want. It is not enough to react. You have to learn to anticipate."

Joel Hawksley, photojournalist
based in Seattle, Wash.

"Shoot all the time, even when you don't have a camera. If you don't have a camera with you, make the photo in your head."

Carlos Alvarez Montero, freelance photographer
based in Mexico City

IDEAS, ONLINE

Lomography

 First, let's note the irony. Lomography is an analogue photography movement, meaning it pushes for the use of film cameras, not digital. But regardless of the old-school equipment, like everything else, its main presence and connective tissue is now online (including lomography.com).

Lomography is built atop a photo mantra of quantity, not quality. The roughly 20-year-old movement encourages amateur photogs to shoot photos anywhere and everywhere, from all angles, at all times, without a second thought—literally.

As one of its Golden Rules commands, "Don't think! Throw your intellectual socialization over board, let the unfiltered flow of information circulate freely, untreated and unrated in your mind. Shoot, feel, perceive and shoot, have fun, shoot whatever catches your eye, whatever attracts you, astounds you, excites you, seduces you."

Your Assignment

 Become a lomographer. Embark on a temporary photo-first existence. Take pictures at random and ad nauseam, from all angles, and without lighting–composition–storytelling concerns. At a self-appointed endpoint or break in your lomographic action, check out your stock footage. Self-critique and ask for outside opinions on any emergent themes and especially poor or standout shots. Reflect on what you learned from the experience overall and brainstorm story ideas connected to the unthinking images you nabbed.

Wait and Wait and Wait

"A lot of what we do is hurry up and wait—and wait and wait. Over the course of my career, I've waited thousands of hours for something to happen. But when it does happen, you've got to be on."

J.L. Sousa

THE SUBJECT STORIES

Connecting to the Person

"Your photo subject should be a person. Always. Unless it is a really cute baby animal doing something only really cute baby animals do. Buildings and open spaces are boring. Even if the event is the opening of a new building or somebody's fancy garden, make sure you get a person in there."

Katie Paysinger, photographer based in Ore.

"You have to draw the reader into the photo with some kind of connection to the person being photographed. The connection such as 'If I was him, I'd be pissed too!' or 'What is she so happy about?' or 'I also remember that crazy day when I graduated from college.'"

Paul Aiken, photo and video editor,
Daily Camera, Colo.

ASSIGNMENT ALERT!

The Verb Test

"People in action is the key to capturing a news photo. If something isn't happening in the frame—if a verb can't be used to describe the content—then it's most likely neither newsworthy nor captivating."

Jeffrey Basinger, former photo editor, *The Daily Barometer*, Oregon State University

Your Assignment

Grab your phone or a camera, head out, and snap some verbs. Specifically, capture a photo series of people in action, each shot displaying a different verb. Sure, a few common ones—smiling, jogging, studying—are fine. But seek out more playful and bizarre action words as well.

Ego Ego Ego

"One major mistake among young photographers: Ego Ego Ego. Too many arrive at a scene cameras blazing, using their equipment to intimidate or awe. They make images and leave—no thank you, no eye contact, no connection. We don't have a right to make images of people. It is a privilege, and should be respected."

Kainaz Amaria, multimedia trainer, National Public Radio

"**The best photographers have the ability to hide in plain sight**, in that they spend enough time with their subject that the photos they take almost seem as if they are from the perspective of a fly on the wall."

Viktors Dindzans

"Try to put your subjects at ease within seconds of their doors opening. You have to immediately figure out if you're going to address a person as Bob or Mr. Jones. If you pick the wrong way to come at a person, it may affect your entire interaction with him for the session and that may ultimately affect the reporter's interaction with him."

J.L. Sousa

"You have to care about the people you are shooting and what they are going through, even if you disagree with everything they are doing. I didn't say like them. I said care about their situation."

Paul Aiken

"I use comedy when appropriate. I like to get people to laugh when I photograph them. It helps loosen them up, and laughter makes for a better photograph."

Jeffrey Basinger

"Something I hear all the time when I arrive at someone's home or business: 'What do you want me to do?' I tell them to ignore me. I don't want people to perform for me. My job as a photojournalist is to capture life and reality as it happens, not some contrived, sanitized version of it."

J.L. Sousa

"I show subjects the photos on my LCD screen as I take them, which helps build trust. They want to know they are in good hands."

Jeffrey Basinger

"Once you have a photo, it is very important you follow through by taking down the proper information. Nothing like having your photo in the paper only to have it totally misspelled or the wrong name altogether."

Tom Peel, chief photographer, *The Indiana Gazette*, Pa.

"Find a subject you are passionate about and then get as close as you can without getting punched in the face. That's all I've ever done."

Jake Dobkin, photographer based in Brooklyn

"Get close. OK, now get closer."

Sonya Hebert

IDEAS, ONLINE

Dear Photograph

The tagline is confusing: "Take a picture of a picture from the past in the present." But its premise is actually simple. In each post, the blog Dear Photograph (dearphotograph.com) features a user-submitted photo of a present-day location that is personally significant to them—often linked to their childhood or a major event like a wedding, graduation, or prom.

The twist: Each present-day photo has a past photo placed atop a portion of it, showing the same exact scene from years before. This past photo often features the individuals who took the present one. The past and present shots are then tied together with a brief memory, shared in the form of a letter, one that begins with the greeting, "Dear Photograph."

The result: what one reader calls "a nostalgic sort of experience."

For example, last summer, a man took a photo of the street on which he lives, noting a father had taught his son to ride a bike the previous week. In the forefront of the photo, he holds an older photo, one featuring his own father teaching him to ride a bike 30 years before—on the same street.

Your Assignment

Embrace the nostalgia. Tell the stories behind the old photos kept in boxes, scrapbooks, social networks, and digital folders by people in your coverage area. Share the stories in their own words, with the visuals included.

Search for potential themes around which to organize the nostalgia, such as seniors reflecting on freshmen photos near graduation or underclassmen speaking about photos of their first big childhood trips just prior to Spring Break.

Also, consider extending Dear Photograph's presence to a real-world field trip. Travel with a story subject to a spot of past significance, as a means of framing or fleshing out their narratives.

DON'T BE AFRAID OF THE DARK

Doing Things Your Own Way

"At assignments, I avoid hanging out by all the other photographers. Instead, I try to find 'my shot.'"

Scott Strazzante, photographer, *The Chicago Tribune*

Zigzag

"A mentor once told me, 'When everyone else zigs, you zag.' After graduate school, I found myself in a photo internship for a local mid-sized daily newspaper covering the Minnesota Twins spring training in southwest Florida.

"I stood amidst a pack of other shooters making the same images from a slightly different angle. I was focused on a famous player signing baseballs for adoring kids draped over the partition, a pretty Florida sky in the background.

"At one point, I looked past the athlete and watched an ancient, shirtless man dragging a nail-bottomed sled back and forth across the baseball diamond. When I ventured over and struck up a conversation, I learned the man was a legend amongst groundskeepers. I chatted with him for a bit, then came back the following week and compiled a short feature on him.

"The story, accompanied by a single image that encompassed the front page of the feature section, above the fold, ultimately helped me land a staff job at the paper. It all came back to my mentor's advice: When everyone else zigged, I zagged."

Tristan Spinski, documentary photographer based in Fla.

"Photojournalism can be artistic, but there's a time and place. Don't try and out-do yourself when it comes to unique and 'artsy' shots. Although it is important to always shoot creatively, you also need to realize what is practical. **Not every shoot is going to win you an award**."

Alex Trautwig, former photo editor, *The Heights*, Boston College

"Know your audience. You would be surprised what people think is good. The random cute kids and dog photos won't impress a colleague, but they will be the ones you receive the most calls about. Countless times, I have captured a photo illustrating a house fire, sports play, or disastrous storm—images I thought were impressive. I do not receive a single call from the community. But on a last-minute scramble to find wild art to fill a page, snapping photos of a dog and owner running in the park, I receive many personal calls on how the photo was 'incredible,' 'wonderful,' and 'made my day.'"

Jason Halley

"Be patient about getting the right shot, especially if you have time to wait. Magic happens when you get the combination of a good moment and good light."

Karla Gachet, freelance photographer
represented by Panos Pictures, Quito, Ecuador

"When everyone is about to get off work is when I start to work. This is the golden hour, when the light from the sunset can easily create beautiful scenery and long shadows."

Jason Halley

ASSIGNMENT ALERT!

The Vampire Photographer

"Don't be afraid of the dark. Some of the most dramatic photos can be taken at night with available light."

Tom Peel

Your Assignment

Temporarily morph into a vampire photographer. Wait for the sun to set, and begin documenting the people, places, events, and creatures of the night on your campus or surrounding community. Avoid turning to flash when snapping or Photoshop lightening tools when editing. Instead, see what you can capture, via simple point-and-clicks, in the dark.

Some Hokey Thing

"Don't stage photos. Staged photos just end up looking rather cheesy and, well, fake. When readers look at your photo, you don't want them to roll their eyes and keep going because it looks like some hokey thing they have seen on someone's Facebook."

Aly Durrett, former photo editor,
The Northerner, Northern Kentucky University

"One of the most limiting factors holding back new photographers is fear. Fear to take risks. Fear to have a point of view. Fear of failure. Photographers who are taught by others tend to be told what they can and cannot do. 'No tilting!' 'Follow the rule of thirds!' 'Don't put the horizon in the middle of the frame!' 'Get closer!' Photographers should instead find their own way. Develop your voice over time and try not to mimic other shooters. **The best images are made on the edge of failure**."

Scott Strazzante

ASSIGNMENT ALERT!

Dare to Suck

 "The difference between a good photographer and a bad photographer is that a good photographer has taken more bad pictures."

Travis Dove, freelance photographer based in Durham, N.C.

"Do not think in terms of good or bad work. Focus on being as genuine as possible and pushing yourself out of your comfort zone. As one of my professors used to say, 'Dare to suck.' "

Peter Earl McCollough, street photographer based in San Francisco

Your Assignment

 Take McCollough's dare. For your next assignment, shoot a series of photos that purposefully break the rules or adhere to the most cringe-worthy clichés. Share with classmates and friends to see if they can determine where you doggedly went wrong. Subsequently, brainstorm what could be done to capture better images to replace each awful one.

IDEAS, ONLINE

Photo Slideshows

An online photo slideshow is occasionally the perfect method to share a story independently or complement other elements of a multimedia story package.

Slideshows boast numerous strengths. They offer a more comprehensive, visual glimpse at something or someone. They highlight aspects or individuals otherwise left out of a text-driven or single-shot story. They show changes over time. And they more powerfully and directly connect readers with featured subjects.

Fuse the photos with audio narratives and video bursts for even livelier presentations.

A few ideas for slideshow-friendly stories:

Behind the scenes: a look at the private side of newsworthy and everyday people, places, and events.

Example

The moo of a cow. The rev of a tractor engine. The clank of gates. The thump of boots. The splash of hose water. The scrape of a rake and shovel.

These ambient noises accompany photos featured in a 2008 narrative slideshow focused on a college student who also runs a Tennessee dairy farm.

The black-and-white photo set, titled "Dairy King" (thedairyking.blogspot.com), strolls through what appears to be a typical day on the farm.

Along with the moos, revs, clanks, and scrapes, the photos are overlaid with the voices of the farmer and his family briefly discussing the rigors, routines, and larger rationale behind the student's farm focus.

Fringe elements: a glimpse at individuals and activities on the edge of major news, entertainment, and sports events such as protestors at a bill signing or tailgaters at a big game.

Post-disaster: a surveying of the damage and recovery tied to natural and manmade disasters, social troubles such as homelessness, and personal tragedies such as the loss of a loved one.

Street style: a sampling of local fashion choices or everyday on-the-ground activities.

Crowdsourced shots: submitted by the public and sharing numerous perspectives from major events like a graduation ceremony or during times like Homecoming or Halloween.

Retrospectives: a visual reflection of the previous week, semester, year, sports season, or the life and times of someone or something newsworthy. Most popular on the personal level: a day in the life. Others focus on personal journeys—from pregnancy and study abroad to Olympics training and a fundraising drive.

Example

Since January 2000, Noah Kalina has snapped a headshot photograph of himself—every day. He posts the photos on his website Noah K. Everyday (everyday.noahkalina.com). The result: a click-and-scroll photographic evolution of one man's aging, outfits, home, and facial hair. According to the director of the famed Musée de l'Élysée, "There is nothing comparable in the history of photography."

SITE ALERT!

Use these programs to help you build and publish online slideshows, including those integrating photos, audio, and video:

Animoto (animoto.com), "a video creation service that makes it easy and fun for anyone to create and share extraordinary videos using their own pictures, video clips, words, and music"

Soundslides (soundslides.com), "a rapid production tool for still image and audio web presentations"

VUVOX (vuvox.com), "an easy-to-use production and instant sharing service that allows you to mix, create, and blend your personal media—video, photos, and music into rich personal expressions"

Exploring Through Your Own Eyes

"When on assignment, take the safe picture you know an editor is expecting and then start exploring through your own eyes. Work the scene for as much time as you have."

Melissa Cherry, multimedia journalist, *The Herald*, S.C.

"When I review contact sheets, I enjoy when the photographer is trying to work something out through her viewfinder. There is a sense of searching for the light, narrative, gesture, and geometry to align in a single frame. That is always the ultimate challenge. **Photographs can be like notes for the writer or sketches for the painter**. They are ideas that lead to new ideas that then lead to *the* photograph."

Emilio Bañuelos

"To be a good writer, you have to read a lot. The same is true about photography. **Look at a lot of pictures**. I mean a lot. Copy them. Then change things up."

Jeffrey Basinger

"One of the best pieces of advice I ever read was, 'Learn the rules of photography and then go out and break them.' My advice is to do what feels right to you. Absorb as many different styles of photography as you can, then choose things that resonate with you, and gradually develop your own unique style."

Scott Strazzante

"While I feel that I have taken many good photos over the years, I'm always thinking that my best photo will be my next photo."

Tom Peel

CHAPTER 15

An Immersion of Ideas

Illustration by Yee Hung Lim

Brian Dzenis is a devoted member of what he calls "Team Bacon."

Along with journalism, Dzenis, a Temple University student, has publicly declared his enjoyment of three things most in this world: "sports, bacon, and foods that include bacon."

While editor-in-chief of *The Temple News*, the student newspaper at the Philadelphia school, he tested his bacon adulation and general carnivorousness by agreeing to not eat meat for a full month.

The challenge was part of "Vices," a creative series published within the *News* "that challenges what we think we need." As the paper explains, "For each segment, a different writer will give up something he or she 'can't live without.' We watch them land safely or crash and burn."

Past *News* staff have temporarily sworn off personal obsessions such as coffee ("Coffee controls my life."); smoking ("I let cigarettes control my life, my happiness, and my sanity."); their smartphone ("My BlackBerry is my life."); and "World of Warcraft" ("To say I like to game is a vast understatement.").

■ "Vices" represents a virtue, and longstanding tradition, within journalism: Sometimes, storytelling requires a little stunt work. Immersion journalism, also called stunt journalism, is a full-bore reporting method that relies on an individual's own experiences just as much as or more than observation and interviewing.

It typically involves a story planned, staged, and told in the first-person by the reporter. It is artificial in that the happening is only news because the reporter decides to leap into it, but it is focused on something very real and preferably newsworthy.

For the stunt to be successful, the reporter must completely submerge within—or entirely avoid—a specific activity, event, trend, or culture. Sometimes, the reporter goes at it alone or undercover. At other times, it is with the full knowledge, consent, and assistance of the people being reported upon.

Either way, its aim is to capture a more thorough, accurate rendering of how certain people live, learn, love, laugh, celebrate, grieve, worship, indulge, abstain, or ultimately see the world.

TYPES OF IMMERSION

Signing Up: joining a large or influential subculture or group, typically one off the beaten path or invisible to the public.

Example

For her book *Nickel and Dimed: On (Not) Getting By in America*, Barbara Ehrenreich went undercover as a minimum-wage employee, experiencing firsthand how hard it is for the country's lowest classes to get by day-to-day.

Diving In: engaging in a particularly niche, extreme, outdated, or even dangerous activity.

Example

For his book, *The Year of Living Biblically: One Man's Humble Quest to Follow the Bible as Literally as Possible*, secular journalist A.J. Jacobs sought to live for a prolonged period by the more famous and obscure biblical rules, while exploring the influence, ironies, and anachronisms of modern religion.

Not Knowing When to Stop: engaging in an ordinary activity to the extremes.

Example

For his breakout documentary *Super Size Me*, Morgan Spurlock ate only McDonalds food for an entire month, documenting the physical, emotional, and social toll it took on him.

Avoiding at All Costs: abstaining from an activity or leaving a subculture, typically one that is mainstream, popular, or powerful.

Example

For her book, *Not Buying It: My Year Without Shopping*, Judith Levine refrained from purchasing a single non-necessity item for 365 days, raising serious questions about our consumer culture along the way.

THE ALWAYS LIST

- **Always** base your stunt report on a newsworthy premise. It should not simply be performance art or outlandish for its own sake. Please, no firsthand *Hunger Games*.
- **Always** engage fully, honestly, and for as long as possible in the experience. Depending on the project, be prepared to live with your stunt work during downtime, nights, weekends, and holidays. From the perspective of Dzenis's *Temple News* quest, no meat means no meat, period. Readers and viewers will see through, and mock, a half-hearted attempt.
- **Always** go back and talk to key people after you wrap up a stunt. Get context. Ensure you understood what you experienced.
- **Always** conduct outside research, interviewing, and document reviews similar to a straightforward news report.
- **Always** plan a ton. With the help of a friend, editor, or mentor, you typically must decide what you will or won't do, how long you plan to engage in the stunt, what your exceptions will be, who needs to be notified in advance, the laws that might impact your endeavor, and what training, education, and special clearance you will need beforehand.

THE NEVER LIST

- **Never** break laws or journalism ethical tenets in your immersive pursuits. For example, donate the money you make during the time you pretend to be homeless or have fellow staff return it to givers 30 seconds after they pass by.
- **Never** judge the groups you join. Or at least be upfront about your initial judgments, the stereotypes you hold, or your lack of knowledge about them. You must be willing to observe

not just how a culture relates to your own, but how it operates in and of itself, a philosophy known as cultural relativism. It is the notion that no one culture is better or worse, just different. Or, in the end, it's all relative.

- **Never** be obnoxious or mischievous. Most immersion journalism reports are mainly about or significantly involve the writers. If you are seen cheating, lying, doing bad things, or constantly expressing smarminess or cynicism, readers won't want to follow you on your journey.

- **Never** go for the easiest, most obvious, or most glamorous immersion. Consider groups and activities that are particularly misunderstood, extreme, or so ordinary they have gone overlooked.

- **Never** lose sight of your ultimate focus: educating the public and bringing fresh attention to a larger newsworthy issue, event, law, behavior pattern, societal norm, or group of people.

IN OTHER WORDS

Illustration by Yee Hung Lim

"Immersion is the best way to develop story ideas. There is nothing better than being in the middle of things and using the advantage of access as a reporter to generate ideas."

Fluto Shinzawa, sports reporter, *The Boston Globe*

"Critics blast stunts as manufactured and contrived, the literary equivalent of *The Bachelorette* . . . But done right, the literary stunt can still be entertaining, illuminating, even sublime. It gives readers a unique perspective on the world, one that only total immersion can provide. Think of it as the difference between reading Census data about Paris and actually flying there and tasting the ham croissants . . . In fact, I think everyone—even those without book contracts—should do stunts. You don't need to grow a beard and wear a linen robe, as I did [for his book *The Year of Living Biblically*]. Try small experiments. Sample a new toothpaste every week. Swear off gossip for a day. Get your news from the opposition channel, be it Fox News or MSNBC. You'll carve new neural pathways in your brain, which is always healthy."

A.J. Jacobs, author and *Esquire* editor-at-large

STUNT WORK PROMPTS

Along with carving new neural pathways, as Jacobs argues, stunt work also enables you to carve out some news. Here are a few stunt story prompts to get you started, all inspired by recent student journalism immersion reports.

Re: Appearance. Alter your physical appearance to explore issues involving perceptions of beauty, superficiality, and everyday discrimination. If you're a brunette, go blonde. If you have perfect teeth, add a prominent gap. If you're clean-shaven and sporting a crew cut, go longhaired and unkempt. If you're thin, sport a fat suit. If you're pale, tan until your actual ethnicity is uncertain. Live out your new appearance in public in various settings, experiencing how it affects others' reactions toward you and how you felt while doing it. Also, reach out to those who actually look like your performance self to learn about their everyday experiences.

Becoming Homeless. Briefly adopt a panhandling persona to experience firsthand its practical rigors, emotional toll, financial realities, and social stigma.

Staying Silent. Stop speaking or verbally communicating in any way for a predetermined amount of time to better understand its relative necessity in the digital age and to observe how and how well your peers truly speak and listen to one other.

Blacking Out. Refrain from using the Internet, social media, mobile and tablet devices, or any and all digital programs and tools. Tie your temporary blackout to a deeper look at societal tech obsessions and routines. Or employ it as a pushback against online restrictions adopted by school or governmental officials.

Arriving on Set. Participate in a campus or community theater production as an extra, minor actor, or stagehand to help you tell a behind-the-scenes tale about what it's really like during prep and rehearsals for a local show.

Cleaning Up. Join your school's overnight janitorial crew to experience firsthand the type of work they do and amount of recognition and pay they receive for it. While you work, collect the stories of your fellow crew. Subsequently, ensure readers have a greater understanding of the people behind the uniforms and cleaning equipment.

AN EXCHANGE OF IDEAS

A Change of Routine

 The exchange is a recurring feature in the book and on my blog, spotlighting advice and exercises from top journalism students, professionals, educators, and advocates.

This exchange comes from Caley Cook. Cook is a journalism professor, student media adviser, and journalist with a decade of experience producing print, broadcast, and online content for outlets such as the Los Angeles Times, *CBS Sports,* The San Diego Union-Tribune, Orlando Weekly, VIBE *magazine, and* The Orange County Register.

Her exchange focuses on a starter stunt of sorts, one aimed at helping you see fresh ideas by only slightly diverting your own daily habits.

The nightmare scenario: You are suddenly stuck in the journalism equivalent of No Man's Land. You cannot think of a good story idea to save your life. You have repeatedly tried to pitch pieces about things you experience in your daily routine, but each time these stories fall flat in news value or you find out they have already been done.

You are not alone. Most journalists face this nightmare at some point early in their collegiate or professional careers. They initially mine their daily lives for story ideas, until they realize their daily routines are, well, shockingly mundane.

Most of us wake up at the same time each morning, eat generally the same food, walk the same way to work or classes, sit in the same place in the office or classroom, talk to the same people, and some of us (gasp!) even wear the same clothes each week.

When we grow accustomed to such a regular schedule, it results in a pretty stagnant perspective. Don't ever become so stuck in your routine that you lose sight of the kinds of oddities, people, structures, or entities that lurk in the world and lead to great story ideas.

Your Assignment

 If you are feeling adventurous, try this one-day stunt to free yourself from the doldrums of routine, refresh your perspectives, and break new ground in your reporting.

Step 1

Write out your normal, day-to-day schedule in as much detail as possible, employing all your senses. For instance, if you usually eat at the same place for lunch each day, write it down. If you usually see the same friend on your walk from class, write it down. If you usually listen to the same music on your iPod after classes, write it down.

Got it all on the page? Great. Just writing down your observations in more detail might help you notice a few new story ideas. But let's not stop there.

Step 2

On a day you select, shake up your entire regular routine. This may involve changes like waking up at an earlier time in the morning, eating at a new place for lunch, walking a roundabout way to your classes, sitting in a different place in the lecture hall, and talking to people you've never spoken to.

This routine rearrangement will take some planning. For example, you may need to map out your walking routes between classes so you avoid your regular paths. Or you may need to download some new tunes to your iPod or buy food so you can prepare lunch at home instead of your usual practice of eating out.

It will take a conscious effort to avoid your regular routine, even the little habits you may have never given a second thought. For example, if you usually go to the same bathroom down the hall in a classroom building, try a new one and pay attention to the graffiti on the walls, anything that needs fixing, or even the quietude of a specific lavatory.

It is helpful to embark on this assignment with a partner, so you can keep each other accountable. Have your partner review your routines from Step 1. Go through each step together, in part so you can pinpoint what you should do or refrain from doing on your chosen non-routine day.

Unfortunately, there will be a few things you will still have to do the usual way. Some of us have to go to work at a specific time or take medication every day or talk to the same teacher during office hours. Do not miss work or class or endanger yourself in any way for this assignment. Just try to temporarily live and perceive as many things as possible differently.

Step 3

On your big day, have a notebook with you at all times. Write down your real-time observations and thoughts in a table with five columns—sight, touch, taste, smell, and sound.

If you are walking down a new hall and see beautiful murals on the walls, jot down a note under *sight* to do a story on campus art. If you eat lunch from a food truck instead of your usual cafeteria, jot down a note under *taste* to do a story about alternative lunch ideas. If you decide to walk a new way home and you overhear two students talking about a professor's fresh approach to teaching math, jot down a note under *sound* to do a profile on the prof.

To be successful in this exercise, you have to be open to the confusion and sensory overload the change of scenery and activity might bring. Those who are resistant to experiencing life in new ways will have trouble here. Try to take more time than you normally would to observe and experience everything happening around you.

What You Might Find

Past students have come across some amazing story ideas from this exercise. For example, for her assignment, Justine from Pennsylvania's Allegheny College decided to wake up earlier than the average college student. As she shared later, "I was not excited about being up at 6 a.m., but I found that our campus was so alive at that time. Workers were clearing snow off the sidewalks, our food service folks were making coffee and chatting about the day, and there were students who were actually up at that time and headed to sports practices. I had no idea about this life of the school before I was up with them."

Justine subsequently wrote a story about the daily grind of off-season weight training for Division III athletes and a separate behind-the-scenes look at what it takes to keep a college campus running during a snowstorm. Both stories stemmed from her earlier wake-up call, and her larger attempt at changing her routine for just a day.

To learn more from Caley Cook, follow her on Twitter @caleycook.

POST-MORTEM

 Post-Mortem is a recurring feature in the book and on my blog, telling the story *behind* **a story, series, or website—in the words of the reporter or editor responsible for creating it.**

The Video Game Challenge

In November 2011, Miles Parks decided to play video games for 24 hours straight. Or in his words, "I was going to sit and game and turn my cerebral cortex into applesauce."

The University of Tampa student journalist, an admittedly light gamer, conducted the multi-player, multi-platform, multi-game experiment in part to better understand his many friends and classmates who "can sit down at one end of an evening and beat up bad guys until the sun rises."

Amid the endless sports games and a helping of Mario Party, Parks kept a running diary and a video log, enabling his audience to slowly follow his descent into cranky numbness.

"Honestly, I'm spent," he wrote after hour 12. "I eat pasta and I can barely even enjoy it. I'm so hungry and so tired and I feel nauseous. My stomach hurts and feels queasy and I've had a headache for five hours . . . I've given up keeping track of my wins and losses. The outcome doesn't really matter anymore."

At the close of the marathon session, he slept heartily and awoke feeling guilty about the time he had wasted in front of the Wii, Xbox, and PlayStation.

Yet, gaming's pull still proved strong. The next night, he watched football at a friend's house. As he recounted in a piece for *The Minaret*, UT's student newspaper, "I get up to leave and he asks if I want to play a game of NHL with him on Xbox . . . 'Just one,' I reply."

In this Q&A, Parks talks more about the challenge's rigors and rationale and video games' role in subverting students' undergraduate experiences.

What motivated you to take on this challenge?

I've been reading a lot of first-person writing over the past few months and it's pretty obvious that if you truly want an entertaining story, you've got to go big and you've got to do something you relate to. I'm in college. Half of my friends spend their lives attached to a television. As I mention in the story, my mom has always drilled into my head that video games are bad for your soul. Basically, I've had these two opposing viewpoints shown to me about a prominent part of pop culture, and I wanted to see who was right. The best way to do that was to write about it.

What are your thoughts on the video game culture you see among students nowadays?

What I've begun to realize is that this culture and these electronics affect everyone differently, similar to drug use. Some people can smoke [ahem, certain illegal substances] and still write papers and get straight As. Others are going to end up on their couch with a bag of Fritos and a 1.8 GPA.

I think the ones who are really obsessed with video games need to take a deep breath and a step back. You're paying your tuition—which for me, at a private university, is upwards of $30,000 a year—to sit in your bedroom or living room. At some point, you've got to take advantage of your environment. It's a cliché, but it's true. You're not going to remember what you did in that game on that couch in 30 years. We're not truly diving headfirst into our education if we're spending even a couple hours a day in front of a television.

What was the toughest part of your 24-hour challenge?

I would say staying motivated within each game. After 15 hours, there comes a time when being down 14 points seems like the largest deficit in college football history. I had to keep trying to win because it's that focus and drive that was probably the most draining part of it all. I lost more than 60 times throughout the adventure. For a competitive guy like myself, that starts to get very, very frustrating.

Also, it was challenging writing the story in a way that didn't come off as insulting to video game enthusiasts, but still ended on a strong note with a clear idea. Writing diary style in chronological order is easy, especially with the help of the video diaries I kept.

I found myself sometimes getting too philosophical. It's a serious issue, but it was still light, funny, and, most importantly, supposed to be an easy read. There's a weird balance there. I was legitimately distraught at the concept of a whole day down the crapper, but I had to write it in a way that didn't feel forced or exaggerated.

At the end of the 24 hours, did you learn any lessons or uncover any truths?

I learned a lot about motivation. It's amazing how quickly it can be zapped from you and be gone indefinitely. Once a day is gone, what's a week? What's a month or a year? You can so easily get into this zone without a clear end where you're just floating along, especially as a student. Video games seem to shift me into that zone, and it's a terrible place to live.

I think the great part about higher education is that we can make it what we want. We can choose almost everything we associate ourselves with. If you end your college days with no job experience, internships, good grades, or memories to show for it, then that stinks. But chances are, you put yourself in a place that led to those outcomes.

ETHICS ALERT!

The Bicycle Theft

In a reporting experiment of sorts last spring, a student at Canada's Wilfrid Laurier University brazenly "stole" a bicycle in public, in broad daylight, in four locations including WLU's campus.

According to Alanna Fairey, the reporter-thief at WLU's campus newspaper *The Cord*, the purpose, in part, was to answer this question: "What would you do if you saw someone stealing a bike by the use of bolt cutters? In a big open space with plenty of people, you'd assume someone would stop them; but as *The Cord* discovered . . . that's not exactly the case. I am not the kind of person that would even steal a chocolate bar, let alone a bicycle. However, as an experiment, I went to several different locations in Waterloo to 'steal' a friend's bike, just to see if others would try and stop me. And the results were shocking."

The most common bystander reactions were purposeful ignorance or lighthearted curiosity, nothing more. As Fairey writes, "After my bike stealing adventures, I can conclude that it is relatively easy to steal a bike in the Kitchener-Waterloo area. People will stare and possibly ask questions, but no one confronted me aggressively or threatened to report me to the police."

The related question: When is it OK, if ever, to carry out faux crimes in public for the purposes of practicing journalism?

IDEAS, ONLINE

The Snowball Fight

When is a snowball fight also a social media revolution? On a wintry day in 2011 in Washington D.C., one ambitious George Washington University student employed Twitter and *The Georgetown Voice* to spread the word about a snowy battle "that would eventually be referenced in one way or another by *The Washington Post*, *LA Times*, *U.S. News & World Report*, NBC DC, and a host of campus media outlets."

GW student Kyle Boyer explains: "The day before the snowball fight, I sent a tweet to @GtownVoice, Georgetown's student magazine and blog, and suggested the idea. About 46 minutes later, they replied and planning began. We created an event page on Facebook and spread the word on Twitter. Within 24 hours, about 600 students from both schools had RSVP'ed . . . There is no doubt that the #gwgusnowdown was historic, as was the snowfall that made it possible. Hopefully, though, students from both schools will hold on to the greater messages of the event. One of those messages is that when organizational skill meets the power of social networking anything can be accomplished."

Your Assignment

Start a snowball fight! More seriously, step back from the journalist's normal role as news gatherer and become a news creator, via social networking. Plan an offbeat campus event requiring student particpation, such as a flash mob. Cover it with video reports, photo slideshows, and real-time tweeting. The key: Follow Boyer's lead and organize something fun and at least marginally newsworthy—connected to a major national story, a pop culture trend, the time of year or, if nothing else, the weather.

CHAPTER 16
Idea Lists

Illustration by Yee Hung Lim

Let's talk lists.

A list can be a very worthy addition to your regular content mix. It educates, entertains, brings out the movie critic within all of us, and prompts massive online commenting and sharing. It organizes and simplifies complex issues. It varies up the traditional story format. And it helps us make sense of the world.

As James Poniewozik, an entertainment news writer who occasionally dabbles in list-making shares, "Lists are incredibly important. They are how we define what matters to us, what we want entertainment and art to do, what we expect of our culture."

They are an especially popular part of college culture. College life is full of lists. There are lists for the top NCAA sports teams, the coolest drinking games, the strangest mascots, the best school mottos, the most inspiring professors, the largest school endowments, the most popular student newspapers, and the highest-paying academic majors (engineering, for those keeping score).

There are separate lists telling students about the best historically black colleges, the best Christian colleges, and the best schools at which to drink, dance, surf, party, and explore illegal drugs such as marijuana. One additional list ranks the happiest schools in America, deduced through analyzing factors such as campus housing, nightlife, dining, and hours of daily sunshine. The happiest school: Claremont McKenna College in California. Harvard University comes in second.

There are also lists touting the best cars to own while in college, the strangest classes to take, the most spirited sports stadiums in which to cheer on college teams, the wildest student sections in those stadiums, the most convenient dorm foods to munch on, the best college foods to devour while drunk, the top fashion trends for students on a budget, and the top student inventions (including a robotic arm run by a Sony PlayStation controller).

There are lists laying out the top mobile apps, laptops, tech gadgets, and textbook alternatives to buy, rent, or download while in school. Other lists focus on study stress busters, grade improvement tips, and techniques to reduce debt from student loans. Still others scream about the best ways to impress professors, earn scholarships, and cheat on exams.

There are lists about the top Twitter feeds for students to follow, students' oft-cited guilty pleasures (#1 ice coffee, #2 sleeping until noon), the top items typically stolen on campus (including iPods, smartphones, and bicycles), and the top gifts to get other students.

A separate list reverses the focus of the latter, instructing students on the 12 things they do not need while in school—including a printer, a big meal plan, campus health insurance, and cable TV. Another list highlights the "dumbest things" students complain about, including parking tickets, cafeteria food, residence hall rules, and roommates. Separate lists offer tips on avoiding the freshman 15, the sophomore slump, senioritis, and post-graduation depression.

Among the most influential lists are the annual rundowns from high-profile organizations and media outlets proclaiming the priciest schools, cheapest schools, brainiest schools (#1 Brown University), most flirtatious schools (#1 Arizona State University), and the best darn schools, period.

Perhaps the strangest college list I have come across was published in *The Miscellany News* at Vassar College. The student newspaper published a review of the "ten best and quirkiest" campus restrooms. While seemingly odd at first glance, the list purporting to help students "find the perfect potty" comes across by its close as the quintessential campus guide.

After all, as the paper notes, "College students are often deprived of many comforts: parentally run laundry services, nights that don't include your neighbors playing Call of Duty at ungodly hours and your own bathroom." By the way, the bathroom earning the top spot on the list sports a sofa, floral wallpaper, gold fixtures, a baby grand piano—and, I hope, working toilets.

TOP 10 LIST OF LISTS

- **Advice**: an instructional summary of tips to follow, steps to take, traps to avoid, and tools to master.

- **Catalogue**: an attempt to capture everything worthy of attention that has been written about a particular person, place, location, subject, or school.

- **Education**: a way of providing information in easy-to-follow, quick-hit chunks, often focused on topics too complex, mundane, or offbeat to be featured regularly in mainstream news stories.

- **Flights of Fancy**: a wish list of sorts often involving exotic locations, high-priced food, cutting-edge gadgets, and more extreme bucket-list adventures.

- **Personal**: an individual's take on a portion of the world or a reflection on an experience.

- **Popular**: a rundown of what's hot, in the news, and being enjoyed or discussed by the masses.

- **Rating**: an objective or opinionated outline of what is considered the best, worst, most, least, longest, shortest, largest, and smallest.

- **Review**: a reflective overview of a particular time period, event, project, or life. A popular offshoot is the predictive list, forecasting what is definitely or possibly coming our way in the near or distant future.

- **Social**: a collection of opinions from numerous people on the same subject, often from staffers at the same outlet or via crowdsourcing.

- **Underground**: a glimpse at people, groups, genres, and aesthetics that are impactful or in vogue, beneath or outside the mainstream.

THE ALWAYS LIST

- **Always** pick topics suitable for listing. Not everything is newsworthy enough or includes enough separate components to be stretched into a full list. At the same time, don't doubt a list's ability to make seemingly dull topics at least passably interesting. I once scrolled through a slideshow list featuring photographs of celebrities yawning. The big reveal: At times, President Obama, Miley Cyrus, and the Dalai Lama yawn without covering their mouths.

- **Always** select a solid number. Your list's length should be clearly labeled and easy to follow, sporting actual numbers, a slideshow clicker, or bolded headers to separate one item from the next. Most of the time, the number of items should follow the list custom of five, seven,

10, 20, 25, or even 100. Just be sure the number never overshadows the content, such as leaving people wondering, "Why are there only nine top schools featured? That's a weird amount. Where's the tenth?" On some occasions, pick a number appropriate to the list's focus. For example, a 2013 Year in Review might call for 13 items.

- **Always** research what you are listing. Lists are often opinionated exercises. Even when built atop data, they involve the creator's personal touch or outright editorializing. You owe it to your audience to not simply feature the first items that come to mind. Follow the same reporting procedures for a list as you would for a regular story.

- **Always** search for subtleties. Look beyond the obvious and instead consider featuring quietly emerging phenomena or the types of activities, issues, people, places, or things not often situated together or ranked against one another. The point of lists, in part, is to bring order and provide fresh perspectives about our experiences, our interests, and our world.

- **Always** explain your selections. The actual items on a list are empty shells. They require context if you want people to take in, learn about, and respond to them. Be sure to include verifiable facts and source quotes to back up your choices. Also, all online lists should feature active links for those interested in further exploration.

THE NEVER LIST

- **Never** overly explain your selections. If you have to provide an especially bloated justification for an item, it's a big clue it may be a weak selection or featured in the wrong spot.

- **Never** overlook the order. Be sure to present your lists in an order that makes sense. Among the most popular orderings: chronological, alphabetical, simply random, or in increasing or decreasing order of rank when coupled with words like best and worst.

- **Never** forget the timing. Specifically, think timely or timeless. A list is often most appreciated during a specific time of year, such as a rundown of things freshmen must know about college shared during fall orientation. If run at the wrong time—say, a Year in Review in March—a list can seem nonsensical. Yet, with the power of Google, more lists are enjoying a search-and-scan permanence. So when crafting a list that could hold up long term, don't weigh it down with too many pop culture references or other aspects that might turn people off if they check it out more than a week after it's posted.

- **Never** play it safe. A "safe" list will be quickly forgotten. Do not be provocative without any accompanying news value, but be sure to create lists people will want to digitally share and comment upon. After all, if you cannot hook people in and keep them reading, what's the point of having a list?

- **Never** turn to lists too often. As a Copyblogger contributor shares, "Too much of a good thing is usually a bad thing, and if you keep writing lists you will soon reach a point where you annoy your readers. It's a great idea to throw in a list once in a while but don't overdo it."

ASSIGNMENT ALERT!

Campus Bucket List

In a pre-commencement piece published in *The Pendulum* at North Carolina's Elon University, a staff writer laid out a list of more than 20 activities students should consider undertaking prior to graduation.

Some are general—racing through sprinklers, stealing a brick from a campus walkway, making a 2 a.m. run to the nearby Walmart, pulling a library all-nighter, and taking a Polar Bear plunge in a freeeeeezing campus lake. Others are Elon-specific. They add up to what the piece calls the "Elon Bucket List."

Your Assignment

Every school should have a bucket list. In the spirit of the *Pendulum* piece, put together a rundown of the activities, events, and rituals students at your college or university should participate in prior to leaving campus. Seek student, alumni, faculty, and staff input via social media and publish the funniest, most popular, and most bizarre responses. Run a contest for the best bucket list viral video.

The key to the list's awesomeness: Go beyond the stereotypical. Attempt to localize a national current event. Select an activity related to a prominent historical landmark, moment, or anniversary on campus. And remember that at least a few items on any modern bucket list must be digital. Also, make sure everything is legal and within the bounds of human decency.

THE FACEBOOK TIMELINE

Last spring, *The Crimson White* at the University of Alabama modeled its entire 32-page Year in Review issue after the Facebook Timeline. Each month sported its own cover photo and status updates related to major campus events. The massive, impressive effort is published proof that lists do not always have to be text-driven, text-heavy, or presented in a rundown readers have come to expect.

IDEAS, ONLINE

Lists as Inspiration

 Along with using lists as inspirations for how to format your stories, existing ones should also provide endless story prompts. As with almost everything worthy of editorial consideration these days, the most inspirational lists are now created and updated online.

Take a look at a few of these featured list sites—a mix of serious, snarky, silly, and almost surreal:

11 Points (11points.com), "because top 10 lists are for cowards"

12 Most (12most.com), "yes, it is a website of lists . . . yet it is also so much more"

List25 (list25.com), "compiles lesser-known intriguing information on a variety of subjects"

Listology (listology.com), "enabling your OCD one bullet at a time"

Listphobia (listphobia.com), "listings from all around the web about design, concepts, nature, and people"

Lists of Bests (listsofbests.com), "create and find lists of products, places, goals, and people"

Listverse (listverse.com), "dedicated to top 10 lists of trivia from a variety of categories"

The Longest List (bit.ly/3ScBfd), "Ever wonder what the longest (insert item) in the world is? You've come to the right place"

Smashing Lists (listpress.com), "top 10 lists—hot and weird"

Top 10 List (top-10-list.org), "focused on lists that intrigue and educate . . . specializing in entertainment, travel, trivia and people"

While checking out the sites, mine the lists' topics, specific selections, omissions, and overall themes for story ideas. Respond with related lists of your own. Target spin-off lists toward a student audience. Or simply brainstorm story ideas connected to various lists—even if an idea's association with a particular list is not immediately clear.

For example, the site Smashing Lists features the "Top 10 Sleepiest Mammals around the Globe." It includes the Southern owl monkey, the nine-banded armadillo, the little brown bat, and the three-toed sloth. It does not include the modern college student.

For many students, sleep is the most precious commodity of their college years, except for maybe alcohol and easy classes. And yet, it remains scarce. As a column in *The Daily Illini* at the University of Illinois at Urbana-Champaign confirms, "With the beginning of a new semester and a new class schedule, students will be getting syllabi, textbooks, and stacks of notebooks. One thing students won't be getting a lot of: sleep." Sleep is also rare within student media coverage. Let's uproot that trend.

ASSIGNMENT ALERT!

Shuteye Stories

Grab some shuteye stories. Find a freshman insomniac. Ferret out a sleep-obsessed sophomore. Profile a junior who always wears pajamas to class. Focus on a senior vampire who sleeps all day and stays up all night. Uncover the craziest places and craziest situations in which students have fallen asleep. Determine the sleep-related disorders most commonly dealt with by campus counselors. Check in on the relative popularity of energy drinks, sleeping pills, and other stimulants. See what early classes are actually like. Attempt a first-person stay-up-all-night report, possibly timed to an appropriate event like an all-night rave or final exam study period.

Tons of possible sleep stories abound—in this case all of them originally spun out from a list involving a three-toed sloth.

CHAPTER 17

Digital and Mobile Story Mining

Illustration by Yee Hung Lim

Stories are forever.

But the way we go about brainstorming, digging, creating, presenting, promoting, and sharing stories is changing. As digital artist and big thinker Joe Sabia said, "In 6,000 years of storytelling, [people have] gone from depicting hunting on cave walls to depicting Shakespeare on Facebook walls."

Journalists have long contended news and feature stories are created in four main physically impacting ways. Your feet need to be begging for a break due to their constant pounding on the streets of your beat. Your voice needs to be hoarse from working contacts. Your stomach needs to be revolting from the bad food you ate during an extended editorial meeting. Or your neck and shoulders need to be sore and cricked from endless phone chatter.

While these still hold true to a certain extent, journalism 2.0 has two new "idea ailments": eyestrain and carpal tunnel syndrome.

Nine out of every 10 journalists nowadays use the Internet to find stories and sources. And the remaining ones are just waiting for their Wi-Fi to reconnect, believe me.

Surfing the net is a real-time, Wild-West-style free-for-all of a brainstorming session. Story ideas and information to flesh out your stories lurk everywhere in the digital realm. A trillion websites, social networks, apps, tools, and programs are at your disposal. Within them, an even more endless array of profiles, posts, multimedia creations, documents, and comments are also waiting to be scanned.

Building off the featured websites and digital reporting suggestions shared in earlier chapters, let's continue mining new media for golden ideas.

TAMING THE WILD WEB

Tips for Brainstorming and Discovering Stories Online

Stay Trendy

Monitor the stories, videos, photos, status updates, tweets, pins, hashtags, and posts earning trending and popular status on leading social networks and news sites. Also, keep an eye out for online content receiving an especially high number of retweets, reblogs, repins, votes, likes, shares, views, and comments. Build off the issues, topics, people, events, and movements at the heart of all this buzzworthy chatter with fresh stories.

Follow the Leaders

Keep track of the thought leaders in various corners of the Internet, including the individuals, outlets, and organizations sporting the most readers, followers, subscribers, friends, or fans. What they say matters—at least to the many who adore or loathe them—and has a greater potential to go viral, provoke controversy, and make news.

Be a Groupie

Join and regularly check group pages and discussion groups on networks such as Facebook and LinkedIn.

Know the Rules

Keep up with national, state, and city cyber laws, along with the Internet usage regulations for all major employers, schools, and Internet service providers in your coverage area. Pay special attention to your own school's social media policies and social media monitoring efforts.

Don't Forget Niche Networks

Outside the realm of Facebook, Twitter, Google+, Pinterest, and other first-tier and second-tier social networks, a boatload of active and wacky web worlds exist. Dogster, Catster, Hamsterer, FarmersOnly, and VampireFreaks are fairly self-explanatory. Ravelry is aimed at knitters, crocheters, spinners, weavers, and dyers. Stache Passions is the world's leading social network and dating service for those sporting and supporting mustaches. The list goes on.

For every age, race, faith, sexual persuasion, job, hobby, pop culture phenomenon, and closet fetish, there is an online community and a bevy of story ideas waiting to be discovered.

Seek Answers, and Questions

Visit sites such as Quora (quora.com) and Yahoo! Answers (answers.yahoo.com), which bring people together through user-submitted questions and answers. Take a look at especially popular, timely, timeless, quirky, and intense Q&As—and spot the ideas embedded within them.

For example, a Yahoo Answers! scan last summer revealed open questions on everything from pediatric cancer, digital art, and the fighting in Syria to Egyptologists, electronic cigarettes, and fears of an impending apocalypse. There are also sillier questions that may be fun to share with your readers and gather rapid crowdsourced responses online. One Yahoo Answers! example: "Hypothetical scenario, Aliens came to earth and said, 'Take me to your leader.' Who would be the leader exactly?" (One of the respondents suggested the IRS commissioner, noting, "The Tax Man is our leader.")

Look for Love

Online dating is an enormous industry and extremely popular activity that deserves more diverse, in-depth reporting. There are dating websites catering to individuals of nearly every faith, ethnicity, age group, geographic location, and sexual desire. Brainstorming more broadly, the digital explosion has also spurred new methods of flirting, fighting, cheating, keeping in touch, and breaking up.

Seek Out Sex.com

Ignoring the sexual underbelly of the Internet is like avoiding features on animals while covering the zoo. Pornography is one of the web's most pervasive, profitable enterprises. There are also endless sex and hook-up personals sites. At some schools, students participate in sexually explicit webcamming for money. Sexting, online sex addiction, Internet sex crimes, and virtual sex including through games like "The Sims" are also constants. Safely stake out these e-sex activities and the arenas in which they occur. Determine their root causes and what they say about our wider digital world and the people enmeshed within it.

Example

Image control within higher education has gone triple-X. Beginning last year, officials at colleges and universities nationwide have been rapidly purchasing domain names sporting the new .xxx URL. Administrators' primary goal with the purchases is protecting their schools' online trademarks. At the same time, the hope is that the web acquisitions will help stop sites springing up that connect their schools with, ahem, sexual innuendo. For example, a Duke University administrator told *The Chronicle*, "We have reserved a number of Duke-related names, things that involve Duke, things that involve Blue Devils." Among the purchases: coachk.xxx and bluedevils.xxx.

Engage the Disengaged

Monitor people and the world, away from the web. Focus on institutions and individuals who temporarily or permanently go without online access or leave a particular community like Facebook (an act known as Facebookicide)—either purposefully or due to forces beyond their control. Tell their stories, including what they have learned, what they feel they have lost, and what they are doing more and less often since cutting back on their web use.

Example

In September 2011, University of Alabama student Matt Mecoli carried out a roughly weeklong "social media blackout" in part to determine his own—and society's—level of social media addiction. "I found giving it up to be an extremely uncomfortable and difficult experience," Mecoli wrote for *The Crimson White*. "The level to which social media permeated my life and how frequently I was using it didn't become apparent until I gave it up."

He recounted that during his blackout he had to stop himself from signing onto services such as Facebook, Twitter, and Skype an average of 16 times each day. He was surprised by how often he turned to them during downtime such as waits at the bus stop or even during boring moments in class.

He also recognized just how much he used social media to keep in touch with friends and family and keep abreast of current events. "I found it shocking when my friends began talking about the Wall Street riots in New York City," he wrote. "I had no idea what they were talking about, and I came to the realization that I'd come to depend on social media: for my news, for my networking, for many of the little tasks that contribute to managing my life."

Think Hyperlocal

Bookmark and regularly check the websites, blogs, list-servs, and social media accounts applicable to your coverage area, including those kept by schools, the local government, businesses, nonprofit organizations, entertainment venues, sports teams, and leaders and celebrity figures.

Go Back in Time

Check out the archives of news sites focused on your coverage area. Search for content posted months or even years ago that is screaming for an update, fresh take, or spin-off.

In addition, explore parts of the web that no longer exist and sites devoted to sharing real-world history in digital ways. Check out the next chapter for an introduction to a helpful website known as the Internet Archive (archive.org). Also, visit the sites below.

SITE ALERT!

CyberCemetery (govinfo.library.unt.edu), "an archive of government websites that have ceased operation"

The National Archives Experience: Digital Vaults (archives.gov/nae), "depicts our astounding national mosaic and tells the stories of the American journey to young and old, scholars and students, cynics and dreamers"

American Memory from the Library of Congress (memory.loc.gov), "free and open access through the Internet to written and spoken words, sound recordings, still and moving images, prints, maps, and sheet music that document the American experience"

Report on Reputation

Examine the digital branding business, including the job of social media manager and online reputation management services like Klout. Also, explore our increasingly viral culture, including the videos, social media feeds, websites, people, and projects that suddenly become Internet famous, for better and worse.

Go Beyond Google

There are tons of websites Google does not locate or properly highlight. There are also loads of other search engines that are designed to pinpoint specific types of sites or conduct specific types of searches. Beyond Ask (ask.com), Bing, and Yahoo!, here is a lucky 13 listing of online engines possibly worth searching.

SITE ALERT!

Acronym Finder (acronymfinder.com), "an online database of abbreviations and their meanings"

Addict-o-matic (addictomatic.com), "instantly create a custom page with the latest buzz on any topic"

Blinkx (blinkx.com), "world's largest video search engine"

CompletePlanet (completeplanet.com), "the deep web directory . . . over 70,000+ searchable databases and specialty search engines"

Dogpile (dogpile.com), "a metasearch engine that fetches results from Google, Yahoo!, Bing, Ask.com, About.com, and several other popular search engines"

DuckDuckGo (duckduckgo.com), "uses information from crowd-sourced sites to augment traditional results and improve relevance"

Help a Reporter Out (helpareporter.com), "connects news sources with journalists looking for their expertise"

NETR Online (netronline.com), "provides many public records and real estate research"

Pipl (pipl.com), "the most comprehensive people search on the web"

Similar Site Search (similarsitesearch.com), "the best place to find similar websites"

Technorati (technorati.com), "real-time search for user-generated media"

Wolfram Alpha (wolframalpha.com), "an online service that answers factual queries directly by computing the answer from structured data, rather than providing a list of documents or web pages that might contain the answer"

YIPPY (yippy.com), "we won't track your activity on our platform, store your history in our browser, monitor or record your searches, store copies of your email, or collect any more personal information than you volunteer"

Dive Into the Invisible Web

A gigantic chunk of the web containing invaluable information is purposefully or inadvertently hidden from searches. Related sites can typically be tracked down through deep web search engines, directed searches (such as those coupling the keyword "database" with your search term), and the search engines on specific sites.

Search for Who Owns and Operates Various Websites

It might provide clues about why certain stances are being taken or why certain facts are being left out. Here are two search engines for domain name ownership to get you started.

SITE ALERT!

Whois.net (whois.net), "your trusted source for secure domain name searches, registration, and availability"

WHOIS (networksolutions.com/whois), "discover who owns a website or domain name by searching our WHOIS database"

Never Look Past the Backstage

Explore the underground foundation of many sites—the coding, content management systems, server rooms, bandwidth capabilities, and those in charge of their creation and daily functionality.

Example

Last summer, OnlineColleges.net published "The Battle for Bandwidth," an infographic breakdown of how students' electronic and digital devices are increasingly devouring and slowing bandwidth at colleges and universities nationwide. Campus bandwidth gobblers now include everything from tablets, smartphones, and iPods to e-readers, smart TVs, and wireless printers. All that network activity requires ever-larger bandwidth capacity, which in turn costs more money and comes with greater expectations. For example, more than 60 percent of students said they would consider moving "if their apartment's Internet speeds were slower than expected."

Play Games—and Explore Gamers

The video game industry is a social and entertainment behemoth bursting with story potential. Last fall, the University of Iowa even offered what is believed to be the first video game journalism course at a major research university. "Computer gaming is as much a part of our lives as movies or journalism," UI's journalism school director said at the time. "It deserves the same rigorous standards of reporting and analysis."

Learn Net Lingo

The terms coined and shared every day to describe various aspects of our digital existence are screaming for related reports and closer analysis. A sampling of new media terms in recent years: mouse potato ("someone who spends all of his or her time on the computer surfing the Internet or playing games, similar to a couch potato"); cellcert ("a concert transmitted via cell phone . . . when a person calls a friend and holds up his or her cell so the friend can also enjoy the show"); textpectation ("the anticipation one feels when waiting for a response to a text message"); and Facebooger ("an unsightly or unwanted comment or post left on your Facebook profile or wall"). Check out Chapter 5, "Words, Letters, and Lots of Ideas," for a rundown on how to conduct regular "Wordy Web Checks."

Let the News—and Ideas—Come to You

Set up RSS feeds, sign up for email alerts, join list-servs, and buy in to the power of active or passive crowdsourcing. Google News Alerts (google.com/alerts) are especially helpful.

SITE ALERT!

 ChangeDetection.com (changedetection.com), "provides page change monitoring and notification services to Internet users worldwide . . . Just fill in the form [and] we will create a change log for the page and alert you by email when we detect a change in the page text."

Simply Stumble

Every once in a while, conduct an organic story search through StumbleUpon (stumbleupon.com). You will happen upon an interesting site or news nugget worth a story almost every time.

Fact-Check

Never accept information presented online at face value. Remember, every site, just like every person, has an agenda. So run fact checks on what you find, similar to the political fact-checking performed by the *Tampa Bay Times* PolitiFact (politifact.com) project.

Analyze E-Commerce

Document the latest trends in online trades, rentals, and sales of goods, services, and skillsets, especially among the biggie sites like Craigslist, eBay, and Amazon. As *Business Insider* reports about the rising influence of the latter retailer, "Google's real rival, and real competition to watch over the next few years is Amazon." Separately, see the next section for a rundown of TaskRabbit.

Pay Attention to Online Advertising

Peek at the pop-ups. Read the banner copy. Sneak into your email spam folder for a quick scan. And monitor the so-called search advertising that appears when you seek out something on Google. Look at the type of ad being run. Check out the funding structures and related revenues. And search for more unique or ethically tricky sponsorships or partnerships.

Gauge the Digital Experiences of the Disabled

Examine the ways in which individuals with mental or physical disabilities use the web and other digital platforms and tools. Outline the roadblocks, unique routines, and the technology assisting them. Also, focus on the online communities in which they participate.

Consider Cross-Cultural Internet Customs

Examine how individual families, schools, religious institutions, ethnic groups, political organizations, age brackets, economic classes, and even entire neighborhoods across the U.S. use, abstain, and interact online in ways very specific to their beliefs, histories, and even economic states.

Travel Beyond the U.S. Web

Similar to the stateside cross-cultural exploration, dive into the gigantic stockpile of active sites, social networks, and online information repositories operated outside our country's real-world borders. Analyze foreign government oversight and control of public Internet use and the larger international community's bedrock digital principles. For example, last year, the United Nations announced, "Free expression online is a basic human right."

SITE ALERT!

 Pulitzer Center on Crisis Reporting (pulitzercenter.org), "an innovative award-winning nonprofit journalism organization dedicated to supporting the independent international journalism that U.S. media organizations are increasingly less able to undertake"

Reporters Without Borders (rsf.org), "a nonprofit organization which defends the freedom to be informed and to inform others"

Transparency International (transparency.org), "the global coalition against corruption"

Get an Education

The Internet continues to hit various parts of primary, secondary, and higher education like a thunderclap. Examine the latest trends in online and hybrid courses, open courseware projects (most prominently at MIT, ocw.mit.edu), digital textbooks, and the many new innovations available for teaching and learning.

Go Underground

Explore the hacker, cyberpunk, illegal downloading, data breaching, and online protest movements that operate outside the mainstream and sometimes the law. Also, look at general Internet security and privacy issues.

Example

Keeping personal information secret online is a sacrosanct principle—unless you're young and in love. *The New York Times* reports that a growing number of teens are throwing digital caution to the wind, sharing their email, social media, and smartphone passwords with their significant others. As one high school senior who shares Facebook and email passwords with her boyfriend explained, "It's a sign of trust. I have nothing to hide from him, and he has nothing to hide from me." The problem with this decision, according to the *Times*, often begins when the young couples break up.

Need Information? Fill in the Blanks

The "automated open records law letter generator" (bit.ly/dtcwnu) is one of the most useful online resources for journalists seeking information through records requests. Created and maintained by the Student Press Law Center, the program takes the details you provide about the information you are looking to obtain and instantly produces a "complete, well-written request" that should increase your chances of acquiring the records without delay.

Find People

And find out more about people—and the places they live—through public records search engines and independent and government sites devoted to population trends.

SITE ALERT!

BRBPub.com (brbpub.com), "your portal to finding public records"

City-Data.com (city-data.com), "we've collected and analyzed data from numerous sources to create as complete and interesting profiles of all U.S. cities as we could"

Population Reference Bureau (prb.org), "provides timely and objective information on U.S. and international population trends and their implications"

SearchSystems.net (publicrecords.searchsystems.net), "the original free public records resource"

U.S. Census Bureau (census.gov), "the leading source of quality data about the nation's people and economy"

WhitePages (whitepages.com), "the world's largest and most trusted source for business and people search"

ZabaSearch (zabasearch.com), "free people search engine includes public records, whitepages, U.S. addresses, phone numbers, and more"

After Reading Stories Online, Keep Scrolling

Read the comments to determine what might have been left out of the main reports, other perspectives worth noting, general reactions, and even insights into the commenters themselves.

Bookmark Your Half-Baked Ideas

Spot a story with spin-off potential? Come across a site chock full of ideas you want to explore later? Drop into a discussion thread you know will come in handy soon? Bookmark them, and visit them again when you have more time. The key: Give the sites memorable names in your bookmarks folder so you will always remember what they are and why you saved them.

Check the Calendars

The calendars featured on the websites of many schools, organizations, teams, and communities often double as story stockpiles. Scan them, and stick a virtual pin in especially interesting upcoming events, special days, intriguing promos, and noticeably active or quiet periods.

Don't Overlook PR

While dismissed as the dark side by righteous journalists, online public relations and marketing vehicles at times boast stories with fantastic potential. Check out corporate, governmental, educational, activist, nonprofit, and personal politician and celebrity websites and affiliated social media. Look past the hype, instead concentrating on events, issues, and achievements worthy of the promotion they are receiving. Consider the sites and feeds as modern press releases. And if you truly smell phoniness or too much over-exaggeration, that is an idea and reporting angle all its own.

Monitor Market Research

OK, the survey methods may be a tad questionable and their desired aims may be disgustingly corporate. But there is a lot to love about the copious amount of corporate-sponsored studies—often known as market research—available online. While possibly not accurate to the percentage or decimal point, the research does provide snapshots into how people (consumers) are living, working, socializing—and enjoying (or not enjoying) various products, services, and habits along the way. If nothing else, the studies' content can be a story-starter—offering clues into what companies and fields are most interested in knowing about their existing or potential customer bases.

SITE ALERT!

 U.S. Commercial Service Market Research Library (export.gov/mrktresearch), "containing more than 100,000 industry and country-specific market reports" created by government-affiliated specialists

Focus on Money, Politics, and Power

A growing number of websites and organizations are tracking the details of government spending, salaries, campaign donations, and the financial influence of lobbyists. A few clicks and a semi-decent search reveal every last payout, contribution, investment, and eye-opening fiscal waste in some way impacting the country or your coverage area. Some sites also provide context and help you analyze this impact.

SITE ALERT!

 Federal Election Commission (fec.gov), "an independent regulatory agency . . . to enforce the provisions of the law such as the limits and prohibitions on contributions, and to oversee the public funding of presidential elections"

LegiStorm (legistorm.com), "a searchable database of U.S. congressional staff salaries"

MapLight (maplight.org), "illuminates the connection between campaign contributions and legislative votes in unprecedented ways"

OpenSecrets.org (opensecrets.org), "the most comprehensive resource for federal campaign contributions, lobbying data, and analysis available anywhere"

U.S. Government Accountability Office (gao.gov), "investigative arm of Congress charged with examining matters relating to the receipt and payment of public funds"

IDEAS, ONLINE

10 Sites Bursting with Ideas

Some websites are especially helpful when you are stuck without any ideas, dying for inspiration, on deadline or simply searching for fresh perspectives. This list is aimed at helping you discover and harness the storytelling potential of a few of these sites, including ones you know about but have never bothered to truly explore.

For a more thorough list and to nominate idea sites of your own, visit College Media Matters.

TED (ted.com), "Ideas worth spreading"

TED Talks are regularly updated videos of mini-lectures and group discussions led by some of the smartest, most successful, most creative, and quirkiest individuals on Earth.

The lecture videos provide fascinating pockets of knowledge touching on nearly every aspect of life as we know it and envision it to be. The talks are especially valuable because of the sources from which they spring. The individuals are often the figures most sought out for their takes on their areas of expertise or big news of the day.

On the website, you do not get a stock quote, a brief sider, or a single story. Instead, you are granted the chance to hear them speak candidly for an extended period of time about a topic about which they are immensely knowledgeable and passionate.

Ideas, and fresh perspectives, will quickly follow. In recent years, talks have touched on a range of topics aching for greater press attention. Some of the talk buzzwords, to give you a clue about their diversity: digital humanitarianism, the 100,000-student classroom, "over-medicalized," "Mathemagic," barefoot movement, filter bubbles, a patent troll, the $8 billion iPod, and something called the "cockroach beatbox."

A FEW SIMILAR SITES

The 99 Percent (the99percent.com), "insights on making ideas happen"

AtGoogleTalks (youtube.com/atgoogletalks), "hosts innovators, world leaders, authors, and more from around the world"

FORA.tv (fora.tv), "the web's largest collection of conference and event videos"

Wonderopolis (wonderopolis.org), "a digital platform for learning, awe, and wonder"

Reddit (reddit.com), "the front page of the Internet"

Arguably the web's ultimate social news experience, Reddit is a tremendously valuable platform to gain a sense of what people are interested in, talking about, and hungry to share.

Some of the stories and content are light on perceived news value, tough to follow, vulgar, biased, and purposefully silly. But it is in many respects the voice of the people—the downtime, dinnertime, barstool, and waiting room chatter.

A headline sampling of the types of content featured at any given time: "The people of Anaheim just stormed a police station"; "Scientists have bioengineered a swimming 'Jellyfish' out of rat heart and polymer"; "Non-Americans: What is the most shocking thing you saw when visiting the United

States?"; "I enjoy driving barefoot. What are your simple pleasures?"; and "Today I was leaving my apartment and heard the guy that lives under me whisper, 'Wow he's actually going out.' What things have you heard people whisper that make you feel pathetic?"

With some scanning and efficient searching, you can regularly corner conversations and breaking news pertinent to your beat. You can also simply make sure you keep up with everyone else.

Finding and utilizing Reddit content is one of the web's most popular activities. Who does it? "Literally everyone does," one online writer confirms. "*Literally everyone.* The Pope shares popular things he sees on Reddit. At any given moment, the most popular thing on Gawker is a post from Reddit or a similar viral site."

A FEW SIMILAR SITES

4Chan (4chan.org), "the largest English imageboard on the web"

9GAG (9gag.com), "the best place where fun creators and bored people meet"

BuzzFeed (buzzfeed.com), "the hottest, most social content on the web"

Delicious (delicious.com), "the world's leading social bookmarking service"

Digg (digg.com), "a place for people to discover and share content from anywhere on the web"

Internet Archive (archive.org), "Universal access to all knowledge"

The world's ultimate digital library contains millions of audio and video recordings, books, other text documents, and software. It is all easily accessible and free. Those collections play second fiddle though to the Internet Archive's most famous invention: the Wayback Machine, a portal transporting users to previous versions of nearly every website.

The site snapshots—at times boasting working links—offer the most complete picture of the Internet. They also contain a ton of potential story ideas. They reveal what sites once looked like, featured, and left out. They might provide a way to get at something people now want hidden. And they may be able to let you see what a webpage looked like on an especially historic day.

To this end, the Internet Archive's special collections also present glimpses at webpages during major events in the Internet age such as the September 11 attacks, Hurricane Katrina, and the transition between the administrations of Presidents George W. Bush and Barack Obama.

The Onion (theonion.com), "America's finest news source"

Satire and straightforward humor are incredibly powerful tools to comment upon current events and at times boil complex issues to their most basic, human level. Online, *The Onion* is an unequivocal leader in both the satire and humor camps.

Its power is built atop staffers' innate ability to recognize absurdities, find the punchline of every serious situation, and publish what we are all thinking but lack the nerve to say.

For example, some headlines published atop online stories last year: "Report: Every Potential 2040 President Already Unelectable Due To Facebook"; "New Study Finds Americans Need 6 Hours Of Sleep At Work"; "Study: Red Meat Takes Years Off Of Cow's Life"; "Commanding General In Afghanistan Has No Idea How War Is Going, Just Trying To Ignore It At This Point"; and "This Article Generating Thousands Of Dollars In Ad Revenue Simply By Mentioning New iPad."

Along with your mainstream, serious-minded daily press checks, occasionally peel back the *Onion* for a different perspective on news of the day and a satirical push toward a possible serious idea.

A FEW SIMILAR SITES

CollegeHumor (collegehumor.com), "funny videos, funny pictures, funny links!"

Cracked (cracked.com), "a funny website filled with funny videos, pics, articles, and a whole bunch of other funny stuff"

Fark (fark.com), "satirical views on interesting, bizarre, and amusing stories, submitted by a community of millions of news junkies"

Funny or Die (funnyordie.com), "funny videos, funny pictures, and funny jokes"

I Can Has Cheezburger (icanhascheezburger.com), "the home of lol cats and lol* (other animals)"

Urban Dictionary (urbandictionary.com), "a veritable cornucopia of streetwise lingo"

As the web's most popular spot for user-submitted slang, Urban Dictionary is a valuable entryway toward understanding what people are excitedly adding to the cultural conversation.

Yes, the entries are opinionated and anonymous—and some are simply incoherent, vulgar, or cliché. But many of the words, phrases, acronyms, and definitions are ripe for contemplation, a quick reaction story, or a full feature report.

The entries often hint at a new online or youth-oriented phenomenon or build off a breaking news event or larger societal shift. For example, a sampling of terms in summer 2012: Olympic Adoption ("the act of changing which country you root for in the Olympics, usually done when your home country's team is terrible"); Chick-fil-Atheist ("a person who loves Chick-fil-A, but not God, and is therefore pissed that Chick-fil-A is closed on Sundays"); Mittconception ("a fundamental belief of Mitt Romney's, based on mistaken understanding of an issue"); and Ann Curry'd ("fired without merit or reason").

The site also sports a growing number of definitions for colleges and universities—some attempting to capture the schools' main thrusts and others simply venting. The nastiest ones, in many ways, are the most intriguing. They cut through the PR muck of school mission statements to reveal a number of potentially newsworthy items: a university's actual underbelly; what everyone takes for granted as true but might possibly be false; how the school is perceived, for better or worse; and the things everyone experiences daily but haven't reflected upon in a while.

A FEW SIMILAR SITES

Banished Words List, Lake Superior State University (lssu.edu/banished)

Word Spy (wordspy.com), "the word lover's guide to new words"

Words of the Year, American Dialect Society (americandialect.org/woty)

Change.org (change.org), "Start, join, and win campaigns for change"

It has become a hub for anger, righteousness, activism, occasional lunacy, outright vengeance, character assassinations, publicity stunts, sheer entertainment, and rampant idealism.

Change.org, known informally as online petition central, has caught on surprisingly strongly since its start. It often serves as the first and most visible point of protest for many perceived and actual wrongs. The site's creators hold it up as "the web's leading platform for social change, empowering anyone, anywhere to start petitions that make a difference."

The signatures and subsequent press attention at times change minds, decisions, or behavior. Mostly though, it is simply a way to vent, raise a point, and bring a tiny bit of notice to a cause.

A sampling of petition titles: "Speak Out Against Walmart's Cruelty to Pigs"; "State of Ohio: Strengthen the Domestic Violence Law"; "Teen Vogue: Give Us Images of Real Girls!" "Jamba Juice: Stop Using Styrofoam Cups that Kill Animals!"; and "Demand Facebook Remove Pages That Promote Sexual Violence."

Monitoring Change.org is a unique way to keep abreast of what is stirring emotions or is abuzz among the online masses or individuals in your coverage area. Potential stories abound within the most-signed, least-signed, and quirkier petitions. It is also a springboard to a more general look at activism trends.

Kickstarter (kickstarter.com), "Fund and follow creativity"

The crowdfunding website Kickstarter helps people finance their passions, inventions, hobbies, and causes. As its motto states, "Fund and follow creativity."

Your task: Adhere to the second part. Follow the latest, most popular, quirkiest, and most controversial projects gaining money and momentum.

The projects seeking public generosity are varied—from a sixth-grader's science fair experiment and a couple's plan to sell their homemade hot sauce nationwide to a voice-activated computer and a photography book featuring more than 150 LGBTQ high school student-athletes.

Check to see how, and how often, projects like these and many others are funded and eventually come to fruition. Determine the larger trends you see embedded in what people are begging others to help them get off the ground. Separately, pitch a project yourself. Or use the site as a leaping point for a more general exploration of independent creative endeavors—from a student's graphic novel to a popular local street artist.

A FEW SIMILAR SITES

 CharityWatch (charitywatch.org), "the independent, assertive charity watchdog that you rely on"

Foundation Center (foundationcenter.org), "the leading source of information about philanthropy worldwide"

Indiegogo (indiegogo.com), "the world's funding platform"

Kiva (kiva.org), "loans that change lives"

TaskRabbit (taskrabbit.com), "Task and errand service by awesome, trustworthy people"

Need someone to buy and deliver groceries to your front door? Need a planner or host for a catered party? Need help assembling furniture you bought at Ikea? For all these things and more, try TaskRabbit.

The online start-up earning tech industry buzz provides people with a platform to ask others to do something for them. From the beginning, its founder Leah Busque envisioned it as "a site where you could name the price you were willing to pay for any task."

As TaskRabbit's tagline similarly states, "Get pretty much anything done by awesome people." The site employs a bidding system aimed at finding the perfect price point for each niche job— typically a happy medium between the maximum someone is willing to spend for a task and the minimum someone is willing to be paid to complete it. To this end, a *Wired* feature calls it "an eBay for real-world labor."

The site is still small in scope, operating at present within a sampling of major U.S. cities. But it plans to expand quickly, leading an ABC News story headline to proclaim, "TaskRabbit: Putting Americans Back to Work, One Odd Job at a Time."

A few examples of the odd jobs featured, along with their opening price estimates: "2 loads of laundry, drop off dry cleaning" ($29–$41); "Pick up my dog's Heartgard medication" ($11–$17); "Someone needed to paint white a picket fence with 2 gates" ($70–$96); "Lead a Yoga group in office" ($42–$58); and "Unfollow uninteresting Twitter accounts" ($28–$38).

Its basic premise and burgeoning success address the questions: What are people most interested in having other people do for them? And what are people willing to do for others in their spare time, while out of work, or to build their personal brands?

For stories, link the site to trends within the service economy, entrepreneurialism, the virtual workforce, the recession, and the many common and quirky skillsets and knowledge bases ordinary people possess.

A FEW SIMILAR SITES

Gigwalk (gigwalk.com), "Instantly mobilize people to do work anywhere"

Skillshare (skillshare.com), "Learn anything from anyone, anywhere"

Wordle (wordle.net), "Beautiful word clouds"

Sometimes words, rearranged or reimagined, reveal compelling insights not visible when they are in their regular form. Wordle helps you carry out this rearranging and reimagining.

It takes words delivered in speeches, songs, research, historical and leaked documents, mission statements, and much more, presenting them as word clouds. It highlights the words appearing most often. And it shows the words out of order, independent of the ones they are aligned with in the original texts. While appearing at first like gobbledygook, the mess can actually crystallize a text's theme. It is a different method of uncovering buzzwords that are especially stressed, under-stressed, or missing entirely.

It can also be a unique way to bring words together, revealing any repetition or trends—the names of classes, the titles of current viral videos, the names of perfume fragrances, the first names of all freshmen students, the words embedded in all crime reports throughout the semester, tweet responses to a major debate, and the job titles of faculty and staff at your school.

A FEW SIMILAR SITES

Tagul (tagul.com), "Gorgeous tag clouds"

Tagxedo (tagxedo.com), "Word cloud with styles"

WordSift (wordsift.com), "Visualize text"

We Feel Fine (wefeelfine.org), "an exploration of human emotion"

We Feel Fine is by far the world's largest online database of human emotion. Using a unique automated search that involves scanning blogs, micro-blogs, and social networks for the phrase "I feel" or "I am feeling," it presents millions of sentiments about how people are feeling about numerous things at any given moment.

The results reveal people's feelings toward their faith, weight, relationships, jobs, politics, holidays, and news of the day. There are 15,000 to 20,000 feelings added each day, all of them organized by demographics such as age, gender, location, and even the weather at that location when the related blog post appeared.

These demographics are searchable, offering users the fascinatingly powerful potential to gauge what certain types of people in certain places are publicly feeling at certain times. The links are also available to the blogs themselves, offering the opportunity to read all related posts in their entirety and contact the writers firsthand.

GO MOBILE

Starter Tips for Your Smartphone Storytelling Adventure

The two-word journalism mantra of the moment: Go mobile.

With most mobile—and tablet—devices, you can capture, edit, and instantly upload photos, video, and audio. You can take notes, tweet, livestream, blog, and write and post full stories. You can contact and interview sources on the fly. You can search for information online and monitor real-time social media chatter. You can crowdsource. You can access many primary documents. You can track down the locations of people, places, and events. You can keep a schedule of interviews and a contacts list of sources. You can create voice memos right after an interview or when inspiration strikes. You can utilize a flashlight app to help you report in the dark.

You can also brainstorm and discover a ton of stories.

To jumpstart your smartphone storytelling adventure, here is a quick-hit list of ideas for the mobile journalist—based on the built-in tools, available apps, and general mobile culture. Unlike the many guides focused on *how* to practice journalism using a mobile apparatus, this list shows you *what* journalism you can produce on your phone better, faster, and more conveniently than any other device.

Shoot Photos the Mobile Way

Embrace your phone's omnipresence, instant capture-and-share abilities, and invisibility. Pull it out, anywhere, everywhere, all the time, around anyone, and snap, snap, snap, share, share, share. With a smartphone as your photographic device, you have a chance to capture life as it really happens. "Like many photojournalists, I've been shooting with my iPhone for a while," Michael Christopher Brown wrote last summer for *Time*. "Using a mobile phone allows me to be somewhat invisible as a professional photographer; people see me as just another person in the crowd."

Embrace Instagram

Take advantage of the image app's "compulsively easy" sharing. Provide a running visual blueprint of where you are and what you are up to while reporting, establishing a more personal connection with your audience. Also, utilize its image-filtering options. They may seem like huge red flags, direct affronts to journalism tenets of honesty and accuracy. But, from the right perspective, the alterations can be perfectly valid, even innovative, storytelling prisms.

The adjustments capture a mood, a person's motivation, a visual theme or framework of sorts, and an artistic purpose. For example, they might provide a clue as to how a depressed or bipolar student sees the world or a surrealist review of how students experienced orientation weekend or a popular campus event.

Separately, harness the app's community angle, geotagging capabilities, and increasingly massive inventory of images to see what people in your coverage area or near a major news event are doing, seeing, and snapping.

Example

The Daily Emerald invented and runs InstaO, a real-time web application that collects and shares all Instagram photos taken on or near the University of Oregon campus. The visual photo stream (dailyemerald.com/instagram-eugene-uo) is a quirky glance at what Oregon students and Eugene, Ore., residents and visitors are shooting, altering, and posting for public consumption.

Start Scanning

Through apps such as 5–0 Radio Police Scanner and Scanner911 Police Radio, tune in to real-time law enforcement chatter in your coverage area or at the spot of a high-profile incident like a school shooting or raging hurricane. Once you learn the lingo and codes, listen, really listen. Pick up on the most repeated or odd incidents being discussed. Grab scoops about out-of-the-blue busts and emergencies. And ask police later about snippets not fully audible or understandable, possibly gleaning a significant story that otherwise would not have been shared.

Scan Another Way

Utilize apps like TurboScan to immediately scan, upload, print, and share all types of documents, signs, posters, business cards, and even whiteboard messages. According to a leading digital magazine, "It's like carrying a copy machine in your pocket."

Dive Into the Livestream

Through apps such as Qik, capture and share real-time video of newsworthy events and personal interviews. Enable your entire campus to attend student government meetings, as they happen. Record a full class led by a professor who is being profiled for his eccentric teaching style. Share the goings-on of tailgaters or workers on the edges of a major sporting event, while the event itself is going on. Stage and stream your own event, bringing together students to reflect on a milestone moment or newsworthy issue.

Augment Reality

Through apps such as acrossair, immediately learn about the places you pass by, including area amenities, GPS locations, related Wikipedia entries, and local photos and tweets. These digital extras may provide ideas you cannot see with your own eyes, including scoops on upcoming events, the online buzz about a hyperlocal controversy, or the skinny on the sordid history of a site you see is now closed. Location-based entertainment apps such as Yelp and social networking apps such as Foursquare offer similar augmented info.

Listen Up, and Start Talking

Through apps such as Audioboo and SoundCloud, record and share newsworthy audio. Focus on capturing raw clips from interviews, speeches, conference calls, and classes. Put together more polished packages such as podcast chats and full audio news reports. And utilize the related audio communities. Check out and search for news within the recordings posted by people in your coverage area or the location in which big news is occurring.

Take Notes

Use the phone as your ultimate unpublished idea inventory. When an idea strikes, jot it down via an app like Evernote. When you pass by an interesting sign, major car crash, or random protest march, snap and send yourself a few photos. When you meet a source bubbling over with newsworthy scoops, input their contact information. When a big interview concludes, sit alone for a moment and talk to yourself, recording your initial thoughts and related ideas—you can even have it transcribed and emailed to you via an audio-to-text app like Vlingo. When a friend mentions a hot new website at lunch, call it up and bookmark it on your mobile web browser for later inspection.

Don't Forget the Phone

Focus on the device itself and its endless fads, apps, technological breakthroughs, and cultural touchstones. Outline the many facets of mobile's integration into our academic, professional, social, political, economic, and love lives. Determine how and where the phones are made. Examine how and where mobile service grids are built and maintained. And investigate how our mobile data is handled, monitored, accessed, and used for and against us.

STORY PLANNING 2.0

Including Digital Options in Every Brainstorming Session

Within mobile and digital media, *how* you tell stories becomes an idea all its own.

Nowadays, all stories have multimedia potential. It is imperative you recognize this potential and unleash it within your own reporting.

To that end, utilize the following graphic as your story planner 2.0—prompting you to consider everything from guiding questions, source suggestions, and data to analyze to crowdsourcing, geotagging, and search engine optimization.

Try it out for a story currently in the brainstorming or initial discovery stage.

Graphic by Mike Trobiano and Brooke Scherer

IDEAS, ONLINE

In Package Form

Standalone text stories are *so* twentieth century. The most powerful, comprehensive storytelling within journalism today comes in package form. Whether created in advance or spur-of-the-moment on deadline, the multimedia and sometimes multi-platform news package contains an array of text, visual, audio, and interactive elements. When done right, they add up to a rich user experience and a full-bore dig into a newsworthy topic deeper than any has gone before.

Here are three examples of standout multimedia news packages created by students—at times with some "adult" supervision or coordination.

North by Northwestern, Dance Marathon

Each March, the online student newsmagazine *North by Northwestern* (northbynorthwestern.com) creates a special site to cover Northwestern University's über-popular Dance Marathon, a 30-hour philanthropy party

Updated throughout the event, it features photos, videos, blog posts, tweets, and crowdsourced responses from the student dancers. In 2012, *NBN* also updated a playable list of the featured music and even tracked one student's heart rate while dancing and another student's calorie intake during the marathon.

In addition, throughout the event, staffers polled participants on whether they would rather engage in sexual activity or grab a shower, publishing the results each time right away in a pie chart. (Deeper and deeper into the dancing, the shower option apparently began to seem most appealing.)

The outlet also published one student dancer's haiku poetry, penned during breaks in the action. As one of them read: "Dancers sway, eyes shut. / Literally two girls snore / While they booty shake."

"DM provides us with an opportunity to do what we do best," said Nolan Feeney, *NBN*'s top editor at the time. "We are able to be there the whole weekend and find ways to tell stories that we couldn't necessarily do with a traditional news format. It also allows us to show off our personality and our voice. *The Daily Northwestern* is a great paper, but I don't think they would be asking Dance Marathon students whether they would rather have sex or a shower four times that day."

University of Miami, "Prescribing Addiction"

Leah is a recovering drug addict in her early twenties who lives alone in a sparse Florida apartment. She calls it "my little kingdom, not a very nice kingdom, but it's mine."

She signed the lease and made the move from her hometown in the northern U.S. to escape a past life loaded with drugs—marijuana, alcohol, acid, ecstasy, cocaine, and, most prominently, pills such as Xanax, OxyContin, and Percocet. "Once I discovered the pills," she said, "everything else was downhill."

Leah is one of the individuals featured in "Prescribing Addiction" (prescribingaddiction.com), a multimedia project published in fall 2011 by University of Miami interactive storytelling students. For the project, a team of designers, coders, and videographers put together a fairly comprehensive report on young adults' battles with prescription medication addiction—without relying upon a single text-based story.

Instead, the special site features video profiles of current and recovering teen and twenty-something addicts. Students also created a set of interactive graphics, including a breakdown of the most common prescription medicine abused. A click on each pill bottle reveals the drug's brand and street names, medical and recreational uses, side effects, and the methods by which they are taken.

A separate "Ask the Expert" graphic allow users to scroll through and select questions for a trio of people "knowledgeable about pill abuse" including a nurse and narcotics officer. Their answers are then provided in brief videos.

News21, "How Safe is Your Food?"

In summer 2011, a team of students from four universities nationwide, mentored by top journalism faculty and professionals, focused on food safety. The 10-week investigative reporting project (foodsafety.news21.com), part of the vaunted News21 initiative headquartered at Arizona State University, uncovered an array of unappetizing truths about foodborne illness, contamination risks, and the lack of food inspections throughout the U.S.

The report earned awards, international attention, and republication in a host of local, regional, and national news outlets. Among the many standout multimedia elements: "Farm to Fork," an interactive graphic outlining each step of the process that brings food such as chicken, cheese, shrimp, and eggs from its initial harvesting or production to our plates. A separate scroll-through graphic offers a state-by-state breakdown of required health department responses to 20 food-related diseases, including Salmonella, Hepatitis A, and Botulism.

CHAPTER 18

Journalism Hackathon

Illustration by Yee Hung Lim

Ready to hack?

Congratulations. If you made it to this page, you have mastered the initial story brainstorming and discovery phase. Your ultimate assignment: the journalism hackathon; a closed-door, extended, hands-on brainstorming session extraordinaire.

It is built atop a modern Silicon Valley invention. As *Wired* notes, hackathons are "[r]elentless programming sessions fueled by hope and coffee. Usually days long, hackathons bring together Silicon Valley's brightest and most sleep-deprived as they attempt to grind out software (and companies based on it)."

■ By comparison, this hackathon is focused on stories, not software. It is a step back from the daily reporting grind, a refueling of your creative energies, and a chance to focus solely on ideas, ideas, ideas.

Working solo or with a small group, a full class, or your news outlet's staff, you will dream up, adapt, flesh out, localize, plan, ponder, and collaborate on tons of potential stories.

The simple, singular goal: come up with as many quality ideas as possible.

PREP WORK

To stage a quality journalism hackathon, you must hold it in the right place, at the right time, and for the right amount of time. You also need to have the right tools and online resources at your disposal. Here are a few planning suggestions to get you started.

Setting

Feel free to stake out almost any area that is multimedia-friendly, food-friendly, and private enough to accommodate occasional shouting, quiet interviews, and stacks of newspapers and pizza boxes. Past journalism hackathons have been held in classrooms, decent-sized newsrooms, a library study room, a residence hall suite, and the corner of a student center lounge.

Timing

Set aside at least a few hours, possibly a full night, or even an entire weekend. Agree upon the general timeframe in advance. Don't cut it too short. The hackathon should feel like a mini-retreat and an experience worth preparing for and diving into full throttle.

Tools

Bring snack food, pens, notebooks, Wi-Fi-enabled laptops and smartphones, and a copy of every issue of your school's student newspaper published over the past two years and from random years before that (as far back as you can grab). Also round up old student yearbooks, recent issues of local newspapers, and student newspapers from other schools. In addition, create a folder on your laptop filled with photos you took the day before of flyers and posters hung around campus, chalked-up campus sidewalks, and random graffiti on walls and bathroom stalls.

To up the socializing component, ask all participants to arrive with a white elephant gift (a purposefully cheap, tacky item). Warn them though: Along with being exchanged, these gifts will also be idea fodder. Keep reading for an explanation.

Online Resources

Prior to the hackathon's start, open your school's website, Facebook, Google, Google+, Google News, Skype, and Twitter on your laptop. Also, load the websites of roughly 30 student newspapers, including some operating at schools nearby and others that are highly acclaimed nationwide.

OK, LET'S HACK

Sit and Talk

At the start, along with any needed introductions, simply talk a bit about what's been going on in your own classes, what friends have been saying about campus life, what you have recently overheard faculty members discussing, what people are posting on Facebook, reposting on Tumblr, and pinning on Pinterest. Jot down ideas as they come. Embrace the chaos, including people talking over each other, odd tangents, and angry riffs.

Play with Words

To continue warming up, indulge in a rapid-fire version of the Brainstorm Something game. (See Chapter 5, "Words, Letters, and Lots of Ideas," for the full version.) First, have everyone shout out a few words, acronyms, and phrases—maybe those tied to your campus, embedded within news of the day, or sporting especially quirky definitions. Subsequently, brainstorm, conduct Google News searches, and search student newspaper website archives to conceive of related ideas both straightforward and bizarre. If you are having trouble getting started, use the following 10 words as triggers:

- Prank
- Hocus-Pocus
- Drama
- #EpicFail
- Nuclear
- Oil Spill
- YOLO

- Founder
- Bibliobibuli (individuals who read too much)
- Yahoo (both the website and the country bumpkin)

Flip Through the Papers

Start by looking closely at the old copies of your own campus newspaper. Scrutinize every story, searching for pieces that deserve a direct update, a full spin-off, or a complete do-over. A few examples: how Homecoming has changed, what former student-athlete stars are doing now, how the family of a dead student is coping years later, and a then-and-now comparison of dining options. Pay close attention to opinion pieces to gain a sense of what issues and events spurred especially impassioned debate during past years. What is their status now?

In addition, check out the advertisements to see what businesses, restaurants, products, and services used to be popular—or at least were trying to be popular—among students. Also, find ads touching on wars, racial and religious issues, lifestyles, and leisure activities that would be considered controversial or out of place today.

Think no treasures exist within old campus newspaper ads? Last spring, *The Daily Collegian* business staff at Penn State University stumbled across a pair of adjoining promos in a September 1975 issue that brought oral sex, sharks, Steven Spielberg, and pornography together for probably the first and last time.

As a post on a *Collegian* blog confirmed, "The now-defunct Garden Theatre placed advertise-ments for a screening of the new movie 'Jaws' . . . or were you more interested in the ad for 'Deep Throat?' According to our beloved business advisor, Candy Heckard, the porno screening ads ran through the late 1980s." The paper labeled the random juxtaposition as "Rated X for eXtraordinary Coincidence."

Page Through the Yearbooks

Examine the yearbooks you scooped up, searching for similarly extraordinary finds. Pay especially close attention to featured photos. Some potentially pertinent details: the old campus infrastructure, student fashions, featured activities and sports that are now defunct, current faculty who previously attended the school as students, and featured students who are now famous alumni.

Look at Pictures

Check out the campus photos you and your colleagues snapped the day before. Brainstorm stories that pop out of the pictured chalk marks, graffiti, flyers, and posters. Focus on the events and social issues they are promoting, the groups promoting them, individuals and organizations who might line up as opponents, and any larger trends or cultural shifts they represent.

Turn to the Outside Press

Scroll through the websites and back issues of other college newspapers. Also, dive into any local newspapers you brought to the hackathon. Pinpoint at least a few stories that can be localized or storytelling methods that can be replicated.

Give Some Gifts

Exchange and unwrap the barrage of tacky gifts that participants are eager to give away, oohing and aahing with mock sincerity. Then, get to work. Brainstorm quirky and newsworthy ideas for every white elephant in the room. Similar to The Story Ideas Sack exercise in Chapter 4, "Fresh Perspectives," build your ideas off each item's name, appearance, age, intended and unintended uses, cultural significance, and simply the first things that come to mind when it is flashed before your eyes.

Have Some Guests Over

Invite special guests affiliated with your school to stop by in person or join the hackathon via Skype or a Google+ hangout. Interview them briefly about what they do, what is happening within their office or organization, and what stories they feel should be covered or covered more often by the campus and local press.

Some suggestions on who to invite: the public information director, athletic director, dean of students, student government president, Greek life coordinator, campus safety director, the head of the alumni association, and an officer in the commuter student club. Also, convince random students and staffers walking by to briefly join the fun. Talk to them about their campus experiences and ask them what stories they would like to see published.

Brainstorm in the Moment

Think about ideas happening on and off campus *now*. Check local and national news websites, Twitter, and Google News during the hackathon. See what might be worth localizing, adapting, or following up on in a few minutes, hours or days.

Just Browse for a Bit

Set aside a few minutes for seemingly aimless web browsing. The twist: Promise prizes for participants who find the strongest ideas on the strangest non-news sites. If you need more direction than that, send everyone to Pinterest, pushing them to generate ideas based on the popular products, pictures, and pinboards.

Turn to Your School Site

Call up and explore a slew of pages, including the course catalog, student demographics breakdown, events calendar, the main sports hub, the clubs and activities page, the campus safety page linking to the most recent annual security report, and the study abroad page featuring a listing of locations where students travel, volunteer, and intern.

SOME OTHER SUGGESTIONS

Put on background music, to stimulate creativity or simply avoid eerie silences.

Collect and upload all ideas to some sort of list. Students in past hackathons have contributed to an open Google doc.

Brainstorm multimedia ideas along with the basic story ideas, including online photo slideshows, video reports, and real-time reporting projects.

Hold a recap presentation at the end. Possibly stage it as a lighthearted contest involving participants speed-pitching their best ideas. Have a top editor, professional journalist, or journalism professor select some winners.

As *Wired* notes about the Silicon Valley hackathons, "These idea-generating marathons double as competitions, and the victor with the best proposal stands a chance of nabbing fame, fortune, and immortality. Or at least a little bit of venture capital."

In this case, consider giving the winners a chance to write stories based on their ideas for possible pick-up by a campus, local, or online outlet. In addition, if you have the funds, give them candy, a gift certificate to the school bookstore, or a free pizza sporting any toppings they'd like.

Let the public in on at least some of the action. Blog or tweet the more promising ideas being brainstormed, in part to grab instant feedback from readers that might include suggestions on other angles, sources, or spin-off stories.

Email me. I'll gladly feature your efforts on College Media Matters. To that end, take photos and shoot video of the hackathon. If you stage it correctly, it will be an experience you will want to remember and boast about on Facebook.

ASSIGNMENT ALERT!

100 Ideas in 15 Minutes

If you do not have the time, ambition, or willing accomplices to stage a full hackathon, follow the Lori Brooks 15-minute plan.

At a few national college media conferences each year, Brooks, the associate executive director of the College Media Association (CMA), presents students with more than 100 story ideas she says she brainstorms beforehand in less than 15 minutes.

Below are 20 of the 101 ideas Brooks pitched in spring 2011 to a packed hall of journalism students attending New York City's CMA convention. The general prompts are aimed at inspiring students to come up with related stories focused on their own campuses. As she shared at the time, "Coming up with story ideas is easy . . . Getting a good angle, finding sources and a strong writer? That's the hard part."

- Odd classes
- Online classes
- Capstone classes
- Blow-off vs. hard classes
- Other ways to get credit
- Study habits/locations/quirks
- Cheating/plagiarism
- Book buying/selling
- Visiting professors
- Alums returning as faculty/staff
- Day in the life: quarterback, student government president, commuter, etc.
- Building names
- Strange student organizations
- High school vs. college (what was cool then, but not now)
- Student-athlete superstitions
- Sports tailgating
- Man (woman?) behind mascot
- Intramural sports
- Drinking games
- Students who . . . play in bands, create art, run websites, shoot photos, follow celebrities, or spend money on cars, shoes, or swords

Your Assignment

Carry out a Brooks-inspired brainstorming speed session of your own. Start the countdown at 15 minutes. Work alone or with a friend. Conceive and jot down as many ideas as possible in quick-hit, stream-of-consciousness style.

Then, consider diving into what Brooks labeled the hard part. Pick a few of the most promising ideas and give them an additional 15 minutes of fame. Brainstorm possible news hooks, related sources to interview and observe, significant facts to ferret out, and a few interactive and multimedia elements to capture or create.

IN OTHER WORDS

"Practice brainstorming story ideas until they practically pour out—until you can come up with 10 fantastic ideas on any given topic on any given day, no matter how seemingly boring the prompt. The more you do it, the better you get at it."

Jackie Burrell, food editor,
Bay Area News Group, Calif.

Illustration by Yee Hung Lim

THREE STAGES OF STORY DEVELOPMENT

Once the ideas pour out of you, you still need to develop them.

According to Sonny Albarado, projects editor at the *Arkansas Democrat-Gazette*, "The keys to a quality news project: Planning, Planning, Planning." In conjunction with Mike Roberts, a trainer and consultant for news organizations across North America, Albarado offers advice on successful planning for the three most important project stages: brainstorming, reporting, and writing.

The Brainstorming Stage

Story Mapping

Map the story idea as a web of interlocking or connected circles, laying out all aspects of the idea. Select the most important part of the "map" as the focus of the story and the reporting to come.

Central Questions

Identify the central question at the heart of your idea. Then set out to answer it.

Premise

Frame your idea as a premise, not a fact, and set out to prove or disprove the hypothesis. Remain open-minded. We repeat, remain open-minded.

Point of View

Write your topic, question, and premise in the middle of a circle. Around the circle, list all the people with a connection to the story idea. Decide which person's point of view might be the best way to report and tell the story.

Reader POV

Ask five questions a reader would ask about the topic. Set out to answer them.

Why x 5?

Ask "why" five times. Each "why" should take you deeper into the topic and closer to the central question or premise.

The Reporting Stage

Involve Your Editor

If you didn't do so in the idea stage, talk through your focused idea with your editor or faculty adviser. Be open to their questions or skepticism; that's their job.

Draft a Project Proposal

The surest way to get buy-in from an editor is to present a detailed, written reporting plan. This can be done before you do any reporting or after you have done some preliminary legwork.

What's in a project proposal? A two-sentence thesis that expresses the single most important idea the story should convey to the reader. Then, brief descriptions of how the story will meet **the High Five standards: News, Impact, Context, Edge, and Scope**.

Revisit the Proposal

Go back to the written proposal periodically and revise it to reflect changes forced by the facts uncovered in the reporting.

Involve Other Players . . . Early and Often

Make sure you and your editor meet with the photo editor, the graphics chief, and the online editor so they know what you're working on and can be prepared for the eventual art assignments and online tie-ins. Do this early enough and the photo editor may decide to assign a photographer to the project right then. But the main purpose is to give the folks who think visually and in online terms a chance to offer their own ideas for enhancing the project. Meet with them often enough, and the path from idea to published project will be a lot smoother. Don't forget to include a page designer in meetings when you're closer to publication.

The Writing Stage

Story Re-Mapping

Re-map the story with all the knowledge gained through your reporting. If you are telling the story through a specific point of view, re-map the story with the selected point of view at the center.

Outline the Story

List key points in the order they will appear in the story. Keep focus, length, and packaging in mind.

Revisit Your Thesis Statement

The key question to ask: Is the central point of the story the same now as when you started? Use the theme statement to help decide what material stays in the story and what is left out.

Select a Story Form

The last question to ask yourself prior to writing your heart out: Is the story best told in the inverted pyramid, block, wine glass, or layer-cake form?

CHAPTER 19
Field Notes

Illustration by Yee Hung Lim

Stories Ripe for Adaptation and Inspiration

"I don't think you can learn to be a good journalist from inside a classroom. You have to get out and experience the challenges in real-time and real-life situations—developing solid story ideas, interviewing reluctant sources, sorting through reams of information and, finally, writing a coherent story under deadline pressure. Every story is a different experience that can't be replicated in a classroom."

Robert Radziewicz, faculty adviser,
The Miami Hurricane, University of Miami

You have hit the journalism of ideas jackpot.

You have unlocked the storytelling treasure chest. You have unearthed the brainstorming goldmine. You are finally cashing in on your reporting credit card rewards.

A flip through the pages that follow will reveal tons of story ideas ripe for adaptation, regardless of where in the world you are covering and the amount of journalism experience you have so far.

Almost every featured idea is directly connected to stories recently published by student press outlets across the U.S., Canada, and in parts of Europe and Asia. So along with a jackpot, a treasure chest, a goldmine, and a big reward, think of this section as the ultimate guide for peer-to-peer content sharing among student journalists worldwide. Or put another way, this is the first major chunk of a journalism textbook in which students play a huge role in teaching themselves.

■ The ideas fall within every essential and popular reporting beat worth mastering—on and off campus. All of them come with assignment prompts to help you get started on related stories of your own. Also, keep an eye out for new media advice, immersion journalism possibilities, ethical issues to think about, clichés to avoid, and spin-off and more offbeat stories to consider exploring when you have the time and the courage.

OK, now a teaser. Among the buzzwords you will come across in this chapter: traumarama, worldsuck, sleep texting, dubstep, SlutWalk, battlegaming, bed bugs, Arab Spring, rat rods, sugar babies, superfans, Adderall, drunkorexia, YOLO, trashion fashion, tightrope walkers, two-ply toilet paper, voluntary amputation, and He-Who-Must-Not-Be-Named.

At the end of the chapter, there is even an idea involving a guy who licks shoes. I am not joking.

Let's start with an oversized somersaulting wolf.

"THE MAGIC OF BEING A MASCOT"

He is nearly seven feet tall. He has wool paws and a massively oversized head. He grooves to Michael Jackson's "Thriller" to entertain the crowds at major sporting events. He is Wolfie, the mascot for Stony Brook University athletics and the star of an engaging profile published in *The Statesman*, SBU's student newspaper.

"The Magic of Being a Mascot" is a behind-the-mask glimpse of everything involved in one student's Wolfie experience—from the "dancing, chest pounding, [and] somersault-rolling" to the larger notion of "what it means to hold 25,000 students in the palm of his paw, to be the representative of an entire university."

Your Assignment

Profile your own school's mascot. Interview and observe the student who currently embodies the character. Chronicle how the student was selected, their practice routine, costume preparation, performance rigors, and the deeper identity issues of being a beloved icon one moment and an anonymous undergraduate the next. Reveal the external mascot mechanisms, including related marketing, athletic department oversight, and university logistics. Talk to alumni who formerly strutted and cheered in costume. And provide a graphic showing the mascot's evolution over time.

NEW MEDIA ALERT!

Shoot a how-to video with a student getting in and out of costume or practicing a popular dance. Run a fun photo slideshow featuring the mascot interacting with fans on campus or in the nearby community. If student sentiment is just so-so on the current mascot, hold an online contest asking students and staff to brainstorm a new one, including desired name, creature type, and clothing choices.

IMMERSION ALERT!

Walk a mile in the mascot's suit for a first-person piece. See from the insider's perspective what it is like to operate in a heavy, oversized costume and play a silent character, along with how the public responds to your presence.

A PURE GARBAGE REPORT

Where does your school's trash go after it is tossed out? The answer may surprise you. For example, the University of Minnesota has not transported any of its waste to a landfill in roughly two years.

Instead, according to *The Minnesota Daily*, most of the school's trash is burned in an incinerator at a nearby energy recovery center—helping produce "enough electricity for 25,000 homes each year."

Like many big campus communities, Gopher Nation is awash in endless stacks of garbage, ludicrously high garbage spending, and even a bit of garbage moneymaking. Some of the numbers: UM shells out $2 million each year to sort and gather roughly 23 million pounds of garbage.

The school also spends $600,000 on recycling, although it makes more than three-quarters of that back, in part by selling the paper, plastic, and aluminum.

Along with the electricity-generating incinerator, technology is changing many other facets of waste management. One example: An increase in the power of trash compactors has enabled UM to drop from five garbage trucks rolling through the campus streets daily to one.

Your Assignment

 Simply put, root through the garbage. Determine how much trash your campus or community produces each semester or year. Confirm how much potential waste is being recycled and how—and how well—area recycling programs work. If there is a way to assess it, figure out the types of item tossed out most often—in academic buildings, the student center, and residence halls.

Separately, break down how much is spent on waste management and what the money is used for. Profile your school's official or de facto waste manager. Outline the most pressing trash and recycling challenges at the moment. And look into other area environmental initiatives or pro-environment organizations.

NEW MEDIA ALERT!

 Provide readers with trashy visuals. Put together videos or photo slideshows of local compost centers, compactors, incinerators, recycling processors, and other garbage-related machines and sites that are typically only smelled, not seen. Provide audio backdrops of employees explaining how the facilities and technology operate.

Capture time-lapse video of an initial holding center for campus garbage or recyclables, as a means of visualizing how high the waste or soon-to-be-renewed goods stack up during the day or week. Separately, construct an online map pinpointing the locations of all campus recycling bins or showing the typical garbage truck routes—supplemented by photos of the waste management employees in action at various stops.

OFFBEAT ALERT!

 Ride with the waste management crew during a morning shift or two. Learn the proper art and etiquette of collecting, compacting, and sorting garbage and recyclables. Or follow a single item's path from creation, distribution, and point of purchase to initial use, recycling, reinvention, and subsequent new use. Separately, keep track of how much trash you personally produce in a single week or other predetermined timeframe. According to the Environmental Protection Agency, the average American throws out 1,600 pounds of garbage per year—4.4 pounds daily. Yikes.

CRAZY CAMPUS TRADITIONS

Dragon Day. Pumpkin Drop. Toast Toss. Polar Bear Swim. Naked Quad Run. At many colleges and universities, crazy traditions are as much a part of campus life as fall football Saturdays and final exams. My favorite: the Healy Howl, a Halloween rite of passage for Georgetown University students involving a midnight campus cemetery howl at the moon.

A somewhat similar shriek sounds twice a year at New York's Vassar College. It is known as the Primal Scream. As *The Miscellany News* explains, "At midnight before the start of exam period, you'll hear hundreds of people screaming in unison on the Quad to de-stress and mark the start of exam week. Though screaming is the chief activity of the tradition, students are also known to streak across the Quad and through the library."

The student newspaper at another New York school, Columbia University, may win the award for longest traditions list. In a special issue published last fall, *The Columbia Daily Spectator* ran through 116 traditions Columbia undergrads should participate in prior to graduation. Among them: "Enter the 116th Street gates and sing 'Roar, Lion, Roar' on the first night of orientation . . . Set foot in all five boroughs. Alternatively, set foot in four and look at Staten Island on the subway map . . . Take Principles of Economics with Sunil Gulati. Become an econ major . . . Discover econ majors have to take econometrics. Become an English major."

Your Assignment

Report upon your school's hallowed, reviled, and quirky traditions—official and unofficial. Get the back-stories, including how they began, evolved, and who plans and participates in them. Gather responses from administrators about how they feel they reflect upon the school. Also inquire into how much students actually know about the traditions in which they are taking part.

PEPSI, COKE, CASH

Pepsi. Coke. Candy. Chips. The sweets and soda that are dispensed daily from campus vending machines add up to a formidable annual sum at schools worldwide. Where there's money, there's news.

For example, Northern Illinois University nabs roughly $500,000 annually in vending machine sales. A report in *The Northern Star*, NIU's campus newspaper, revealed the school allots $270,000 of that commission to academic scholarships for incoming students.

Your Assignment

Nail down how much money vending machines on your campus take in each year. Find out details about the agreement in place between your school and the companies creating the goods and stocking them for sale. Confirm your school's cut of the machines' profits and how that portion is allocated. Specifically, how much of the money goes directly to students, in the form of scholarships or funding for clubs and events?

TWO IDEAS IN ONE

Eating Too Healthy, Exercising Too Much

It is possible to not only eat too healthy, but also to exercise too much. The former is a disorder known as orthorexia. As *The Signpost* at Weber State University explains, "Orthorexia is the fixation on righteous eating and an unhealthy obsession with eating only healthy foods. Like anorexia and bulimia, it can wreak serious damage on the health of someone trapped in the obsession."

A somewhat related activity: over-exercising. "[I]f you start to put other important priorities on the back burner in order to watch that Jillian Michaels workout DVD or go to the gym for hours and hours every single day of the week, then you might be working out a little too much," stresses a feature in *The Daily Titan* at California State University,

Fullerton. "When you have other obligations at home or school and then you begin to cut all of that out of your schedule just to work out, then it can be considered an obsession."

A staff editorial in *The Daily Free Press* at Boston University argues more generally, "Disorders concerning health, food, and exercise—whether it be a binge or a purge or any or all—are extremely concerning, especially in a country like ours where everyone is completely overwhelmed by social pressure to be thin and by a media that is oversaturated with celebrities who serve as 'thinspiration.'"

Your Assignment

Report upon orthorexia and other eating disorders and diet trends among students. Explore the more general culture of "thinspiration"—often linked to pro-ana (pro-anorexic) groups—in your coverage area. Look into the relative healthiness of campus cafeteria offerings. Separately, shadow students who are especially well known for their extreme workouts. Interview fitness center junkies now in recovery. And check in with exercise and sports science professors, confirming the best running-and-lifting regimes for teens and twentysomethings.

ETHICS ALERT!

Avoid stereotyping individuals with eating or exercise disorders as weird. And don't define them solely by their condition. Also, avoid puns and other wordplay involving food, eating, and exercising that might be read as insulting. In general, ensure students understand the implications of having their names run with this type of story and the rushed judgments or false assumptions of some readers that might come with it.

STAFF SALARY DATABASE

The University of Illinois at Urbana-Champaign head football coach raked in $1.06 million in 2011. The university president earned a little more than half of that. And the highest-paid employee at UIUC not in athletics, medicine, or the top tier of the administration: a law professor whose 2011 base pay was close to $300,000.

These snippets are part of a comprehensive salary database put together by *The Daily Illini*. Since its launch, the regularly updated feature has been the most-visited portion of the student newspaper's website every day.

"The most difficult part was actually getting the information," said former *Daily Illini* editor-in-chief Melissa Silverberg. "We filed at least three different Freedom of Information requests and talked with another college paper as well as the *St. Louis Post-Dispatch*, who had both created salary databases on their websites. We just had to figure out the right way to ask for the information so we would receive the entire salary listing, in the correct format. We needed the listings in an Excel document to feed into our database. We didn't want to have to do any retyping of names or salaries because we wanted to avoid any possibility for error on our end."

Your Assignment

 For student journalists at public institutions, utilize Freedom of Information requests to obtain salary information for your school's faculty and staff. For student journalists everywhere, consider other financial database options such as student government budget breakdowns and the Form 990 all schools are required to complete and publicly disclose annually.

Remember, the hard data is only the first step. The numbers tell numerous stories—departmental biases, generation gaps, sudden cash influxes, unexplained raises, and other funding mysteries. Share these stories with readers, using the database as your first primary source. See Chapter 12, "Records Reporting," and Chapter 13, "Data Journalism," for instructions on finding and utilizing this type of information.

ANONYMOUS CONFESSIONS

Anonymity is in. At an increasing number of schools, students are starting, participating in, and obsessing over anonymous online confession boards—in the spirit of the Internet sensation PostSecret. The national collegiate gossip centers such as JuicyCampus and College ACB have disappeared. In their place, campus-specific sharing sites are cropping up.

One example: TerpSecret (terpsecret.wordpress.com) at the University of Maryland. As *The Washington Post* explains, "TerpSecret allows UMD students—or really anyone—to anonymously share secrets about their lives." Its motto: "Pour your heart out. Or just talk sh★t. Whatever works."

A small sampling of the secrets shared by students on the site: "I still think about you all the time and how upset and hurt and angry and used you made me feel . . . so why do I still want you?"; "I would rather be disfigured or disabled in an accident than lose my sense of humor. It's my favorite part about myself and I wouldn't trade it for anything."; and, more lightheartedly, "I pick my nose in my car."

Your Assignment

 Explore the anonymous online confessions culture relevant to your campus. Search for especially bizarre or intriguing communiqués and any larger trends embedded within the types of messages posted. Also, use the online platforms as springboards for more detailed features on the state of student gossip, flirtation, and secret sharing—online, via mobile devices, and in person.

STUDENT DEBT TALES

In February 2010, *The Huffington Post* launched its College section, with stories of debt. Along with spotlighting news from colleges worldwide, the most innovative feature on day one was an original report on undergraduate and graduate student loan debt. *Huffington Post College* (huffington post.com/college) has continued telling students' debt tales, in part through crowdsourced photos and video sent in by students and fresh graduates sharing how much they currently or will soon owe for their higher education experiences.

Your Assignment

Tell the debt stories of students and alumni on your campus or within your coverage area. Explore how individuals especially weighed down with loans are coping. Profile the students and graduates who are creatively solving their debt woes. Also, talk to students' parents about their kids' debt situation. And explain how your school is responding to student financial struggles in a down economy or dealing with any debt woes of its own.

POST-MORTEM

 Post-Mortem is a recurring feature in the book and on my blog, telling the story *behind* a story, series, or website—in the words of the reporter or editor responsible for creating it.

"Tragedy in Transition"

On a historic night more than four years ago, Chris Schaadt's father called him, crying. He told him to hurry home—something had happened to his mother. As Kelly Stroda reported for *The University Daily Kansan*, "It was Election Day 2008—monumental because the first African-American president was elected—but [Schaadt] remembers it for a different reason. It was the last time he would see his mom alive."

Schaadt's story is part of a powerful four-part *Kansan* report that tells the tales of three University of Kansas students who lost a parent during their time in school. It is, as the series headline states, a "tragedy in transition."

The haunting stat that provides grounding for the stories' newsworthiness: **One in 10 individuals deals with the death of their mom or dad before turning 25**. And yet, as a prominent sociology professor is paraphrased telling Stroda, "[T]here is little research conducted on college students and the death of a parent."

Stroda's series begins filling this information gap. She captures the students' heartrending memories of the moment death entered their undergraduate experience, the emotional hole it etched, and their baby steps toward healing.

As she writes in the introduction, "College students who lose a parent are affected emotionally, psychologically, physically, academically, and financially. At the very time they are about to launch independent lives, they lose the people they rely on most for direction."

In this Q&A, Stroda, the *Kansan*'s former editor-in-chief, shares what she learned about life, death, and journalism while writing the series and provides tips for students looking to produce a similar report.

What drew you to the project? What questions were you interested in answering?
The topic was one I'd been thinking about awhile. Then in January [2011], Thomas Robinson, one of KU's star basketball players, unexpectedly lost his mom. The story of his loss and the impact it had on his family was all over the media. I realized, though, that there were plenty of other college students who have suffered the same loss. So, in the end,

I would say my piece was less about questions I wanted answered, but stories I thought deserved to be told.

How did you find students who had lost their parents while at KU?

It wasn't easy. I mostly relied on Facebook and people who knew other people. I joke that it's a miracle I still have Facebook friends after the number of depressing statuses I had looking for college students who lost a parent. The students I spoke with were quite open to telling me their stories. In fact, most said it was relieving to talk about their experiences. Usually, they said they try to not talk about their loss because it might make others uncomfortable. I was the opposite of that.

What surprised you most while reporting?

When I started, I had no idea how much research was out there. Like I said, I mostly just wanted to tell the stories. However, upon trying to find statistics and research for my piece, I was shocked at how little research has been done. The loss of a parent is jolting no matter how old the child is. There is plenty of research about both children younger than 18 and adults who lose their parents at traditional ages, but very little information about college students who lose a parent.

What did you learn from the students?

I learned that sometimes journalism can act as therapy for sources who have been in traumatic situations. Sometimes, they haven't had the chance to talk about their experiences because they don't trust anyone to listen or don't want to make others uncomfortable.

Many people who suffer the loss of a parent feel "silenced"—as if they can't talk about their pain with anyone. Seeing a source cry during an interview was a new experience for me as a journalist. Heck, I even started tearing up during [one especially powerful] interview. How could I not?

What are the keys to mounting a long-term, feature-length report similar to this one?

It's imperative that you give yourself plenty of time to report and write the story. Investigative and feature pieces take many interviews and lots of research. It's not a short-term gig. Second, if you have the luxury to choose the subject you are writing about, make sure it's something you want to write or learn about. If that's not the case, you may not enjoy it or learn as much from the experience.

Third, remember that your sources are more than sources—they are people. They are people who deserve to be respected and listened to. Sometimes, you may have to interview a source three, four, or five times to get the story you want to tell. That's part of good journalism.

Once the reporting is done, how do you organize and write the final stories?
This is definitely the tricky part. Usually, I write down some sort of outline. Nothing extravagant, but just a general direction of where I think the story can go. First, just get what you want to say out. Then, the pieces will come together and make sense. Also, remember that editing is imperative. Bad editing could ruin a potentially great story, so don't be afraid to ask others for help. Separately, a note on combing through background work and interview data: Somehow note important things that strike you during interviews—dates, stories, quotes, etc. You can always look back at those and then try to go in the direction you want to go.

Your Assignment

 Find students who have lost a parent or other loved one during their time in school. Similar to Stroda's efforts, share their stories. Emphasize not only the loss but the healing and how their grief has impacted their experiences in classes, clubs, dorm chats, and internships. Separately, focus on the lives and professional challenges of the grief counselors and trauma specialists who help students cope and recover from significant losses.

NEW MEDIA ALERT!

 Put together a brief video vignette or audio slideshow, enabling the featured students to share their memories and emotions directly to readers in their own words. If possible for the slideshow, overlay the audio with scrapbook photos of the students with the loved ones they lost, tying certain memories to the images on the screen.

SPIN-OFF ALERT!

Focus on students whose homes are broken up during their time in school, not due to a sudden death but through a divorce, a move, or a job loss or transfer.

"THE COST OF CONVENIENCE"

In fall 2009, Hayley Peterson followed the money. Specifically, the *Red and Black* staffer investigated how much money the University of Georgia allotted for trips taken by UGA officials on the school's private plane.

Her subsequent award-winning report, "The Cost of Convenience," revealed an array of high-cost flights, including one taken by the university president to attend a dinner only two hours away by car that totaled $1,363.

Your Assignment

Launch a similar investigation into the travel habits of your school's higher-level administrators and admissions and athletic department recruiters. Determine how much their transportation efforts cost the school. Look into what vehicles, equipment, and services the school owns, rents, and utilizes for travel purposes. Separately, reverse the report's focus. Look into the arrangements and costs associated with invited guests traveling *to* the university.

NEW MEDIA ALERT!

Create a database displaying the amount spent on specific trips or certain aspects of administrator, staff, and faculty travel, including comparisons from past years. Also, put together an online map showing the spots your school's most frequent travelers have visited in recent semesters or throughout their careers.

ETHICS ALERT!

Be sure to put the numbers in context. Compare them with other schools and account for gas price fluctuations and economic inflation. And similar to Peterson's excellent report, give people a chance to clarify certain expenses or the travel budget overall.

THRIFTING

Reduce, Revamp, Rewear. The slogan of a University of Northern Iowa clothing swap last spring also serves as the perfect description for a fashion trend en vogue among students: thrifting.

Students are increasingly vocal champions of this creative and commercial endeavor and the culture it represents. In a straightforward sense, the act of thrifting involves donating or shopping for used fashion, accessories, and dorm decor online or at thrift and consignment shops.

It also relates to the exploding popularity of clothing swaps in which students trade apparel with friends, informally or through campus events and websites such as Swapstyle and Savvy Swaps. And it is at the heart of the rise in students' do-it-yourself fashion shows and themed parties in which clothes must be handmade—composed of older, organic, or recyclable items.

More broadly, the thrifting movement represents a generational shift built atop five basic tenets: old is new, mixing trumps matching, swapping beats shopping, the best things in life are free (or incredibly cheap), and social responsibility is the new black.

Your Assignment

 Report upon the thrifting, clothes swapping, and do-it-yourself fashion movements within your coverage area. Profile their most impassioned and stylish supporters. Accompany a die-hard thrifter on a shopping or swapping excursion, documenting their finds, exchange techniques, and overall thrifting philosophy. And get a firsthand sense of how the thrift fashion social networks operate.

IMMERSION ALERT!

Go thrifting or partake in a clothes swap. Determine what you found especially enlightening, exhilarating, and challenging about the experience. In a larger sense, stage a so-called trashion fashion show, featuring students modeling their most creative homemade ensembles.

SPIN-OFF ALERT!

Investigate the latest buzz surrounding the ethical apparel push, fashion-themed parties, on-campus pajama fashion, the nudist subculture, and the nerd chic phenomenon recently popularized by a few NBA stars.

STUDENT SUICIDE

The top half of the newspaper's front page features only the image of a noose, tied taut, hanging over the masthead. Beneath it, the main headline of the related story is summed up in a single word: Suicide.

In an issue of *The Eagle News* at Florida Gulf Coast University, top editors sought to raise awareness about the alarmingly high number of college students who commit suicide each year. Depending on how related data is gathered and interpreted, the taking of one's own life is often cited as the leading or second-leading cause of death among undergraduates nationwide.

"I can list statistics and facts and figures all day long, but unless you've gone through it [having suicidal thoughts] yourself it's not going to really get to you," said Mike Ricci, the *Eagle News* managing editor at the time. "If you really see the first-person accounts of someone who has been there, who has had those feelings of suicide, that's when you kind of put yourself in their shoes. It makes people realize just how real it is."

In that spirit, Ricci focuses in the newspaper's main report on those who have grappled with and gotten past suicidal thoughts and actions such as cutting, and others still dealing with the fallout from the suicide of someone close to them.

"The person who does it never feels the pain directly," said an FGCU student who lost a friend and classmate to suicide. "It's the community who feels the pain. When someone takes their own life, you don't expect it, so it's almost like taking a sucker punch from Mike Tyson right in the gut."

Your Assignment

Report upon the culture and lasting impact of student suicides or attempted suicides on your campus. Document the number of related incidents and the responses of RAs, crisis counselors, and law enforcement officials. With great tact, profile people who have attempted suicide in the past and are willing to share their stories. And speak to suicide survivors—the friends and loved ones the victims leave behind.

Also, explore the controversial online suicide subculture, including pro-suicide websites in which users actually encourage each other to carry out the act and provide instructions on how to do it. Taking a wider-angle lens, profile individuals dealing with depression and other unseen mental and emotional conditions.

ETHICS ALERT!

Be careful about reporting the circumstances of specific suicides in too much detail, especially if it may hurt the families of the deceased or sicken readers.

WALKING BACKWARD, SHOWING OFF

One of the more lucrative campus jobs for students involves pointing, walking backward, and spouting the wonders of the school they call home. Tour guides are compelling figures. They often serve as the first and most visible points of reference for prospective students and their families. They are trained to focus on a school's highlights, even while sometimes experiencing its lowlights and underside.

They also occasionally tell white lies. A University of Virginia historian grew so concerned about tour exaggerations he now requires a meeting with all UVA student guides to ensure they know the facts about the school they are selling. As *The Washington Post* reports, "At the country's most historic colleges, some of the wildest tales handed down through generations of students and retold to campus visitors have only kernels of truth in them—if any at all."

Your Assignment

Report upon the challenges and quirks of this iconic campus job. Put together a profile or day-in-the-life feature of an especially eager guide. Determine what guides secretly loathe about the position or cannot believe they have to say out loud. Examine the innovative and digital-friendly initiatives being implemented on tours or related portions of your school's website. And assess what guides are exaggerating or failing to mention.

NEW MEDIA ALERT!

Create a video montage showing student guides working their magic at different spots, interspersed with interview snippets. (Just steer clear of a final product that looks like an admissions office creation.) Make a separate video featuring students' takes on what they would say about the school if granted tour guide status. Construct a text-based slideshow of the most common or crazier questions student guides have been asked. And if it does not yet exist, create an interactive digital tour of campus and popular surrounding areas. Utilize text, audio, photo, and video pop-ups to provide the real story behind the student experience at prominent spots.

IMMERSION ALERT!

Serve as a campus tour guide to experience the rigors of the job firsthand. Determine for yourself what is being especially stressed, exaggerated, and outright fabricated and what visitors find most interesting, confusing, and repellent about the school.

OFFBEAT ALERT!

Building off the UVA historian's efforts, create an interactive quiz about your school's hallowed myths and historical facts.

HANDICAPPED SPOT CHECK

In spring 2009, journalism students at the University of Minnesota Duluth tweeted from parking lots across the UMD campus. Their aim: verifying how many handicapped spots were available on a mid-morning weekday.

The Twitter report fleshed out a student newspaper story regarding complaints about a lack of free handicapped spaces near campus buildings. "The assignment for students," a local news report noted, "was to team up and take laptops to each parking area of the campus at the same time, checking the 58 parking spots designated for drivers with physical handicaps and posting the status of each space immediately."

What did they find? Only a few spots were free.

Your Assignment

 Confirm the number of free spots in your school's parking lots during a given day or time—handicapped and regular. Extend the free-space checks to library study nooks, cafeteria seats, computer lab workstations, and dorm lounge chairs. Follow the lead of the UMD handicapped spot search and report your findings in real time.

SPIN-OFF ALERT!

 Focus on other facets of your school's parking culture. Investigate commuter lot security. Follow the money made from parking permits and fines. Examine ticketing regulations. Profile the staff responsible for distributing parking tickets. And observe the process students go through to contest them. Separately, report upon your school's outside towing, paving, and streetlight contracts. And identify students' more creative and illegal parking methods and nearby spots serving as unofficial free garages or lots.

THE "ACADEMIC STEROID"

Studying for finals. Paying attention in class. Simply wanting to feel wired. The explosion of illegal Adderall use by students has many root causes—and a number of unintended side effects.

The pill's medical purpose is to help individuals with ADHD (Attention Deficit Hyperactivity Disorder) and narcolepsy. Yet, it's being increasingly co-opted by college students looking for an academic edge or a head-trip. Apparently, full-time students are twice as likely to illegally use Adderall as individuals their age who are not in school or only enrolled part-time.

The results of this so-called FADerall: a running debate about whether the "academic steroid" is equivalent to actual cheating; student Adderall dealers who make oodles of cash selling the pills; student Adderall addicts whose sleep schedules, brains, and bodily functions are thrown off; students with verifiable ADHD who face increased peer pressure to pass along pills to friends; and medical professionals wary of promoting an academic doping revolution by prescribing the pills to students who do not truly need them.

Your Assignment

 Investigate Adderall use on your campus. Find out if it is a major part of underground student life and residence halls' black markets. Explore why students take the pills and how school officials, health and wellness staffers, academic counselors, campus security, and local law enforcement are handling various aspects of the boom.

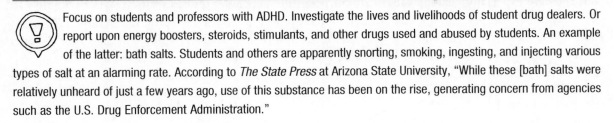

SPIN-OFF ALERT!

Focus on students and professors with ADHD. Investigate the lives and livelihoods of student drug dealers. Or report upon energy boosters, steroids, stimulants, and other drugs used and abused by students. An example of the latter: bath salts. Students and others are apparently snorting, smoking, ingesting, and injecting various types of salt at an alarming rate. According to *The State Press* at Arizona State University, "While these [bath] salts were relatively unheard of just a few years ago, use of this substance has been on the rise, generating concern from agencies such as the U.S. Drug Enforcement Administration."

"CAN YOU DUB IT?"

College students remain "dazed by the dub." Student newspapers nationwide confirm dubstep has officially implanted its beat into the campus music and dance scenes. As *The Pipe Dream* at Binghamton University reports, "It's the fastest-growing music genre of the 21st century. So can you dub it?"

Dubstep is a sub-genre of the electronic music movement begun in Britain that also includes breakcore, fidget, house, jungle, and trance. It is described as nasty, filthy, and grimy—by its supporters. But its emergence at or near schools has been celebrated for providing students with "orgasmic vibrations that just make you want to move your body."

Your Assignment

Follow the beat. Determine how and to what extent dubstep has carved out a musical niche within your coverage area. Also investigate other emerging musical genres competing for local club and house party airplay.

NEW MEDIA ALERT!

Put together a photo slideshow featuring students dancing to dubstep music at a local club or dorm bash. Use a dubstep song obtained via a free music-licensing website as the slideshow's soundtrack. Separately, compile video footage of student DJs or college radio station staffers discussing dubstep's popularity and their attempts to define the sub-genre's sound. It should lead to entertaining clips—an actual definition is tough to pin down in words.

RAT ROD CULTURE

Rat rods are especially beat-up older cars purposefully kept in crappy condition. "As a response to the traditional and pristine hot rod culture," a feature in *Flux Magazine* at the University of Oregon notes, "rat rods glorify rust and age and are meant to look cartoonishly sinister . . . Everyone seems to have their own notion as to what makes the perfect rat rod—the highlighted appeal being the idea of raw, incomplete vehicles that intimidate grandmothers everywhere."

Your Assignment

 Explore the rat rod culture within your coverage area. Tell the stories behind the especially decrepit vehicles and what they mean to their owners.

NEW MEDIA ALERT!

 The cars are the stars. Capture and present a slideshow of shots showing the vehicles in all their ugly glory, at times with their owners behind the steering wheel, gazing under the hood, or looking on proudly from the side of the road.

SPIN-OFF ALERT!

 Profile road racers, mechanics, car salesmen, or taxi drivers. Separately, report upon alternative-fuel cars, drunk driving accidents, or individuals without cars who commute long distances daily via the train, subway, bus, a bicycle, or their own two feet.

ACADEMIC HYPERINFLATION

College students' grades are going up—and it may have nothing to do with the quality of their work. "For the past thirty years, grades and grade point averages in private and public universities have risen significantly," a report in *The Student Voice* at the University of Wisconsin-River Falls, notes. "[S]tudents should be aware that the 'A' they are striving for may not be as big a deal as they once thought it was."

The latest study by leading grade-inflation researchers Stuart Rojstaczer and Christopher Healy confirms an "A" is now the most common mark earned by undergraduate students. Meanwhile, the "C" grade is decreasing and "D" and "F" are almost out of the grading equation altogether.

What has spurred such academic hyperinflation? Apparently, it's not hard work. As a student writes in *The Hoya* at Georgetown University, "Students today study less, party more, and spend more hours in time-consuming and academically distracting internships and extracurricular activities than at any time in the past. Clearly then, something larger is at work."

In a Q&A with *The Chronicle* at Duke University, Rojstaczer connects higher grades with the rising expectations of students and their families. Simply put, they see high marks as a suitable reward for the high amount they are shelling out for their education. "In a sense," said Rojstaczer, "people are buying GPAs."

Economic factors may also lead some schools to look the other way when students under-achieve—even to the point of failure. For example, a 2011 report in *The Chicago Tribune* revealed Chicago State University officials had been allowing students with "D" averages to remain enrolled—and paying school fees. Some students apparently were given permission to soldier on with grade point averages of 0.0.

Your Assignment

Investigate the grade inflation situation at your school. If possible, look into obtaining actual grade distributions for certain classes, majors, programs, and professors. Or simply try to get the scoop on any official or unofficial grading requirements presented to faculty by deans and department chairs. Also, gather feedback from students and their parents. Among the questions to ask: Do students expect an "A" just for showing up?

Separately, check out your school's policies for dealing with those not measuring up academically. Profile the tutors and academic counselors responsible for working with those in GPA jeopardy. And report upon a student once destined for dismissal who has turned things around.

"CONCUSSIONS AND REPERCUSSIONS"

A frightening brain disease is increasingly being spotted in former football players, linked to the frequent hits they sustain on the field.

According to *The Minnesota Daily*, the degenerative disorder "is similar to Alzheimer's, but it takes hold at a much younger age . . . Its onset may occur months or years—even decades—after a player's last concussion. Its symptoms, like Alzheimer's, begin with memory loss and eventually progress to full dementia."

The award-winning feature, "Concussions and Repercussions," spotlights an important element of sports reporting: After the games, winning streaks, seasons, and careers conclude, the stories continue.

Your Assignment

Talk to athletic trainers and sports medical staff to uncover the most common and serious injuries suffered by student-athletes in various sports. Follow an athlete during rehab for an extended profile. Check in with alumni who suffered career-ending or life-altering injuries while in school to see how they are faring now.

HUMAN SEXUALITY, UNDER DEBATE

One of the most spirited recent debates at Northwestern University brewed over the value of human sexuality. It began when Northwestern officials temporarily dropped a popular human sexuality course from the curriculum, in response to a mega-controversy caused by an optional sex-themed demonstration held after a class session.

As *The Daily Northwestern* reported, "The 600-person course, taught by psychology Prof. John Michael Bailey, is one of the largest at NU. The after-class events, which range from a question-and-answer session with swingers to a panel of convicted sex offenders, are a popular feature of the class." The event that fell under nationwide scrutiny proved more explicit than usual, involving a woman performing for students with a "motorized sex toy."

It triggered an explosion of media attention and a university investigation. Separate ethics complaints filed by an outside clinician alleged the performance "may have exposed minors to a public sex act and knowingly inflicted psychological damage upon present students."

A number of students fought those charges and spoke out against the school's decision to drop the course. One Northwestern junior who previously took human sexuality wrote, "Learning about the evolutionary, physiological, psychological, and sociological factors at work challenged the way I previously thought, or, perhaps more appropriately, had not thought, about sex. I am grateful for having gained this valuable experience and concerned that the university is planning to deny it to future students."

Your Assignment

Explore human sexuality and its role within your school's curriculum. Find out if there are any official or unofficial limits placed on the teaching of more sexually explicit topic areas. Gauge student reactions to the class. Explore the teaching philosophy of the professor who most often leads it. And with the instructor's permission, attend a class or two. What was taught? What were the readings and assignments? And how engaged were students with the lessons?

NEVER HAVE I EVER . . .

The trio described it as a venture into the unknown, "a world where archers, jousters, and warriors band together." In a piece published in *The Rocky Mountain Collegian* at Colorado State University, two student reporters and a photographer described their first foray into battlegaming, an unconnected offshoot of the live action role playing (LARP) community.

The battlefield report was the opening feature of a larger *Collegian* series: "Never Have I Ever." The series documented staffers' experiences with activities they had never tried before.

For "Never Have I Ever . . . Battlegamed," the student team joined a battlegaming group one afternoon in a local park to engage in a war game. They described the basic scene, the rules, the costuming, and the rush of the battle—"each army destroying the other side a few times before stopping for a water break." As one member of the *Collegian* trio admitted, "Who knew that hitting each other with foam swords could be so much fun?"

Your Assignment

 Head into battle. Report upon the battlegaming and larger LARP communities within your coverage area. Also explore the cosplay and online role-play cultures. Separately, focus on local historical reenactments, improvisational comedy troupes, high-tech flight simulations, and children's make-believe games.

SPIN-OFF ALERT!

 Follow the lead of the *Collegian* series overall. Do something you have never done before. Work the security night shift. Participate in a mock debate. Attempt to master a rhythmic gymnastics routine. The opportunities are endless. Regardless of what you select, the key to your role-play report's success: Play to the human element. A feature of this type should be built atop the people participating in the activities—the student journalist first-timers and the experienced individuals acting as their guides.

ESSAY BAN

A college in Maryland temporarily banned a student from setting foot on campus due to an essay he wrote. In fall 2011, the Community College of Baltimore informed one of its students, an Iraq War veteran, he was suddenly no longer allowed to attend classes. Administrators even issued a "notice of trespass," making it illegal for him to be on CCB's grounds.

The cause for their concern: "War is a Drug," an essay the student wrote for an English class that he later submitted to the monthly campus newspaper. According to a CNN report, the piece "details what [the student] calls his addiction to killing."

A portion of the essay: "I got used to killing and after a while it became something I really had to do. Killing becomes a drug, and it is really addictive . . . I still feel the addictions running through my blood and throughout my body. When I stick my blade through his stomach or his ribs or slice his throat it's a feeling that I cannot explain, but feels so good to me."

The student said the essay was simply a means to cope and describe an emotion experienced to different degrees by some veterans—and not meant to hint at any machinations for civilian violence. CCB administrators were not swayed, allowing him back on campus only after he passed a psychiatric evaluation. "When you look in the era of post-Virginia Tech and the content and the nature that he wrote about in the article, it caused us concerns," said a college spokeswoman. "We had to take some action against [the student] to ensure the safety of the college."

Your Assignment

 Explore the people and process behind campus suspensions and full dismissals, including how the banned students and staff are investigated, informed, removed, monitored, and possibly rehabilitated.

SPIN-OFF ALERT!

 Focus on individuals with post-traumatic stress disorder. Or profile campus ROTC chapters or student military veterans.

TWO IDEAS IN ONE

Animals, Alive and Stuffed

Each fall, students arrive on campus with tons of stuffed animals. They often sport silly names. They sit prominently on residence hall beds and shelves. They are furry. They are squeezable. And they are among students' closest childhood companions.

As a student of mine at the University of Tampa once shared about her beloved Teddy bear, "Ever since 9/11, I've had Teddy. When I was little, I always thought of him as my protector. I had been really shaken up by the terrorist attack, but with Lieutenant Teddy by my side, I would never have to be afraid . . . Going away to college and settling into a home away from home can be hard for some students. With a little help from a stuffed animal, blanket, pillow, or even a sweater, students . . . have found settling into school to be a lot easier."

Students are also enjoying evermore freedom at some schools to have their real-life pets included in all parts of their college experience—sometimes to the extremes. For example, according to an administrator at Florida's Eckerd College, "A couple of years ago, we had one young lady whose dog actually walked across stage with her at commencement."

Your Assignment

 Sniff out the stuffed and live animals residing on your campus. Tell the stories of how they came into students' lives and what they mean to them now. Focus on students with more unusual pets or especially large, colorful, or quirky stuffed animal collections. Separately, investigate your school's pet policies. Also, don't forget faculty and staff pets. And check if there are any pet–owner lookalikes. Remember the stuffed and live animals are the starting points. The real stories are about the people who love and spoil them.

NEW MEDIA ALERT!

 Whether full of life or simply stuffed, animals demand a spotlight, in this case a photo slideshow. Include a mix of animal-only and animal-and-owner shots. Along with the current images you take, seek out older scrapbooked shots, when the dogs were puppies, the cats were kittens, and the college students were kids. And audio record students' pet and teddy bear tales, including them as narrations in the slideshow.

OFFBEAT ALERT!

 Create a map highlighting the places where stuffed animals' real-life counterparts are indigenous. Or tell the story of how your own school's stuffed animal mascot is selected, created, marketed, shipped, and sold.

COSTS OF CAMPUS 911

In fall 2010, *Arizona Daily Wildcat* staff writer Jazmine Woodberry wondered about the emergency phones that shine under blue lights across the University of Arizona campus. There are similar devices at many schools—often marked, well lit, and situated in high-traffic and out-of-the-way areas.

Woodberry put together her report based on the following questions: How much do the phones cost the school? How often are they used? How are the calls handled? And what are the most common situations prompting people to push the buttons?

The answers she found were somewhat surprising. These are expensive suckers. They are hardly ever used to report actual trouble. And campus police do not record the calls people place on them.

"With nearly half a million dollars spent on close to 200 blue light emergency phones and call buttons and no direct record of usage for each $7,800 phone, their function and purpose are more speculative than conclusive," Woodberry confirmed. "'We get a call from the blue phones just about every day,' said UAPD Public Information Officer Sgt. Juan Alvarez. Few of those calls though, Alvarez noted, were emergencies, as people will ask for directions, escorts, or push them as a late-night joke."

Your Assignment

 Look into the status and costs of the emergency phone system on your campus. Attempt to determine how often the phones are used. Figure out how much the school is shelling out for their installation and upkeep. Get the scoop from campus safety about the most common types of call they field. And with officers' permission, carry out a test call to learn firsthand how the phones work.

"THE ANTICIPATION, NOT THE NUDITY"

At first, it seems like the perfect campus job. Earn $18 per hour for only a few hours' work per week. Be part of the school's arts community. And, oh yeah, you may have to be partially or fully naked.

Colleges and universities worldwide employ student models, paying them to pose—at times sans clothing—while their peers paint and sketch them.

A past report in *The Dartmouth* student newspaper profiled Julia Marks, one such model at Dartmouth College. For Marks, the most nerve-wracking part was "the anticipation, not the nudity." There were nerves about whether she would know anyone in the class, nerves about being stared at nonstop while forced to remain completely still, and separate nerves about how she should act if she saw the student artists on campus after the session wrapped.

Your Assignment

 Inquire into the existence of a paid student model program at your school. Determine how student models are solicited, and gauge their relative eagerness toward signing up. Also, find out how the nudity aspect is handled and what student artists think of the full-frontal contact they experience with someone they might later see in the cafeteria. Separately, confirm what the models think of the portraits their peers create.

NEW MEDIA ALERT!

With permission, shoot video of a portrait session, later mixing in interviews you capture with the model, student artists, and overseeing art professor. Be sure to film from start to finish, including following the student model earlier in the day as they prepare mentally and maybe physically for the session and the presentation of the portraits in class or an exhibition.

ETHICS ALERT!

Unlike the actual modeling session, for the video, no nudity is needed. Use appropriate cuts and camera angles to obscure or steer clear of that specific part of the scene.

TWO IDEAS IN ONE

Internet Famous

One of the more popular images co-opted by the online masses is actually an old photo of a University of New Hampshire student.

As *The New Hampshire* reported, while a UNH freshman, Griffin Kiritsy "was interviewed and photographed for an article in *Reader's Digest* about technology affecting people's everyday lives. It was featured in both the print and online version of the magazine." Sporting jeans and his sister's UNH hoodie, Kiritsy posed wearing a backpack and holding a mobile phone, embodying the clean-cut collegian 2.0.

It has become the photo that defines him. During summer 2011, it popped up on the website quickmeme.com and later went viral as part of the exploding college memes phenomenon. It is known as the "College Freshman" meme. "It's a weird experience," said Kiritsy. "At first it wasn't a big deal, but now people are coming up to me and are like, 'Hey, you're that guy.' . . . I think it's hilarious. There are a million images of college freshmen online, and they picked me."

If he had enrolled, Kiritsy would have certainly earned high marks in Internet Famous Class. Internet Famous is a digital media course at Parsons New School for Design in New York City. A few years back it gained national attention for its focus on helping students create viral media projects.

More specifically, as one of the instructors previously told his students, "This class is all about the art and science of getting hits, getting eyeballs, extracting stuff out of the attention economy—views, comments, blog links . . . followers, MySpace friends."

Your Assignment

 Find and profile individuals within your coverage area who have experienced some measure of Internet fame, through their active efforts or due to elements out of their control. Also, detail how various courses at your school are teaching digital branding or audience building. Separately, search for alums whose post-graduation lives have been in some way impacted by the "Google prints" they formed while still in school.

IMMERSION ALERT!

 Attempt to go viral. Collect ideas from classmates, colleagues, and readers about what you should do to gain the attention of local websurfers or netizens worldwide.

SPIN-OFF ALERT!

In spring 2012, the University of Rochester went viral with a music video created by its Office of Admissions, featuring students rapping about the awesomeness of the school. It grabbed more than 90,000 hits on YouTube in the first four months of its posting. It was billed as a wonderful marketing tool for the university and part of a new wave of admissions efforts nationwide. As *Washington Post* higher education reporter Jenna Johnson wrote, "In the arms race of creating the most viral admissions video, several universities have jumped on the *Glee* bandwagon, written musical numbers and filmed their students dancing through campus."

Explore your own school's viral admissions efforts and its more general digital marketing campaigns. Profile the individuals responsible for the school's digital brand overall. And determine the visitor totals for various parts of your school's website.

"IS IT VANDALISM OR IS IT ART?"

"Only GOD can judge me! . . . I eat yogurt . . . Where words fail, music speaks . . . Sidewalks are just suggestions . . . You never realize how shallow your life was until you become a mother . . . Please let us express ourselves."

A bathroom stall at the University of North Carolina Wilmington is overrun with these random statements, and many more. Altogether, they add up to a funny, quirky, and one-of-a-kind glimpse into the minds and moods of UNCW students.

As a staff writer for *The Seahawk* at UNCW argues in an opinion-editorial, "The bathroom stalls contain some of the more honest writings of the students on this campus. We do a ton of writing to get through our courses, but all of it is written for someone else with the knowledge that it will be judged. There is no fear of judgment when writing on a bathroom stall because no one will know you wrote it."

Graffiti, in general, has long been an omnipresent backdrop to many parts of all college and university campuses. The online student outlet *NeoJourno* at the University of Hawaii confirms, "It can be found on buildings, overpasses, sidewalks, and even on bathroom stalls. It has existed since ancient times, dating back to the glory days of the Greek and Roman Empires. Is it vandalism or is it art?"

Your Assignment

Explore the graffiti chalked and scrawled around your campus or coverage area. Be on the lookout for common sayings, styles, or themes. Also, take note of more offbeat words, phrases, acronyms, and drawings, and funnier or more interesting running conversations. Determine whether any particular statements speak for the student body or address current community concerns.

Detail the response of school officials and law enforcement to the graffiti, along with student opinions of the scrawls. Profile student graffiti artists. Observe art and design classes that incorporate graffiti styles or perspectives into their lesson plans. Also, through a scan of your student newspaper archives, uncover any especially famous or controversial graffiti incidents on campus—a defaced iconic statue perhaps or a protest mark-up of a prominent portrait.

NEW MEDIA ALERT!

Produce an interactive standalone site featuring photos of graffiti touching on major campus issues, with rollover or pop-up captions objectively explaining the issues being addressed and links to news coverage for those wanting to learn more. Or create a set of memes featuring images of popular campus spots. Overlay each meme image with bits of "digital graffiti," including words and phrases lightheartedly and seriously suggested by students. The question: What *should* be scrawled on certain buildings and statues?

OFFBEAT ALERT!

With school officials' approval, create a temporary free speech wall on campus, enabling students to write or draw whatever they want. Grab video or photos of students scrawling on it or strolling by it. And assess the themes and debates that emerge.

RECREATION SPORTS FEES

Students at Ohio State University pay a combined $14 million in student fees each year that go toward funding OSU recreational sports, a report in *The Lantern* confirms. How is that money put to use exactly? Umm, well, as of spring 2012, OSU officials were not exactly able to say.

During an investigation into the funding, the school gave *The Lantern* numerous runarounds that boiled down to one basic sentiment: There is no organized, itemized list outlining how the rec fees are spent.

It is a considerable oversight given the amount of money involved and its connection to the larger set of fees students pay at schools worldwide. For example, as *The Lantern* explained, "Fees such as the Rec Sports fee, the Student Activity fee, the Student Legal Services fee, the Student Union Facility fee, and the COTA Bus Service fee are not included in the posted cost of tuition . . . In a four-year period, students at OSU [each] pay $3,676 in required fees."

Your Assignment

Carry out some recreational, and financial, reporting. Start by looking into the student rec services offered at your school. Gather student assessments about their quality, popularity, and financial worth. Nail down how much students pay in rec fees, individually and overall. Determine how the money is allocated, including the amount of student input involved in the process. Compare your school's rec fees with those paid by students at other schools.

NEW MEDIA ALERT!

If you can obtain an itemized breakdown of how rec fees are spent, create a photo slideshow of the uniforms, equipment, employees, and facilities receiving funding, with captions confirming the amount allocated for each. Or put together an interactive database listing the current breakdown, along with the comparable numbers from previous years.

OFFBEAT ALERT!

Follow a ragtag recreational sports team with a crazy name from its first practice to its amazing playoff run—capturing the joy of sport, the priceless camaraderie, and the varying quality of the athletic talent displayed along the way. While recreational sports (sometimes known as club or intramural sports) are often left out of student press coverage in favor of interscholastic awesomeness, many students who compete bring true zeal and interesting back-stories to their fields of play. They deserve an occasional spotlight.

SPIN-OFF ALERT!

Investigate the larger fees system, including its likely rise over time and what it is used to fund. Highlight lesser known activities and organizations that exist due to fees support. And uncover any seemingly misused fees or over-funded projects and clubs.

MEAL PLAN WASTE

At the University of North Carolina at Chapel Hill, "25 percent of all meals bought through campus dining plans are wasted each semester."

The high percentage, revealed last spring by *The Daily Tar Heel*, prompted a student–administrator blame game. Students claim they are forced into meal plans that require them to pay for excess food, while the dining director argues students are at least partially at fault for purchasing plans that "don't match their lifestyles."

Depending on the perspective, the "waste money" is not simply going to waste—the funds are used to keep dining services operating. In addition, the wastefulness also apparently keeps meal prices down. According to the DTH, "If students were to eat every meal they purchased, meal plan prices would be higher, [the dining director] said. 'For a plan that includes 14 meals per week, we charge $6.67 (per meal),' he said. 'You would never see an all-you-can-eat meal for $6.67 anywhere else.'"

Your Assignment

Take a fresh look at campus food costs. Explore every facet of the meal plan options available for students at your school, including their total costs per semester and the amount and type of input students have in shaping them. Confirm how much meal plan prices have risen in recent years, comparing the rise to general inflation and the rate of increase for your school's tuition, room and board, student fees, and textbook expenses. And figure out the percentage of meal plans wasted each semester and how much money this waste is costing students.

NEW MEDIA ALERT!

Run a photo slideshow of select food and drinks available at breakfast, lunch, and dinner in the campus dining halls, accompanied by the prices students technically pay for them via their meal plans and what they cost at a local supermarket, wholesaler, and restaurant.

IMMERSION ALERT!

Avoid the dining hall and other campus markets and eateries for a few weeks. Instead, head off-campus, mooch off friends, and call your parents for an edible care package. Record all expenses, the food and drinks consumed, and a running set of responses to the experience. And create a subsequent health comparison between what you chowed down at various mealtimes and what you would have eaten in the dining hall.

TWO IDEAS IN ONE

Gender Matters

At a rising number of colleges and universities—in middle America and along the coasts—students are protesting, passing resolutions, and publishing commentaries in support of a single hyphenated buzzword: gender-neutral.

The push for gender-neutral campus housing and restroom options is part of a larger student-led fight on some campuses for greater "transgender inclusiveness." *The Oklahoma Daily* at the University of Oklahoma hails it as the heart of "this generation's civil rights movement."

The Daily Texan at the University of Texas reported last February more than 100 schools currently offer gender-neutral housing programs nationwide, a huge leap in the last six years. As a University of Chicago student wrote separately for *USA TODAY College*, "[S]ome students say an environment without gender labels has become an integral part of their college experience . . . Gender-neutral colleges can be a safe and comfortable place for students who are transgender or who don't identify with their biological sex."

Gender identity became an especially big issue last spring at American University. A day after ending his tenure as student government president at American University, Tim McBride revealed in an op-ed in *The Eagle* campus newspaper that he is transgender and was ready to begin publicly identifying himself as a woman, Sarah.

As McBride wrote in the piece, headlined "The Real Me," "For my entire life, I've wrestled with my gender identity. It was only after the experiences of this year that I was able to come to terms with what had been my deepest secret: I'm transgender . . . As SG President, I realized that as great as it is to work on issues of fairness, it only highlighted my own struggles. It didn't bring the completeness that I sought. By mid-fall, it had gotten to the point where I was living in my own head. With everything I did, from the mundane to the exciting, the only way I was able to enjoy it was if I re-imagined doing it as a girl. My life was passing me by, and I was done wasting it as someone I wasn't."

Your Assignment

Document local gender-neutral fights and facilities. Share the stories of students whose sexuality, physical make-up, or general body type outcasts them in some way from the mainstream. And profile organizations and activists fighting for LGBTQ issues.

ETHICS ALERT!

Be mindful of the gender identification you use for transgender individuals. In almost all cases, respect the wishes of the individuals you are sourcing or featuring.

TRAUMARAMA

One word, four syllables, lots of blushing: Traumarama. The term, first coined by *Seventeen* magazine, involves life happenings so embarrassing they "make even the most dignified college student's skin crawl."

Last spring, *The Edge*, a magazine supplement of *The Pendulum* student newspaper at Elon University, published a related piece headlined "Elon's Own Traumarama." It shared first-person accounts from students about their especially cringe-inducing accidental cleavage exposures, urinary faux pas, walks of shame, black eyes, and missed kisses.

A portion of one traumarama: "My roommate last year had an unfortunate problem when she gets really drunk—she tends to wet the bed after she gets back from partying. One weekend we were out having fun at a party when we decided we wanted to go home. Since no one was capable of driving at that point, I called a guy friend to come pick us up, and we decided to just sleep over at his house. After giving my roommate and I his bed while he slept on the couch, I woke up first the next morning—and discovered that my roomie had peed herself all over his bed!"

Your Assignment

 Lightheartedly report upon the traumaramas involving students, faculty, and staff at your school, possibly themed around relationship, social, dorm, or classroom incidents. More seriously, detail the experiences of students with social phobias or mental or physical conditions that cause them embarrassment or extreme public discomfort.

NEW MEDIA ALERT!

 Through a check of the student press archives and chats with alumni and longtime employees, create an online timeline featuring the most shocking and legendary traumaramas at your school.

IMMERSION ALERT!

 Stage a single dramatic traumarama or a series of small ones, secretly recording and later attempting to interview a sampling of passersby. Your aim is to capture the levels of caring and human connection in public, observed in part by whether strangers will assist the faux traumarama victim, ignore what is happening, or even laugh and point.

STUDENT SHOOTERS

By day, they are students. By night, they are shooters. After dark, many female students morph into shot girls, or shooters, selling alcohol by the shot at local bars and clubs.

A UPIU report profiling a student shooter focused on her work over the course of a single night—from her intense make-up and costuming preparation to her not-so-subtle flirtations employed to sell drinks and earn money. At one point, men seeking drinks "make it rain," tossing dollar bills above the shooter's head to indicate their interest in purchasing shots.

Your Assignment

Explore the shooter culture at your school. Examine the popularity of this side-job among undergraduates and its perceived perks and downsides. Similar to the UPIU write-up, follow a student shooter on a typical shift, including their preparation beforehand and what happens after last call.

NEW MEDIA ALERT!

Video inside a private club or bar may be tough. Instead, grab as much audio as you can. Sounds of a lively drinking establishment and snippets of the student's interactions with patrons will be nice accompaniments for a still image slideshow.

IMMERSION ALERT!

Experience the challenges and benefits of shooter work firsthand. Spend a night or full week on your feet, selling shots, interacting with customers, and mingling with other shooters and bar and club employees.

OFF-CAMPUS HOUSING

With an increasing number of students selecting off-campus housing options, the legality and living conditions of local rental units are more significant than ever.

For example, *The Spectrum* at the University at Buffalo reported, "Every year, thousands of UB students risk their lives by renting homes that violate city and state building codes. In an eight-block radius within [an area near campus], 75 landlords rent properties that total hundreds of violations." *The Spectrum* found fault with the shady, often-absentee landlords, the local government whose inspectors were not doing their jobs, and the school for not monitoring students' choices more closely.

Your Assignment

Detail the living conditions faced by students in off-campus housing. Determine why students decide to live in specific spots and the problems they most frequently have. Investigate the related inspection process and landlord reputations, along with the university's role in overseeing off-campus housing decisions.

Teach as well as report. Run a sider outlining the websites students should visit, the university officials and government agencies they should contact, and the questions they should ask when checking on a property or landlord.

STUDENTS WITH DISABILITIES

Kedric Kitchens is in the minority. Not for his race, gender, or religious beliefs, but for his mode of transportation. Kitchens, a University of Oklahoma student, uses a wheelchair to travel across campus.

From his perspective, the trips are much more difficult than they should be. "The world is designed and built for the majority," he writes in a column for *The Oklahoma Daily*. "Therefore, it's unsurprising that being in a wheelchair makes getting around on a day-to-day basis a bit of a challenge. This is a universal truth anywhere you go, and OU is no different."

He describes being forced to take circuitous routes in order to reach the few building entrances accessible to those with disabilities. He confirms at times being forced to head up ramps that are too steep or centrally located, leaving him to push through crowds and feel like he is on display. He relates needing "a little help or a lot of luck" in order to get through some buildings' closed or locked doors. And he respectfully criticizes building elevators that are sometimes much too tiny for those in wheelchairs and take so much time to rise and fall that Kitchens says he can "knit a sweater in the time it takes for the door to open."

"If all you know of me is this story, you probably think that I hate this school," he concludes his column. "Nothing could be further from the truth. I love the University of Oklahoma. And on a daily basis, none of these things prove the least bit insurmountable. But things could be improved greatly."

Ultimately, the experiences described by Kitchens are a window into a much wider range of challenges faced by college students with all types of disabilities.

Your Assignment

 Look into your own school's level of compliance, as outlined by the Americans with Disabilities Act (ADA). Get the official statement on services offered, but also be sure to check things out for yourself. Most importantly, talk to students with disabilities about their experiences and suggestions for ADA-related improvement. Publish or post the ADA guidelines for restrooms, dorm rooms, classrooms, and campuses in general. You may be surprised how many students and staff you educate.

IMMERSION ALERT!

 Temporarily feign a disability. With the help of a knowledgeable guide, respectfully adopt a physical disability to determine firsthand the challenges of living with it day-to-day and the infrastructure gaps on campus and in your home, workplace, and community.

TWO IDEAS IN ONE

Book Nooks and Rare Finds

A study spot. A nook to relax. A computer lab. A group meeting pad. Among the many roles modern college and university libraries serve for their students, information center may no longer be chief among them.

University of Southern California student Rebecca Gao says her student peers "grossly underutilize the libraries' resources." In a column for *The Daily Trojan*, Gao argues libraries' digital offerings and special collections are especially going to waste due to a mix of student apathy and poor publicity efforts by schools. The result: a Google-only approach to student research that casts aside "in-depth, credible, and thorough" sources for those that are free, easy to understand, and only a click away.

Gao's assessment is doubly troubling when considering the value and diversity of items on display within many libraries' special collections. For example, as *The Dartmouth* shared last fall about the Dartmouth College special collections library, "[T]hough rarely used by most Dartmouth students for coursework, [it] features thousands of historical artifacts that include books, letters, and more eclectic items that you might not expect to find in an Ivy League library."

Among the more eclectic items: a lock of George Washington's hair, a fireman's helmet owned by former vice president Nelson Rockefeller, letters written by Winston Churchill to an American man who shared his name, and the final draft of the screenplay for the classic film *Animal House*.

Your Assignment

Report upon student research methods in various classes and academic programs. Separately, explore your school's library at different times of the day and semester, confirming how and how much students are utilizing it. Also, examine the most interesting, rare, and newsworthy finds in the library archives or special collections area. Focus particularly on works and items that might lead to greater understanding about the history of your school or coverage area.

NEW MEDIA ALERT!

With great care, and the permission and help of a librarian, use Scribd (scribd.com) or another social publishing site to post paper archives as viewable, even searchable, PDFs. Leave George Washington's hair out of this process.

PAY-FOR INTERNSHIPS

Forget low-paid and unpaid labor. The latest trend in student work experiences: paying *for* internships. Specifically, there has been a recent rise in the use of placement agencies. These agencies require students—or more typically their parents—to fork over hefty fees in exchange for help landing an internship in the field and city of their choice.

They provide a foot in the door for students without connections, but take away an essential attribute needed by traditional internship applicants: ambition. As *The Wall Street Journal* reports, "The whole idea of paying for internships is jarring to parents accustomed to finding work the old-fashioned way—by pounding the pavement. Critics say the trend risks deepening the divide between the haves and have-nots."

Your Assignment

 Report upon the paid, unpaid, and paid-*for* internship trends at your school. Gauge the perspectives of students, Career Services, and local employers on the rising use of internship placement agencies. More generally, determine the most common internship positions and the more popular fields in which students are attempting to intern. Share the stories of students' more creative and impacting internships. And find fresh graduates forced to segue into the real world with an internship instead of a job due to the down economy or their field's competitiveness.

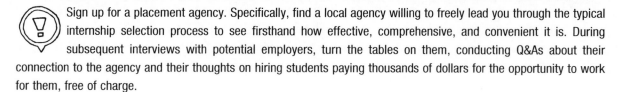

OFFBEAT ALERT!

Sign up for a placement agency. Specifically, find a local agency willing to freely lead you through the typical internship selection process to see firsthand how effective, comprehensive, and convenient it is. During subsequent interviews with potential employers, turn the tables on them, conducting Q&As about their connection to the agency and their thoughts on hiring students paying thousands of dollars for the opportunity to work for them, free of charge.

MALE CAPPER

The baseball cap is the ultimate young male fashion accessory. It is the non-essential clothing item undergraduate guys are likely to spend the most time picking out each morning. The most interesting aspect of this daily selection process is that it no longer revolves around hometown favorites or actual rooting interests. Instead, more male students are picking out the hat that best fits the rest of their outfit.

Yet, while team loyalty may no longer be as big of a factor, cap loyalty remains at an all-time high. As a column by a male student cap-lover in *The Louisville Cardinal* at the University of Louisville explains, "Most fashion elites would classify a worn, faded, and tired men's baseball cap as a fashion blunder . . . However, ask us to part with our beloved baseball cap and you are asking for a war. These thoughts and feelings regarding our most beloved garment lies deep in the emotional realm alongside our thoughts of our first teenage love . . . Whether it be a baseball logo hat, a name brand cap or a cap that features your favorite collegiate team, this cap may be more important than our eventual firstborn. Women, heed notice that I speak only the truth."

Your Assignment

 Investigate male baseball cap mania on your campus. Observe the styles, teams, sports, and color schemes most often represented. Profile any especially avid cap collectors and wearers. Determine how your own school's caps are designed and how well they sell.

NEW MEDIA ALERT!

 Create a time-lapse video featuring photos of a single cap-wearing student. The student should take self-portrait shots each morning for an entire semester or academic year. The key is displaying the different caps and clothes selected, in part to better visualize the male urge to match their headgear with the rest of their outfits. Separately, put together a narrative slideshow displaying students' favorite caps, overlaid with anecdotes about why they matter to the students. Or, more playfully, construct an online map displaying the locations of each school or team featured on the caps owned by an impassioned student collector.

OFFBEAT ALERT!

 Tell the story of a student's favorite cap, from the cap's perspective—from initial design specs and creation to the point of sale and subsequent journeying atop the student's head. Think caps lead quiet, fitted lives? As the Louisville student shares about his favorite headgear, "It has been run over, caught fire, been submerged in a lake, lost, found, and even bogarted by police. I tell you, if this hat had a memory, it probably should be in therapy."

RISE OF THE SPEEDY SENIOR

According to a report in *The Eagle* at American University, there are an "increasing number of students that graduate early from universities across the nation." The so-called speedy senior typically graduates a semester or full year early, taking advantage of AP credits, course overloads, and summer and winter break sessions.

Sometimes, the speedsters are spurred by academic ambitions or a general impatience to enter the job market. But mostly, they are motivated by the opportunity to stave off debt. As the *Eagle* found, "Though many students acknowledged that they would be giving up opportunities like studying abroad, interning, or taking more electives by graduating early, they explained that saving money is more important."

While it is better for students' bank accounts, it is troublesome for schools' bottom lines. As *The Cornell Daily Sun* reports, "The upswing in early graduations has begun to put a financial burden on the colleges, which do not receive expected tuition dollars when students graduate early."

Your Assignment

 Find out how many students in your school's current graduating class are speedy seniors. Assess whether there has been an increasing number of early graduates in recent years. Gauge the reactions of administrators on how the speedsters are helping or hurting themselves and the school. And check on what the student masses think about the early graduation option.

BRINGING THE SIDELINES TO LIFE

In anticipation of a recent college football season, Stanford University student Cyrus Pinto looked to the sidelines. The *Stanford Daily* sports writer believes one key to the success of his school's football squad is the passion of its supporters. As he explained in a column, "We need fans to be loud . . . We are competing with schools that have student sections two or three times our size, so to match their noise level, each of us has to be two or three times as loud."

Who was Pinto calling upon to pump up the volume of students in the stands? Superfans. As he wrote, "They are the guys and gals that paint their bodies, ring their cowbells, and/or are in the band. They help make football craziness mainstream on campus. All we need to do is spread their knowledge and passion to the rest of the student body. And this will be key to not just keeping students' butts in the seats . . . but to creating more effective cheering and yelling."

The superfan is a special breed of athletic enthusiast. Superfans have long been part of the college sports world—typically clumped together with friends and classmates in special student sections or cheering alone with the fervency of rabid dogs. Yet, superfandom goes far beyond simply cheering your heart out.

Superfans arrive super early on game day. They feed off watching warm-ups, player introductions, and the energy of the gathering crowd. They dress up—sporting carefully applied body paint or mascot-style costumes. They not only cheer the loudest but the smartest, delivering witty rehearsed chants and only shouting when it is most conducive to inspiring their own teams or infuriating the opponents. They are loyal, never abandoning their teams during a losing streak or even a stretch of bad seasons. And they have an almost encyclopedic knowledge of their teams' histories, players, coaches, and recruiting classes. True superfans can also break down the strengths and weaknesses of their teams' opponents on demand.

Your Assignment

 Examine the superfan subculture on your campus. Profile the most impassioned fans for various sports. Detail the most revered and quirky traditions of teams' supporters. Separately, report on fan apathy among certain sports and during certain times of year.

NEW MEDIA ALERT!

 Plan and execute a time-lapse video of superfans preparing and taking part in a big game, including applying body paint, tailgating, cheering their hearts out, and socializing and talking with friends about the game after its conclusion.

SEXUAL ACTIVISM

In spring 2011, the attention of many activists shifted to York University in Toronto after a local police officer speaking at a campus safety event advised female students to not "dress like sluts" to avoid being sexually assaulted. The comment prompted worldwide backlash and the birth of a new movement named for its chief activity: the SlutWalk.

The provocatively titled protest march involves women—and men—strolling in public while dressed in a sexually suggestive manner. It is aimed at eliminating the misperception that clothing choices cause sexual violence. Among the signs carried by the walkers: "Don't tell me what to wear; tell men not to rape."

Adrienne Edwards, a University of Pennsylvania student, writes that the walks also relate to a larger push for greater respect. "It is not just about feminism, it is not just about violence; it is about a common concern for our fellow human being," she argues. "[T]he marches are begging the question, if we do dress like sluts, what then? Are we not still entitled to the same respect that any other human walking this Earth does? It challenges everyone to think about how we relate to other different people. Is it really OK to disrespect the homeless man you saw on the street today? Is it really OK to disrespect someone perceived as less powerful than you? Is it really OK to disrespect a woman because of what she is wearing?"

Your Assignment

Explore the SlutWalk movement at your school or within your community, including its supporters and opponents. Extend the focus to the larger issues the movement addresses, including more provocative clothing styles and generational divides regarding style and sexuality perspectives. Also, outline school rules and even legal requirements regarding attire worn in residence halls and in public.

Separately, explore the general culture of activism on your campus. Profile the professors and administrators with activist histories who are willing to tell their tales. Outline the most popular current student causes. And share stories of student activists' efforts.

NEW MEDIA ALERT!

Livestream a SlutWalk or other area activist event. Produce an audio slideshow featuring activists making their most compelling arguments in support of their causes, in 60 seconds.

OFFBEAT ALERT!

Tell the story of activism from the point of view of the object, issue, or group being fought for or protested against. For example, follow the creation, harvesting, and distribution of food produced via slave labor. Or share the story of a popular tech gadget produced overseas in poor factory conditions.

TWO IDEAS IN ONE

An Alcohol Education

An online alcohol education course incoming freshmen nationwide are required to complete is "ineffective and may actually encourage irresponsible drinking," according to *The Red and Black* at the University of Georgia.

Apparently, many students see the hours-long program—called "My Student Body"—as a waste of time, something they click through while multi-tasking. Some even use it as a resource to learn *more* about how to get drunk, the exact opposite of its intended purpose. Yikes.

As a UGA student wrote in a focus group report cited by *The Red and Black*, "I thought [the My Student Body course] was great! It taught me all sorts of new tricks for drinking so I didn't look so naïve coming into college!"

Students' unofficial use of the course as a pro-drinking seminar is especially newsworthy given the prevalence of student drinking ailments and deaths. As the *Michigan Tech Lode* at Michigan Technological University states, "Approximately half of all full-time college undergraduate students report abusing alcohol at least once a month . . . nearly 50 students die a year from too much alcohol consumption and over 1,800 students die a year from alcohol-related motor vehicle crashes."

An increasing number also fall prey to conditions such as drunkorexia. The five-syllable word has become the most publicized new disorder impacting college students. The affliction, which leaves students hungry and at times hungover, involves "starving all day to drink at night."

As *The Daily Pennsylvanian* at the University of Pennsylvania explains, drunkorexia centers on students "bingeing or skipping meals in order to either compensate for alcohol calories consumed later at night, or to get drunk faster . . . At its most severe, it is a combination of an eating disorder and alcohol dependency."

Drunkorexia surged into the spotlight most prominently in fall 2011 after an eye-opening study by University of Missouri researchers revealed "one in six students said they restricted food in order to consume alcohol within the last year."

To help combat the consequences of such behavior, more schools are granting amnesty to students who report friends' or their own alcohol-related emergencies. The official pardon, known as the Good Samaritan Policy, aims to ensure students don't avoid calling for medical help for fear of being cited for underage drinking or on-campus alcohol possession.

Your Assignment

Examine the alcohol culture on your campus, including dangerous drinking trends such as drunkorexia and the student groups leading responsible drinking campaigns. Also, take a sobering look at your school's alcohol education and awareness programs, including how students view them and how much the school spends on them.

If incoming students are required to complete the My Student Body course—as they seem to be nearly everywhere—outline what they think of it and their suggestions for improving it. Also, investigate what the course actually entails, including the questions asked, information offered, and the style in which everything is presented.

NEW MEDIA ALERT!

 Post a running blog series maintained by an admitted drunkorexic, journaling what they eat and drink during a given week or set of weekends. Separately, present a screenshot slideshow of sample questions and information featured in the My Student Body course.

OFFBEAT ALERT!

 Create an infographic sharing the top "tricks for drinking" the My Student Body course ironically provides underage students.

THE PLEDGE PROCESS

A column last year by a Dartmouth College student outlining the many degrading acts he endured while pledging a fraternity earned national attention for its extremely candid glimpse at hazing.

As Andrew Lohse wrote in the piece, headlined "Telling the Truth," "I was a member of a fraternity that asked pledges, in order to become a brother, to: swim in a kiddie pool full of vomit, urine, fecal matter, semen, and rotten food products; eat omelets made of vomit; chug cups of vinegar, which in one case caused a pledge to vomit blood; drink beers poured down fellow pledges' ass cracks; and vomit on other pledges, among other abuses. Certainly, pledges could have refused these orders. However, under extreme peer pressure and the desire to 'be a brother,' most acquiesced."

Your Assignment

 Use the column as a trigger for a fresh look at your school's hazing practices and reporting procedures. Investigate the existence of hazing in any form among student groups, including Greek organizations and athletic teams. Explore how much of it is considered illegal or against school rules. Depending on its pervasiveness, tell the stories of those who have been through it and those who were in charge of dishing it out.

Also, look into the official procedures surrounding hazing complaints. Profile the point-people who carry out related investigations. And detail how oversight and enforcement work with student groups operating from off-campus housing.

NEW MEDIA ALERT!

Create a photo slideshow or video report following a single fraternity or sorority pledge class as they endure the process of becoming full-blown brothers or sisters. Put together a photo rundown of the funnier, more public, and more lighthearted hazing stunts, such as the odd clothes, props, and facial hair some pledges and new student-athletes must wear, carry with them, or grow. Construct an online map highlighting the spots where campus hazing has occurred, providing background information in the map's pop-up captions.

ETHICS ALERT!

Be extremely careful about reporting on alleged hazing or any form of degradation without seeing it with your own eyes or confirming it through multiple trusted sources. You should honor the requests of current and former pledges to remain anonymous in some cases, but be wary of campaigns to simply take down a team or organization a few people don't like. Also, be sure you understand the full context of a particular ritual or event before labeling it hazing or against the law or the school's code of conduct.

BED BUG BITES

They are nocturnal, live off the blood of people and animals, measure only "about one-third the width of a dime," and regularly cause big, big problems worldwide. Bed bugs are some of the creepiest, most persistent little buggers infesting bedrooms, clothing, couches, backpacks, and pets. In late 2010, the federal government sponsored a Congressional Bed Bug Forum and approved $50 million in funding to combat their spread.

The creatures have plagued residence halls since higher education's start. An outbreak last year at the University of Nebraska-Lincoln grew into a hysteria labeled "bed bug-gate." It began when a female student in a UNL residence hall saw the "parasitic insects" on her roommate's bed. "I had my boyfriend kill them because bugs freak me out," she told *The Daily Nebraskan*. "After they were dead I didn't think anything else about it and just went to bed . . . [But] that night I couldn't go to sleep, I kept feeling these pinches of nerve pain all over my legs and arms." She woke up the next morning with bite marks on her legs.

Housing staffers and exterminators later set traps, fumigated rooms, tossed infected dorm furniture, purchased a carbon dioxide machine to freeze them, inspected every campus dorm room, and even employed a trained bed-bug-sniffing rat terrier named Spots to help ferret them out. Total estimated cost for the effort: $100,000.

Your Assignment

 Investigate the bed bug situation on your campus or within your community. Outline the infestation prevention and treatment methods and personnel—don't forget the trained pooches. Also, profile individuals with bed bug horror stories or actual scars. In a larger sense, detail the money spent and steps taken by school officials to keep campus buildings clean and up to code.

OFFBEAT ALERT!

 Create a series of memes displaying the reactions of bed bugs to various places they inhabit on campus, aimed at satirizing well-known school ephemera, stereotypes, current events, and gossip.

CALLING FOUL

In the pantheon of campus club sports, the most undervalued, underpaid heroes may just be the student officials. Over the course of numerous seasons and for multiple sports, a core group of students does its part to ensure everyone is following the rules. As a Texas Tech University student flag football official told *The Daily Toreador*, the benefits of the assignment are numerous: "It gets me out in my community, it gives me exercise, gets me running around, and interacting with the student body."

Your Assignment

 Look beyond the games and team rankings that represent a large majority of club sports coverage. Instead, explore what it is like to officiate the on-campus contests, along with the training and tests students must pass. Profile the students who take on the gig, capturing their motivations for doing it and how the endeavor interacts with their current interests and larger life goals.

IMMERSION ALERT!

If you have the sports knowledge and the gusto, take up the officiating challenge for a game or two. Document every step of your referee journey, including what rules were toughest to memorize, what decisions were toughest to make on the fly, what it is like dealing with impassioned athletes and fans, and how you were able to assess the quality of your work after the game.

SPIN-OFF ALERT!

Sports reporting is most often focused on the games, the athletes who play them—and at times the coaches and team owners who have a hand in shaping them. There are many, many others though whose first jobs, side jobs, and sole jobs revolve around sports. They are indelible parts of the larger sports narrative—and worth interviewing, observing, or profiling. Some examples: announcers, athletic recruiters and scouts, athletic trainers, groundskeepers, scoreboard operators, Sports Information Office employees, sports psychologists, sports technology researchers, student-athlete tutors, and team chefs.

MARRIED STUDENTS

A small but prominent subset of students within higher education is balancing marriage and a full course load. In a video report last spring by *The Daily Titan* at California State University, Fullerton, married students cited a range of real-world challenges, including finances, time apart from their spouses, and competing work–life commitments.

They often face additional challenges on campus. For example, in a letter to the editor published in *The Branding Iron* at the University of Wyoming, a married student expressed her "concern and irritation with the lack of support for married students on campus." As she writes, "When I got married, I assumed there would be some benefits for my spouse also. But there are not. There is no health insurance option (and as students this is hard to get when jobs or schools do not provide it or some help for it), there is no gym discount, and the married student housing is lacking in number. This seems like a problem to me . . . You have to ask yourselves: how many of your students are married?"

Your Assignment

Start by answering that question. Determine the number of students at your school who are engaged, married, separated, divorced, pregnant, and full-blown parents. Share snippets of what life is like for married students specifically, on and off campus. And, building off the *Branding Iron* letter, detail what life is like for their spouses. Be sure to include LGBTQ students who are legally married or involved in marriage-like domestic partnerships. Also, examine your school's stance toward students who are married—gay and straight—including whether it provides related health insurance options, special housing, or perks for their significant others.

EXTINGUISHER EXPLORATION

In January 2012, *The Signal* at Georgia State University confirmed a quarter of the 7,000 fire extinguishers housed on GSU's campus are past due.

"A spot check of fire extinguishers . . . in the parking garages and secluded areas of various buildings revealed expired extinguishers," the paper reported. "A more serious concern for administrators . . . is that students do not know where fire extinguishers are located or what to do in case of a fire."

Your Assignment

Carry out a fire drill. Determine how many fire extinguishers are standing ready on your campus or inside highly trafficked buildings within your coverage area. Outline their purchase and maintenance procedures, costs, and overseeing personnel. Check to see if any are past their expiration dates, along with confirming what that means exactly. In addition, report upon other elements of fire safety required by law to be supervised by your school. Determine how the school measures up in that supervision.

Conduct man-on-the-street interviews to gauge the public's general familiarity with fire safety protocol, such as the location of extinguishers, emergency exits, and proper evacuation procedures. Separately, look into the amount and type of fire alarm incidences on campus, along with the pranks and campus security test runs.

NEW MEDIA ALERT!

Stage an undercover video tour of fire extinguishers in dorms, academic buildings, and parking garages, in part to determine their accessibility and whether any are past due. Or put together a brief instructional video featuring a local firefighter explaining how to effectively operate an extinguisher.

OFFBEAT ALERT!

Tell the story of a single extinguisher located on campus. Using its unique ID code, document its journey from creation and assembly to purchase, placement, maintenance, and checks. It provides a great grounding for a larger look at these strange devices we pass by multiple times every day but never think twice about.

ADDICTION, ON THE RUN

Wes Trueblood is a recovering addict.

He once "stole from his grandmother's church group and snuck change from his niece's piggy bank" to pay for drugs. At rock bottom, a few years back, he said goodbye to his sister, drank, popped pills, and drove until his mind hit oblivion—and his Ford Escort flipped into a ditch.

He survived. Soon after, he started running. He is unable to stop. As an award-winning profile in *Indiana Daily Student*'s *Inside* magazine at Indiana University shared, Trueblood is addicted to the so-called runner's high. He needs to run at least 12 miles a day, every day, to satiate his need for an exercise and adrenaline fix.

"At the end of every run, the internal battle continues," *Inside* staff writer Rachel Stark reported. "Trueblood can't outrun something inside of him, because when he stops, the demons catch up. So he'll just keep running, as much as he can, for the rest of his life. It's all he knows [how] to do."

Your Assignment

Report upon various forms of addiction and their consequences within your coverage area. Profile individuals currently or formerly addicted to acts, substances, and entities such as smoking, sex, exercise, cleanliness, the Internet, video games, alcohol, drugs, shopping, gambling, and the spotlight. And examine the outlets that feed or help them fight their addictions.

TWO IDEAS IN ONE

"A Simple Prick, Slash, or Burn"

 A growing movement among students and many others makes ear piercing and the basic forearm tattoo look like child's play. Real body modification is built atop individuals who "test the waters and push the envelope," including through tongue splitting, teeth filing, 3D body implants, scarification, body suspension, and voluntary amputation.

As a feature in *The Red and Black* at the University of Georgia begins, "Metal and flesh are in harmony—at times. With body modification, a simple prick, slash, or burn can be used to ornament or manipulate the body. Some do it for pain. Others for pleasure. And others are just curious."

One body modification of sorts especially widespread at the moment: fake baking. According to Reuters, indoor tanning is now more common than smoking. One consequence has been the rise of tanorexia, identified as both an addiction and a disease. Tanorexics currently run rampant on many college campuses. They are identifiable by their orange-brown, leathery skin, tanning salon membership cards, and the strange tan line under their arms caused by the position in which they lay in the tanning beds.

"The tanning industry targets the college-age demographic," *The Apache Pow Wow* at Tyler Junior College in Texas notes. "That's the generation most easily influenced by what is portrayed in the media, which currently glorifies having a sexy, glowing tan." Unfortunately, that glow comes with dangers, including skin cancer and an increased blood flow to the brain that creates an addiction on par with smoking and drinking.

Your Assignment

 Document the steel-and-ink culture on your campus. Profile individuals who have opted for more common and extreme body modifications. Also, seek out locals who serve as tattoo artists and professional piercers. Attend and observe classes that teach it. Stop by local organizations geared toward specific types of body modification. Share the stories behind the modifications undertaken by students, faculty, and staff.

Separately, shine a light on local tanning trends. Focus on current and recovering tanorexics and the salons that darken them so conveniently. Report upon the related dangers, psychological motivations, and pop culture influences.

NEW MEDIA ALERT!

Create a time-lapse video of a student's body modification procedure. Run a slideshow of various modifications, overlaid with audio of people explaining what they mean. Crowdsource the crazier and more memorable tattoos and piercings people have received.

IMMERSION ALERT!

If you are the especially adventurous type, modify your body. Consider a range of short-term mod options to better understand the appeal and related public response. A few possibilities, some more extreme than others: temporary tattooing, play piercing, cell popping, hair feathering, non-piercing jewelry, and body glitter.

CLICHÉ ALERT!

Unless truly fresh or newsworthy, avoid stories on how tattoos and other body modifications cost students jobs or have become symbols they regret. Those pieces have been published a million times before.

SPIN-OFF ALERT!

Focus on the people and processes involved in liposuction, plastic surgery, or chemotherapy. Profile individuals whose bodies have been modified via permanent hearing aids, voice boxes, and prosthetic limbs. Or tell the stories behind individuals' limps and scars.

A "BALANCE SPORT REVOLUTION"

Slacklining, a pursuit centered on finding the perfect balance, has reached a tipping point among students. The activity involves walking ever-so-carefully across shaky nylon webbing typically tied between two trees about a foot from the ground. BBC News describes it as "the trampoline meets the tightrope." Separate enthusiasts consider it a mere hobby, a rock-climbing training technique, a form of "moving meditation," or a full-blown "balance sport revolution."

In numerous spots nationwide, students have become the faces of this revolution. As the *Columbia Missourian* at the University of Missouri explains, "College students have especially taken to slacklining because it is relatively inexpensive, can be set up almost anywhere, and is extremely entertaining."

Student slackliners do recognize the whole set-up appears slightly outlandish to those not familiar with the practice or its purpose. As a University of Delaware student admits, "We look like we're walking a tightrope, so [student passersby are] like, 'Where's the circus?'"

Your Assignment

 Report upon the "balance sport revolution" within your coverage area. Profile local slackliners. Explore the environmental impact of the tree-tying component. Extend the focus to more extreme sports and activities, including body boarding, bungee jumping, cliff jumping, hang gliding, skydiving, snowboarding, and windsurfing.

IMMERSION ALERT!

 Join the circus. Attempt slacklining for yourself.

OFFBEAT ALERT!

 Feature students whose various physical abilities, knowledge bases, and skillsets would combine to form a campus circus of sorts, such as trapeze artists, jugglers, animal tamers, acrobats, tightrope walkers, fire breathers, contortionists, and clowns.

EARLY CLASSES, HIGHER GRADES

As students select their courses for each upcoming semester, one schedule tidbit they should keep in mind: To boost your GPA, an 8 a.m. class might be worth waking up for. College students enrolled in early classes apparently earn higher grades. One study by researchers at New York's St. Lawrence University literally found a slight drop in student grade point averages for each hour a class starts later.

The numbers push for a reversal of the "dreaded 8 a.m. class" stereotype, built atop the image of bleary-eyed undergraduates who would rather be anywhere else. They also argue for a striking turnabout on the traditional thinking that late afternoon or evening classes allow for more sleep and, in turn, more engaged students. Instead, according to the study, a morning class often pushes students to get to sleep earlier, complete work more efficiently, and, most importantly, stay sober—all of which helps their grades.

Your Assignment

Stake out the morning class scene at your school. Document the general student and professor attitudes toward early-riser courses. Single out classes that serve as especially inspiring wake-up calls or creatively use the morning hour to their advantage. Scroll through the current course listing. Confirm how many classes qualify for morning status, compared with the number of classes held in the afternoon, evening, and any time (including independent studies and online). If you are able to obtain a full grading breakdown, run a crosscheck of student marks in earlier and later classes, possibly using easy comparisons such as sections of the same course held at different times.

OFFBEAT ALERT!

Revise the academic transcripts of a few willing students. Replace the names of the courses they have completed with the time periods in which they were held. Subsequently, determine how their GPA fluctuates—not by major or core requirements—but by the time of day their classes were scheduled. Does the higher-achieving morning theory hold up?

TWO IDEAS IN ONE

Weight of a (Fresh) Man

The Freshman 15 is actually the Freshman 3. According to a report in *Social Science Quarterly*, first-year students at colleges and universities only gain a bit more than three pounds during their first two semesters in school.

The "myth-debunking" finding is the first major blowback against the Freshman 15 phenomenon since its introduction into the media and public lexicon more than 20 years ago. According to the *Los Angeles Times*, "The first mention of 'Freshman 15' came . . . in 1989 in *Seventeen* magazine. By the late 1990s, use of the 'Freshman 15' term in articles had risen significantly and (shockingly!) about half . . . did not refute or question the reality of 'Freshman 15.'"

Mainstream magazines and college media regularly run articles obsessing about how students can avoid the dramatic weight gain. As an opinion piece in a student newspaper at a Michigan college shares, "Education typically isn't the only thing you gain in college. Looked in the mirror lately? Many college kids have a case of the Freshman 15. And many students don't even realize it until their pants are too tight."

In actuality, according to the study, those pants for the most part will still be a perfect fit by the end of the year. According to the study's co-author, "There are a lot of things to worry about when you go to college. However, gaining 15 pounds your freshman year is not one of them."

Along with issues of weight gain, extreme weight loss has become a micro-beat all its own within the modern news media. Related diet and exercise plans, food brands, weight-management programs, mobile apps, and inspirational weight loss stories have all worked their way into the news cycle.

For example, in respect to the latter, last spring the *Reporter* at the Rochester Institute of Technology featured a rotund student's efforts to shed more than half his body weight. In a year, RIT undergraduate Nate Finch lost roughly 125 pounds, chronicling the efforts on his blog, Weight of a Man (weightofaman.com).

As he wrote in his opening post, "Obesity is a huge issue and I know that. I don't want to be that guy getting winded walking up the stairs anymore. I want to be that guy that can run up 10 flights of stairs, and be able to resume normally at the end. I want to be the guy the women turn their heads for, not the guy they turn their heads away from. Most of all, I just want to feel good in my body."

Your Assignment

 Feature the weight gain issues and weight loss efforts of individuals in your coverage area. Report upon your school's food science and nutrition programs and classes. Explore the social networks and digital tools aimed at helping those with weight issues. And determine once and for all whether, on your campus, the Freshman 15 is a myth to be debunked or an actual phenomenon.

NEW MEDIA ALERT!

 Following Finch's lead, chronicle a student's extreme weight loss journey via a blog, Twitter feed, and a Flickr photo set showing their (hopefully) receding pants or dress size.

FIGHTING WORLDSUCK

DFTBA. The five-letter acronym is also a call-to-arms. Simply put: Don't Forget to Be Awesome. The saying is a core component of nerdfighting, a cult movement gaining traction on many campuses.

Nerdfighters are a loose collection of geeky do-gooders who attempt to enact positive change in the real world and online. "[A] nerdfighter just tries to fight against worldsuck," *The Butler Collegian* at Butler University explains. "Worldsuck: In essence, all the bad and/or stupid things in the world."

For example, at California's Chapman University, a campus nerdfighting club carries out "positive pranking." As *The Panther*, Chapman's student newspaper, confirms, "Instead of playing ding-dong-ditch, they would leave a Hostess CupCake with an inspiring note on a doorstep, and instead of toilet-papering a house, they would hang Tootsie Pops on trees."

At the University of Notre Dame, *Observer* columnist Elisa DeCastro suggests taking up similarly positive, productive activities. "Increase awesome," she implores readers. "Write a book, discover a new species, build a time machine—or just put stuff on your head and do a funny dance. (What? It's fun!) Big or small, find some way to share your nerdy passions with the world."

Your Assignment

 Explore your own school's nerdfighting culture and its most committed converts. More generally, report upon the volunteer work individual students, campus groups, and classes are carrying out. And profile the most generous donors to area schools and charities. Separately, examine the nerdfighting tenet, in reverse. Investigate the more common or heinous campus pranks, personal attacks, and cyberbullying incidents.

IMMERSION ALERT!

 Dish out kind words, hugs, high-fives, or free gifts on camera for people who walk by. Gauge the public reactions to the niceties. And stop a few individuals right after for instant interviews about their own history with random acts of kindness.

TWO IDEAS IN ONE

Bike Shares, Long Boards

 University students, professors, and staff are riding bicycles in record numbers. As campuses expand, gas prices surge, and parking spaces dwindle, more bikes are being put to use to travel to and from classes, club meetings, sporting events, and social hangouts.

One effort being put into place or expanded at an increasing number of schools to meet spoke-and-wheel demand: bicycle-sharing programs. For example, at Michigan's Oakland University, a single bike with bad brakes has grown over the past two years into a campus-wide initiative featuring a fleet of more than 250 pink women's bicycles available for student use free of charge. As *The Oakland Post* reports, "They may be pink, but these trusty transporters demand some respect."

Another increasingly popular mode of transport on and near campuses: the longboard. It is longer than a skateboard and loosely akin to a surfboard with wheels.

"You've seen them around campus, you've seen them downtown, and you've seen them skated on with bare feet, sneakers or sandals," *The DePaulia* at DePaul University notes. "Longboards have been a part of our culture for the past 60 years and have gradually become a part of our campus within the last three."

The rise is attributed to the boards' abilities to gain more speed, roll smoother, and glide for greater distances than traditional skateboards. As one young longboarder shares, "When I ride, I feel like a navigator of my environment. I feel at one with the geography of the land, as I use it to my advantage to propel me forward. Riding is a relief from the everyday, standstill life."

Your Assignment

 Inquire into local biking and longboarding cultures. Break down school and community sharing programs, competitions, and gathering points. Profile especially impassioned bicyclists and longboarders, including those who endure arduous commutes or create or collect a high number of boards.

NEW MEDIA ALERT!

 Feature a slideshow of especially creative bikes and boards owned by local individuals, including those adorned with personal touches linked a bit to who they are.

IMMERSION ALERT!

 Get on a board. Learn the basic gist, more extreme tricks, and proper etiquette of longboarding firsthand. Temporarily travel solely via longboard, determining its benefits, difficulties, and the public reactions it provokes while in motion.

OFFBEAT ALERT!

 Pull together livestream video of a dedicated bicyclist's morning or afternoon commute, seeing and hearing things from the rider's point of view (maybe via a small helmet camera and microphone).

SLEEP TEXTING

While they sleep, some students snore. Some dream. And a growing number text. Sleep texting has recently become a phenomenon worthy of attention in student and professional press circles. It has joined sleepwalking, sleep paralysis, and old-fashioned nightmares as one of the more common things that occur while undergraduates and others are grabbing some shuteye.

As *The Lantern* at Ohio State University explains, "Sleep texting is as simple as it sounds: a person will respond or send out a text message in the middle of their sleep. Most people who do this usually do not remember doing it and it usually doesn't make much sense." For example, a University of Georgia senior told *The Red and Black*, "I've done it several times before and they've been coherent and incoherent. One time, I accidentally asked for a pizza."

One possible cause of this slumbering text craze: FOMO or the Fear of Missing Out. Students are increasingly obsessed with being connected—to their high-tech devices, social media chatter, and their friends. The goal is to ensure they are present or in the loop when an incident worthy of a viral video or funny status update occurs.

In a Huffington Post write-up last spring, a Georgetown University student confirmed FOMO "is a widespread problem on college campuses . . . Even when we'd rather catch up on sleep or melt our brain with some reality television, we feel compelled to seek bigger and better things from our weekend. We fear that if we don't partake in every Saturday night's fever, something truly amazing will happen, leaving us hopelessly behind."

Your Assignment

Focus on the FOMO phenomenon, and the behaviors like sleep texting it draws out. Profile mobile-and-Internet addicts, along with those who purposefully steer clear of the unending madness by not purchasing a smartphone or signing up for Facebook.

More generally, explore the dying art and shifting definition of alone time, especially in a world in which "solitude has become stigmatized," according to a *Daily Pennsylvanian* column. As it shares, "Technology has complicated our notion of what being alone really means. If you're by yourself in your bedroom with your phone on and Facebook open, are you really alone?"

NEW MEDIA ALERT!

Pull together an interactive timeline displaying the wildest or most significant can't-miss moments in your school's history or just within the past academic year. Separately, post an illustrative slideshow featuring students' more heartfelt, random, and funny "sleep texts."

SPIN-OFF ALERT!

Explore other after-dark activities and conditions including insomnia, stargazing, snoring, walks of shame, late-night work shifts, night eating syndrome (NES), and all-night study sessions.

"THE EXPERIENCE OF HOMESICKNESS"

As students return to school at the start of each semester, there is one especially nagging feeling many bring with them: homesickness. Whether it involves missing family, pets, friends, or the comfort of the familiar, homesickness is undoubtedly as embedded within higher education as Spring Break and Saturday football.

Its emotional impact has not abated in the digital age, even amid the many tools making long-distance connections more convenient.

As Susan J. Matt, the author of *Homesickness: An American History*, explains, "Today, college students, members of the military, immigrants and other folks far from home certainly can call or text their families, connect on Facebook, use Skype, and be in touch in a way their ancestors could only dream of. For many people, this makes being away from family easier. On the other hand, some people say that having all that contact with home without actually being there heightens the feeling of homesickness, because you know exactly what you are missing out on . . . Technology definitely has changed the experience of homesickness, but it hasn't eliminated the feeling."

Your Assignment

 Hone in on homesickness—the emotion, the causes, the consequences, and the potential cures. Profile students who deal with bouts of it, including those on campus and in far-flung places due to study abroad and internships. Feature the spots on or near campus that remind individual students of home. Travel with students to their childhood homes or hometowns to learn a bit about where they come from and who they are away from campus. And discuss students' take on the digital impact Matt describes.

OFFBEAT ALERT!

 Profile students who are not homesick but sick of home. Specifically, share the stories of students who rarely if ever return home due to a troubled upbringing, family rift, or the inconvenience or time it takes to get there. Inquire into their semester break routines and what life is like for someone who does not have a place they long to go home to.

"THE WHOLE PREMISE OF ANNUAL GIVING"

"As government funding for the nation's colleges dwindle due to budget cuts and a sputtering economy, private donations to higher education have increased," a *USA TODAY College* report confirmed last spring. The two most pressing related questions for many students and young alumni: How much should you give back to your university after graduation? And when should the giving begin?

Schools often ask senior students to join the donor ranks prior to graduation, in hopes of instilling an immediate and lasting sense of indebtedness and connection to one's alma mater. Faced with the prospect of enormous student loans, impending graduate school payments, or meager starting salaries, some students are too financially strapped to make an early donation. Others, however, simply do not buy into the concept.

For example, in February 2012 at Princeton University, a senior student spurred campus-wide debate after calling "the whole premise of annual giving . . . problematic." In a guest column published in *The Daily Princetonian*, Emily Rutherford argued the idea of alumni simply passing along money to their alma maters is a narrow way of conceptualizing "giving back."

Rutherford also took issue with the notion that she is forever bonded to the university financially because it offered her enrollment, memorable experiences, and financial aid. "I'd like to think I've shown my gratitude for my scholarship throughout the past four years: trying my hardest at my schoolwork, remaining very involved in institutional committee work and other kinds of campus activism, and serving as a mentor to younger students," she wrote. "And now my commitment is done. I didn't sell Princeton my soul for a financial aid grant; I don't owe the university for the rest of my life."

Upon its publication, the piece triggered close to 200 online comments, a large majority nastily ripping into the student as ungrateful for her Ivy League education. According to one commenter, "Donating isn't about doing something 'morally good,' it's about helping a university that has given you so much, and will not be able to do so for future generations if students stop giving."

Your Assignment

Report upon student and alumni giving at your school. Gather the related donation figures. Observe the fundraising apparatus in action. Interview and feature fundraising chairs, big-time and minimal donors, individuals unable to donate due to financial difficulties, and those like Rutherford who do not buy into the premise. Detail the quirkiest and most complicated strings attached to past donations. And explore the motivations behind donations linked to very specific student scholarships and school programs.

NEW MEDIA ALERT!

Create an interactive graphic displaying donation levels to your school over time. Provide details on the allocation of those funds. And outline how big a part donations play in the school's total revenue, compared with public assistance, student tuition and room and board, athletics and merchandising, and other areas.

SPIN-OFF ALERT!

Share the stories of the individuals responsible for the largest donations in school history or those whose funding earned them naming rights on campus buildings and other facilities.

THE FIGHT FOR TWO-PLY

The University Daily Kansan fought for two-ply—and won. Last spring, the student newspaper at the University of Kansas published an editorial calling for thicker, more durable toilet paper to replace the oft-ripped one-ply in all campus restrooms.

The commentary complemented a news story in which students said they were similarly chapped. As one student shared, "The toilet paper is so thin, it rips and it's frustrating as you attempt to tear it off the dispenser. I would never TP a house with this stuff."

Months later, the school announced a switch to two-ply, prompting campus-wide praise. A KU senior told the *Kansan* at the time that while he used to "hold it" until getting off campus because of the low-quality toilet paper, "Now that there's a better product, I'm willing to give it another shot."

Your Assignment

Address the state of TP quality, consumption, and cost on your campus. Assess who makes the purchasing decisions and the relative happiness of students with both the ply and availability. Throw in paper towels, hand soap, hand dryers, and urinal, toilet, and stall installation and repair for a complete restroom financial picture.

SUGAR BABIES

A growing number of mostly female students are engaging in romantic, sexual, and apparently financial relationships with gentlemen often old enough to be their fathers—or even grandfathers.

They are known as sugar babies. Under a mutually acceptable agreement, some or all of the young women's financial needs are taken care of by their older beaus, including clothes, cars, food, trips, and tuition and room and board.

As one man who runs a company overseeing such arrangements explained to *The Tulane Hullabaloo* at Tulane University, "The press likes to compare it to prostitution, but it really isn't. Once, Dr. Drew asked one of the sugar babies why she didn't strip, and she answered that stripping is degrading for her, but being a sugar baby is more like dating and having a generous person who is willing to help her—perhaps a more extreme form of dating, but dating nonetheless."

Your Assignment

Search for sugar babies at your school. Share their stories and possibly those of the older professionals who enter into relationships with them. Answer readers' most pressing questions, including how they first meet, routinely interact, arrange payments, maintain secrecy, and determine an end date for the arrangement.

ETHICS ALERT!

Recognize that while supporters might deem it "extreme dating," many others' perceptions will hover in the prostitution category. Be careful about inserting judgment, sarcasm, or even open-to-interpretation wordplay into the headlines or main piece. And strongly consider protecting the identities of all related interviewees and possibly even being vague on the places and times their meet-ups happen.

TWO IDEAS IN ONE

Common Readings and Campus Portraits

Diversity issues are present on every campus beyond the gender spread, skin color, and birthplaces of the student body and staff. Sometimes, they are also hanging on the walls and assigned as readings.

For example, last spring, *The Harvard Crimson* reported on the homogeneity of individuals featured in artwork displayed at Harvard University—and a professor determined to make them more diverse. As the *Crimson* confirmed, "[O]f the approximately 750 oil paintings that hang throughout the campus, about 690 of them feature white males. From marble busts to stained glass, Harvard's art collection is stunningly grand and yet remarkably homogenous."

Separately, a day after the *Crimson* portrait piece, *The Cornell Daily Sun* published an op-ed by a Cornell University professor criticizing the selection of a novel all freshmen are required to read as "particularly insensitive vis-à-vis diversity issues on campus." As he asked, "How are our Arab and Muslim students supposed to read this novel? Where is their representation in it? More broadly, what kind of a message does it send to underrepresented 'minorities' about their representation on campus? That is, what kind of a critical inspection did it receive in terms of the diversity baggage it brings with it?"

Your Assignment

Examine who and what are featured in the artwork displayed on your campus. Also, confirm who created them. Assess the overall diversity of the creators and creations, in respect to gender, race, ethnicity, class, and even time period. Dive deeper by investigating art purchasing and display decisions, including the amount and type of student input. In addition, analyze the diversity of the artists and art genres studied within your school's art program.

Separately, investigate the selection process surrounding "common readings" at your school. Confirm the criteria for choosing the finalists and ultimate winner. Report upon the characteristics shared by recent readings, in respect to the diversity or homogeneity of the authors, main characters, central plot locations and time periods, and the main themes and worldviews espoused.

NEW MEDIA ALERT!

Stage a visual crowdsourcing. Lightheartedly request digital student self-portraits to diversify the offerings hanging on campus building walls. They may be drawn in any style, but should focus on displaying the students' main characteristics, passions, or life goals. Feature the portraits and brief backgrounds about the student artists on a digital wall you erect.

YOLO

Carpe Diem is dead. *Gather ye rosebuds* has withered. *Live life to the fullest* is so last year. The latest dream-big-be-bold phrase is actually an acronym, one that has been fervently adopted and scorned in equal measure by students and the general public: YOLO or You Only Live Once. It is a text-and-tweet-friendly reminder about the benefits of seeking sheer enjoyment, adventure, and risk during our brief time on Earth.

Many students have publicly demeaned it as nothing more than a silly phrase their peers are whispering and hashtagging when engaged in irresponsible behavior. Others, though, see its potential.

As Ashley Dye wrote for *The Ball State Daily News* at Ball State University, "I see it as a fun little fad. It reminds me of 'Hakuna Matata,' but without a warthog and a meerkat singing about it

. . . Too many people (myself included) can work themselves to death and forget about an important part of a healthy life—mental health. Remember 'all work and no play makes Jack a dull boy'? If shouting '#YOLO' is what keeps you from pulling a *The Shining*, then do it."

Your Assignment

Wrangle up YOLO stories and status updates, along with a firm handle on its subculture within your coverage area. Extend its basic premise to more lighthearted glimpses at the latest adventure sports and extreme travel trends. Or take more serious looks at individuals with out-of-balance lifestyles due to factors such as substance abuse, a mental condition, economic despair, or sheer workaholism. Also, use the acronym as a foundation for a feature on student side-passions—the hobbies, start-up companies, and sports that compete for their time and attention between classes, studying, and socializing.

TWO IDEAS IN ONE

The Snitch is Loose, Harry is Lost

The University Daily Kansan described the sports match-up in three words, each getting their own sentence: "Rivalry. Competition. Broomsticks."

The University of Kansas student newspaper article was previewing a "Border Showdown" between KU and the University of Missouri. As the last word of the opening description hints, the piece was describing a sport most people do not associate with intercollegiate athletics.

Among the many phenomena the Harry Potter book and film series has spawned—a theme park, the Pottermore website, HP fan fiction and conventions, and Daniel Radcliffe's film career—perhaps none is quirkier and currently en vogue than Quidditch.

The sport, based in fiction, is catching on among real-world students at an astonishingly high number of schools globally. Students play on the ground instead of in the air, but dutifully take on the various roles described in J.K. Rowling's books including keepers, seekers, chasers, and beaters.

A UPIU report calls Quidditch "a sport combining elements of rugby and basketball; the exception: players are running with a broomstick in between their legs."

College Quidditch sprang to life in 2005 in Vermont. Middlebury College students formed the first intramural league and the International Quidditch Association. Currently, hundreds of teams have formed at schools in almost every state and more than a dozen countries. A Quidditch World Cup is held. The NCAA recognizes the sport. And rivalries have begun to form, including between KU and Mizzou.

Among the cheers sounded at the matches, some by fans dressed in Potter regalia, perhaps the best is the one voiced by the referees. As they scream to squads to kick things off, "The snitch is loose!"

Separately, a much more dispiriting HP phenomenon is also on the loose and growing: Post-Potter Depression. PPD attempts to identify the loss being experienced by rabid and casual fans related to the creative end of *Harry Potter*, a series that has entertained and defined many current collegians since grade school.

As University of Michigan student Proma Khosla writes in *The Michigan Daily*, "I've been with Harry since I was eight years old. That's well over half my life, and for all that time, there has always been something to look forward to in the world of Potter. Even since the last book and the empty feeling of knowing it was the end, there was always this last movie. It was a pleasant, unreachable future, distant enough that I didn't need to worry about losing Harry forever. But that day has come."

Your Assignment

 Observe and report upon Quidditch teams competing within your coverage area. Separately, check in with students on the current state and focuses of their HP fandom. Profile any especially severe PPD sufferers, those who consider the permanent end to the series as an evil on par with He-Who-Must-Not-Be-Named. Identify the condition's most common, acute symptoms. Determine the pop culture creations that have at least somewhat supplanted the public's Potter obsession. And explore the classes and clubs in some way incorporating Rowling's series into their activities or identities.

SPIN-OFF ALERT!

 Reaching beyond the HP stratosphere, explore the growing number of niche online communities built around an intense love of a certain book series, TV show, film, or even celebrity. Separately, aside from Quidditch, report on other smaller, non-marquee or offbeat sports, games, and athletic-style events taking place in your coverage area. Some examples: board games, competitive cheerleading, dog shows, Humans vs. Zombies, paintball, the Special Olympics, spelling bees, ultimate Frisbee, and videogame contests.

UNUSUAL COURSES, MAJORS

College sweethearts and beer pong battles come and go, but an academic major stays with you forever—at least on your résumé or as small talk on a first date. Most students travel the expected route. But a few opt for more interesting experiences.

Among the more random academic majors offered at schools nationwide: equine journalism, comic book art, bowling industry management, boilermaking, bakery science, and nanoscience or "the study of objects one-billionth of a meter in size."

Individual courses can be even stranger, often at the whim of the professors who create them. Some of the most out-there college classes of recent vintage: The History, Politics and Taste of Chocolate, Underwater Basket Weaving, The Art of Walking, and Zombies in Popular Media.

Your Assignment

Explore out-of-the-box majors, minors, and course offerings at your school. Also, determine the offbeat majors and courses that students, professors, and even the university president would love to see created and permanently added to the curriculum.

ETHICS ALERT!

Be sensitive here. It is easy to simply poke fun at the unusual, but these majors and courses are most likely truly worthwhile—at least in a specialized sense. The odder courses especially are often the professors' passion projects, motivating them to throw their hearts and souls into leading them. Examine that passion and make it visible to readers in your report.

REVOLUTION, WHILE ABROAD

In late January 2011, Drake University student Ian Weller sat on the balcony of an 11th-floor apartment, looking out over the calm that was Cairo, Egypt. At the start of his study abroad in the historic city, Weller wrote about his group's "'ready to take on the world' mentality" and his personal contentment. As he shared on his blog, A Bulldog Abroad, "Steam comes off my freshly made cup of tea . . . as the sun starts to warm up the city. It will get up [to] 70 today, and I couldn't be happier."

The tea went cold a few moments later. Cairo's calm splintered into protests days after that—and then spread nationwide, part of the larger Arab Spring. Through the chaos—and Internet restrictions—he shot photos and wrote before being transported safely to Prague. He figures the experience makes a heck of a story, one that includes an especially memorable start: "So, I was once evacuated from Egypt during a revolution . . ."

Your Assignment

Seek out study-abroad students living and learning in more turbulent spots. Detail their daily safety precautions and the myths that have been shattered for them after spending some time in the countries. Also outline the factors that go into the school's decision-making about where to send students and when to steer clear of a troublesome area.

NEW MEDIA ALERT!

 Construct an online map outlining the spots students are studying—and working and volunteering. Include first-person video and blog-style accounts from the students about their experiences abroad, sharing perspectives about the areas not featured in mainstream news reports.

TWO IDEAS IN ONE

Helicopters and Boomerangs

Certain moms and dads just don't know when to quit. Even with their kids grown up and enrolled at a school far away, they continue to restrict, coddle, and fuss over their academic, professional, and social lives with an eye-opening vigor. So-called helicopter parents have hovered over higher education for years, but recently rose again to A-list prominence within the student and professional media for their continued interference in their children's lives.

These parents constantly phone, text, email, and tweet at their undergraduate kids, along with monitoring all social media activity. They contact professors, admissions counselors, and even employers to promote their children or check on the status of their work. They try to "Facebook friend" their son's or daughter's classmates and significant others. And they ensure they have a say in every major and minor life decision—even when it leaves their children exasperated, rebellious, or clinically depressed.

Separately, whether they are helicopters or hippies, parents are also playing an increasingly extended role in students' post-graduation lives—in part by providing food and shelter.

Right after commencement, a growing number of college graduates are heading home, diploma in hand and futures on hold. They are the boomerangers, young twentysomethings who are spending their immediate college afterlife in hometown purgatory. Most move back into their childhood bedrooms due to poor employment or graduate school prospects or to save money so they can soon travel internationally, engage in volunteer work, or launch their own business.

A brief homestay has long been an option favored by some fresh graduates, but it has recently reemerged as a defining activity of this student generation. "Graduation means something completely different than it used to 30 years ago," a student columnist wrote last year for *The Collegiate Times* at Virginia Tech. "At my age, my parents were already engaged, planning their wedding, had jobs, and thinking about starting a family. Today, the economy is still recovering, and more students are moving back in with mom and dad."

Your Assignment

 Profile the hovering parental units and the children putting up with or rebelling against them. Also, find and feature current, former, and soon-to-be boomerangers connected to your school. In a related sense, report upon the experiences of students who were homeschooled or who live at home throughout their undergraduate careers.

EDIBLE DUMPSTER DIVING

Some people are so determined not to waste even a morsel of grub they will literally dive in dumpsters to preserve them. It is one of the more extreme acts related to a unique food ideology known as freeganism. Freegans express supreme pride in local and organic food, along with a disdain for the discarding of anything that might still be even the least bit edible.

As Penn State University student Nathan Pipenberg writes in *The Daily Collegian*, "If you stick your head into a dumpster, the first thing that you notice is the smell—a delicious mix of rancid cooking oil, rotten fruits, and mold. When you jump all the way into a dumpster, you start thinking about what other people would think if they saw you standing ankle-deep in garbage bags. But if you really check out a dumpster, there's one discovery that will stick with you after the smell washes away and you accept your questionable habits—there's a lot of food in those things. Good, clean, healthy food that we can eat. Loads of it. And it ends up in the trash every day."

Your Assignment

Explore the freeganism movement within your coverage area. Observe and profile the so-called dumpster divers. Document their finds. Grasp the activity's related legal issues. And garner responses from the restaurant and business owners whose garbage is being surveyed and plucked.

IMMERSION ALERT!

Dumpster dive. Rummage through some dumpsters or a campus cafeteria trash area to uncover (hopefully) edible food. Depending on the quality of your haul, partake of the secondhand items. For an even more intense stomach-churning experience, attempt to eat only items recovered from dumpsters for a set period of time, monitoring your weight, mood, and cravings along the way.

SPIN-OFF ALERT!

Report upon the slow food, locavore, and sustainable food movements. Focus on individuals and trends related to religious-based dietary routines and restrictions. Or localize a part of the increasingly influential fair trade movement.

THE SHOE LICKER

His Twitter account bio features a poem: "Lookin in the mirror. Checkin My hair. What Kinda shoes have you got on there? Bitch I'm Jamie, and I like lickin' shoes." The "personal interests" on his Facebook page: "Men's boots, Licking shoes, Being exceptionally creepy."

He is the Tampa Bay Shoe Licker. The young man apparently roams the city's historic Ybor neighborhood looking to lick—yes, lick—the dirtied soles of people's shoes.

In a column published in *The Hawkeye* at Florida's Hillsborough Community College, a student once described an encounter with this brazen-tongued mystery man.

A snippet: "I spotted a young man dressed in a concert T-shirt and jeans headed toward us, almost running. He was probably around 25, but his face looked innocent, almost child-like . . . The unnamed man flirtatiously raised an eyebrow as he glanced up and down [the writer's friend] Drew's body, stopping at his feet. I laughed at the nervous look on my friend's face, not familiar with being ogled. 'Hey man,' said the stranger, 'what kinda shoes are those? They're nice.' . . . Quicker than I'd ever seen anyone move before, the man dropped to his knees and balanced his weight on his palms as he squatted in front of my friend. He was clearly not fazed by the sticky, grimy, possibly urine-soaked pavement of 7th Avenue. Exhibiting unusual strength for such a skinny, petite guy, the man lifted one of Drew's Nikes. He stuck his tongue out and slowly, almost sensually, licked the entire length of the shoe from bottom to top, as if it were a pool of water and he'd been lost in the desert for weeks."

Your Assignment

 For this story, you are on your own. My only advice: Do not attempt a first-person report.

For more story ideas, visit collegemediamatters.com.

CHAPTER 20

The Sales Pitch

Illustration by Yee Hung Lim

The Final Stage in Your Storytelling Evolution

"A great idea deserves a great pitch. It shows editors you have initiative and enthusiasm, exactly what they are looking for in a reporter. I remember the first time I pitched two ideas to a national newspaper. One got accepted—and ended up as a published story. Emboldened, I pitched some more. It was like an addictive drug. I was hooked. I spent more time chasing freelance stories as a final-year student than on my own schoolwork—and it taught me much more about the craft of journalism than any textbook could."

Serene Luo, journalist, Singapore

You cannot just brainstorm, report, write, and revise a story.

To be published, you also have to sell it.

Nowadays, an increasing number of stories are pitched by email, during real-time video chats or within a Google doc. They also continue to be pitched occasionally over the phone. But they still occur most often in person, on the spot, amid lots of stares, sighs, feedback, and expectations.

THE ART OF THE PITCH

Pitching a story in person can be intimidating. It can be easy to lose control. And it can often be tough to carry it out the way you pictured it in your head.

Use these 10 guidelines to perfect your in-person pitch.

Prepare

After the creative spark, research the idea. Ensure it has legs. Find some fun facts or side issues possibly worth bringing up. Identify the main questions people will have about it. Then come up with the answers. Soon after, pitch the story in your head. Do it in front of a mirror. Grab a pet or a friend and have them play the role of cynical editor. Carry out a long-form pitch at first. Don't worry about rambling. Then slowly whittle it down and sharpen it up.

Keep it Conversational

At the actual pitch session, use your preparation and practice to enable you to speak freely, not be reined in. Trying to remember lines will inevitably lead to a stumble. Go with the flow. Speak from the heart. Make eye contact. Smile. And be prepared for offbeat questions or empty stares.

Follow the 60-Second Rule

Keep your initial pitch to a minute, at most. An overly long "sell" will only work against you. If you have a golden idea, people will immediately spot the gleam. At times, even a minute is too long. Can you pitch your idea in 10 seconds flat?

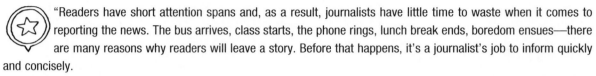

ASSIGNMENT ALERT!

The 10-Second Pitch

"Readers have short attention spans and, as a result, journalists have little time to waste when it comes to reporting the news. The bus arrives, class starts, the phone rings, lunch break ends, boredom ensues—there are many reasons why readers will leave a story. Before that happens, it's a journalist's job to inform quickly and concisely.

"This can be troublesome for young journalists, who have the tendency to weigh down their stories at the beginning with unnecessary details and background information.

"To combat this problem, I have introduced an exercise into my reporting classes. Students are sent out on assignments. Before they can begin writing, they must tell the rest of the class in 10 seconds or fewer what their story is about. When faced with such time constraints, students—after some practice—will automatically begin filtering out unnecessary information and get to the heart of their stories. This, in turn, reflects in their writing. The lesson is useful for journalists of all ages and experience levels: Get to the point and get there quickly."

Jim Rodenbush, news adviser, *The Daily Collegian*, Penn State University

Your Assignment

Pitch. Pitch. Pitch. Embrace Rodenbush's quick-pitch call-to-arms. Brainstorm 10 story ideas. Then pitch each of them rapid-fire to your colleagues, classmates, friends, or dorm suitemates. Get to the heart of each story in no more than 10 seconds. Have someone hit a buzzer when your time is up. No breaks are allowed. When the buzzer sounds, move on to the next pitch. When complete, get feedback on what pitches succeeded and failed. Watch a video or listen to a recording of your effort and engage in a brutal self-critique. Revise pitches that went off track or ran long. Hone in on their 10-second essence. Then, assemble another group and repeat the process. Pitch. Pitch. Pitch.

Pitch the Room

Explain the idea in a context your audience will grasp. Toss in references to their own lives or how the issue you want to explore is impacting them.

Cite Something, Anything

Back up your opening salvo with a trusted outside source or two. Maybe it's a recent article from a national news outlet on a similar topic. Maybe it's data from a recent report. Depending on the story, it could even be a Twitter hashtag. For the record, the lowest citations on the pitch totem pole: a personal anecdote or a vague eyewitness account. They may breed great stories of course, but they don't inspire a ton of confidence about an idea's potential larger impact. Go with something outside of your personal sphere, if possible.

Don't Oversell

When our ideas are first forming, we all think we have the next Watergate. But it is important to recognize your story's actual scope and relative significance. Pitch it appropriately to your audience. And let the content speak for itself. Unless your confidence level about the pitch is supremely high, resist the temptation to trumpet your own idea as amazing or the scoop of the year while you are pitching it.

Stop Talking—That Means You

Once you roll out the main pitch, be ready for an initial reaction of silence, followed by head nodding, and maybe a "hmm" or two. People often need a moment to process an idea, even a great one. Let that processing play out. Avoid spewing additional information that might derail an otherwise on-target pitch.

Go on a Charm Offensive

Along with initial silence, you may also be met with full-on skepticism about an idea's merit or your ability to report upon it. If this happens, do not—I repeat, do not—go on the defensive. Simply reiterate the main idea and share additional information that might buoy it in the skeptics' eyes. Recognize that most of the time, the questions that feel like attacks are just people's ways of warming up to an idea and fully picturing it. If all else fails, have a back-up idea for another angle or reporting method through which you might tell the story. Sometimes that will be the final push that gets you the OK to move forward.

Be Ready to Discuss the Next Step

The best-case scenario is a full acceptance of your pitch, combined with excitement and questions about how you will flesh out the story. Have at least a barebones plan in place for how you will report upon it, the sources you will track down, and the multimedia elements you will incorporate.

On the Flip Side, Be Ready for Defeat

Some ideas don't sell. Be open to feedback that might provide you with a related topic to tackle. And while you should briefly fight for your story with a smile, don't ruin relationships over it or earn a reputation as someone who does not accept rejection. Tomorrow is another day. And another outlet might be interested in your pitch.

FREELANCE, FREELANCE, FREELANCE

As a student within journalism 2.0, publishing pieces is generally accomplished in one of four ways: join an existing campus publication, start your own outlet or blog, land an internship or other work experience with a professional media outlet, or freelance, freelance, freelance.

Let's break down how to find success with those last three words.

Three Keys to Know Upfront

Sell the Story First

The power of a pitch is in the idea. It needs to be fresh, newsworthy, and in line with what the outlet you are pitching typically publishes or sometimes craves.

Think Ahead

Recognize when the timing is right for your idea. Pitches sometimes play out weeks, even months, before a story will be reported and finally published. Brainstorm about upcoming events and the next big thing, not simply what is happening now.

Rely Upon Email

Email is modern journalism's main freelance vehicle. For the most part, unannounced phone calls or random tweet queries are considered tacky.

The Right Spot

Find the Right Home for Your Story

The types of outlets student freelancers most often consider: the college newspaper or other campus media, the local mainstream or alternative press, a respected national news outlet, a respected independent blog, a school alumni magazine, national and local organizations seeking related industry coverage for their websites and magazines, and national online outlets with relatively open calls such as *USA TODAY College*, AOL's Patch, and the Yahoo! Contributor Network.

Get Help

Ask professors, advisers, alumni, and more experienced peers for recommendations on potential freelance outlets. They are often plugged into parts of the local, national, and online journalism scenes and might be able to offer a valuable suggestion or contact.

Know the Outlet You're Pitching Inside Out

Pick up the publication. Check out the site. Read the stories! And search the bylines—paying special attention to pieces penned by freelancers. Grasp the stories' general specs—length, organization, focus area, source diversity, and writing style. If nothing else, at least ensure the piece you plan to pitch has not recently appeared in the outlet.

Start Small

Avoid pitching the more vaunted outlets until you have some link-worthy clips, the teeniest bit of name recognition, and, most importantly, experience. You might only get one chance to impress an editor. Being bold and slightly overreaching has the potential to pay off. But waiting until you are truly ready—and boasting a portfolio that immediately piques an editor's interest—will greatly increase your dream gig acceptance rate.

The Search

Find an Actual Person to Pitch

Avoid "To Whom It May Concern" messages or general email addresses.

Pitch a Connection

In the freelance universe, a blind pitch is the equivalent of asking a stranger for spare change. Strive to find even the scantest connection to the person or news outlet you are pitching—maybe a mutual friend or former professor who suggested reaching out, a shared alma mater, a quick chat at a conference you both recently attended, or your appearance in a story the outlet published months before. Read the contact person's bio on the outlet's website. Google her. Search for a Twitter feed or LinkedIn profile. And if they write as well as edit, read their recent featured work.

Search the Sites First

Many news media websites list freelance instructions and related email addresses, often on a Contact, About Us, Submission, or FAQ page. For more prominent outlets, simply Google the name along with something like "freelance contact" or "freelancer FAQ."

The Format

Be Brief

If editors open a pitch email with an eye-gouging chunk of text, your message and freelance dreams will head straight to the digital trash. Instead, to meet with freelance success, keep your pitch short, and your personal history shorter. Introduce yourself with a single sentence. Spare another sentence to provide a smidgen more about your life or work experience, especially if it fits with your planned story focus or format. Pitch your story in the next sentence. And close with the big sell on why your proposed story matters and why it is perfect for that outlet.

Sell Yourself Along with Your Idea

If asked, be sure to briefly explain why you are the right person to tackle the idea you are pitching—given your location, access to key events or sources, unique perspective, related expertise, or the speed with which you can produce something the editor wants.

Construct the Pitch Like a Letter

Even include a formal greeting and salutation, instead of a generic "Hi" and "Later." At the same time though, understand the vibe of the outlet you are pitching. If it is run more informally, addressing a person by their formal title versus their first name may lose you points instead of gaining their favor. It is a game of chance, one you almost always win by erring on the side of professionalism.

Close with an Email Signature

At the end of an e-pitch, include your full contact information, most importantly your mobile phone number, email address, and links to either your blog, student news outlet, or online portfolio. Feature the latter links only if they help sell yourself and your pitch.

Avoidance Issues

Avoid Overselling

Hiding your student status or being a braggadocio is a pitch of death for a young freelancer. Most of the time, those messages are met with laughter, eye-rolls, or furrowed brows—followed by a quick delete.

Avoid Conflicts of Interest

You may have the inside scoop on a story, but if it comes because your father, best friend, or professor is involved, you may have to serve simply as a source instead of the reporter.

Avoid Mistakes

Make sure the pitch is polished. Consider it the equivalent of a strong handshake and combed hair during an interview. It is the first impression. Read it over one last time before clicking "Send." Have a friend check it for spelling and grammar faux pas.

The Indirect Pitch

Write *About* Someone, Instead of to Them.

It is an indirect pitch method increasingly popular in the digital realm. Specifically, craft a quality blog post or story about an individual or outlet you are attempting to impress. Hope for a tweet of thanks, a comment beneath the post, an embedded link of recognition on their site, or a quick private email filled with praise. After that connection is established, without seeming too overeager, respond with a pitch.

Establish Yourself Independently

One other way to get on outlets' and editors' radars: Build a following and slowly morph into a fresh or expert voice within the field you want to write about. Online is one big ballroom party—gaining a steady readership, spots on blogrolls, lots of retweets, and other mentions will make people curious about you and lead to many more email responses and pitch acceptances.

Rejection

Accept Silence as Rejection

Don't bug someone repeatedly if you have not received an answer to a pitch. A lack of an email reply is almost always a clear two-word answer: not interested.

Expect Rejection

As famed British author Neil Gaiman advises, "Swear, shrug, write the next thing."

Once Accepted

Map Out Your Story

Do it prior to your pitch. In some cases, you might even want to report and write a full draft beforehand as well. If an editor really wants it, the requested turnaround time might be quick. The initiative you show in already having it complete will be noticed, and appreciated.

Be Flexible

An editor might like only a portion of your pitch. He might request a different angle for its main focus. Or he might use your idea as the springboard for a desired story only marginally related. Be open to any and all suggestions within reason. Fight for your main idea if you feel strongly about its potential, but never be so beholden to your initial pitch that you lose out on the chance to write a fun related story.

Supersede Assignment Expectations

Track down more, or more esteemed, sources. Show extra care in the writing. Submit the story ahead of deadline. Impress the outlet, enough for them to add you to their regular freelance roster. The only area in which to avoid going the extra mile: word count.

Pick Your Battles Carefully

During the editing process, fight for the facts and story portions you hold sacred, but don't earn a reputation as indignant or incorrigible. Journalists talk.

Recognize Times are Changing Re: Pay

Many outlets have a standard freelance rate. If it involves a negotiation, ask for what you deserve without being greedy and see if compensation for extras such as travel, lodging, food, and event tickets are available.

Get Organized

Ensure you obtain press passes and event access. Also, confirm how you are aligned with the outlet and how, and how much, you can throw its name around during your reporting.

Be Prepared to Do Everything

You will most likely report and write the story, take related photos and video, and upload everything and insert links.

After It's Posted

The Story's Posting is Only the Beginning

Promote it professionally on your social media feeds, your blog, and your online portfolio. Interact with commenters beneath the story if the outlet allows or encourages it. Share it with all the sources. If you have access to the editing bay, read it over and fix any mistakes you spot after it's been posted.

One Story Begets Another

A successful freelancer never lingers too long over a single published piece. The best time to pitch more stories is the immediate aftermath of a recent published one. One great idea and story is wonderful. Becoming a reliable contributor though is priceless. For example, according to Linda Bates, the driving and travel editor for *The Vancouver Sun*, "As much as I'd like to give new writers a chance, I increasingly rely on a 'stable' of about 15 freelancers whom I know are reliable, accurate, creative, and it seems happy to work with me. I just don't have time for handholding, rewriting, confrontation, or last-minute fact checking. Become someone who can be counted on to produce great work with no drama. You'll be a stable horse in no time."

YOUR PERSONAL FREELANCE VEHICLE

Along with pitching and freelancing for other outlets, one increasingly popular option for those seeking to publish and share their ideas: starting your own blog, website, or independent reporting operation.

Though student entrepreneurs are not new, more and more of them are taking advantage of the upheaval in the media world to stake their claim. If you are up for the challenge, stake your own claim. Even if it fails, it shows you possess courage, a spirit of innovation, a digital mindset, and oodles of entrepreneurialism to spare.

Here are some general guidelines for launching and maintaining your own blog, site, or full-blown news outlet while still in school.

Starting Up

First, Find a Niche

And stick to it. It might be within a field or industry, a coverage area, a geographical location, or your school.

Be Genuine

Start the blog or site for a purpose *other* than getting your name known or simply sharing your cute slice of life with the world. If you are posting simply to be seen or to impress employers, readers will either see right through it or find you uninteresting. Instead, write about a valuable topic and boldly enter the fray. Ensure it doesn't reek of informality or over-promotion.

Think Branding and SEO

Give your venture a name and a tagline that stand out, represent what it's all about, enable Google to quickly and easily recognize it through search terms, and compel readers to click and check it out.

Go With What You Know

When selecting a focus, build off your own experiences or flesh out your own interests. It will make it easier to update on slow days and after the adrenaline rush of the start-up period wears off. It will also help you more quickly establish a personal voice. Readers know and appreciate when someone is writing about something they "get" and greatly enjoy. They will respond by more enthusiastically liking what you write—and you. This is important. On most sites, along with the content, the creator is the star.

Also Value What You Don't Know

Expertise is not necessarily the answer. In recent years, some of the most interesting, impacting digital platforms and news operations have been started by admittedly inexpert, even immature, college students. With the media landscape upending so fast—and many traditional institutions and veterans who supposedly know better remaining resistant to change—fresh thinking, wide-eyed optimism, and even outright naïveté can be the keys to online success. So, along with what you know, consider what you *don't know* to be a blessing.

Content and Design

Keep it Fresh

Update regularly. It is harder to do than you think. Outside the realm of eating, sleeping, commuting, and general hygiene, most of us hardly do anything every day or nearly every day. To help, establish a posting schedule. Remember, you have classes, homework, the football season, social media, and a social life competing for your attention.

Maintain a Consistent Tone

While certainly allowing for exceptions, produce content of similar length, style, interactivity, and personal inflection so readers begin to know what to expect and potential employers quickly spot the singular vision you have laid out.

Be an Endpoint, Not a Portal

Aggregation has its place, but the Internet is currently overcrowded with sites simply building off or directing people toward others' work. Add something to the mix. Whenever possible, publish original content.

Employ Multimedia in Spots

If your site begins to reek of too much text, usher in some video, audio, photo slideshows, and graphical elements to break things up. Try out a few, see what your audience likes, and what you most enjoy capturing or creating. Think of them as one more way to lure an audience and build your brand.

Use Posts as Starting Points for Other Freelancing

Upon completing and publishing content you consider especially bold or eloquent, consider where else it might go. Once fleshed out or adapted, your better posts may have second lives as freelance pieces for established news sites. Your blogwork is doubly helpful in this regard. It pushes you to produce worthy content. And, over time, it makes you a known quantity—someone much more likely to have a pitch accepted by an editor at an established outlet.

Choose the Best Platform

Selecting the right service for your blog or site is paramount to a successful start-up experience. Base your decision on the amount and type of interactivity you want to foster, the types of posts and multimedia elements you want to incorporate, and your level of design and programming skills.

Identity and Interactivity

Invite Interactivity

Serve as a sounding board as much as a personal voice. Start discussions. Ask questions. Run instant polls. Invite others to write guest posts. Think dialogue, not monologue.

Expect Quiet at First

Daily traffic may be in the single digits for months at the start. You may go weeks without a comment. Be persistent. Evaluate traffic patterns to see if certain types of content garner more hits or comments. And quickly build off an especially popular or well-received post with related follow-ups.

Be Optimistic and Constructive

You can at times gain attention by attacking bigger names or expressing smarminess or cynicism, but it may not be the attention you want. Establish an identity built atop positivity. It offers many more long-term potential rewards.

Earn Your Reputation Organically

Do not ask for attention on day one or expect kudos for having a single cool post or a week's worth of strong content. Blatant egomania or exhibitionism will be rebuffed, ignored, or mocked by many.

Write About Other Sites and Bloggers

Keep those posts upbeat. Ask to interview and feature them. Journalists are suckers for attention. Put together a decent profile. Boom. You are on their radar.

Address Big Issues of the Day

Depending on your site's focus, regularly monitor, report, and comment upon the most significant or gossiped news at any given moment. It will heighten your blog's connectivity to the wider web, sell your site as in the loop, and test your real-time writing and information-gathering instincts.

Collaborate

Reach out to others in your coverage area or across the wider web to expand your outlet's reach and updating frequency. Even consider contacting a local news outlet, journalism organization, or department at your own school to determine if an affiliated student voice is needed. You will be surprised at how many organizations, schools, and outlets are seeking fresh content aimed at their membership, readership, or student body. They may even be willing to pay—by sponsoring your site or creating a student–professional hybrid arrangement.

You Can Keep Your Identity Muted or Secret, at First

If your start-up is edgier or outside the box, feel free to build it up anonymously or pseudonymously. It is a generally accepted practice in the blogosphere and online journalism arena, depending on a site's content and tone. If it hits big, reveal yourself.

NETWORKING

Humble is *so* 20th-century. Brag is the new black. Along with selling your story ideas, selling yourself is paramount within journalism 2.0. We are all our own brands. Our value rests in our experiences, know-how, perspectives, work ethic, and passion—and how well we communicate these aspects of ourselves with others.

As Elora Walsh, the former editor-in-chief of *The Clarion Call* at Clarion University of Pennsylvania, advises, "Don't let the stress of being a freshman make you put yourself in a corner. Get out there and build a name for yourself."

Before sharing your wondrousness with others, you need to recognize and organize its components for yourself. Enter the brag notebook. "A brag notebook is one centralized place to store copies of your résumé, essays, awards, certificates, transcripts, and anything else that shows off your awesomeness," the top-notch student advice site HackCollege states. "Whenever you have to fill out an application for something and need to remember all the neat things you've done, check your brag notebook."

Start building your own brag notebook right away. It might be an actual physical scrapbook, a Word document, an online bookmarks folder, a public or private blog, a social media account, or a set of smartphone notes.

20 Things to Include in Your Brag Notebook

1 Published Work

The web is fluid and unreliable, so be sure to do more than simply bookmark and forget about the pieces, posts, photos, and multimedia packages you publish. Take screenshots. Copy and paste the content into a file or folder permanently stored on your desktop. And possibly even print out copies as well.

2 Notable Classwork

Include reporting assignments, essays on the future of journalism or media entrepreneurialism, standout class presentations, and first-person reflection pieces of any kind. You will most likely never share these items, but they may come in handy when searching for the right wording to start off a cover letter or a scholarship, fellowship, or graduate school essay.

3 Awards

Save the certificates and programs confirming your selection, along with any nominating letters written on your behalf.

4 Reference Letters

Also maintain a running list of potential references, with their updated job titles and contact information.

5 Work Experience Outline

Include your campus and professional media experiences—the basic responsibilities and notable achievements.

6 You 2.0

Keep a links listing of everywhere you operate on the web. Track the visitor totals for your blog, the followers to your Twitter and Pinterest accounts, the likes for your Facebook page and YouTube channel, and the reposts from your Tumblr content. Also, track the online mentions of you and your work, including within the established news media, more reputable personal sites, prominent aggregators, your school website, and journalism organization sites.

7 Transcripts

Maintain digital and print copies, including at least a few of the official signed-and-sealed versions provided by the registrar. Also keep a list of all classes in which you have enrolled and excelled that are in any way related to journalism, media, and other pertinent areas such as entrepreneurialism, the tech sphere, or global affairs.

8 Digital List

Keep track of the multimedia and web skills, programs, and platforms you have mastered. Give special notice to web design prowess, mobile mastery, and video, photo, and audio capture, editing, and presentation know-how. In addition, don't overlook what you may consider elementary or obvious skills or areas of comprehension—everything from WordPress, Facebook, YouTube, and Twitter to Tumblr, Pinterest, Storify, and Prezi.

9 Correspondence

Save emails and other private messages denoting your greatness. They may serve as springboards to future reference letters or as reminders about achievements you should more actively promote.

10 Professional Affiliations

Keep track of your relevant organization involvement and conference and workshop participation. Along with noting your general membership status and leadership responsibilities, list unofficial endeavors such as local high school outreach, freshmen orientation involvement, and requests to speak to a university gateways course or introductory journalism seminar.

11 International Experience

Inventory your foreign language aptitude and cross-cultural knowledge, including what you have acquired through related classes, study abroad participation, organization involvement, volunteer work, and leisure trips.

12 Reading List

Keep a record of the great books and pieces of journalism you read and journalism heroes you study, especially the ones who inspire you so much you may mention them in a future cover letter, application essay, or interview.

SITE ALERT!

 One suggested reading list: "The Top 100 Works of Journalism in the United States in the 20th Century," http://bit.ly/9FkhOs.

---

13 Ideas

Keep an unofficial rundown of your amazing ideas for stories, full-blown publications, mobile apps, websites, and digital revenue restructuring. Pair this with a separate file containing your random thoughts about your passion for journalism and the world—and how you hope to make a difference in both.

14 Ready-to-Adapt Answers

HackCollege suggests having answers to commonly-asked graduate school, internship, and job application questions: "For example, 'Describe a moment of challenge and discuss how you overcame it' and 'Why do you want to be a _____ [Insert career choice here].' If you rewrite your response to these every single time, you're wasting time. Why not just write it once and every time you apply for something, edit the paper slightly to tailor it for the specific application?"

15 Pre-College Memorabilia

Consider saving symbolic items such as the class newspaper you created in second grade or the high school yearbook in which you were named "Most Likely to Succeed." You never know what might trigger an idea for a personal reflection essay or act as a discussion starter when speaking to a supervisor, potential employer, or admissions committee.

16 Photos of You

Have at least a few images of you dressed up and looking professional—headshots and full body shots. Save them in appropriate formats and with the appropriately high resolution so they can be sent or accessed via Dropbox (dropbox.com) without delay.

17 Academic Reflections

At the end of each important class, make a list of your accomplishments (including an especially standout essay or project), feedback your professor provided, and what you learned from the class. When you ask for a reference letter or make conversation with a potential employer who considers a particular professor a mentor or friend, these tidbits may prove invaluable.

18 Other Experiences

Keep track of your non-journalism activities, organization involvement, volunteering, summer work, and on-campus employment. Also, make note of your more general hobbies and quirkier skills like the board games or celebrity impressions at which you excel.

19 Beats

Keep a running tally of the beats you cover during classes, campus media assignments, and professional stints. Stick to the beats you truly master. Jot down what you learn about how to report upon them and the advice you would give to student reporters following in your stead.

20 Important People List

Keep a list of all important and semi-important journalism, media, and political people you meet during workshops, conferences, internships, and classes. Collect and organize their business cards or homepages.

Also, track the whereabouts of friends and classmates. Like you, upon graduation, many of your peers are going places, branching out, moving up, and making names for themselves. You will be surprised at how often you will rely upon them to help you land a job, arrange an introduction, provide the dish about a potential employer, or present you with a spare bed and hot meal when you are traveling through their city. It's not just what you know, but who you know that will help you achieve success.

Online Portfolios

Put Together an Online Portfolio

Building off the brag notebook, students who want to work in journalism and media should sport a public website touting personal highlights. But simply having one is not enough.

Here are some tips to help you construct a professional, visually pleasant portfolio that will catch an employer's eye and motivate them to want to learn more and hire you.

First, Figure Out Your Portfolio's Purpose

Are you aiming to market yourself as a media professional in general? Are you looking to highlight one particular skill-set such as your photography work or sports reporting? Are you seeking to simply build your personal brand and creatively express yourself?

Include Only What You Need

A portfolio is not your brag notebook. It is not meant to be a scattered, overflowing receptacle of all your accomplishments, interests, stories, jobs, and classes. You want to spotlight a few parts of your life and work that will best serve your branding or job hunt.

A portfolio typically features some or all of the following, laid out in a variety of ways: a basic résumé tailored toward the type of career or internship you are seeking; a links listing of your published stories and multimedia work; a brief "About Me" page describing your experience and a tiny bit about your personality and interests to give employers a glimpse of you as a person; a short list of professional references; and a list of your digital skills and program mastery.

Choose a Professional Address

It is almost always best to simply stick with your name as your web domain. It is easier for employers to remember. It pops up faster and higher in Google results. And it ensures you do not unknowingly pick an address that will confuse people or even offend them.

Keep the Design Simple and Professional

It should look like a portfolio, not a blog. It should also reflect your work and personality. For example, a photographer's portfolio should be awash in images.

Avoid Errors at All Costs

If you cannot even perfect a page aimed at selling yourself, why should an employer trust you to get things right for them?

Keep it Timely

Add new projects soon after they are published. Double check all links to be sure they are still active and take visitors to the right spots.

Provide Context

Explain a bit about the news outlets you interned for, your student newspaper, the stories you wrote, the jobs you held, and even possibly your school. Never assume an employer will know about these things. Depending on how far they are from your campus, hometown, or reporting beat, they may need more of an introduction.

Ensure Standout Items Stand Out

A three-part, front-page series you wrote for the local newspaper that stirred mega-buzz and legislative action should not just be included as links. Briefly explain the work you put in, its prominent placement in the paper, and its public and industry reception.

Classwork Can Count

Don't be afraid to feature especially innovative classwork, especially multimedia projects.

Show, Don't Tell

Erase any adjectives you use to describe your work, skills, or goals. Instead, let the experiences speak for themselves.

Think Visual

Include photos, page samples, embedded video, graphics, or other eye-catchers to better sell your work and entice the employer to stick around longer. Just be careful of copyright issues when including mastheads, logos, and published content.

Consider Including a Video Profile

One trend among portfolio sites is a brief introductory video. It is typically embedded into the homepage or the "About Me" page. If you create one of your own, keep it short—90 seconds to two minutes tops. Talk briefly about who you are, your experiences, career goals, and general interests or what makes you unique. Tape it outside with sunlight, grass, and trees or in a newsroom or other space stimulating to the eye. Be passionate. Act natural. Smile.

Include a Photo of Yourself

If you are comfortable with it, posting a headshot or other tasteful portrait helps you come to life a bit in employers' eyes. Steer clear of tiny, poor-quality or overly conceptual shots, or those in which you look especially young or unprofessional.

Hype Your Social Media Self

Along with your email address, prominently display links to other areas of the web in which you have an active presence such as Facebook, Google+, Pinterest, Tumblr, Twitter, YouTube, and the blogosphere. Employers are increasingly interested in hiring students who utilize various social media and know their way around buzzworthy sites. One warning: Only lead people to parts of your web self you want them to see or that further underscore your professionalism and active digital participation.

SITE ALERT!

If not turning to LinkedIn or WordPress, here are 10 portfolio sites to consider. Some are completely free, while others offer free platform hosting to varying degrees.

about.me (about.me), "a free service that lets you create a beautiful one-page website that's all about you and your interests"

Behance (behance.net), "the leading online platform to showcase and discover creative work"

Carbonmade (carbonmade.com), "an online portfolio service that helps show off your work"

Cargo (cargocollective.com), "a creative publishing platform where everything . . . is built around the work shared by its members"

cuttings.me (cuttings.me), "free portfolio tool for journalists, bloggers, and writers"

Flavors.me (flavors.me), "allows anyone to make a branded web presence in minutes, using aggregated content from around the web"

Moonfruit (moonfruit.com), "design your site the way you want it and we'll make sure we publish it correctly for web, mobile, and social"

Portfoliobox (portfoliobox.net), "a web-tool you can use to create a high class online portfolio"

Pressfolios (pressfolios.com), "easily build and manage an online portfolio of newsclips—no technical expertise required whatsoever"

SHOWN'D (shownd.com), "aims to provide users with a centralized hub to maintain a portfolio and secure employment"

Social Media

Build a Social Media Empire

Along with the endless storytelling potential it offers, a social media presence is a must for networking, story sharing, and gaining post-graduation employment.

Here are some tips to launch, professionalize, and increase the following of your social media accounts.

Read Through Your Profile Bios

Analyze what they say about you. Then, determine if they say what you want potential employers to read and think about you. Depending, delete and revise to better reflect your professional self.

Constantly Update Your Bios

Do not think of them as one-off, sedentary, all-encompassing general blurbs. They should reflect the latest, greatest version of you, hyping new affiliations, sites, projects, and life stages. A fresh profile will keep followers informed of your goings-on in a much more permanent way than your scattered status updates and tweets. And it is a clear sign of your account activeness, confirming to followers and friends you value keeping your digital presence relevant and up-to-date.

Make Your Bios Blue

Specifically, ensure they feature as many live links as possible. It shows you are plugged in and gives followers or potential followers easy access to other parts of the web featuring your excellence.

Fill In and Flesh Out

There is only one thing worse than having no social media presence—having an empty shell of one. Simply launching a foursquare (foursquare.com) account or typing your name into a LinkedIn profile is not enough. Employers will not blink before dismissing an applicant who has no followers, barely any updates, or a lack of any interesting activity.

Have a Purpose

After you create a new social media account but prior to your first posting, sit in a quiet room and reflect on your purpose for having it. Think about the tone you want to adopt. Determine the type of information you want to share. Without at least a barebones plan of attack, you may unwittingly come across like a troll, a fraud, or what I like to call "a lost digital puppy."

Sit Back, Click Around, Search, and Read

You just may learn something. Try to get a feel for the rhythms of each platform—the type of content posted, the amount and type of user interaction that takes place, the epic fails people get pilloried for, and the times when streams become noisy or quiet.

Post Interesting Content

It is the most obvious, under-utilized secret to social media success. The users who earn acclaim and followings share fresh perspectives, witty insights, probing questions, and eye-opening information.

Adopt a Personal Tone

Recognize that you will need to share some part of your personal self. Decide in general what that will encompass—from your first impressions on big news of the day to photos of the extra dessert you just ordered at the restaurant.

Engage, Engage, Engage

Comment on others' updates. Respond to tweets. Post a response video. Ask big questions. Share others' work.

Monitor Your Activity and Feedback

Scrutinize the retweets, likes, shares, traffic, and comments. Recognize the types of content your users or the wider web most enjoy. Subsequently, create and share more of that content.

Play the Full Field

Avoid in-jokes and too many one-on-one references that will simply confuse or clutter your followers' streams. Your updates should be accessible and understandable to everyone most of the time.

Reach Out to the Biggies

Follow and, when appropriate, respectfully interact with more influential thought leaders within journalism and your coverage areas. They may promote you to social media fame or at least provide you with tips on what everyone will be talking about on a given day.

Share and Promote Your Work, to a Point

No one begrudges a link to a new blog post, a promo about an upcoming speaking gig, or an occasional reminder about a new reporting project you need sources for. But don't engage in promotion overkill. Other users will become annoyed or start reading your updates as commercial, not human.

Think Visual

On most social networks, words are no longer enough. Users want to see real-time, Instagrammed photos, raw video, animated GIFs, primary documents, and interactive graphics.

Invest Wisely

Pick one or two platforms to especially devote your time. They should fit with your interests, skills, and professional area. Dip your toes in the water of many networks, if you like. But recognize there is only so much time in a day. Your work will reach a wider audience and you will impress employers more by being omnipresent and effective on a small number of platforms than a small presence on many.

Think Small

Along with the biggie networks, consider participating in smaller or more offbeat communities, including forums, discussion boards, list-servs, closed Facebook pages, blogs with active commenting, or more nebulous online subcultures in which your interests or expertise may make you a valuable member.

Feature Social Media in Your Stories

Users respect journalists who understand the value of social media as an information source and know how to incorporate it into their work. It can be an extra enticement to have people click on and share your work.

Join the Journalism Network

Invest in the Industry

Attend and participate in the events at which journalists gather. Interact on the social media platforms journalists most often use. Stay informed and discuss media and technology news. Visit and contribute to the more lighthearted online journalism communities. Experiment with and comment upon the steady stream of new journalism tools, reporting methods, and publishing platforms. And follow the latest journalism job and freelance opportunities.

Simply put, join the journalism network. Here is how to get started.

Read Journalism, Media, and Technology News

Click on, scroll, and scan your favorite insider sites daily. It keeps you clued in to what the professional and educational sides of the industry are buzzing about. It provides you with potential freelance and blog fodder. And it should occasionally teach you a thing or two about how to report or at least how to avoid messing up so badly your work goes viral.

SITE ALERT!

Here is a sampling of 15 highly trafficked, reputable sites covering various aspects of the news, media, and tech spheres. Most boast new content each day or week.

10,000 Words (mediabistro.com/10000words), "where journalism and technology meet"

American Journalism Review (ajr.org), "national magazine covering all aspects of print, television, radio, and online media"

College Media Matters (collegemediamatters.com), "a leading student journalism industry blog that aims to tell the story of college media 2.0" (Disclosure: This is my site!)

College Media Review (cmreview.org), "the flagship publication of College Media Association, Inc., the nation's largest organization for advisers and advocates of college student media"

Columbia Journalism Review (cjr.org), "a watchdog and a friend of the press in all its forms, from newspapers to magazines to radio, television, and the web"

Innovation in College Media (collegemediainnovation.org), "a group discussion about the future of college media"

JimRomenesko.com (jimromenesko.com), "a blog about media and other things I'm interested in"

Mashable (mashable.com), "social media news and web tips"

Mediagazer (mediagazer.com), "presents the day's must-read media news on a single page"

Nieman Journalism Lab (niemanlab.org), "a collaborative effort to figure out the future of journalism"

PBS MediaShift (pbs.org/mediashift), "tracks how new media—from weblogs to podcasts to citizen journalism—are changing society and culture"

Poynter MediaWire (poynter.org/category/latest-news/mediawire), "media industry news and commentary"

Student Press Law Center (splc.org), "advocate for student free-press rights"

TechCrunch (techcrunch.com), "group-edited blog about technology start-ups, particularly the web 2.0 sector"

Wired (wired.com), "in-depth coverage of current and future trends in technology, and how they are shaping business, entertainment, communications, science, politics, and culture"

Take Part in Online Journalism Communities

Along with the serious news outlets, blogs, and aggregators, there are a number of more informal, beloved havens for journalists to let loose and digitally share a laugh. Every once in a while, enjoy the laughter yourself, bond with classmates and friends over a related post or tweet, and learn a bit about how journalists think and unwind along the way.

SITE ALERT!

 Here is a short list of some of journalism's most popular informal communities—built atop a mix of satire, one-liners, and crowdsourced venting.

Fake AP Stylebook (twitter.com/FakeAPStylebook), "style tips for proper writing"

Journalism Student Problems (journalismstudentproblems.tumblr.com), "it goes way beyond AP Style"

#LikeACollegeJourno (likeacollegejourno.tumblr.com), "when #Whatshouldwecallme met #partylikeajournalist"

Overheard in the Newsroom (overheardinthenewsroom.com), "features quotes overheard in newsrooms, all submitted by journalists, often laced with booze, blood, and sexual tension"

Stuff Journalists Like (stuffjournalistslike.com), "a satirical blog about journalism and the media. Created by two journalists while waiting for sources to call them back"

Join a Journalism Organization

International, national, regional, and local journalism and media organizations offer a range of student perks. These include membership and conference registration discounts, scholarships, summer or winter boot camps, job search assistance, résumé critiques, mentoring, awards, chapter funding, and conference panels and paper calls for student presenters.

Become a member of an organization or two that fit your niche interests or demographic. Start a related campus chapter. Participate in their annual events. And get to know the student, professor, and professional members.

Here is a starter list of organizations worth checking out. Some are more scholarly, geared toward professionals or require membership from a news outlet not an individual, but they are all very beneficial and provide lots of informal networking.

American Copy Editors Society (ACES), copydesk.org, "a professional organization working toward the advancement of editors"

Asian American Journalists Association (AAJA), aaja.org, "to provide a means of association and support among Asian American and Pacific Islander journalists"

Associated Collegiate Press (ACP), studentpress.org, "the largest and oldest national membership organization for college student media in the United States"

Association for Education in Journalism and Mass Communication (AEJMC), aejmc.com, "a nonprofit, educational association of journalism and mass communication educators, students, and media professionals"

College Broadcasters, Inc. (CBI), askcbi.org, "represents students involved in radio, television, webcasting, and other related media ventures"

Investigative Reporters and Editors (IRE), ire.org, "a grassroots nonprofit organization dedicated to improving the quality of investigative reporting"

National Association of Black Journalists (NABJ), nabj.org, "an organization of journalists, students, and media-related professionals that provides quality programs and services to and advocates on behalf of black journalists worldwide"

National Association of Hispanic Journalists (NAHJ), nahj.org, "dedicated to the recognition and professional advancement of Hispanics in the news industry"

National Lesbian & Gay Journalists Association (NLGJA), nlgja.org, "an organization of journalists, media professionals, educators, and students working from within the news industry to foster fair and accurate coverage of LGBT issues"

Online News Association (ONA), journalists.org, "a nonprofit membership organization for digital journalists"

Society of Professional Journalists (SPJ), spj.org, "dedicated to the perpetuation of a free press as the cornerstone of our nation and our liberty"

The Society for News Design (SND), snd.org, "an international organization for news media professionals and visual communicators—specifically those who create print/web/mobile publications and products"

Attend Workshops and Conventions

They are the best spots to schmooze with journalism peers and major players, learn oodles of useful news media knowledge in a short time, and leave energized and bursting with ideas.

Here is a quick rundown of conferences to consider attending, along with the usual timeframes they are held and the websites offering more information about them.

Computer-Assisted Reporting Conference, Feb.–Mar. (ire.org)

ACP National College Journalism Convention, Feb.–Mar. (studentpress.org/acp)

CMA Spring National College Media Convention, March (collegemedia.org)

International Symposium on Online Journalism, April (online.journalism.utexas.edu)
National Conference of the American Copy Editors Society, April (copydesk.org)
Broadcast Education Association Convention, April (beaweb.org)
Investigative Reporters and Editors Conference, June (ire.org)
NABJ Convention & Career Fair, June (nabj.org)
UNITY Convention, August (unityjournalists.org)
AEJMC Conference, August (aejmc.com)
Online News Association Conference, September (journalists.org)
SPJ/RTDNA Excellence in Journalism, September (spj.org)
Society for News Design Annual Workshop, October (snd.org)
CBI National Student Electronic Media Convention, October (askcbi.org)
ACP/CMA National College Media Convention, Oct.–Nov. (studentpress.org/acp)

AN EXCHANGE OF IDEAS

Land a Job and Impress People

 The exchange is a recurring feature in the book and on my blog, spotlighting advice and exercises from top journalism students, professionals, educators, and advocates.

This exchange comes from Meredith Cochie. Cochie is a former journalist who helped build the New Media Journalism master's program at Full Sail University, where she is currently a course director. She also previously served as director of the University of Florida's Summer Journalism Institute.

Her exchange focuses on helping journalism students stand out from the job-seeking masses and land a position worth bragging about on Facebook.

First, be a know-it-all. More specifically, be a know-it-all about what you want to be a know-it-all about. Journalists need to know about the world in general and should have near-encyclopedic knowledge of one field or subject in particular. As the classic saying goes, "Know a little about a lot and a lot about a little."

If you want to report on sports, fashion, or movies, dive in. Study the history. Read related daily news. Identify and write about emerging trends. Participate in online discussions.

Share your knowledge breadth and depth in mixed company, including in front of potential employers. Just don't overdo it. Asinine should not become a three-syllable synonym for you.

Get a Real Email Address

Potential employers' first perceptions of you may veer into the unprofessional category if you contact them with a personal email containing a cringe-worthy nickname, potty humor, or odd word–number configurations. Two whoppers students actually used when reaching out to me in the past: tequilas69@hotmail.com and tupac4evah@yahoo.com.

Make an Impression in Person

Get out of your comfort zone of texting and emailing people and talk to them in person—beyond Facebook, Twitter, and the Internet at large. Venture into the real world. Go to events. Cold call. Don't be afraid to approach decent-looking strangers.

I once met an overzealous student who politely and repeatedly accosted me with business cards, clips, and questions about job prospects. Guess what? He stood out to me. Some of his early approaches were a bit abrupt and artless, but his overall persistence and speak-to-strangers-in-positions-of-power courage enabled him to earn a name for himself, one he has backed up over time with quality work.

In the digital age, when anything but an email back-and-forth makes some students break out in cold sweats, those who man up and introduce themselves to people they don't know have an edge.

Hustle, Without Being a Pimp

Work über-hard to stand out in some way. Tweet, blog, and build an online presence and a professional individual brand. Otherwise, you are in this big group of normal people and you won't stand out at all.

Don't Be Late

Arrive promptly for all interviews and other get-togethers with potential employers, colleagues, and mentors. When you are late, you look rude—and silly.

Write

Tons. A lot. All the time.

Build, Don't Burn, Bridges

The people you know are often just as important as what you know and where you've worked when attempting to land jobs and make new connections. So play nice, keep in touch, lend a hand, be a pal. To be clear though, you should not simply collect contacts to be called upon for favors later. Phoniness, like Saran Wrap, is see-through.

Don't Overlook the Handshake

When you shake hands with someone, use your hand, not a dead fish. The art of the handshake is simple. Be firm without breaking bones. Make eye contact without being creepy. And lean in without inching too close.

Focus on the Cover

Look at your current cover letter one last time, then rip it up. Most applicants' letters scream unmemorable or middle-of-the-road. So do their job prospects. Your goal: Be bold. Do something different. Inject some life into it. Remember, it's the first chance an employer has to vet you. Hook them with the lede sentence. Show them who you are and why they must hire you immediately. If you cannot sell your fabulousness in five paragraphs or 500 words, you will not be given a second look.

Get More Involved in Less

If you are participating in more than five extracurricular organizations, cut back. Otherwise, it tells people you are willing to take part in things you don't really care about, probably just to make yourself look good. Well, it doesn't. Potential employers and graduate school admissions counselors want to see you truly commit to a few things and grow with them.

For more digital journalism advice from Meredith Cochie, follow her on Twitter @journamaven.

HOW TO UN-IMPRESS PEOPLE

Building off Cochie's treatise, here is one last set of professionally oriented tidbits—on what *not* to do during the job and internship application process. Hint: It involves bragging, being pushy, and screwing up.

So, in full snarky fashion, here is some advice on how to dismay people from hiring you.

Overstate Your Experience or Awesomeness

You are not fluent in Spanish if all you know is hola. You are not a video journalism expert because you once uploaded a home movie to YouTube. You are not an academic counselor because you helped a student with homework for a week. You are not a senior reporter for your student newspaper after writing a few restaurant reviews. You are not a major media voice because a single post on your personal blog was retweeted.

Oversell Yourself

Keep messages to potential employers short. Get right to the point. Only your immediate family is interested in your entire life story. Also, avoid a crazy amount of attachments or a long listing of links. Include just a few links, and use bit.ly to keep them short. Use Dropbox for files, and convert them all to PDF.

Make Mistakes

Avoid fact, spelling, and grammar errors on your résumé, cover letter, and within all email communication. Keep published clips containing mistakes out of your application package. And just because an editor responds with a friendly email, it does not mean you are now free to use Internet acronyms or suddenly drop formalities or correct punctuation when corresponding with her.

List an Unhelpful Professional Reference

Do not include the name of an individual who will barely remember you or not have kind things to say about you. Similarly, do not list someone without first asking their permission and occasionally reminding them, so they will be ready when an email or call comes.

Include a Vague Résumé Objective

Your objective when submitting your résumé somewhere should be clear: You want a job! Including generalities about personal growth, helping the team, or gaining professional experience is a waste of valuable résumé space and an insult to your potential employer's intellect. If you are hell-bent on having an objective, keep it simple: Your objective is to obtain _____ [Insert position title here] with _____ [Insert company name here].

Rebellious Reporter Child

Illustration by Yee Hung Lim

10 Last Story Idea Tips Your Mom Wouldn't Approve Of

"Always think outside the box. What aren't officials telling you? What angle haven't you thought of? A story can never have too many sources. You can never have enough story ideas. No, you probably won't be the next Woodward or Bernstein. But pursue every story like you are."

Christian Hill, staff writer, *The News Tribune*, Wash.

Your mother is not always right.

When it comes to the journalism of ideas, the most time-tested, unquestioned, seemingly commonsense motherly maxims miss the mark—and in certain cases need to be upended. And so, in this one instance, I am advocating becoming a rebellious reporter child.

Building on this tongue-in-cheek premise, atop all the other advice related to brainstorming, discovering, developing, and selling stories shared so far, here is one last set of serious pointers aimed at helping you grab the most—and best—story ideas.

Stop Working So Hard

See a movie. Take a walk. Grab a hot shower. Go for a swim. Play "Guitar Hero." Call an old friend. Do your laundry. Bottom line: Every so often—especially when your emails, assignments, and stress levels are up and your sleep, confidence, and creativity are down—take a break.

It will reset your addled brain. It will refocus you on the bigger picture. It will help you separate the significant from the silly on your to-do list. It will ensure great ideas keep flowing. And it will stop you from physically, mentally, and journalistically burning out.

"It's very easy, especially for young journalists, to stay connected at all times to work by constantly checking email, Facebook, Twitter, cellphones, etc.," said Wendy Reuer, a reporter for *The Forum of Fargo-Moorhead* in North Dakota. "The important thing is to know how to separate your time. Journalists have to carve out time that is not work-related, some time to unplug. Stories and issues will certainly plague a reporter long after they've left work and there will be times you sit up in bed in the middle of the night because you remembered something that should have gone into your story. Still, if there is no separation, a burnout is likely to come much faster."

Don't Stay in School

Study hard. Make friends. Get the most out of campus life. But sometimes, step away from it. At least a few times each semester, physically and intellectually break free of the so-called college bubble. Attend a community event. Take a short road trip. Join a nearby book club. Read world news. Chat up the man at the bus stop. Volunteer with an organization that supports a cause you believe in. Mentor local children. And, yes, call your mother.

These experiences, lessons, people, and places will stir laughter, learning, and a spurt of ideas that cannot be found in a syllabus, dorm room, or classroom. Journalism is a contact sport. It requires exposure to, and interaction with, the outside world.

As Brandon Szuminsky, a columnist and copy editor at *The Uniontown Herald-Standard* in Pennsylvania, shares about his own work, "When I start to get in a rut and think that there aren't any good stories out there, I get out of the newsroom and drive on the highway. When I'm out there, I make it a point to note each car that whizzes past on the other side of the road. On any given day it's easy to overlook that they're there, but I try to imagine the people inside. Each and every one of those drivers is going somewhere specific. They all have hopes and dreams, challenges and struggles. They each have a family and a job and a passion. It reminds me that there are stories everywhere. And just like the cars in the other lane, the fact I don't always notice them doesn't mean they're not there. You just have to focus to see them."

Talk to Strangers

Journalists, it is said, are an odd species. They are one of the only groups of people who like to constantly surround themselves with people they *don't* know. Friends you can trust and respected sources on your beat are sacrosanct. But they can also become fallbacks, or obstructions to a wider view of the world. There are many, many more people all around you—and some would be thrilled to tell you something you don't know.

Read Pulp

There is almost no worse activity than writing or brainstorming with a mushy or unwilling brain. Reading opens it up, exposes you once more to words, plot, and ideas. To get your synapses firing, a textbook, journalism how-to, classic biography, or a website sharing big news of the day might do. But don't discount the easy reading, especially if it is the only option available or the only one you feel motivated to devour. Check out a glossy magazine cover to cover. Scroll through TMZ. Read a sappy novel or mystery thriller. Giggle or cry over a tale or two from *Chicken Soup for the Soul*. Then, go write. I promise, the words will flow more easily.

Be the Center of Attention

Become gregarious instead of practicing the journalism instinct of listen, listen, listen. Specifically, in the right setting and with the right group of people, open up and steer the conversation toward you for a change. What do you find yourself talking about? What prompts the most response from your audience? What are you surprised to find yourself so passionate or knowledgeable about? You might just have a story or series flowing from your own mouth.

Waste Time Online

Casually scrolling through endless scores of websites is often held up as the epitome of apathy. Pure time-suck, I believe, is what my younger brothers call it—not that it stops them from doing it, a lot. But with a journalistic refocus, you can transform your aimless browsing from a "suck" to a score. During your next online dawdle, don't just seek out gossip, life advice, entertainment news, and videos of laughing babies and cute cats. Search for ideas.

The best part about the Internet: You can stumble across tons of random information without warning. And that information can exist as portals to endless potential stories and sources. So the next time you are out of quality ideas, my three words of advice: Pure time-suck.

Don't Dream Big

Some stories are grand in scope. Most are not. Lose the instinct to only conceive of ideas that will require months of legwork, tons of funding, and secret vault access in order to carry out a proper report. Just as often, come up with stories that are more grounded in reality and doable by your deadline. Often, these initially smaller stories can lead to bigger ones. Even while ascending Mount Everest, climbers stop at camps along the way.

Eat Sweets Before Dinner

Or pizza. Or drink coffee or Red Bull. Basically, be occasionally open to consuming anything that will give you a rush or slow ramp-up of energy. Often it is tempting to work hard and do without, or promise yourself a reward only after the work is done. Instead, reward yourself early on. The sugar and carbs will add pizzazz to your brainstorming and reporting efforts. Don't abandon healthy food or a well-rounded diet, but sometimes stake out the sweets that will get you going.

Act Like You Were Born Yesterday

Admit stupidity. Look at something through ignorant eyes. Whittle an issue down to its most elementary level. These are each powerful ways to crystallize, uncover, and sell stories to a mass audience.

As Shira Schoenberg, a political journalist reporting for *The Springfield Republican* and MassLive.com, shares, "Some of the best stories I've written are the ones in which I've felt the stupidest. Yes, it may be embarrassing to call an economist and ask 'What's a derivative?' or 'What's a mortgage-backed security?' But if you don't know, chances are your readers won't know either. If you can explain the concept in plain English, they'll keep reading."

Require Proof of Your Mother's Love

Don't accept anything at face value. Avoid being pulled into a seemingly fantastic scoop without also getting the facts. Never let a great idea stop you from seeing what is really happening. Even the most trusted sources and self-evident truths must be vetted. As the saying goes, if your mother says she loves you, get a second source. OK, this one actually relates to a piece of motherly advice I agree with: If it sounds too good to be true, it probably is.

Bibliography

Unless cited in the following pages, the advice of all professional journalists, student journalists, journalism professors, and student media advisers and advocates featured in the text was collected during in-person, phone, and email interviews I conducted.

Chapter 1: The Idea Stage

Opening Quote

Arthur Gelb, *City Room* (New York: Berkley Books, 2003): 373.

Introduction

"#96: Roman Mars, Host of the 99% Invisible Podcast," *The Conversation Hub*, April 3, 2012: theconversationhub.com/96-roman-mars-host-of-the-99-invisible-podcast.

"99% Invisible," *How Sound*, December 28, 2011: howsound.org/2011/12/99-invisible.

"99% Invisible #07- 99% Alien," *99% Invisible*, December 19, 2011: 99percentinvisible.org/post/1314197574/episode-07-99-alien-download-embed-share.

"99% Invisible-49- Queue Theory and Design," *99% Invisible*, May 18, 2012: 99percentinvisible.org/post/18984374836/episode-49-queue-theory-and-design.

Mark Lukach, "'99% Invisible': The Awesome Little Radio Show about Design," *The Awl*, May 4, 2012: theawl.com/2012/05/99-invisible-design-radio-show.

"Radiolab Presents: 99% Invisible," *Radiolab*, December 12, 2011: radiolab.org/blogs/radiolab-blog/2011/dec/12/radiolab-presents-99-invisible.

"Roman Mars," *Design Matters with Debbie Millman*, April 6, 2012: observermedia.designobserver.com/audio/roman-mars/32498.

WOW Stories

Angela Son, "Students Install Hot Tub on North Campus," *The Michigan Daily*, February 22, 2012: www.michigandaily.com/news/mystery-hot-tub-north-campus.

"Hot Tub on Roof of University of Michigan Building is Mystery," *The Huffington Post*, February 24, 2012: www.huffingtonpost.com/2012/02/25/hot-tub-on-roff-_n_1301010.html.

Kellie Woodhouse, "Mystery Hot Tub: Who Installed the 'Bubbler' on the Roof of a University of Michigan Building?" *AnnArbor.com*, February 24, 2012: annarbor.com/news/students-install-hot-tub-on-roof-of-university-of-michigan-building.

"Any Journalism Story Ideas?" *Yahoo Answers!*, February 5, 2008: answers.yahoo.com/question/index?qid=20080209194243AAWZXXs.

A Thumping Pulse

Nick Dean, "Living Social: College Newsrooms Revisiting Ethics Policies for the Twitter Generation," *Student Press Law Center Report* 32.3, Fall 2011: 30: splc.org/news/report_detail.asp?id=1611&edition=56.

A Standout Story Idea

Christian Hill, Advice originally shared in "Beyond the Byline: 735 Tips Every Reporter Should Know Before Setting Foot in a Newsroom," edited and self-published by Dan Reimold in 2009.

Chapter 2: A Journalism Life

Audrey Scagnelli, "Prevent a Dorm Fire," *College & Cook*, Winter 2012: 26–29: collegeandcook.com/2012/01/16/winter-2012.

Malcolm Gladwell, *What the Dog Saw: And Other Adventures* (New York: Little, Brown and Company, 2009).

The Stuff of Life

"Press," *FOUND Magazine*: foundmagazine.com/press.

Assignment Alert: The Reporter and the Record Egg

Jennifer Levitz, Advice originally shared in "Beyond the Byline: 735 Tips Every Reporter Should Know Before Setting Foot in a Newsroom," edited and self-published by Dan Reimold in 2009.

Chapter 3: People Stories

People Often Profiled

Rob Bradfield, "No Prayers? No Problem," *The Baylor Lariat*, November 15, 2011: baylorlariat.com/2011/11/15/no-prayers-no-problem.

Brandon Lee, "Triples, Trimesters, and Trials," *The Famuan*, April 18, 2012: thefamuanonline.com/sports/triples-trimesters-and-trials-1.2731122.

Stereotyped Sources

Lindsey Gelwicks, "Waiting to Kiss," *Ball Bearings Magazine*, December 7, 2011: ballbearingsonline.com/story.php?id=1665.

Chimamanda Ngozi Adichie, "The Danger of a Single Story," TED, July 2009: ted.com/talks/chimamanda_adichie_the_danger_of_a_single_story.html.

The Little Guys

"Remarks by the President at Barnard College Commencement Ceremony," The White House Office of the Press Secretary, May 14, 2012: whitehouse.gov/the-press-office/2012/05/14/remarks-president-barnard-college-commencement-ceremony.

Ideas, Online: Crowdsourcing

"Passport Verification Officer Demands Bribe..!!" I Paid a Bribe, August 18, 2012: ipaidabribe.com/bribe-central/passport-verification-officer-demands-bribe.

Robert Niles, "A Journalist's Guide to Crowdsourcing," *Online Journalism Review*, July 31, 2007: ojr.org/ojr/stories/070731niles.

Chapter 4: Fresh Perspectives

Adichie, "The Danger of a Single Story."

In Other Words

Kate Kompas, Advice originally shared in "Beyond the Byline: 735 Tips Every Reporter Should Know Before Setting Foot in a Newsroom," edited and self-published by Dan Reimold in 2009.

Three Perspectives to Seek Out

Lou Carlozo, "Why College Students Stop Short of a Degree," Reuters, March 27, 2012: reuters.com/article/2012/03/27/us-attn-andrea-education-dropouts-idUSBRE82Q0Y120120327.

Daniel Drake, "A Shout-Out to Dropouts," *The Mooring Mast*, April 18, 2012: mast.plu.edu/2012/04/shout-out-to-dropouts.html.

Andrew Duffy, "Bedless in Bobst," YouTube, April 16, 2011: youtube.com/watch?v=cdUTv6vmt7g.

Shamus Khan, Priscilla Ferguson, Kate Levin, Herbert Gans, Elisabeth Ladenson, and Allan Silver, "The Way We Were," *The Eye* (the magazine of *The Columbia Daily Spectator*), April 28, 2011: eye.columbiaspectator.com/?q=article/2011/04/28/way-we-were.

The Opposite Attraction

Joe Fox, "I'm Not a Doctor . . . Kitten Cuteness Hard to Resist for Any Cat Lover," *The Post*, May 6, 2012: thepost.ohiou.edu/content/im-not-doctor-kitten-cuteness-hard-resist-any-cat-lover.

Joe Fox, "I'm Not a Doctor . . . Motorcyclists Cruise in Circles for Loud Show," *The Post*, April 22, 2012: thepost.ohiou.edu/content/im-not-doctor-motorcyclists-cruise-circles-loud-show.

The Inanimate Perspective

Sarah Hutchins, "Wanted," *Inside* magazine (the magazine of the *Indiana Daily Student*), April 12, 2010: http://idsnews.com/news/inside/story.aspx?id=75152.

Phantom Story Syndrome

Josh Korr, "Why Not Writing a Story is Innovation," *Publishing 2.0*, December 8, 2008: publishing2.com/2008/12/08/why-not-writing-a-story-is-innovation.

Jeff Jarvis, "The Journalism of Filling Space and Time," *BuzzMachine*, November 4, 2008: buzzmachine.com/2008/11/04/the-journalism-of-filling-space-and-time.

Chapter 5: Words, Letters, and Lots of Ideas

"What the Words of the Year Say about Us," Touré, *Time*, January 5, 2012: ideas.time.com/2012/01/05/what-the-words-of-the-year-say-about-us.

Some Word Stories

Joey Becerra, "More Than Just a Beautiful Plume," *The Daily Titan*, October 31, 2011: dailytitan.com/2011/10/more-than-just-a-beautiful-plume.

Suzy Strutner, "'The Compliment Guys' Hope to Create Friendlier Environment by Praising Passersby on Bruin Walk," *The Daily Bruin*, May 5, 2010: dailybruin.com/index.php/article/2010/05/compliment-guys-hope-create-friendlier-environment.

Richard Pérez-Peña, "Stutterer Speaks Up in Class; His Professor Says Keep Quiet," *The New York Times*, October 10, 2011: nytimes.com/2011/10/11/education/11stutter.html.

Post-Mortem: WKU, A to Z

Molly English, "Q is for Queen: Student Discovers Passion through Dressing in Drag," *The College Heights Herald,* February 17, 2012: wkuherald.com/diversions/article_fd274df6–591e-11e1-b64d-0019bb30f31a.html.

Rialda Zukic, "J is for Juggler: High School Hobby Helps Student Relax," *The College Heights Herald*, November 12, 2010: wkuherald.com/diversions/article_3ebfdb12-edfe-11df-aa6f-0017a4a78c22.html.

Read Everything

Staff, "What We Learned From Reading Every Last Word of 14 Magazines," *The 6th Floor Blog* (kept by staff of *The New York Times Magazine*), May 9, 2012: 6thfloor.blogs.nytimes.com/2012/05/09/what-we-learned-from-reading-every-last-word-of-14-magazines.

Chapter 6: Timely Ideas

"Mount Pleasant in 24 Hours," *The CM Life*, October 14, 2009: cm-life.com/24mp.

The Power of Old

"Civil War: 150 Years Later," *The Daily Tar Heel*, April 18, 2011: dailytarheel.com/multimedia/6335.

Allison Goodman, "Hurricane Andrew: 20 Years Later," *The Miami Hurricane*, August 23, 2012: themiamihurricane.com/2012/08/23/hurricane-andrew-20-years-later.

Assignment Alert: A Special Edition

Dan Reimold, "Sampling of Student Press 9/11 10th Anniversary Coverage," *College Media Matters*, September 10, 2011: collegemediamatters.com/2011/09/10/sampling-of-student-press-911-10th-anniversary-coverage.

Adrienne LaFrance, "OC Register Assigns 70 Reporters to Cover One Baseball Game," *Nieman Journalism Lab,* April 5, 2012: niemanlab.org/2012/04/oc-register-assigns-70-reporters-to-cover-one-baseball-game.

The Long News

Kirk Citron, "And Now, the Real News," TED, February 2010: ted.com/talks/kirk_citron_and_now_the_real_news.html.

Ideas, Online: Real-Time Reporting

David Simpson, "The Power of Live Tweeting," *AdviserDavid*, August 17, 2012: adviserdavid.wordpress.com/2012/08/17/the-power-of-live-tweeting/.

Chapter 7: Trendy Ideas

Hayley Brooks and Ali Kokot, *The Daily Pennsylvanian*: thedp.com/staff/hayley_brooks_and_
ali_kokot.

Common Trend Stories

Ted Burnham, "Battling The Bottle: Students And Industry Face Off Over Water," *The Salt* (food
blog kept by *National Public Radio*), February 12, 2012: npr.org/blogs/thesalt/2012/02/
12/146692656/battling-the-bottle-students-and-industry-face-off-over-water.

Rachel Getzenberg, "Foreign Students Have Higher Rates of Cheating Than American Peers," *The
GW Hatchet*, March 26, 2012: gwhatchet.com/2012/03/26/foreign-students-cheat-more-
than-american-peers.

Spring Cleaning

"Spring Cleaning Special: Ten Things to Toss Out," *The Washington Post*, April 19, 2009: washington
post.com/wp-dyn/content/opinions/outlook/index_20090418.html.

"Twelve Things the World Should Toss Out," *The Washington Post*, Spring 2010: washington
post.com/wp-srv/special/opinions/outlook/spring-cleaning/index.html.

"Outlook's Third Annual Spring Cleaning List," *The Washington Post*, Spring 2011: washington
post.com/wp-srv/special/opinions/outlook/spring-cleaning-2011/

"Outlook's Fourth Annual Spring Cleaning," *The Washington Post*, Spring 2012: washington
post.com/opinions/its-time-to-toss-the-all-volunteer-military/2012/04/19/gIQAwFV3TT
_story.html.

Assignment Alert: Reexamine, Reinvent, or Scrap

LS Observations Editor, "Why On Earth Are We Still Writing Essays?" *Leeds Student*, April 24, 2012:
leedsstudent.org/2012–04–24/ls2/observations/why-on-earth-are-we-still-writing-essays.

Trendspotting Fever

Jack Shafer, "Bogus Trend Week—The Readers Take Over," *Slate*, November 12, 2010: slate.com/
articles/news_and_politics/press_box/2010/11/bogus_trend_weekthe_readers_take_over.html.

"Stuff Journalists Like—#24 Trends," *Stuff Journalists Like*, January 2009: stuffjournalists
like.com/2009/01/trends.html.

Daniel Radosh, "The Trendspotting Generation," *Radosh.net*: radosh.net/writing/trends.html.

Assignment Alert: Cure the Fever

Elspeth Reeve, "Bang the Trend Slowly," *The Atlantic Wire*, June 7, 2012: theatlanticwire.com/
national/2012/06/bang-trend-slowly/53289.

Chapter 8: Criminal Ideas

Everyday Crimes

Emily White, "I Never Owned Any Music to Begin With," *All Songs Considered* (blog kept by *National Public Radio*), June 16, 2012: npr.org/blogs/allsongs/2012/06/16/154863819/i-never-owned-any-music-to-begin-with.

Emily Biggs, "PLU Students Swipe without Swiping," *The Mooring Mast*, March 22, 2012: mast.plu.edu/2012/03/plu-students-swipe-without-swiping.html.

Post-Mortem: Move the Story Forward

Mary Toth, "Penn State Scandal: Newspaper Shows Pure Courage," *The Baltimore Sun*, November 22, 2011: articles.baltimoresun.com/2011–11–22/news/bs-ed-penn-state-newspaper-letter-20111121_1_pure-courage-penn-state-patriot-news.

Liz Brody, "Meet the Woman Who Exposed Jerry Sandusky," *Glamour*, February 2012: glamour.com/inspired/magazine/2012/02/meet-the-woman-who-exposed-jerry-sandusky.

"The 2012 Pulitzer Prize Winners: Local Reporting": pulitzer.org/citation/2012-Local-Reporting.

Criminal Elements

Zach Crizer, "Ex-Felon Moves Forward," *The Collegiate Times*, April 13, 2011: collegiatetimes.com/stories/17378/ex-felon-moves-forward.

Assignment Alert: Nearby, Offenders

Mat Wolf, "DPS Takes Notice of Registered Sex Offender Contacts on Campus," *The Daily Emerald*, February 17, 2011: dailyemerald.com/2011/02/17/dps-takes-notice-of-registered-sex-offender-contacts-on-campus.

Post-Mortem: The Tweetalong

Stephanie Schendel, "Police Ridealong Tweets: Feb. 3," *The Daily Evergreen*, February 3, 2012: dailyevergreen.wsu.edu/public/readmore.castle?id=1782.

Chapter 9: Location, Location, Location

Jordan Bentz, "High Desert Calling," *Flux Magazine*, Spring 2011: 56–61: fluxstories.com/archive/2011.php.

Some Featured Places

"Special Report: The Chrysler Property," *The Review*, Fall 2009: udreview.com/chrysler.

The Always List

Dan Reimold, "Brian Stelter at #NYC12: 10 Tips to Stand Out in School, Land Dream Job, Survive Print Apocalypse," *College Media Matters*, March 19, 2012: collegemediamatters.com/2012/03/19/brian-stelter-at-nyc12–10-tips-to-stand-out-in-school-land-dream-job-survive-print-apocalypse.

Over & Back

Matt Stevens and Maya Sugarman, "Over & Back," *The Daily Bruin*, October 2010: overandback.dailybruin.com.

Cailly Morris, "Malibu of the Midwest: Surfing in Sheboygan," *Curb Magazine*, November 20, 2011: curbonline.com/2011/11/20/surfing-the-elements.

Assignment Alert: The International Exchange

Wiktoria Parysek, "Uncovering the World of Internationals," *The Daily Pennsylvanian*, June 23, 2011: thedp.com/article/2011/06/wiktoria_parysek_uncovering_the_world_of_internationals.

Questionable Places

Lane DeGregory, "Miami Sex Offenders Limited to Life Under a Bridge," *Tampa Bay Times*, August 16, 2009: tampabay.com/features/article1027668.ece.

Nathalie Miraval, "Nine Animals Died in Harvard-Affiliated Laboratories," *The Harvard Crimson*, January 23, 2012: thecrimson.com/article/2012/1/23/Animals-Testing-Lab.

Susana Cobo, "Cambodia: Life in Sewage," *Tusk Magazine*, Spring 2012: tuskmagazine.fullerton.edu/Sewage.html.

Ideas, Online: Worlds Without People

Alan Taylor, "A World without People," *The Atlantic*, March 15, 2012: theatlantic.com/infocus/2012/03/a-world-without-people/100264.

Mapping

Brandee Easter, "Map of Tornado Damage and Volunteer Opportunities," *The Crimson White*, May 7, 2011: cw.ua.edu/2011/05/07/map-of-tornado-damage-and-volunteer-opportunities.

Chapter 10: The Local Angle

Jeff Jarvis, "New Rule: Cover What You Do Best. Link to the Rest," *BuzzMachine*, February 22, 2007: buzzmachine.com/2007/02/22/new-rule-cover-what-you-do-best-link-to-the-rest.

Dan Reimold, "NextGen Journal Gives College Students' Spin on Global Events," *PBS MediaShift*, May 9, 2011: pbs.org/mediashift/2011/05/nextgen-journal-gives-college-students-spin-on-global-events129.html.

To Fit Your Readership

Chase Hopkins, "How Will the State Budget Affect the College?" *The Flat Hat*, April 26, 2012: flathatnews.com/2012/04/26/how-will-the-state-budget-affect-the-college.

Amanda Sieradzki, "When the Parade's Over, Party Beads Find a New Life," UPI, April 1, 2011: upi.com/Top_News/US/2011/04/01/When-the-parades-over-party-beads-find-a-new-life/UPIU-9211300235567.

Peer-to-Peer Story Sharing

Dan Wetzel, "Sandusky Remained a Presence around Penn State Last Week," *Yahoo! Sports*, November 7, 2011: rivals.yahoo.com/ncaa/football/news?slug=dw-wetzel_sandusky_penn_state_presence_last_week110711.

Brenda Medina, "Penn State Scandal Prompts Colleges, and States, to Review Policies on Reporting Crime," *The Chronicle of Higher Education*, November 15, 2011: chronicle.com/article/Penn-State-Scandal-Prompts/129792.

Chapter 11: Building a Beat

The Micro-Beat

Ryan Frank, "Q&A: How Can My College Paper Make a Digital Transition?" *The Garage* (blog kept by *The Daily Emerald*), July 9, 2012: thegarage.dailyemerald.com/2012/07/09/qa-how-can-my-college-paper-make-a-digital-transition.

Post-Mortem: The Homicide Beat

Adrienne LaFrance, "After a Deal Falls Apart, Homicide Watch D.C. is Going on Hiatus," *Nieman Journalism Lab*, August 14, 2012: niemanlab.org/2012/08/after-a-deal-falls-apart-homicide-watch-d-c-is-going-on-hiatus.

Chapter 12: Records Reporting

Doug Brown, "'Cope Court' Donor Withdraws $1 Million Gift," *The Daily Kent Stater*, January 6, 2012: kentwired.com/cope-court-donor-withdraws-$1-million-gift.

Doug Brown, "The Courting of Cope: Behind the Scenes of a $1 Million Withdrawal," *The Daily Kent Stater*, February 12, 2012: kentwired.com/the-courting-of-jason-cope-behind-the-scenes-of-a-$1-million-withdrawal.

Daily Kent Stater Editors, "Our View: Fraudulence Shouldn't be Overlooked," *The Daily Kent Stater*, January 9, 2012: kentwired.com/our-view-fraudulence-shouldnt-be-overlooked.

An Exchange of Ideas: A Reporter's Main Course

Patricia Boh, Brooks Igo, and Natalie Posgate, "Sweeping Rape under the Rug," *The Daily Campus*, May 1, 2012: smudailycampus.com/news/sweeping-rape-under-the-rug-1.2863843.

Paula Lavigne, "What's Lurking in Your Stadium Food?" *ESPN Outside the Lines*, 2010: http://sports.espn.go.com/espn/eticket/story?page=100725/stadiumconcessions.

Ideas, Online: The April 16th Documents

"April 16th Documents," *The Collegiate Times*: collegiatetimes.com/databases/april16th-documents.

Greg Esposito, "Tech Newspaper Posts Documents Related to April 16 Shooting Online," *The Roanoke Times*, December 19, 2008: roanoke.com/news/roanoke/wb/188264.

Assignment Alert: Performer Contracts

Katie McHugh, "What He Wanted: An Exploration of Mac Miller's Concert Requests," *The Allegheny Campus*, February 10, 2012: alleghenycampus.com/2012/02/10/wanted-exploration-mac-millers-concert-requests.

Chapter 13: Data Journalism

"Universities Collected £50m in Library Fines, Figures Show," *The Guardian*, January 7, 2012: guardian.co.uk/education/2012/jan/07/universities-collected-50million-library-fines.

"Library Can't Trace Your Late Book Fees," *Leeds Student*, February 24, 2012: leedsstudent.org/2012–02–24/ls1/ls1-news/library-cant-trace-your-late-book-fees.

LS Web Editor, "Book, Fine and Sinker," *Leeds Student*, March 25, 2011: leedsstudent.org/2011–03–25/ls1/ls1-news/book-fine-and-sinker.

An Exchange of Ideas: Numbers Are the Story

Ioanna Makris, April Cunningham, and Caroline Courtney, "Million-Dollar Bust," *The Daily Toreador*, October 26, 2011: dailytoreador.com/news/article_9802d34c-ff90–11e0-b8cb-0019bb30f31a.html.

Mark Newman, "Maps of the 2008 U.S. Presidential Election Results," November 4, 2010: www-personal.umich.edu/~mejn/election/2008.

Ideas, Online: Data Visualization

"International Number Ones: Because Every Country is the Best at Something," *Information is Beautiful*: informationisbeautiful.net/visualizations/because-every-country-is-the-best-at-something.

Assignment Alert: Start with the Census

Al Tompkins, "How Journalists Can Mine Census Data for Stories about Their Changing Communities," *Al's Morning Meeting*, December 21, 2010: poynter.org/latest-news/als-morning-meeting/111792/how-journalists-can-mine-census-data-for-stories-about-their-changing-communities.

Chapter 14: Photojournalism Ideas

Matt Stamey, "Faces of Katrina," YouTube, June 12, 2009: youtube.com/watch?v=0873rI0E2ww.

Ideas, Online: Photo Slideshows

Noah Kalina, "Noah Takes a Photo of Himself Every Day for 12.5 Years," YouTube, September 4, 2012: youtube.com/watch?v=iPPzXlMdi7o.

Chapter 15: An Immersion of Ideas

Brian Dzenis, "Editor-in-Chief Survives without Meat for Month-Long Vices Challenge," *The Temple News*, November 7, 2011: temple-news.com/living/2011/11/07/editor-in-chief-survives-without-meat-for-month-long-vices-challenge.

Jessica Argondizza, "Dungeon Raider Logs Off 'World of Warcraft,'" *The Temple News*, October 25, 2010: temple-news.com/living/2010/10/25/dungeon-raider-logs-off-world-of-warcraft.

Ashley Nguyen, "Coffee Addict Goes Cold-Turkey," *The Temple News*, October 11, 2010: temple-news.com/living/2010/10/11/coffee-addict-goes-cold-turkey.

Jasmine Offor, "'Crackberry' Addict Shuts Down Connections in Four-Day Challenge," *The Temple News*, October 18, 2010: temple-news.com/living/2010/10/18/crackberry-addict-shuts-down-connections-in-four-day-challenge.

Alexis Sachdev, "Smoker Extinguishes a Habit for Four-Day Challenge," *The Temple News*, November 1, 2010: temple-news.com/living/2010/11/01/smoker-extinguishes-a-habit-for-four-day-challenge.

Types of Immersion

Barbara Ehrenreich, *Nickel and Dimed: On (Not) Getting By in America* (New York: Metropolitan Books, 2001).

A.J. Jacobs, *The Year of Living Biblically: One Man's Humble Quest to Follow the Bible as Literally as Possible* (New York: Simon & Schuster, 2007).

Judith Levine, *Not Buying It: My Year Without Shopping* (New York: Free Press, 2007).

In Other Words

A.J. Jacobs, "In Defense of Literary Stunts," *Wired*, May 11, 2012: wired.com/underwire/ 2012/05/pl_ajjacobs.

Post-Mortem: The Video Game Challenge

Miles Parks, "24 Hours to Game," *The Minaret*, November 30, 2011: theminaretonline. com/2011/11/30/article20424.

Ethics Alert: The Bicycle Theft

Alanna Fairey, "How Easy is it to Steal a Bike in Waterloo?" *The Cord*, March 28, 2012: the cord.ca/?p=4580.

Ideas, Online: The Snowball Fight

Kyle Boyer, "How to Organize a Revolution (Or a Snow Fight)," *The Washington Post*, February 19, 2010: voices.washingtonpost.com/campus-overload/2010/02/how_to_organize_a_revolution_ o.html.

Chapter 16: Idea Lists

James Poniewozik, "All-TIME 100 TV Shows," *Time*, September 6, 2007: entertainment. time.com/2007/09/06/the-100-best-tv-shows-of-all-time/#how-i-chose-the-list.

Dan Reimold, "A List of the Best College Lists: Top Mascots, Twitter Feeds, Fashion Trends," *USA TODAY College*, October 5, 2011: usatodayeducate.com/staging/index.php/campus-beat/a-list-of-the-best-college-lists-top-mascots-twitter-feeds-fashion-trends.

The Always List

"30 Celebrities Yawning," *The Huffington Post*, May 15, 2012: huffingtonpost.com/2012/05/15/sleep-celebrities-yawning_n_1518370.html

The Never List

Muhammad Saleem, "7 Things You Need to Know about Writing Lists That Work," *Copyblogger*, August 1, 2007: copyblogger.com/writing-lists.

Assignment Alert: Campus Bucket List

Nick Massa, "Elon Bucket List," *The Pendulum*, May 13, 2010: elon.edu/pendulum/Story. aspx?id=3880.

Ideas, Online: Lists as Inspiration

"Top 10 Sleepiest Mammals around the Globe," *Smashing Lists*: smashinglists.com/top-10-sleepiest-mammals-around-the-globe.

Chapter 17: Digital and Mobile Story Mining

Joe Sabia, "The Technology of Storytelling," TED, May 2011: ted.com/talks/joe_sabia_the_technology_of_storytelling.html.

Taming the Wild Web

Gloria Lloyd, "University Purchases .xxx URLs," *The Chronicle*, November 22, 2011: duke chronicle.com/article/university-purchases-xxx-urls.

Jay Kennedy and Matt Mecoli, "Social Media Blackout (Video)," *The Crimson White*, October 5, 2011: cw.ua.edu/2011/10/05/social-media-blackout-video.

Matt Mecoli, "The Social Media Blackout," *The Crimson White*, October 5, 2011: cw.ua.edu/2011/10/05/the-social-media-blackout-2.

Staff Writers, "The Battle for Bandwidth," *OnlineColleges.net*, August 1, 2012: onlinecolleges. net/2012/08/01/the-battle-for-bandwidth.

"IGN Partners with the University of Iowa to Kick Off Video Game Journalism Program," *PRNewswire*, August 21, 2012: prnewswire.com/news-releases-test/ign-partners-with-the-university-of-iowa-to-kick-off-video-game-journalism-program-166943666.html?utm_expid=43414375–18.

Nicholas Carlson, "Forget Apple, Forget Facebook: Here's the One Company That Actually Terrifies Google Execs," *Business Insider*, August 15, 2012: finance.yahoo.com/news/forget-apple-forget-facebook-heres-184209532.html.

Andrew Couts, "United Nations: Free Speech Online is a Basic Human Right," *Digital Trends*, July 6, 2012: digitaltrends.com/international/united-nations-free-speech-online-is-a-basic-human-right.

Matt Richtel, "Young, in Love and Sharing Everything, Including a Password," *The New York Times*, January 17, 2012: nytimes.com/2012/01/18/us/teenagers-sharing-passwords-as-show-of-affection.html.

Ideas, Online: 10 Sites Bursting with Ideas

Jeff Sonderman, "Slate Writer: BuzzFeed Pillages Reddit for its Viral Photo Posts," *Poynter MediaWire*, June 27, 2012: poynter.org/latest-news/mediawire/178955/slate-writer-buzzfeed-pillages-reddit-for-its-viral-photo-posts.

Alexa Tsotsis, "TaskRabbit Turns Grunt Work Into a Game," *Wired*, July 15, 2011: wired.com/magazine/2011/07/mf_taskrabbit.

Chris Cuomo, Brinda Adhikari and Maggy Patrick, "TaskRabbit: Putting Americans Back to Work, One Odd Job at a Time," *ABC News*, September 29, 2011: abcnews.go.com/US/taskrabbit-putting-americans-back-work-odd-job-time/story?id=14626495.

Go Mobile

Michael Christopher Brown, "An iPhone in the DRC: Photos by Michael Christopher Brown," *Time*, August 16, 2012: lightbox.time.com/2012/08/16/an-iphone-in-congo-photos-by-michael-christopher-brown.

Chapter 18: Journalism Hackathon

Bryan Lufkin, "Storyboard: Steven Leckart on Silicon Valley's Grueling Hackathons," *Wired*, February 28, 2012: wired.com/magazine/2012/02/storyboard-hackathons.

"Rated X for eXtraordinary Coincidence," *Collegian Biz Buzz* (blog kept by *The Daily Collegian*): collegianbizbuzz.tumblr.com/post/17981766357/rated-x-for-extraordinary-coincidence.

Chapter 19: Field Notes

"The Magic of Being a Mascot": Josh Seidman, "The Magic of Being a Mascot, The Life of Wolfie," *The Statesman*, April 22, 2010: sbstatesman.com/the-magic-of-being-a-mascot-the-life-of-wolfie786.

A Pure Garbage Report: Greta Kaul, "Raking in Recyclables," *The Minnesota Daily*, March 29, 2012: mndaily.com/2012/03/29/raking-recyclables.

Crazy Campus Traditions: Ruby Cramer, and Molly Turpin, "Vassar Dictionary: Your Guide to Acronyms, Nicknames and Life on Campus—Word by Word," *The Miscellany News*, June 16, 2009: miscellanynews.com/meet-vassar-college/the-2012–2013-vassar-dictionary-your-guide-to-acronyms-nicknames-and-life-on-campus-word-by-word-1.2749161.

Crazy Campus Traditions: Spectator Staff, "116 Columbian Traditions," *The Columbia Daily Spectator*, August 27, 2012: columbiaspectator.com/2012/08/27/116-columbian-traditions.

Pepsi, Coke, Cash: Meaghen Harms, "Vending Machine Money on Campus Helps Educate Others," *The Northern Star*, March 22, 2011: northernstar.info/campus/article_c9d751b2-54ec-11e0-9744-00127992bc8b.html.

Eating Too Healthy, Exercising Too Much: Mary Watson Capron, "Orthorexia: Healthy Eating or Harmful Fad?" *The Signpost*, April 11, 2011: wsusignpost.com/business/orthorexia-healthy-eating-or-harmful-fad-1.2156814.

Eating Too Healthy, Exercising Too Much: Sarah Fernandez, "Exercising Too Much," *The Daily Titan*, May 16, 2011: dailytitan.com/2011/05/exercising-too-much.

Eating Too Healthy, Exercising Too Much: Staff Editorial, "Everything in Moderation," *The Daily Free Press*, February 23, 2010: dailyfreepress.com/2010/02/23/staff-edit-everything-in-moderation.

Staff Salary Database: "Salary Guide," *The Daily Illini*, Fall 2011: dailyillini.com/page/salary_guide_2011.

Staff Salary Database: Dan Reimold, "Salary Database Most Popular Part of Daily Illini Site," *College Media Matters*, February 28, 2011: collegemediamatters.com/2011/02/28/salary-database-most-popular-part-of-student-papers-site.

Anonymous Confessions: Michael S. Rosenwald, "Maryland Students Spill Their Secrets," *The Washington Post*, February 1, 2012: washingtonpost.com/blogs/rosenwald-md/post/maryland-students-spill-their-secrets/2012/01/31/gIQAAij5hQ_blog.html.

"Tragedy in Transition": Kelly Stroda, "Tragedy in Transition," *The University Daily Kansan*, Spring 2011: kansan.com/news/2011/may/10/tragedy-transition-when-death-interrupts-college.

"The Cost of Convenience": Hayley Peterson, "The Cost of Convenience," *The Red and Black*, November 13, 2009: redandblack.com/news/the-cost-of-convenience/article_159fc964-a23c-503d-abf7-f6a137985880.html.

Thrifting: Kirsten Tjossem, "Swap 'Til You Drop," *The Northern Iowan*, April 26, 2012: northern-iowan.org/features/swap-til-you-drop-1.2736305.

Thrifting: Emily Boudreau, "Do It Yourself and Make It Your Own," *The Michigan Daily*, March 15, 2011: michigandaily.com/arts/crafts-notebook.

Student Suicide: Mike Ricci, "Suicide: Leading Cause of Death among College Students," *The Eagle News*, March 20, 2012: eaglenews.org/suicide-leading-cause-of-death-among-college-students-1.2717742.

Walking Backward, Showing Off: Jenna Johnson, "U-Va. Historian Corrects Student Tour Guides," *The Washington Post*, April 13, 2012: washingtonpost.com/local/education/u-va-historian-debunks-campus-myths-for-student-tour-guides/2012/04/13/gIQAzTW0FT_story.html.

Handicapped Spot Check: John Hatcher, "Students Use Twitter to Report on Disabled-Parking Spots," *Poynter*, March 9, 2009: poynter.org/uncategorized/94553/students-use-twitter-to-report-on-disabled-parking-spots.

The "Academic Steroid": Corrie Mitchell, "Students Turn to Adderall for Assistance During Finals Week," *The Captain's Log*, April 13, 2011: thecaptainslog.org/2011/04/13/students-turn-to-adderall-for-assistance-during-finals-week.

The "Academic Steroid": Ehsun Forghany, "Adderall: A College Love Story," *The California Aggie*, November 29, 2010: theaggie.org/2010/11/29/adderall-a-college-love-story.

The "Academic Steroid": Becki Steinberg, "Beating the Adderall Curve," *The Daily Pennsylvanian*, February 16, 2011: thedp.com/article/2011/02/beating_the_adderall_curve.

"Can You Dub It?": Carter Lyles, "Gainesville Gets Dazed by the Dub," *The Independent Florida Alligator*, February 17, 2011: alligator.org/the_avenue/music/article_c4cf26a2–3a3b–11e0–906d-001cc4c002e0.html.

"Can You Dub It?": Dariya Bunchuk, "British Music Genre Gains Stateside Momentum," *The Pipe Dream*, February 17, 2011: bupipedream.com/release/4198/british-music-genre-gains-stateside-momentum.

"Can You Dub It?": Mick Hammock, "The Rise of Electronic Music," *NextGen Journal*, September 26, 2010: nextgenjournal.com/2010/09/the-rise-of-electronic-music.

Rat Rod Culture: Leighton Cosseboom, "Trash My Ride," *Flux Magazine*, May 12, 2010: fluxstories.com/2010/05/trash-my-ride-2.

Academic Hyperinflation: Hannah Lenius, "Grade Inflation Causes Concern," *The Student Voice*, February 10, 2011: uwrfvoice.com/index.php/news/article/3111.

Academic Hyperinflation: Catherine Rampell, "A History of College Grade Inflation," *The New York Times*, July 14, 2011: economix.blogs.nytimes.com/2011/07/14/the-history-of-college-grade-inflation.

Academic Hyperinflation: Melissa Dalis, "Buying A's," *The Chronicle*, July 15, 2011: bigblog.dukechronicle.com/news/buying-as.

Academic Hyperinflation: Michael Fischer, "Short-Sightedness on Grade Inflation," *The Hoya*, January 26, 2011: thehoya.com/opinion/fischer-short-sightedness-on-grade-inflation-1.1917817.

Academic Hyperinflation: Jodi S. Cohen, "Hundreds Who Got Aid at Chicago State Should Not Have Been Enrolled," *The Chicago Tribune*, August 10, 2011: articles.chicagotribune.com/2011–08–10/news/chi-hundreds-who-got-aid-at-chicago-state-should-not-have-been-enrolled-20110810_1_financial-aid-map-funding-enrollment.

"Concussions and Repercussions": Austin Cumblad, "Concussions and Repercussions," *The Minnesota Daily*, November 5, 2009: mndaily.com/2009/11/05/concussions-and-repercussions.

Human Sexuality, Under Debate: Patrick Svitek, "Class Sex Toy Demonstration Causes Controversy," *The Daily Northwestern*, March 1, 2011: dailynorthwestern.com/campus/class-sex-toy-demonstration-causes-controversy-1.2501746.

Human Sexuality, Under Debate: Ali Elkin, "Elkin: What We Lose by Repressing Sex in the Classroom," *The Daily Northwestern*, May 10, 2011: dailynorthwestern.com/forum/elkin-what-we-lose-by-repressing-sex-in-the-classroom-1.2561904.

Essay Ban: Jennifer Rizzo, "Veteran Who Wrote about Need for Violence Barred from College Campus," *CNN*, November 23, 2010: edition.cnn.com/2010/US/11/22/veteran.violence.article/index.html.

Animals, Alive and Stuffed: Stef Crocco, "Safe Companions," *The Minaret*, April 6, 2012: theminaretonline.com/2012/04/06/article21976.

Animals, Alive and Stuffed: Kevin Thibodeaux, "Students Cherish Childhood Memories, Bring Stuffed Animals to College," *The Daily Reveille*, November 9, 2011: lsureveille.com/entertainment/students-cherish-childhood-memories-bring-stuffed-animals-to-college-1.2668568.

Animals, Alive and Stuffed: Ryan Lytle, "Bring Your Pet to College," *U.S. News & World Report*, May 19, 2011: usnews.com/education/best-colleges/articles/2011/05/19/bring-your-pet-to-college.

Costs of Campus 911: Jazmine Woodberry, "How High is the Phone Bill?" *Arizona Daily Wildcat*, November 30, 2010: wildcat.arizona.edu/index.php/article/2010/11/how_high_is_the_phone_bill.

"The Anticipation, Not the Nudity": Zeke Turner, "The Life of a Student Nude Model," *The Dartmouth*, February 5, 2007: thedartmouth.com/2007/02/05/opinion/of.

Internet Famous: Joel Kost, "America's Freshman: TNH Talks with UNH's Reluctant Internet Sensation," *The New Hampshire*, February 20, 2012: tnhonline.com/america-s-freshman-1.2789055.

Internet Famous: "Internet Famous Class," *Current TV*, February 3, 2009: current.com/technology/89780332_internet-famous-class.htm.

Internet Famous: Jenna Johnson, "U of Rochester Admissions Creates Hip-Hop Music Video," *The Washington Post*, March 14, 2012: washingtonpost.com/blogs/campus-overload/post/u-of-rochester-admissions-creates-hip-hop-music-video/2012/03/14/gIQAcvdPCS_blog.html.

"Is it Vandalism or is it Art?": James Edmonds, "Erasing Stall Graffiti is Like Burning Shakespearean Sonnets," *The Seahawk*, February 21, 2012: theseahawk.org/op-ed/erasing-stall-graffiti-is-like-burning-shakespearian-sonnets-1.2790155.

"Is it Vandalism or is it Art?": Megan Oshiro, "Graffiti: Vandalism or Art?" *NeoJourno*, November 28, 2011: blog.hawaii.edu/neojourno/2011/11/28/graffiti-art-or-vandalism.

Recreation Sports Fees: Thomas Bradley, and Sarah Stemen, "Nearly $14M Annually in Rec Sports Fees: Where Do They Go?" *The Lantern*, January 17, 2012: thelantern.com/campus/nearly-14m-annually-in-rec-sports-fees-where-do-they-go-1.2743381.

Meal Plan Waste: Katie Quine, "Meal Plan Waste at UNC," *The Daily Tar Heel*, February 6, 2012: dailytarheel.com/index.php/article/2012/02/meal_plan.

Gender Matters: The Daily Editorial Board, "It's More Than a Housing Issue—It's about Respect," *The Oklahoma Daily*, March 7, 2012: oudaily.com/news/2012/mar/07/editorial-its-more-housing-issue-its-about-respect.

Gender Matters: Alexa Ura, "Student Organization Proposes Gender Inclusive Housing," *The Daily Texan*, February 29, 2012: dailytexanonline.com/news/2012/02/29/student-organization-proposes-gender-inclusive-housing.

Gender Matters: Samuel Levine, "Finding Your Way in Gender-Neutral Housing," *USA TODAY College*, November 10, 2011: usatodayeducate.com/staging/index.php/ccp/finding-your-way-in-gender-neutral-housing.

Gender Matters: Sarah McBride, "Op-Ed: The Real Me," *The Eagle*, May 1, 2012: theeagleonline.com/opinion/story/the-real-me.

Traumarama: Kyra Gemberling, "Elon's Own Traumarama," *The Edge* (magazine kept by *The Pendulum*), May 6, 2012: elonpendulum.com/2012/05/elons-own-traumarama.

Student Shooters: Shannon Siegel, "One Night as a Shooter," UPIU, May 4, 2011: upiu.com/culture-society/2011/05/04/One-Night-as-a-Shooter/UPIU-2501304537507.

Off-Campus Housing: Andrew Wiktor, "Reaching New Heights: Off-Campus Safety Issues Endanger UB Students," *The Spectrum*, April 27, 2011: ubspectrum.com/news/reaching-new-heights-1.2208676.

Students with Disabilities: Kedric Kitchens, "Campus Access Not Always Easy Despite Improvements," *The Oklahoma Daily*, September 6, 2011: oudaily.com/news/2011/sep/06/column-campus-access-not-always-easy-despite-impro.

Book Nooks and Rare Finds: Rebecca Gao, "Digital Libraries Wasted," *The Daily Trojan*, August 24, 2011: dailytrojan.com/2011/08/24/digital-libraries-wasted.

Book Nooks and Rare Finds: James Peng, "Scouring the Special Collections," *dartbeat* (blog kept by *The Dartmouth*), August 20, 2012: dartbeat.com/2012/08/20/rauner.

Pay-For Internships: Sue Shellenbarger, "Do You Want an Internship? It'll Cost You," *The Wall Street Journal*, January 28, 2009: online.wsj.com/article/SB123310699999022549.html.

Male Capper: Miles Parks, "Baseball Fans Faithful to Fashion, Not Hometown Team," *The Minaret*, April 7, 2011: theminaretonline.com/2011/04/07/article17985.

Male Capper: Jason Kratzwald, "Mi Sombrero Viejo," *The Louisville Cardinal*, March 26, 2002: louisvillecardinal.com/2002/03/mi-sombrero-viejo.

Rise of the Speedy Senior: Nancy Lavin, "Early Graduation on the Rise," *The Eagle*, April 25, 2011: theeagleonline.com/news/story/early-graduation-on-the-rise.

Rise of the Speedy Senior: Dan Robbins, "Surge in Early Graduation Rates Forces Cornell to Make Adjustments," *The Cornell Daily Sun*, February 1, 2011: cornellsun.com/section/news/content/2011/02/01/surge-early-graduation-rates-forces-cornell-make-adjustments.

Bringing the Sidelines to Life: Cyrus Pinto, "Fan Forum: Red Zone Needs 'Superfans,'" *The Stanford Daily*, May 24, 2011: stanforddaily.com/2011/05/24/fan-forum-red-zone-needs-superfans.

Bringing the Sidelines to Life: Desiree Pettiford and Nichole Seguin, "Becoming a 'Super Fan,'" *The Oakland Post*, March 15, 2011: oaklandpostonline.com/2011/03/15/uncategorized/becoming-a-super-fan.

Bringing the Sidelines to Life: David Pedersen, "The Art of Superfanning," *The Gustavian Weekly*, March 18, 2011: weekly.blog.gustavus.edu/2011/03/18/the-art-of-superfanning.

Sexual Activism: Raymond Kwan, "Don't Dress Like a Slut: Toronto Cop," *Excalibur*, February 16, 2011: excal.on.ca/news/dont-dress-like-a-slut-toronto-cop.

Sexual Activism: Adrienne Edwards, "In Defense of Slutwalks," *NextGen Journal*, June 17, 2011: nextgenjournal.com/2011/06/in-defense-of-slutwalks.

An Alcohol Education: Briana Gerdeman, "Alcohol Course Called 'a Joke': Students Hold Focus Group," *The Red and Black*, May 3, 2011: redandblack.com/news/alcohol-course-called-a-joke-students-hold-focus-group/article_7cd28dbf-4a97–514a-83d5–5942de9c84b4.html.

An Alcohol Education: "Global Campus Alcohol Problems," *Michigan Tech Lode*, February 28, 2012: mtulode.com/news/2012/02/28/global-campus-alcohol-problems.

An Alcohol Education: Laura Cofsky, "'Drunkorexia' a Prevalent Disorder on College Campuses," *The Daily Pennsylvanian*, March 20, 2012: thedp.com/index.php/article/2012/03/binge_drinking_and_eating_disoders_may_be_problematic_at_penn.

An Alcohol Education: "Drunkorexia: No Eating, More Drinking," *The Marquette Tribune*, October 25, 2011: marquettetribune.org/2011/10/25/news/drunkorexia-no-eating-more-drinking-bg1-me2-td3.

The Pledge Process: Andrew Lohse, "Telling the Truth," *The Dartmouth*, January 25, 2012: thedartmouth.com/2012/01/25/opinion/lohse.

Bed Bug Bites: Justice Jones, "Bedbugs Discovered in One Abel Dorm Room," *The Daily Nebraskan*, January 13, 2012: dailynebraskan.com/news/bedbugs-discovered-in-one-abel-dorm-room-1.2685308.

Bed Bug Bites: "Bedbug Cover-Up: University of Nebraska Lincoln Tried to Hide Infestation, Students Say," *The Huffington Post*, February 2, 2012: huffingtonpost.com/2012/02/02/bedbug-cover-up-university-of-nebraska_n_1250473.html.

Bed Bug Bites: "UNL to Search Every Dorm Room for Bedbugs," *Kearney Hub*, March 21, 2012: kearneyhub.com/news/local/article_adddd872–4dad-11e1–88bb-001871e3ce6c.html.

Calling Foul: Rocio Rodriguez, "Students Learn Flag Football Officiating," *The Daily Toreador*, August 31, 2011: dailytoreador.com/lavida/article_5c1db3bc-d450–11e0–9420–001a4bcf6878.html.

Married Students: Kelly Elmore, "UW Spouses Lack Benefits," *The Branding Iron*, January 10, 2012: brandingirononline.info/2012/01/10/uw-spouses-lack-benefits.

Married Students: Kiley Buschhausen, "Challenges Facing Married Students," *The Daily Titan*, April 5, 2012: dailytitan.com/2012/04/challenges-facing-married-students.

Extinguisher Exploration: Tim Miller, "Georgia State Working to Remove Expired Fire Extinguishers," *The Signal*, January 10, 2012: gsusignal.com/news/georgia-state-working-to-remove-expired-fire-extinguishers-1.2684238.

Addiction, on the Run: Rachel Stark, "Runner's High," *Inside* magazine (the magazine of the *Indiana Daily Student*), April 11, 2011: idsnews.com/news/inside/story.aspx?id=81007.

"A Simple Prick, Slash, or Burn": Randy Schafer, "Body Modifications 'Push the Envelope,'" *The Red and Black*, January 8, 2012: redandblack.com/variety/body-modifications-push-the-envelope/article_8e558332–7969–51c0-a049-dc58e9bc2979.html.

"A Simple Prick, Slash, or Burn": Madeline Munoz, "Toxic Tanning," *The Apache Pow Wow*, February 12, 2011: tjcnewspaper.com/student-life/toxic-tanning-1.1977270.

"A Simple Prick, Slash, or Burn": Sarah Greufe, "Opinion: Tanning is an Addiction," *The TCU Daily Skiff*, August 26, 2011: tcu360.com/opinions/2011/08/13074.opinion-tanning-addiction.

A "Balance Sport Revolution": Sarah Schweppe, "Slackliners Asked Not to Use Campus Trees for Sport," *The Daily of the University of Washington*, August 17, 2011: dailyuw.com/news/2011/aug/17/slackliners-asked-not-use-campus-trees-sport.

A "Balance Sport Revolution": "Slacklining: The Trampoline Meets the Tightrope," *BBC News*, May 28, 2011: bbc.co.uk/news/uk-13583411.

A "Balance Sport Revolution": Megan May, "Slacklining Becoming Popular in Columbia," *The Columbia Missourian*, July 13, 2011: columbiamissourian.com/stories/2011/07/13/slacklining-around-columbia.

A "Balance Sport Revolution": Lana Schwartz, "Slacklining: Tightropes Are No Longer for the Circus," *The Review*, October 4, 2010: udreview.com/mosaic/slacklining-tightropes-are-no-longer-for-the-circus-1.1664735.

Early Classes, Higher Grades: Rebecca R. Ruiz, "To Earn an 'A,' Set the Alarm Clock Early," *The New York Times*, September 9, 2011: thechoice.blogs.nytimes.com/2011/09/09/to-earn-an-a-set-the-alarm-clock-early.

Weight of a (Fresh) Man: Valerie Strauss, "'Freshman 15' Weight Gain a Myth, Study Says," *The Washington Post*, November 1, 2011: washingtonpost.com/blogs/answer-sheet/post/freshman-15-weight-gain-a-myth-study-says/2011/11/01/gIQATa4RdM_blog.html.

Weight of a (Fresh) Man: Shelby Newsom, "A Humorous Perspective on the Dreaded Freshman 15," *The Index*, October 4, 2011: kzindex.wordpress.com/2011/10/04/a-humorous-perspective-on-the-dreaded-freshman-15.

Weight of a (Fresh) Man: Kayla Jonsson, "Study Shows Students Gain Less Than 15 Pounds Freshman Year," *The Daily Texan*, November 2, 2011: dailytexanonline.com/news/2011/11/02/study-shows-students-gain-less-than-15-pounds-freshman-year.

Weight of a (Fresh) Man: Rosie Mestel, "'Freshman 15' Weight-Gain Myth Debunked," *Los Angeles Times*, November 2, 2011: articles.latimes.com/2011/nov/02/news/la-heb-freshman-15-weight-gain-myth-debunked-20111102.

Weight of a (Fresh) Man: Danielle Delp, "Eight Months and 100 Pounds," *Reporter*, March 16, 2012: reportermag.com/article/03–16–2012/eight-months-and-100-pounds.

Weight of a (Fresh) Man: Nate Finch, "Just Getting Started," *Weight of a Man*, June 24, 2011: weightofaman.com/just-getting-started.

Fighting Worldsuck: Caitlin O'Rourke, "Nerdfighters Unite," *The Butler Collegian*, October 25, 2011: thebutlercollegian.com/2011/10/nerdfighters-unite.

Fighting Worldsuck: Breana Fischer, "Awesome-ness Versus 'World Suck,'" *The Panther*, December 5, 2010: thepantheronline.com/a-e/awesome-ness-versus-world-suck.

Fighting Worldsuck: Elisa DeCastro, "How to Be a Nerdfighter," *The Observer*, October 6, 2011: ndsmcobserver.com/viewpoint/how-to-be-a-nerdfighter-1.2632744.

Bike Shares, Long Boards: Sara Schonfeld, "Professors See Biking as Scenic and Economical," *The Daily Pennsylvanian*, October 3, 2011: thedp.com/index.php/article/2011/10/professors_see_biking_as_scenic_and_economical.

Bike Shares, Long Boards: Shelby Reynolds, "Bike Share Program Wants 'Respect,'" *The Oakland Post*, September 14, 2011: oaklandpostonline.com/2011/09/14/campus/bike-share-program-wants-respect.

Bike Shares, Long Boards: Kyle Widenski, "Longboarding Trend Spreads from California to Chicago," *The DePaulia*, May 16, 2011: depauliaonline.com/sports/longboarding-trend-spreads-from-california-to-chicago-1.2227763.

Sleep Texting: Stephanie Kariuki, "Rising Problem of Sleep Texting Not Dreamed Up," *The Lantern*, December 4, 2011: thelantern.com/campus/rising-problem-of-sleep-texting-not-dreamed-up-1.2724378.

Sleep Texting: Kinne Chapin, "Fear of Missing Out," *The Huffington Post*, March 2, 2012: huffingtonpost.com/kinne-chapin/fear-of-missing-out_b_1317633.html.

Sleep Texting: Hayley Brooks and Ali Kokot, "A Case for the Lone Luncher," *The Daily Pennsylvanian*, March 29, 2012: thedp.com/index.php/article/2012/03/hayley_brooks_amp_ali_kokot_a_case_for_the_lone_luncher.

"The Experience of Homesickness": Dan Reimold, "Professor Explores the Role of Homesickness in American History," *USA TODAY College*, January 24, 2012: usatodayeducate.com/staging/index.php/campuslife/professor-explores-the-role-of-homesickness-in-american-history.

"The Experience of Homesickness": Susan J. Matt, *Homesickness: An American History* (Oxford: Oxford University Press, 2011).

"The Whole Premise of Annual Giving": Coburn Palmer, "College Donations on the Rise as Government Funding Falls," *USA TODAY College*, March 30, 2012: usatodayeducate. com/staging/index.php/ccp/college-donations-on-the-rise-as-government-funding-falls.

"The Whole Premise of Annual Giving": Emily Rutherford, "Beyond Annual Giving," *The Daily Princetonian*, February 27, 2012: dailyprincetonian.com/2012/02/27/30100.

The Fight for Two-Ply: Marshall Schmidt, "KU Flushes Its One-Ply Toilet Paper," *The University Daily Kansan*, August 27, 2012: kansan.com/news/2012/08/27/ku-flushes-its-one-ply-toilet-paper.

The Fight for Two-Ply: Marshall Schmidt, "One-Ply Toilet Paper Rubs Students the Wrong Way," *The University Daily Kansan*, November 8, 2011: kansan.com/archives/2011/11/08/one-ply-toilet-paper-rubs-students-the-wrong-way.

The Fight for Two-Ply: Billy McCroy, "Editorial: Quality Toilet Paper Worth Extra Cash," *The University Daily Kansan*, November 15, 2011: kansan.com/archives/2011/11/15/editorial-quality-toilet-paper-worth-extra-cash.

Sugar Babies: Jessica Appelbaum, "Sugar Babies at Tulane," *The Tulane Hullabaloo*, September 16, 2011: thehullabaloo.com/news/campus_news/article_c2629d52-e0af-11e0–8a55–001a4bcf6878.html.

Common Readings and Campus Portraits: Ethan G. Loewi, "Painting a New Path at the Kennedy School," *The Harvard Crimson*, March 5, 2012: thecrimson.com/article/2012/3/5/women-portraits-kennedy-school.

Common Readings and Campus Portraits: Eric Cheyfitz, "The Life of Diversity at Cornell: A Response to the Reading Project," *The Cornell Daily Sun*, March 6, 2012: cornellsun.com/section/opinion/content/2012/03/06/life-diversity-cornell-response-reading-project.

YOLO: Keren Baruch, "F> It, YOLO," *The Spectrum*, March 19, 2012: ubspectrum.com/opinion/f-it-yolo-1.2822904.

YOLO: Ashley Dye, "The Dyessertation: Do As You Please," *The Ball State Daily News*, April 30, 2012: bsudailynews.com/the-dyessertation-do-as-you-please-1.2737214.

The Snitch is Loose, Harry is Lost: Dan Reimold, "Is the Hottest Sport in College . . . Quidditch?" *USA TODAY College*, September 28, 2011: usatodayeducate.com/staging/index.php/campus-beat/is-the-hottest-sport-in-college-quidditch.

The Snitch is Loose, Harry is Lost: Cristina Valcarcel-Lopez, "Quidditch: Its Entrance into the Real World," UPIU, March 17, 2011: upiu.com/culture-society/2011/03/17/Quidditch-Its-Entrance-into-the-Real-World/UPIU-1281300400200.

The Snitch is Loose, Harry is Lost: Proma Khosla, "Saying Goodbye to a 'Harry Potter' Childhood," *The Michigan Daily*, July 4, 2011: michigandaily.com/arts/harry-potter-notebook.

Unusual Courses, Majors: "100 Hilarious College Courses That Really Exist," *OnlineUniversities.com*, October 21, 2009: onlineuniversities.com/blog/2009/10/100-hilarious-college-courses-that-really-exist.

Revolution, While Abroad: Ian Weller, *A Bulldog Abroad*, February 1, 2011: ianwellerdrake. blogspot.com/2011_02_01_archive.html.

Helicopters and Boomerangs: Jenna Johnson, "University of Virginia's Sullivan: 'You Might Be a Helicopter Parent If . . .'" *The Washington Post*, August 22, 2011: washingtonpost.com/ blogs/campus-overload/post/university-of-virginias-sullivan-you-might-be-a-helicopter-parent-if/2011/08/22/gIQAu1K0WJ_blog.html.

Helicopters and Boomerangs: Jennifer Ludden, "Helicopter Parents Hover in the Workplace," *National Public Radio*, February 6, 2012: npr.org/2012/02/06/146464665/helicopter-parents-hover-in-the-workplace.

Helicopters and Boomerangs: Madeline Hennings, "Grads Become Parental Burdens," *The Collegiate Times*, January 19, 2012: collegiatetimes.com/stories/19048/grads-become-parental-burdens.

Edible Dumpster Diving: Carolea Casas, "'Freeganism' Challenges Wasteful Attitudes Towards Perishable Foods," *The Puget Sound Trail*, February 17, 2012: trail.pugetsound.edu/ 2012/02/%E2%80%98freeganism%E2%80%99-challenges-wasteful-attitudes-towards-perishable-foods.

Edible Dumpster Diving: Nathan Pipenberg, "'I Am a Dumpster Diver, and I Eat Trash,'" *The Daily Collegian*, April 11, 2012: collegian.psu.edu/archive/2012/04/11/i_am_a_dumpster_diver_and_i_eat_trash.aspx.

The Shoe Licker: Danica Jordan, "Ybor Got Sole," *The Hawkeye*, April 1, 2012: hawkeyenews.net/ news/2012/04/01/ybor-got-sole.

Chapter 20: The Sales Pitch

Freelance, Freelance, Freelance

Neil Gaiman, May 1, 2012: neil-gaiman.tumblr.com/post/22199971613/mr-gaiman-have-you-ever-written-something-absolutely.

Networking

Elyse, "Why You Should Create a Brag Notebook," *HackCollege*, April 3, 2012: hackcollege. com/blog/2012/04/03/why-you-should-create-brag-notebook.html.

Conclusion: Rebellious Reporter Child

Opening Quote

Hill, Advice originally shared in "Beyond the Byline: 735 Tips Every Reporter Should Know Before
Setting Foot in a Newsroom."

Index